YAKUZA MOON

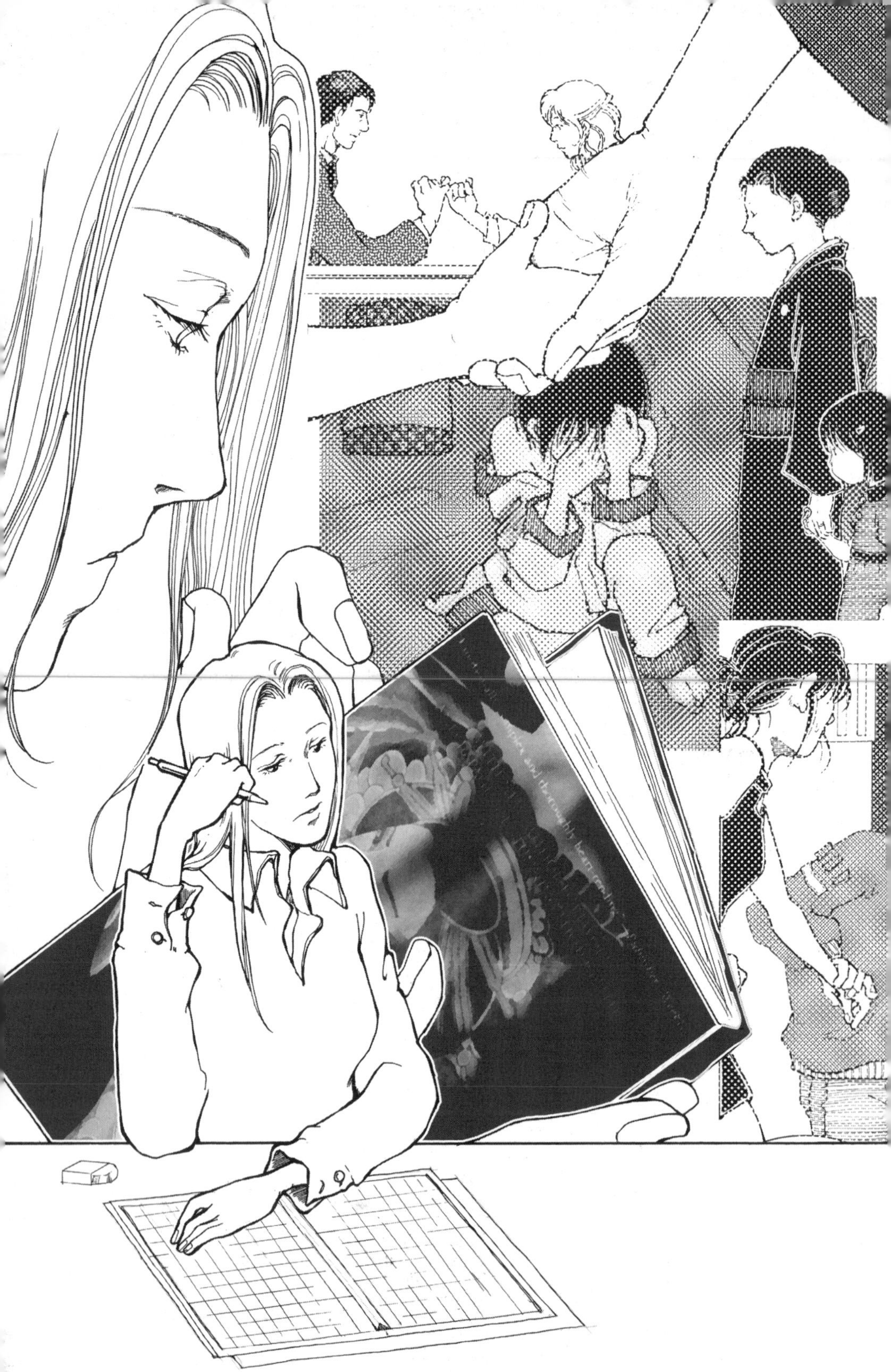

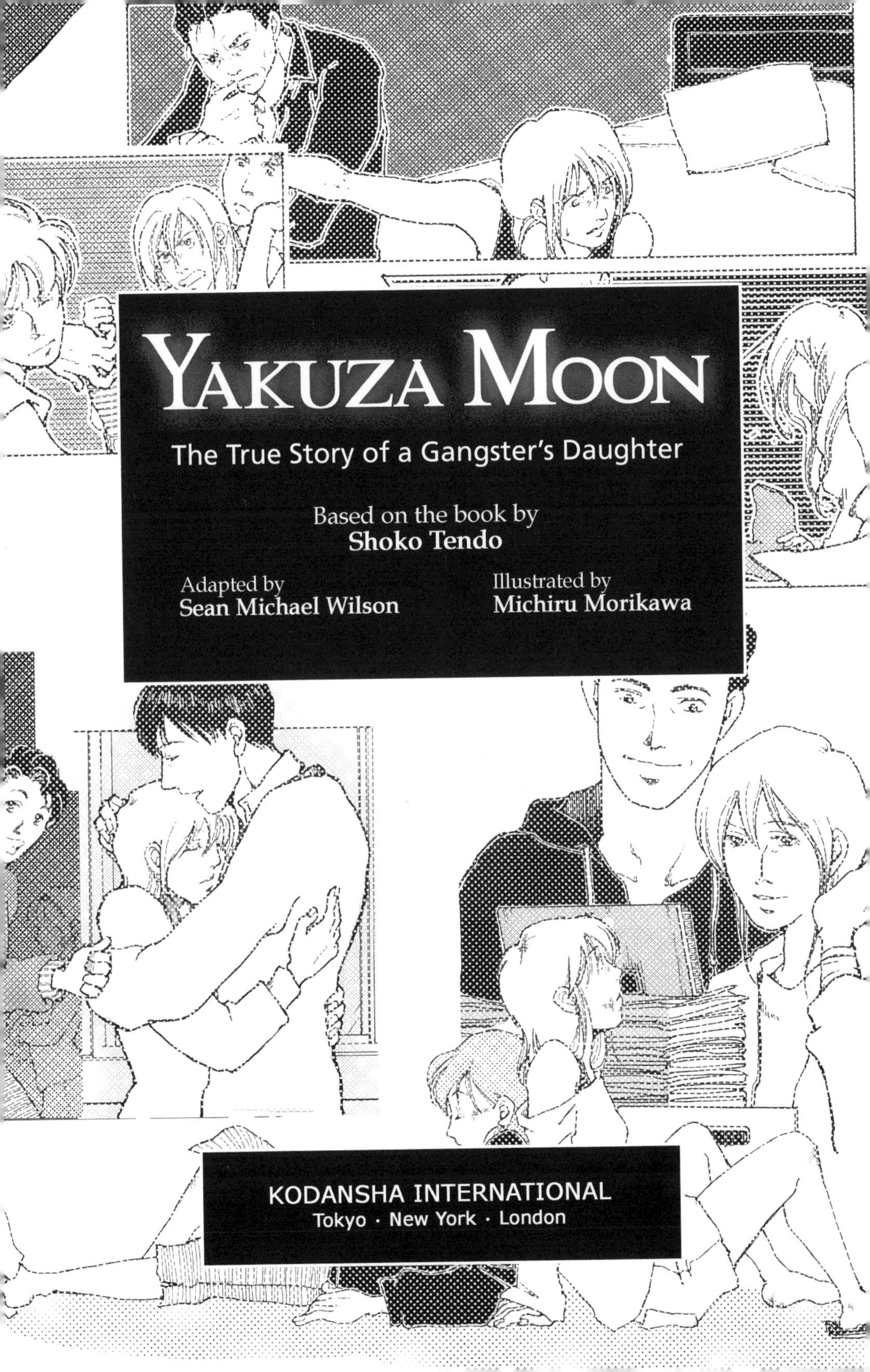

YAKUZA MOON

The True Story of a Gangster's Daughter

Based on the book by
Shoko Tendo

Adapted by
Sean Michael Wilson

Illustrated by
Michiru Morikawa

KODANSHA INTERNATIONAL
Tokyo · New York · London

Based on the English version of *Yakuza Moon: Memoirs of a Gangster's Daughter* by Shoko Tendo and translated by Louise Heal, first published by Kodansha International.

Distributed in the United States by Kodansha America, LLC, and in the United Kingdom and continental Europe by Kodansha Europe Ltd.

Published by Kodansha International Ltd., 17–14 Otowa 1-chome, Bunkyo-ku, Tokyo 112–8652.

ISBN 978–4–7700–3146–4

First edition, 2011
19 18 17 16 15 14 13 12 11   10 9 8 7 6 5 4 3 2 1

Library of Congress Cataloging-in-Publication Data

Wilson, Seán Michael.
  Yakuza moon : the true story of a gangster's daughter / by Shoko Tendo ; adapted by Sean Michael Wilson ; illustrated by Michiru Morikawa. -- Manga ed., 1st ed.
      p. cm.
  Adaptation of: Yakuza moon : memoirs of a gangster's daughter / Shoko Tendo ; translated by Louise Heal. 2008.
   ISBN 978-4-7700-3146-4
  1. Tendo, Shoko, 1968---Comic books, strips, etc. 2. Yakuza--Japan--Comic books, strips, etc. 3. Children of gangsters--Japan--Biography--Comic books, strips, etc. I. Morikawa, Michiru, 1973- II. Tendo, Shoko, 1968- Yakuza na tsuki. English. III. Title.
   HV6453.J33Y3582 2011
   364.1092--dc22
   [B]
                    2010054301

www.kodansha-intl.com

CONTENTS

CHAPTER 1

Floating Clouds

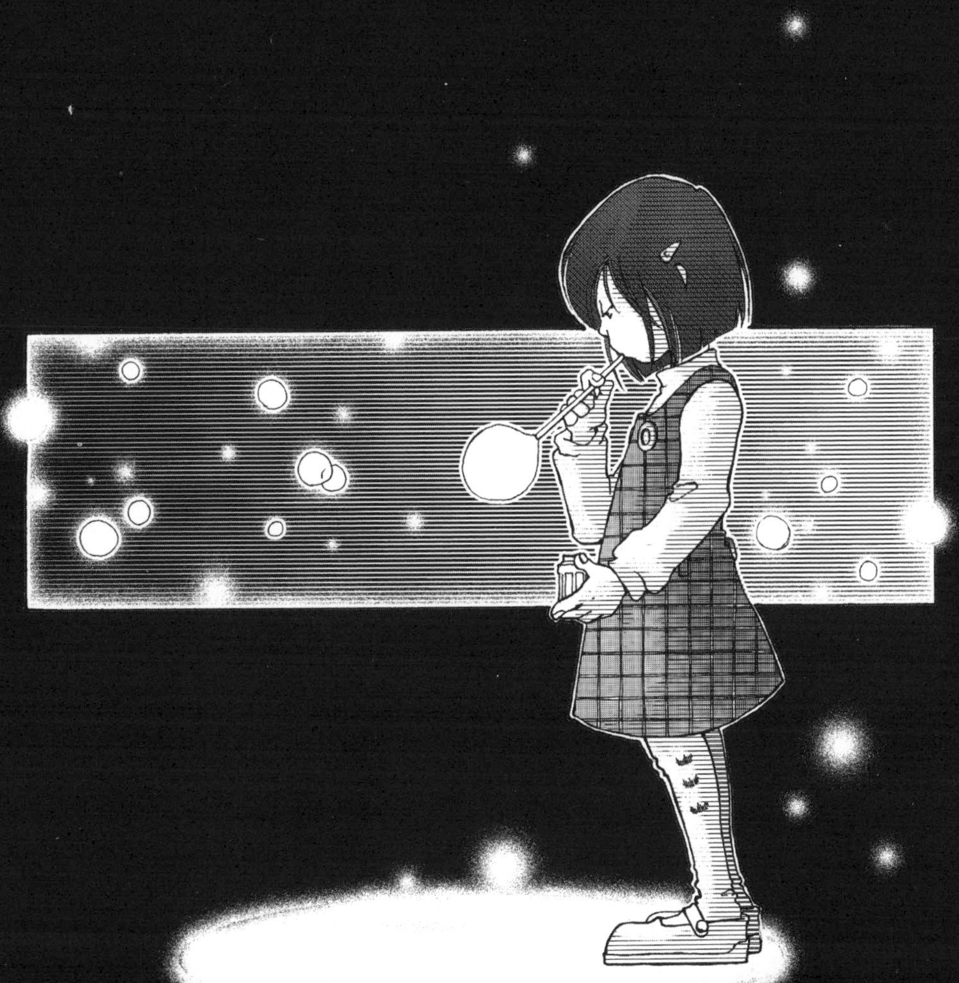

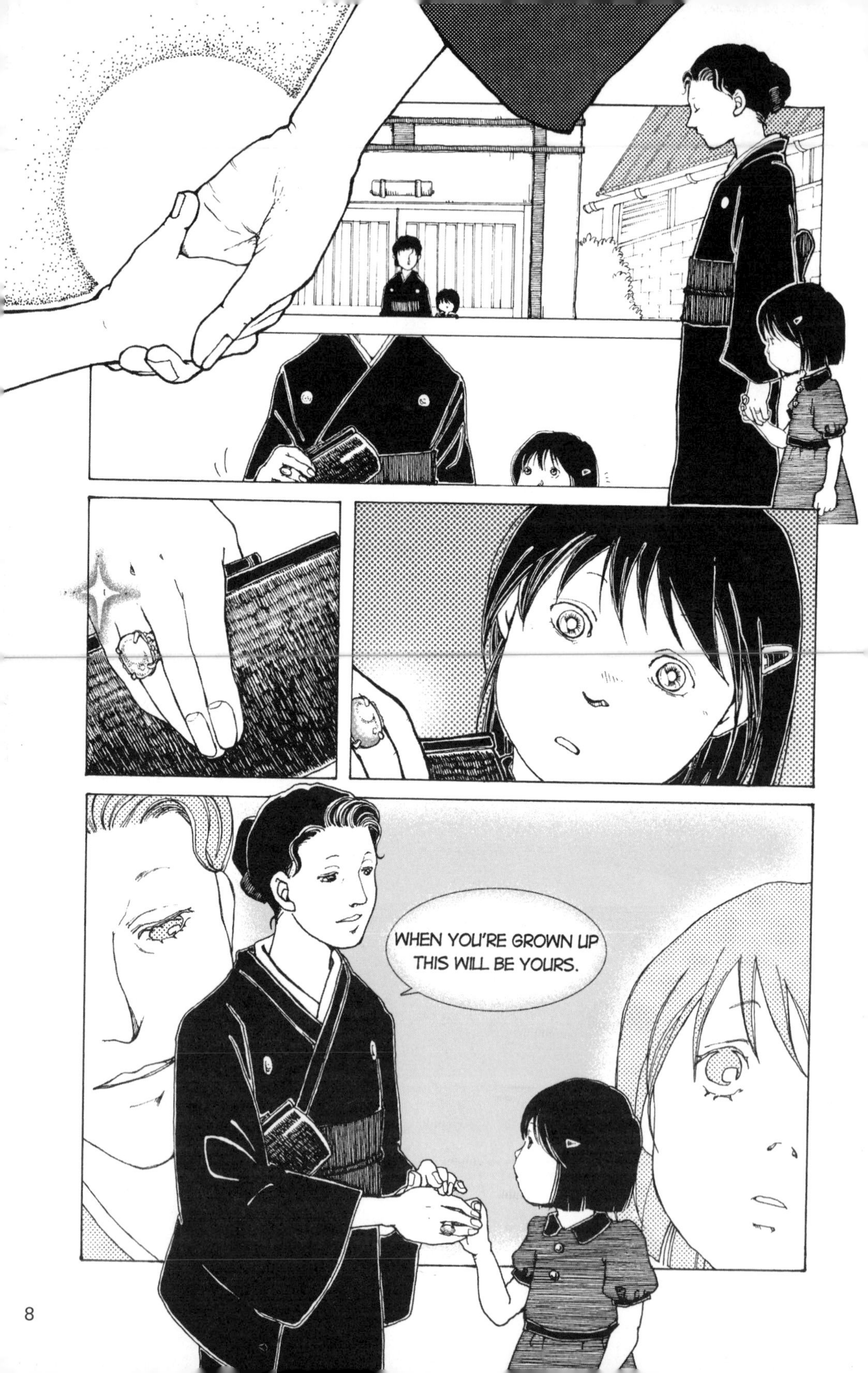
WHEN YOU'RE GROWN UP THIS WILL BE YOURS.

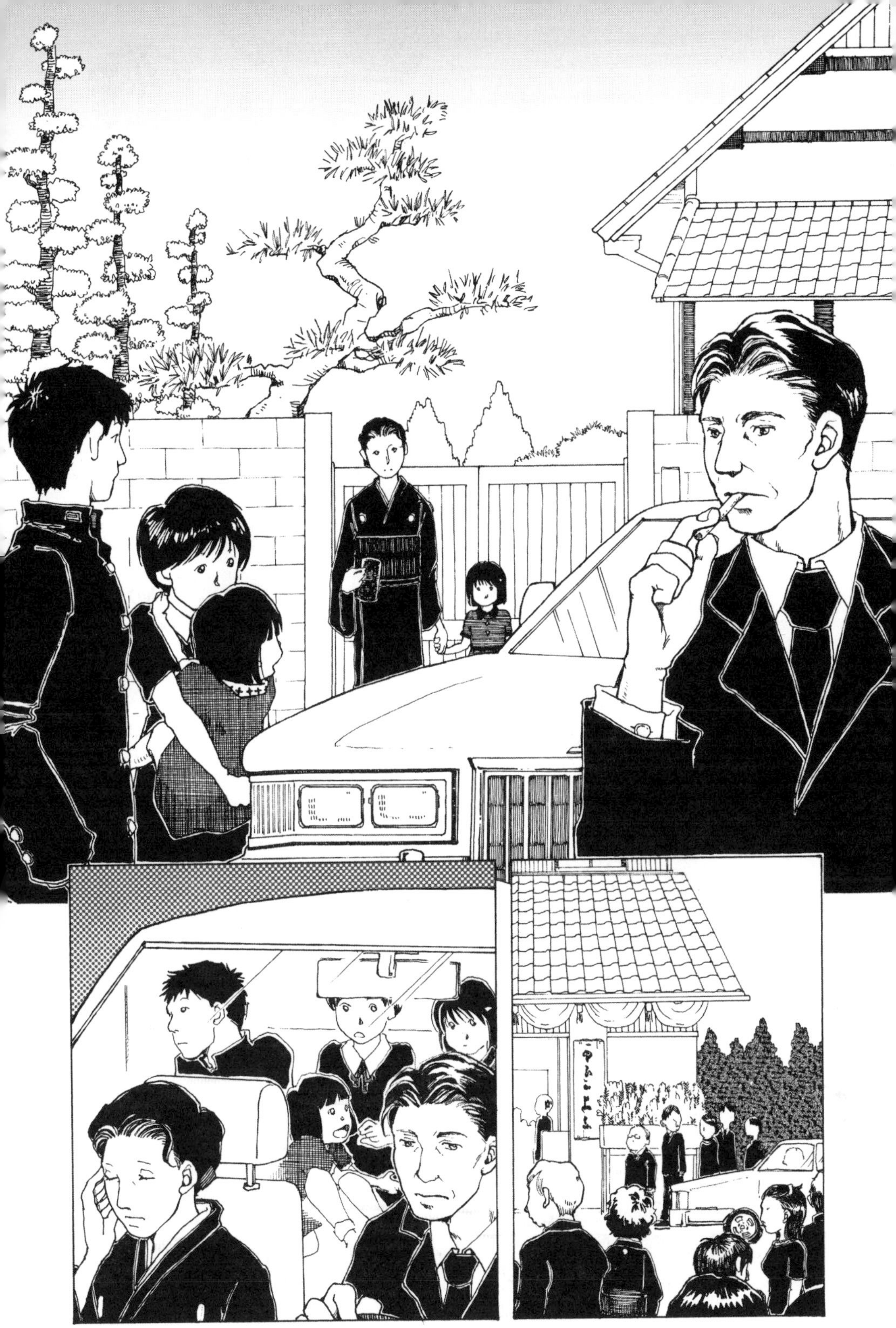

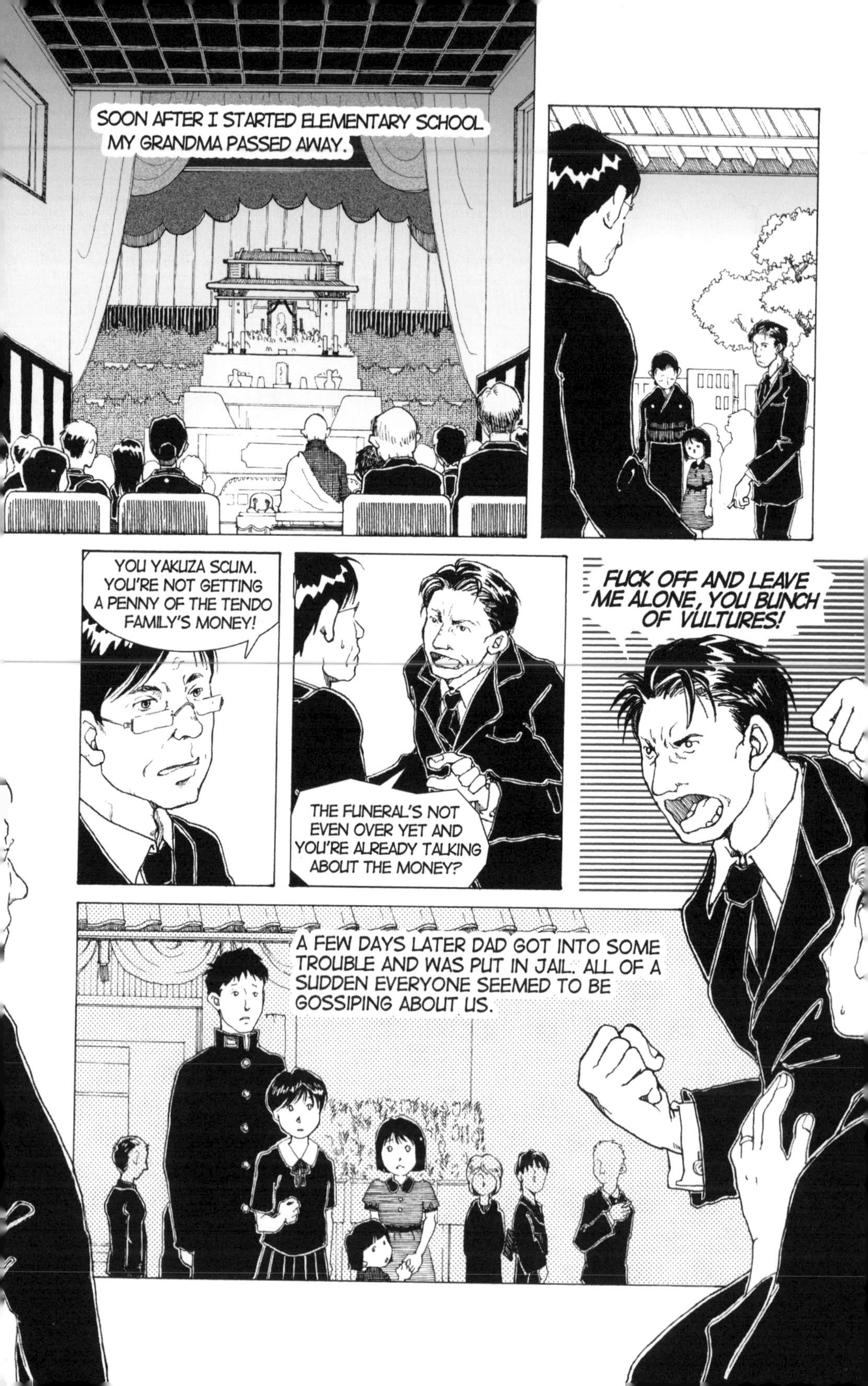

SOON AFTER I STARTED ELEMENTARY SCHOOL MY GRANDMA PASSED AWAY.
YOU YAKUZA SCUM. YOU'RE NOT GETTING A PENNY OF THE TENDO FAMILY'S MONEY!
THE FUNERAL'S NOT EVEN OVER YET AND YOU'RE ALREADY TALKING ABOUT THE MONEY?
FUCK OFF AND LEAVE ME ALONE, YOU BUNCH OF VULTURES!
A FEW DAYS LATER DAD GOT INTO SOME TROUBLE AND WAS PUT IN JAIL. ALL OF A SUDDEN EVERYONE SEEMED TO BE GOSSIPING ABOUT US.

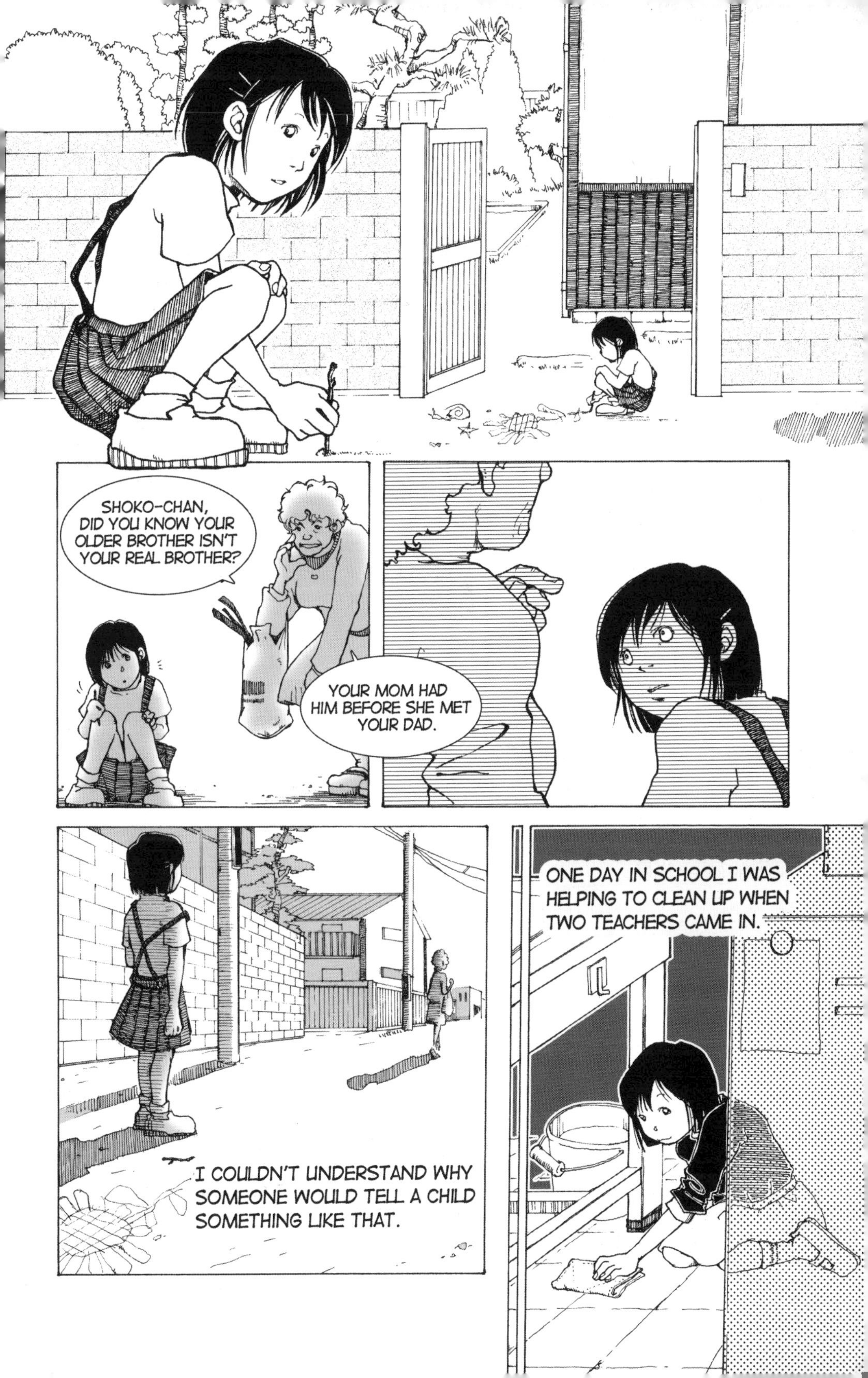
SHOKO-CHAN, DID YOU KNOW YOUR OLDER BROTHER ISN'T YOUR REAL BROTHER?
YOUR MOM HAD HIM BEFORE SHE MET YOUR DAD.
I COULDN'T UNDERSTAND WHY SOMEONE WOULD TELL A CHILD SOMETHING LIKE THAT.
ONE DAY IN SCHOOL I WAS HELPING TO CLEAN UP WHEN TWO TEACHERS CAME IN.

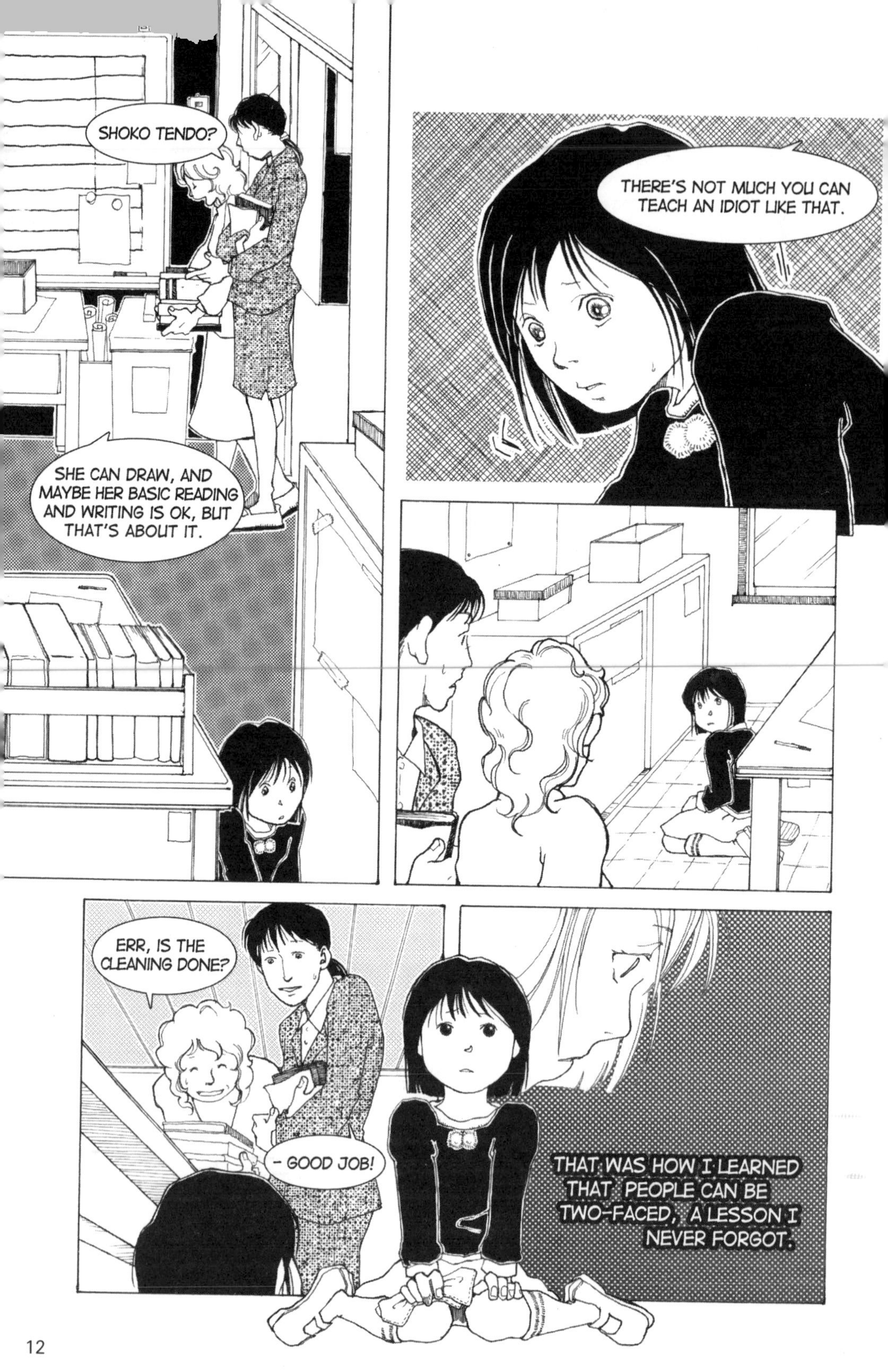
SHOKO TENDO?
SHE CAN DRAW, AND MAYBE HER BASIC READING AND WRITING IS OK, BUT THAT'S ABOUT IT.
THERE'S NOT MUCH YOU CAN TEACH AN IDIOT LIKE THAT.
ERR, IS THE CLEANING DONE?
- GOOD JOB!
THAT WAS HOW I LEARNED THAT PEOPLE CAN BE TWO-FACED, A LESSON I NEVER FORGOT.

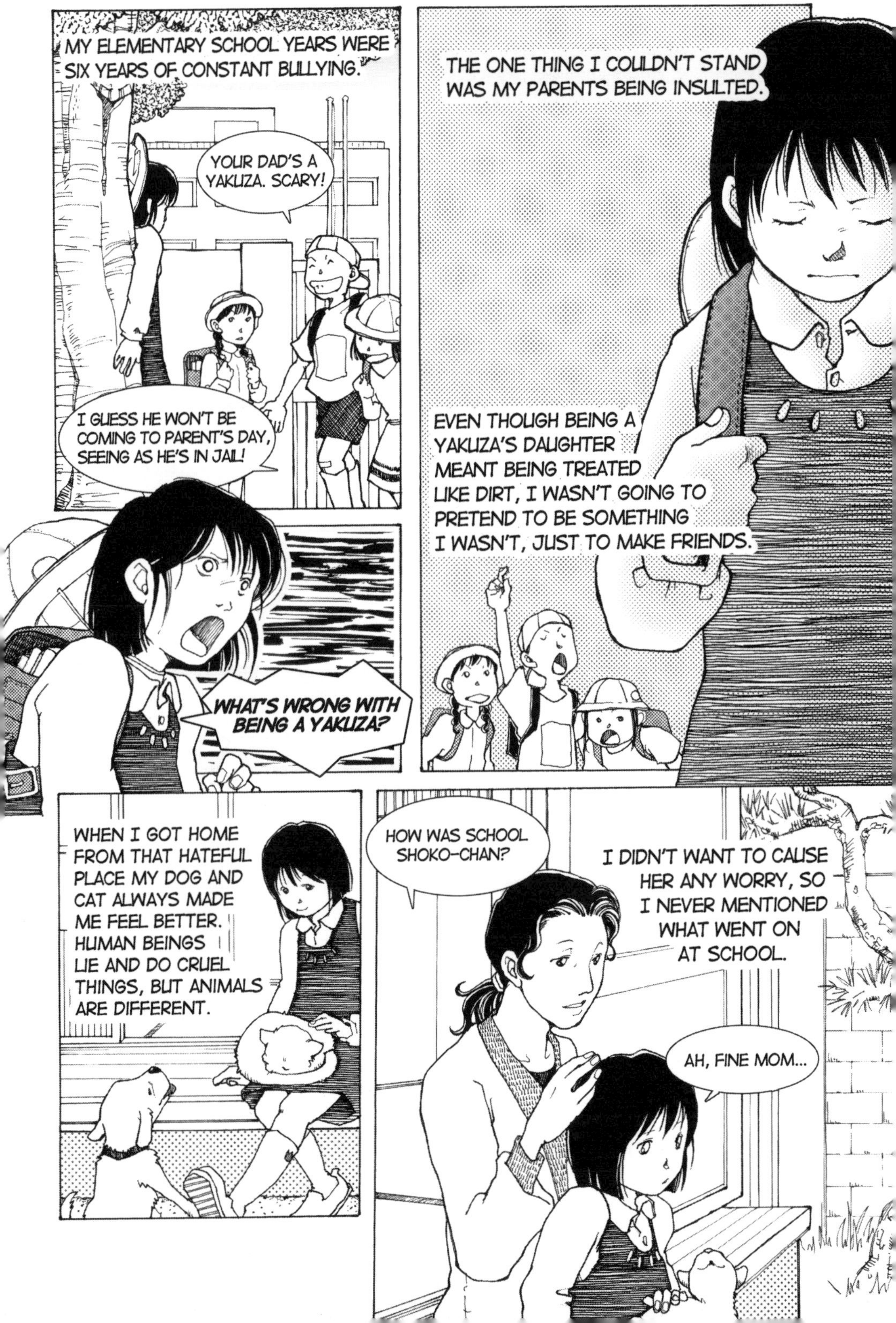

MY ELEMENTARY SCHOOL YEARS WERE SIX YEARS OF CONSTANT BULLYING.
YOUR DAD'S A YAKUZA. SCARY!
I GUESS HE WON'T BE COMING TO PARENT'S DAY, SEEING AS HE'S IN JAIL!
WHAT'S WRONG WITH BEING A YAKUZA?
THE ONE THING I COULDN'T STAND WAS MY PARENTS BEING INSULTED.
EVEN THOUGH BEING A YAKUZA'S DAUGHTER MEANT BEING TREATED LIKE DIRT, I WASN'T GOING TO PRETEND TO BE SOMETHING I WASN'T, JUST TO MAKE FRIENDS.
WHEN I GOT HOME FROM THAT HATEFUL PLACE MY DOG AND CAT ALWAYS MADE ME FEEL BETTER. HUMAN BEINGS LIE AND DO CRUEL THINGS, BUT ANIMALS ARE DIFFERENT.
HOW WAS SCHOOL SHOKO-CHAN?
I DIDN'T WANT TO CAUSE HER ANY WORRY, SO I NEVER MENTIONED WHAT WENT ON AT SCHOOL.
AH, FINE MOM...

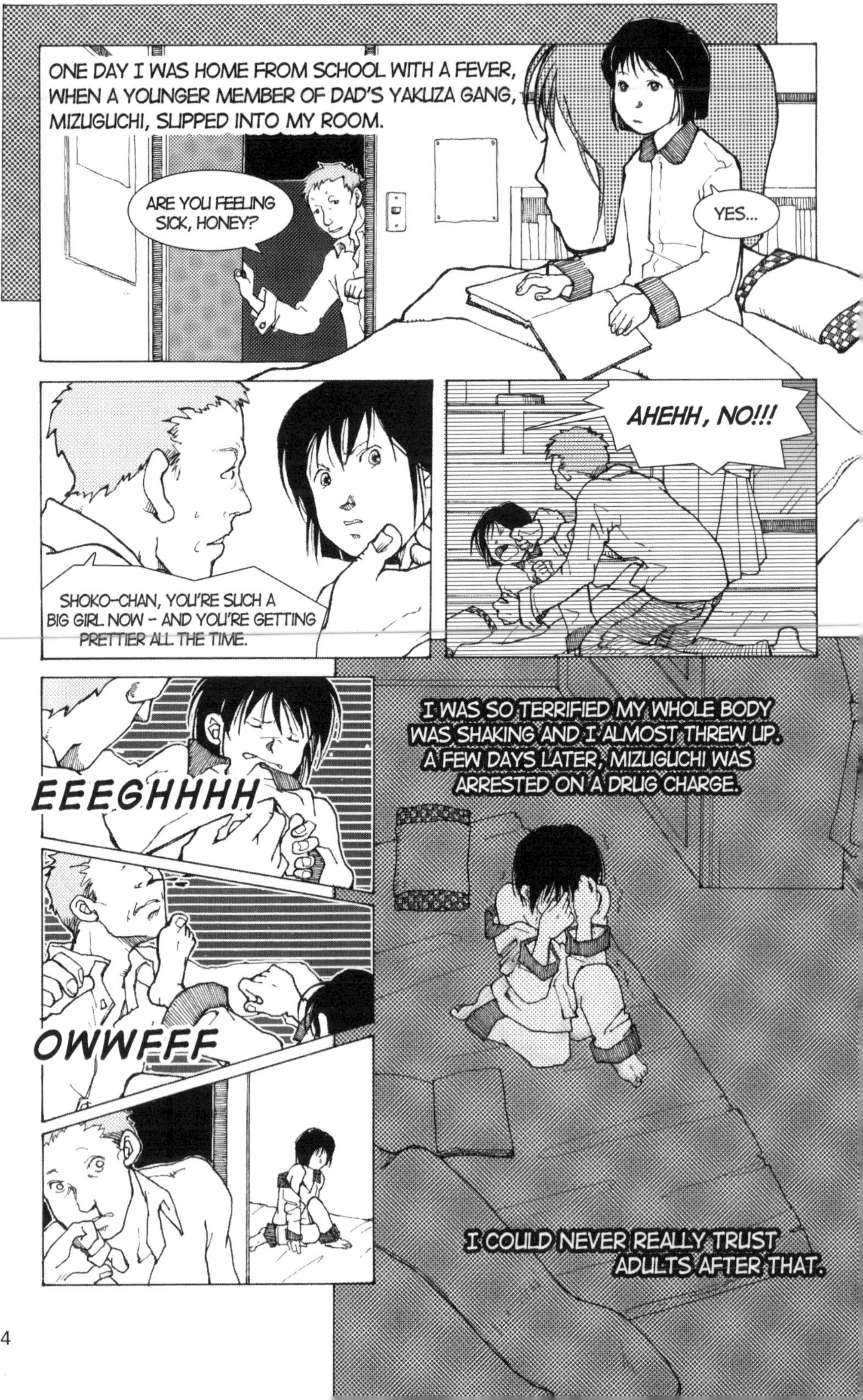
ONE DAY I WAS HOME FROM SCHOOL WITH A FEVER, WHEN A YOUNGER MEMBER OF DAD'S YAKUZA GANG, MIZUGUCHI, SLIPPED INTO MY ROOM.
ARE YOU FEELING SICK, HONEY?
YES...
SHOKO-CHAN, YOU'RE SUCH A BIG GIRL NOW - AND YOU'RE GETTING PRETTIER ALL THE TIME.
AHEHH, NO!!!
EEEGHHHH
OWWFFF
I WAS SO TERRIFIED MY WHOLE BODY WAS SHAKING AND I ALMOST THREW UP. A FEW DAYS LATER, MIZUGUCHI WAS ARRESTED ON A DRUG CHARGE.
I COULD NEVER REALLY TRUST ADULTS AFTER THAT.

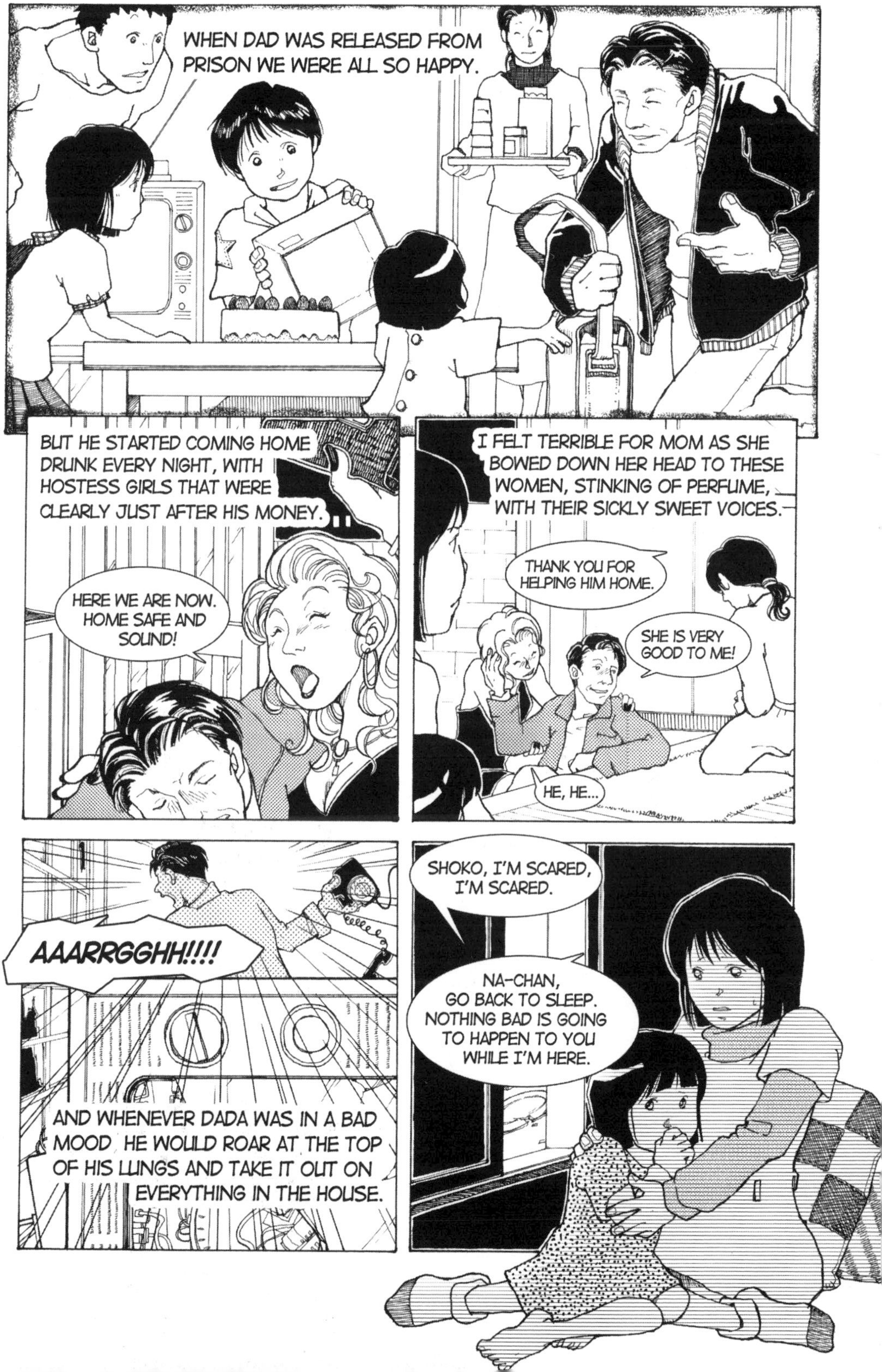
WHEN DAD WAS RELEASED FROM PRISON WE WERE ALL SO HAPPY.
BUT HE STARTED COMING HOME DRUNK EVERY NIGHT, WITH HOSTESS GIRLS THAT WERE CLEARLY JUST AFTER HIS MONEY.
HERE WE ARE NOW. HOME SAFE AND SOUND!
I FELT TERRIBLE FOR MOM AS SHE BOWED DOWN HER HEAD TO THESE WOMEN, STINKING OF PERFUME, WITH THEIR SICKLY SWEET VOICES.
THANK YOU FOR HELPING HIM HOME.
SHE IS VERY GOOD TO ME!
HE, HE...
AAARRGGHH!!!!
AND WHENEVER DADA WAS IN A BAD MOOD, HE WOULD ROAR AT THE TOP OF HIS LUNGS AND TAKE IT OUT ON EVERYTHING IN THE HOUSE.
SHOKO, I'M SCARED, I'M SCARED.
NA-CHAN, GO BACK TO SLEEP. NOTHING BAD IS GOING TO HAPPEN TO YOU WHILE I'M HERE.

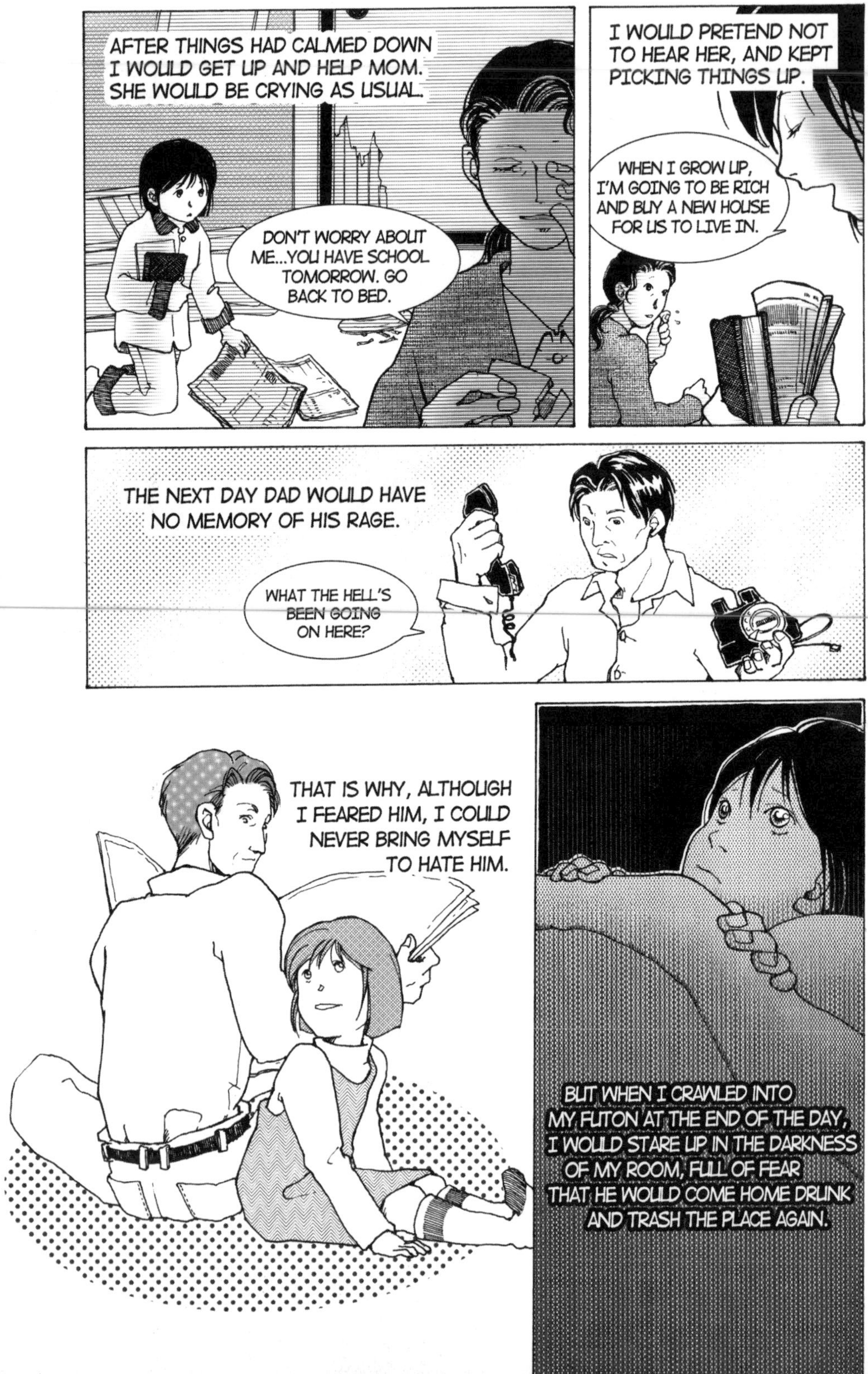
AFTER THINGS HAD CALMED DOWN I WOULD GET UP AND HELP MOM. SHE WOULD BE CRYING AS USUAL.
DON'T WORRY ABOUT ME...YOU HAVE SCHOOL TOMORROW. GO BACK TO BED.
I WOULD PRETEND NOT TO HEAR HER, AND KEPT PICKING THINGS UP.
WHEN I GROW UP, I'M GOING TO BE RICH AND BUY A NEW HOUSE FOR US TO LIVE IN.
THE NEXT DAY DAD WOULD HAVE NO MEMORY OF HIS RAGE.
WHAT THE HELL'S BEEN GOING ON HERE?
THAT IS WHY, ALTHOUGH I FEARED HIM, I COULD NEVER BRING MYSELF TO HATE HIM.
BUT WHEN I CRAWLED INTO MY FUTON AT THE END OF THE DAY, I WOULD STARE UP IN THE DARKNESS OF MY ROOM, FULL OF FEAR THAT HE WOULD COME HOME DRUNK AND TRASH THE PLACE AGAIN.

CHAPTER 2

Cheap Thrills

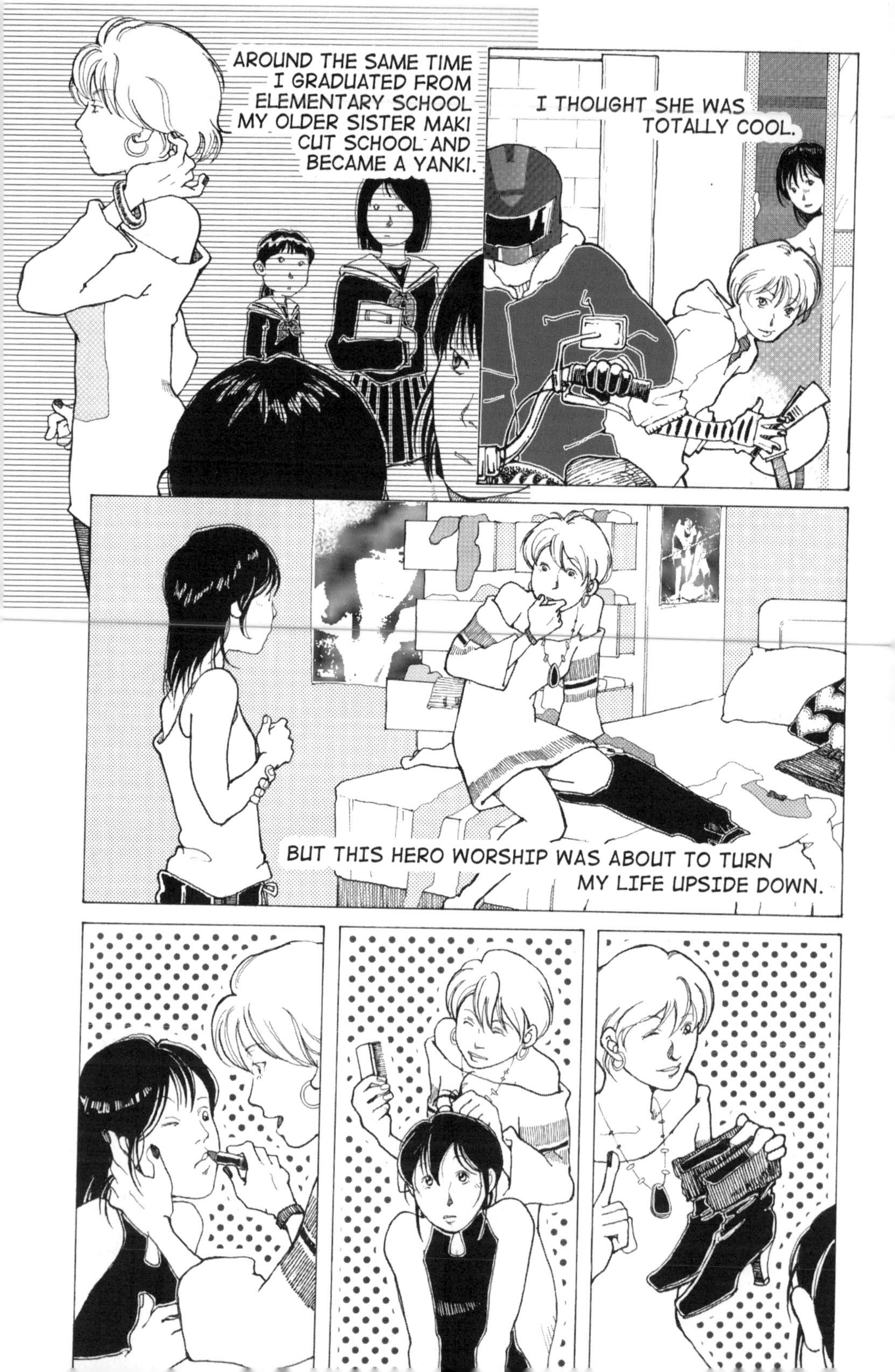

AROUND THE SAME TIME I GRADUATED FROM ELEMENTARY SCHOOL MY OLDER SISTER MAKI CUT SCHOOL AND BECAME A YANKI.
I THOUGHT SHE WAS TOTALLY COOL.
BUT THIS HERO WORSHIP WAS ABOUT TO TURN MY LIFE UPSIDE DOWN.

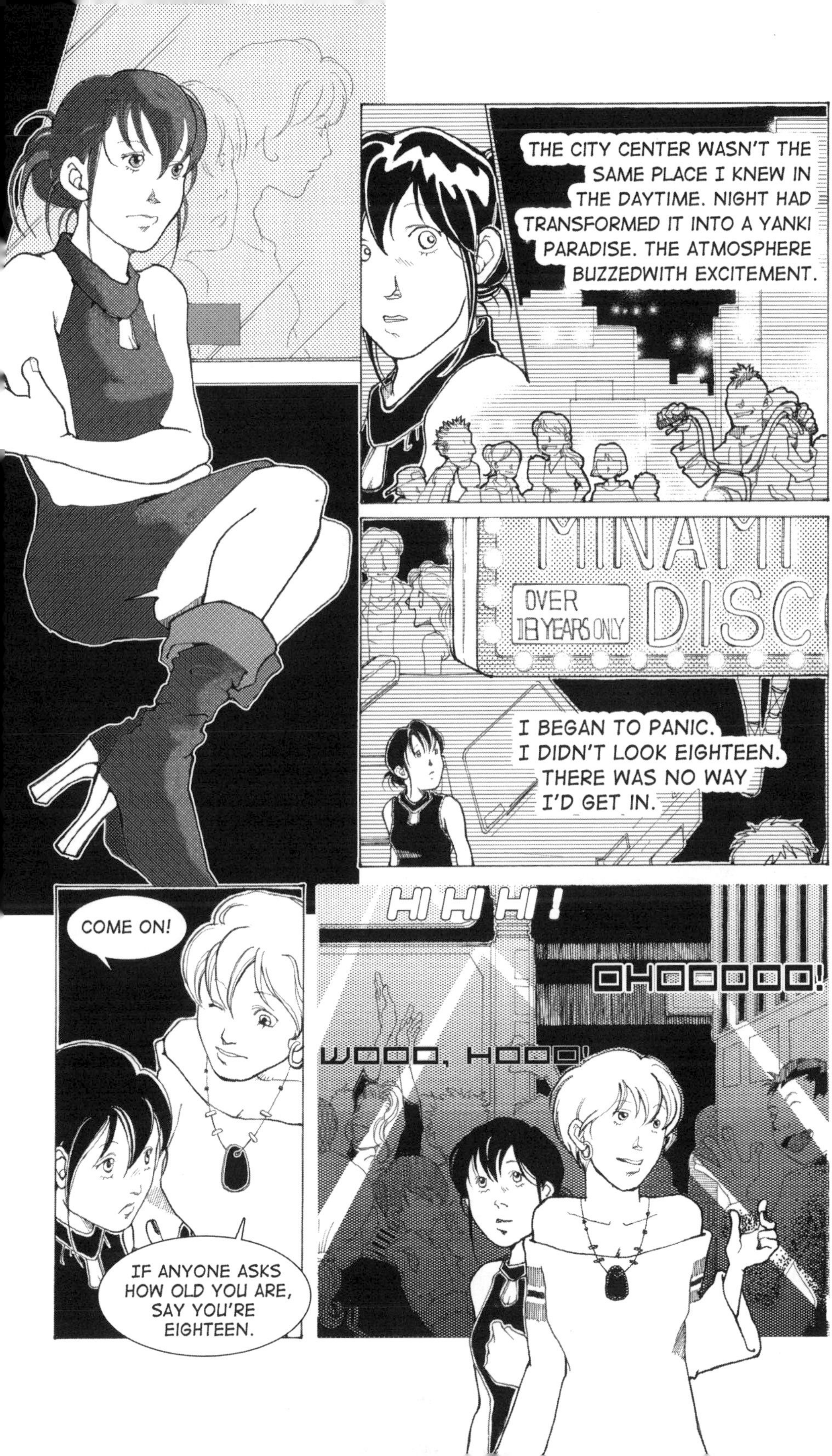
THE CITY CENTER WASN'T THE SAME PLACE I KNEW IN THE DAYTIME. NIGHT HAD TRANSFORMED IT INTO A YANKI PARADISE. THE ATMOSPHERE BUZZEDWITH EXCITEMENT.
MINAMI DISC
OVER 18 YEARS ONLY
I BEGAN TO PANIC. I DIDN'T LOOK EIGHTEEN. THERE WAS NO WAY I'D GET IN.
COME ON!
IF ANYONE ASKS HOW OLD YOU ARE, SAY YOU'RE EIGHTEEN.
HI HI HI!
OHOOOOO!
WOOO, HOOO!

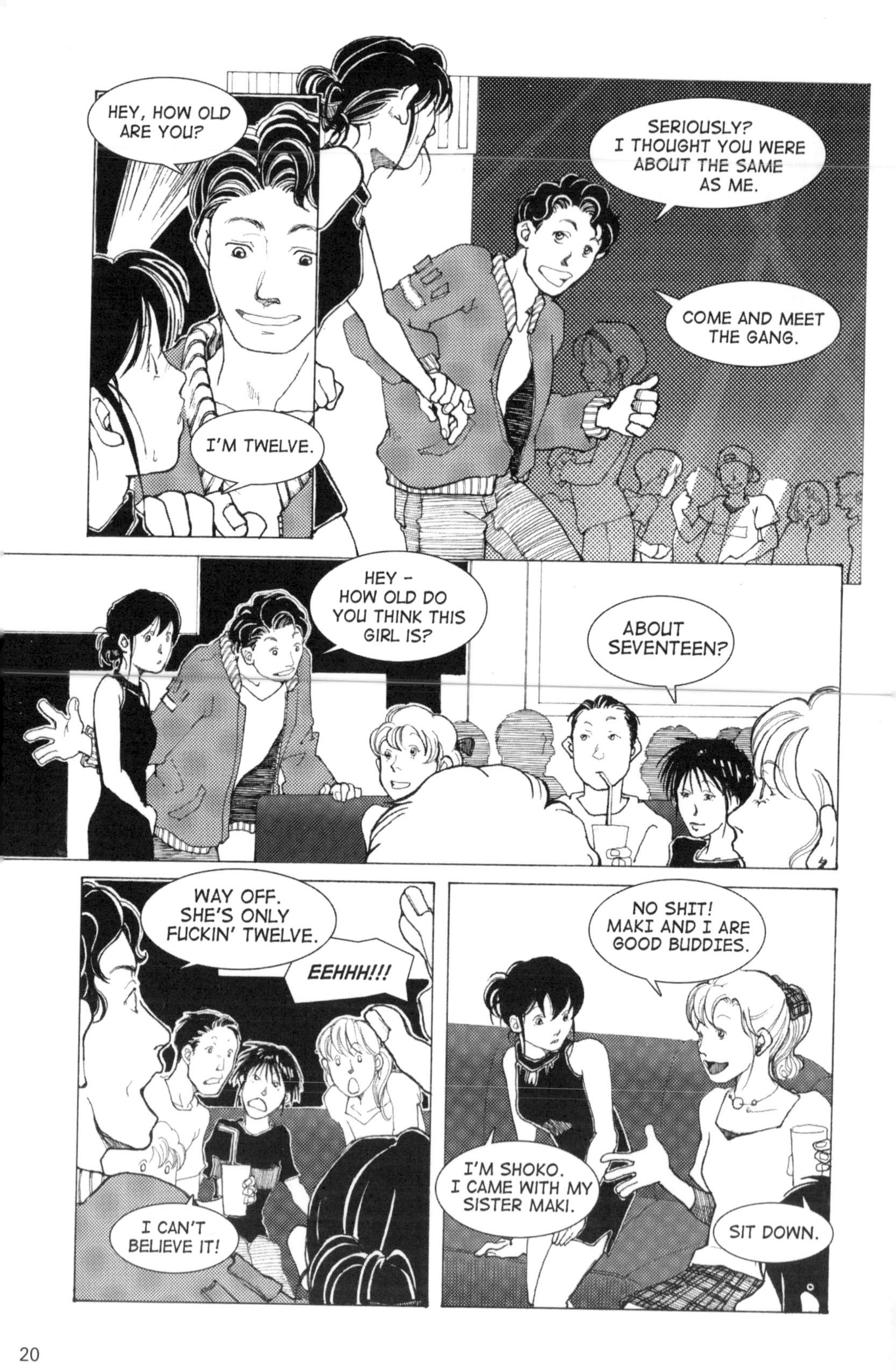
HEY, HOW OLD ARE YOU?
I'M TWELVE.
SERIOUSLY? I THOUGHT YOU WERE ABOUT THE SAME AS ME.
COME AND MEET THE GANG.
HEY - HOW OLD DO YOU THINK THIS GIRL IS?
ABOUT SEVENTEEN?
WAY OFF. SHE'S ONLY FUCKIN' TWELVE.
EEHHH!!!
I CAN'T BELIEVE IT!
NO SHIT! MAKI AND I ARE GOOD BUDDIES.
I'M SHOKO. I CAME WITH MY SISTER MAKI.
SIT DOWN.

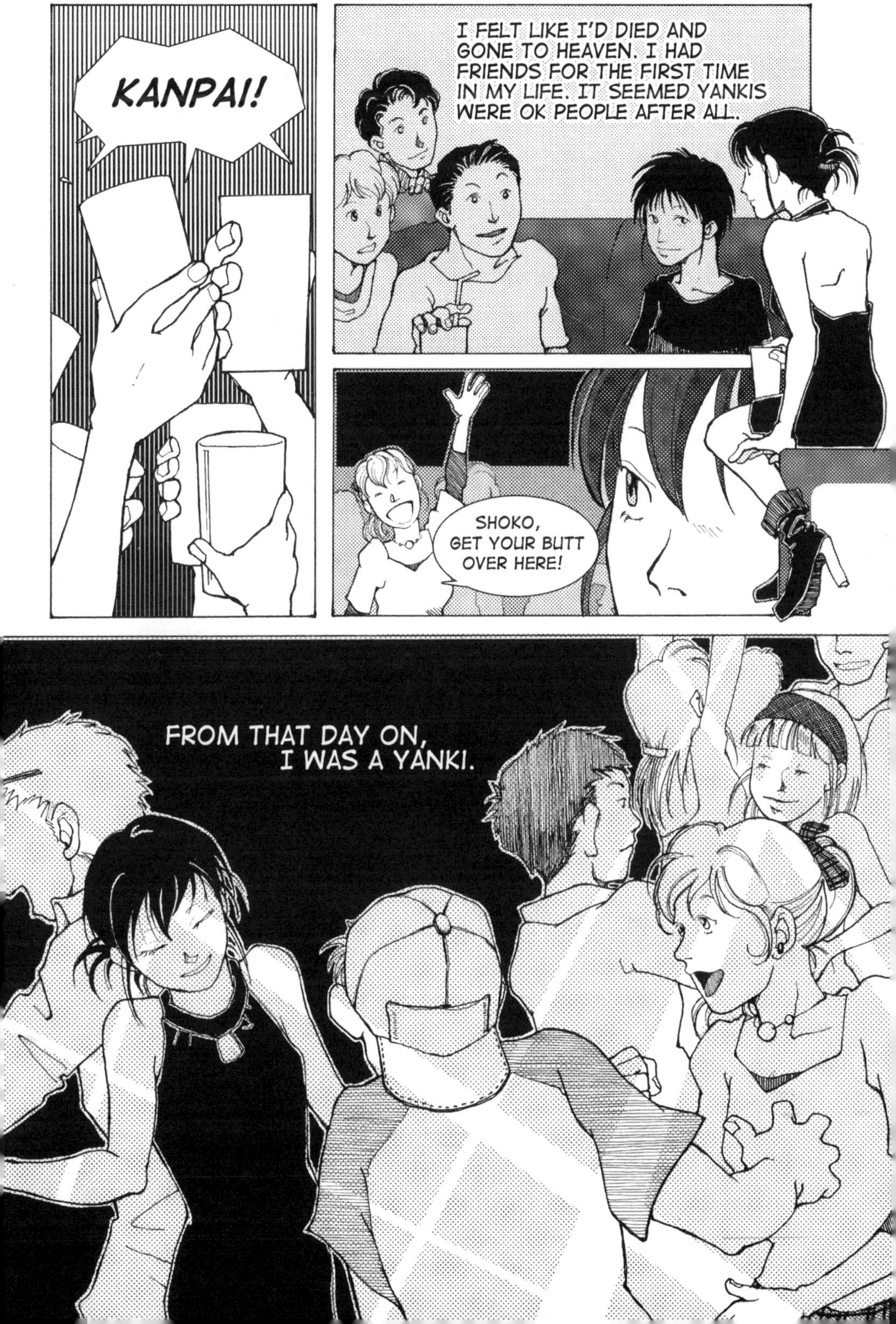
KANPAI!
I FELT LIKE I'D DIED AND GONE TO HEAVEN. I HAD FRIENDS FOR THE FIRST TIME IN MY LIFE. IT SEEMED YANKIS WERE OK PEOPLE AFTER ALL.
SHOKO, GET YOUR BUTT OVER HERE!
FROM THAT DAY ON, I WAS A YANKI.

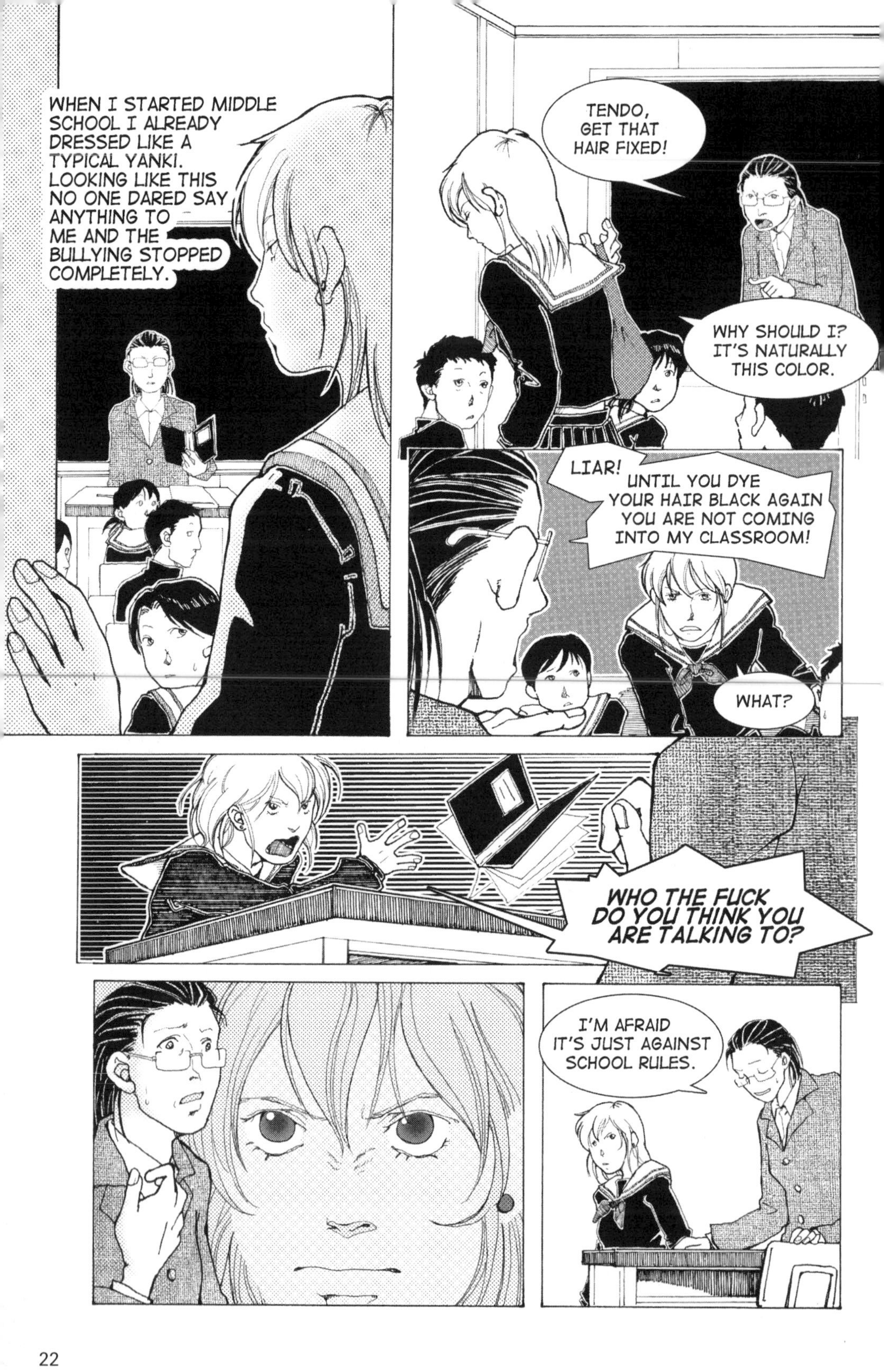
WHEN I STARTED MIDDLE SCHOOL I ALREADY DRESSED LIKE A TYPICAL YANKI. LOOKING LIKE THIS NO ONE DARED SAY ANYTHING TO ME AND THE BULLYING STOPPED COMPLETELY.
TENDO, GET THAT HAIR FIXED!
WHY SHOULD I? IT'S NATURALLY THIS COLOR.
LIAR!
UNTIL YOU DYE YOUR HAIR BLACK AGAIN YOU ARE NOT COMING INTO MY CLASSROOM!
WHAT?
WHO THE FUCK DO YOU THINK YOU ARE TALKING TO?
I'M AFRAID IT'S JUST AGAINST SCHOOL RULES.

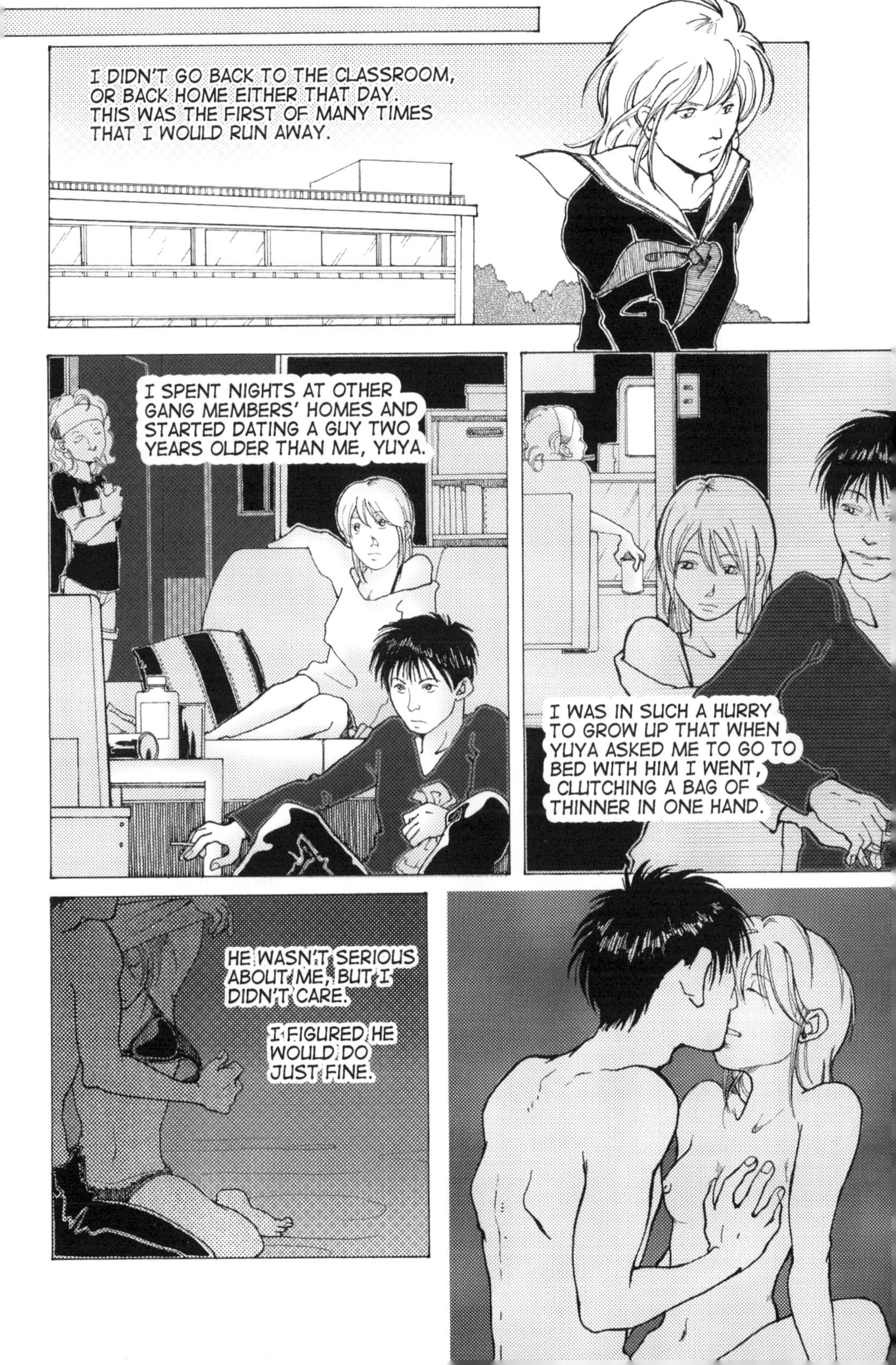
I DIDN'T GO BACK TO THE CLASSROOM, OR BACK HOME EITHER THAT DAY. THIS WAS THE FIRST OF MANY TIMES THAT I WOULD RUN AWAY.
I SPENT NIGHTS AT OTHER GANG MEMBERS' HOMES AND STARTED DATING A GUY TWO YEARS OLDER THAN ME, YUYA.
I WAS IN SUCH A HURRY TO GROW UP THAT WHEN YUYA ASKED ME TO GO TO BED WITH HIM I WENT, CLUTCHING A BAG OF THINNER IN ONE HAND.
HE WASN'T SERIOUS ABOUT ME, BUT I DIDN'T CARE.
I FIGURED HE WOULD DO JUST FINE.

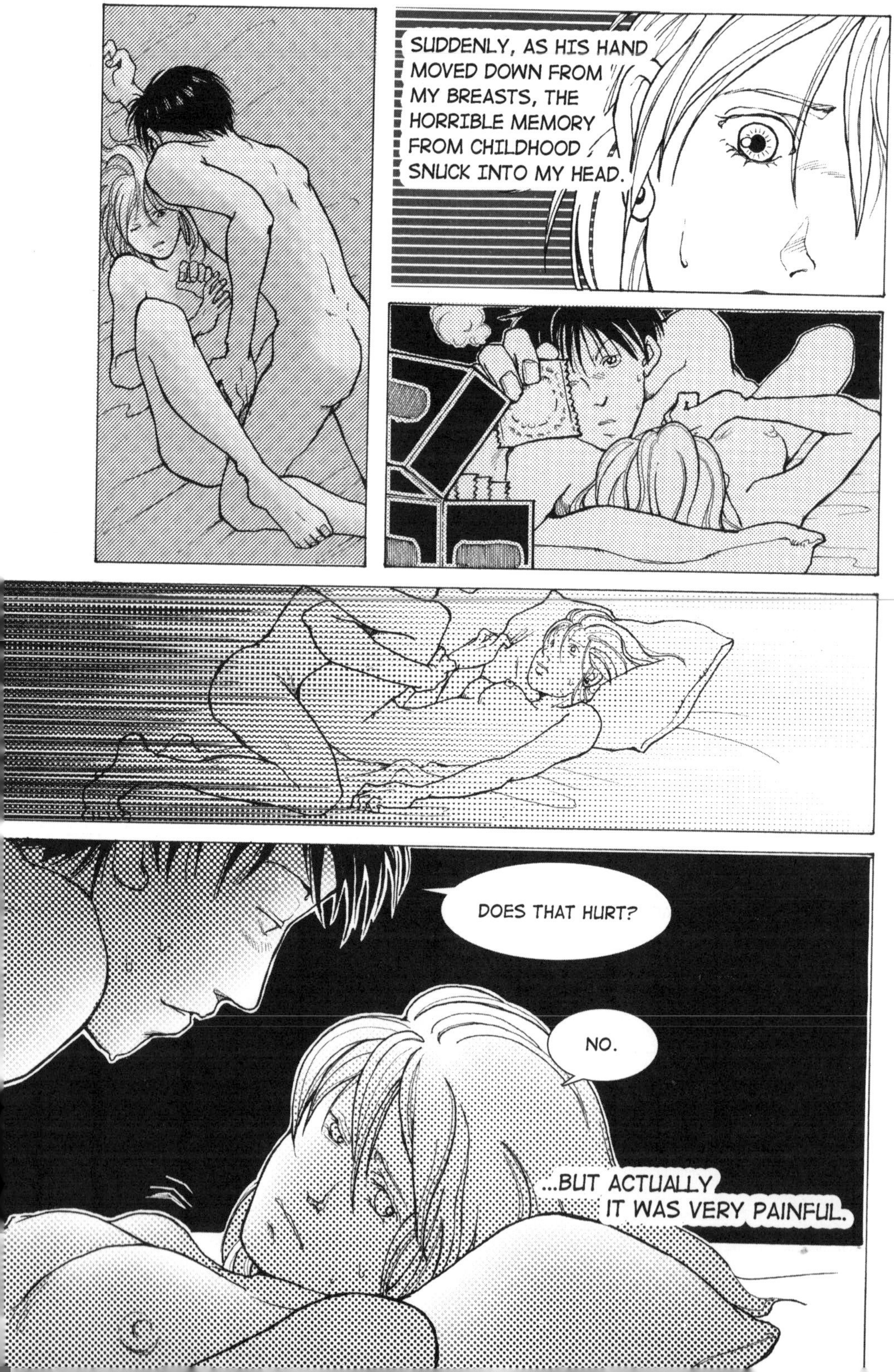
SUDDENLY, AS HIS HAND MOVED DOWN FROM MY BREASTS, THE HORRIBLE MEMORY FROM CHILDHOOD SNUCK INTO MY HEAD.
DOES THAT HURT?
NO.
...BUT ACTUALLY IT WAS VERY PAINFUL.

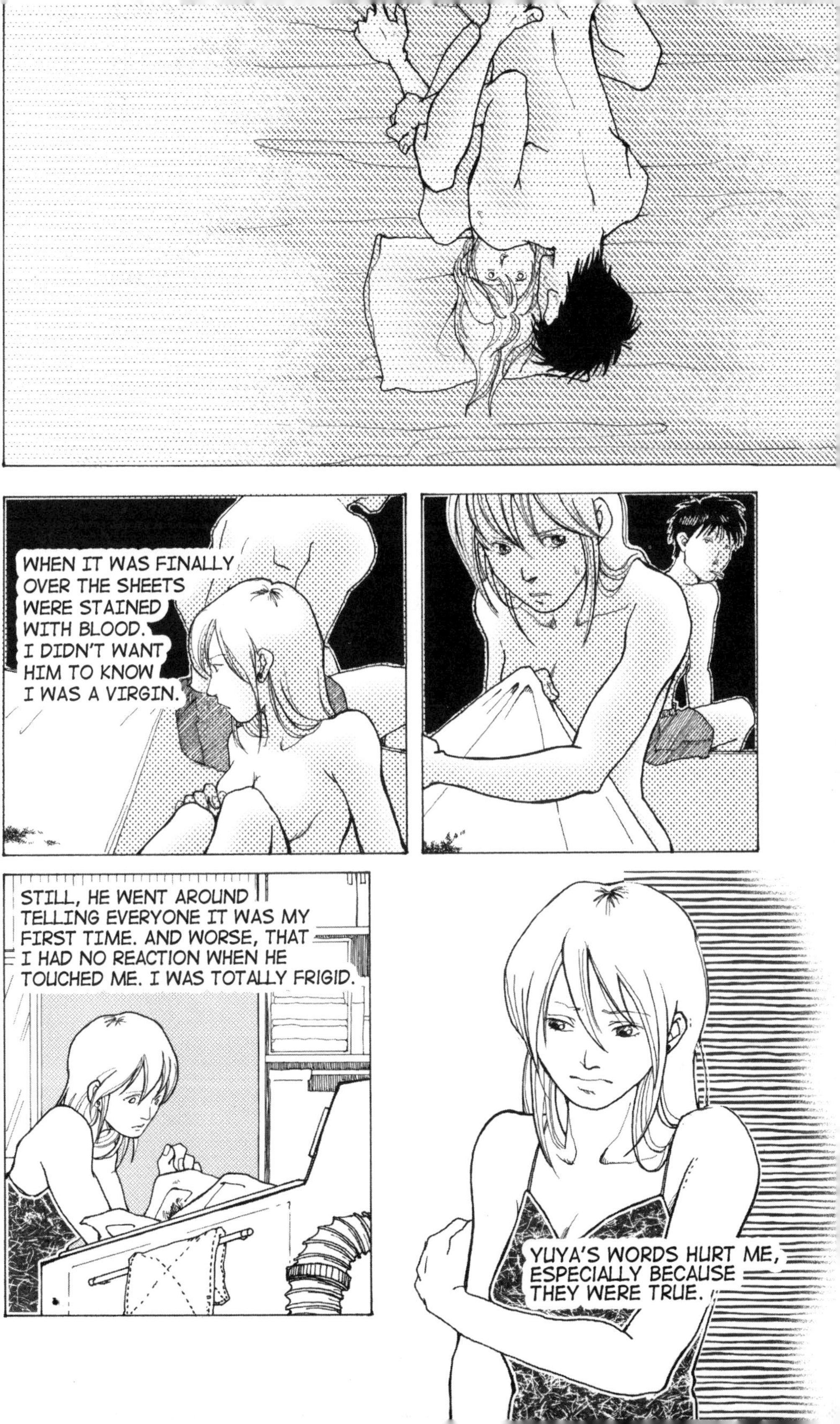
WHEN IT WAS FINALLY OVER THE SHEETS WERE STAINED WITH BLOOD. I DIDN'T WANT HIM TO KNOW I WAS A VIRGIN.
STILL, HE WENT AROUND TELLING EVERYONE IT WAS MY FIRST TIME. AND WORSE, THAT I HAD NO REACTION WHEN HE TOUCHED ME. I WAS TOTALLY FRIGID.
YUYA'S WORDS HURT ME, ESPECIALLY BECAUSE THEY WERE TRUE.

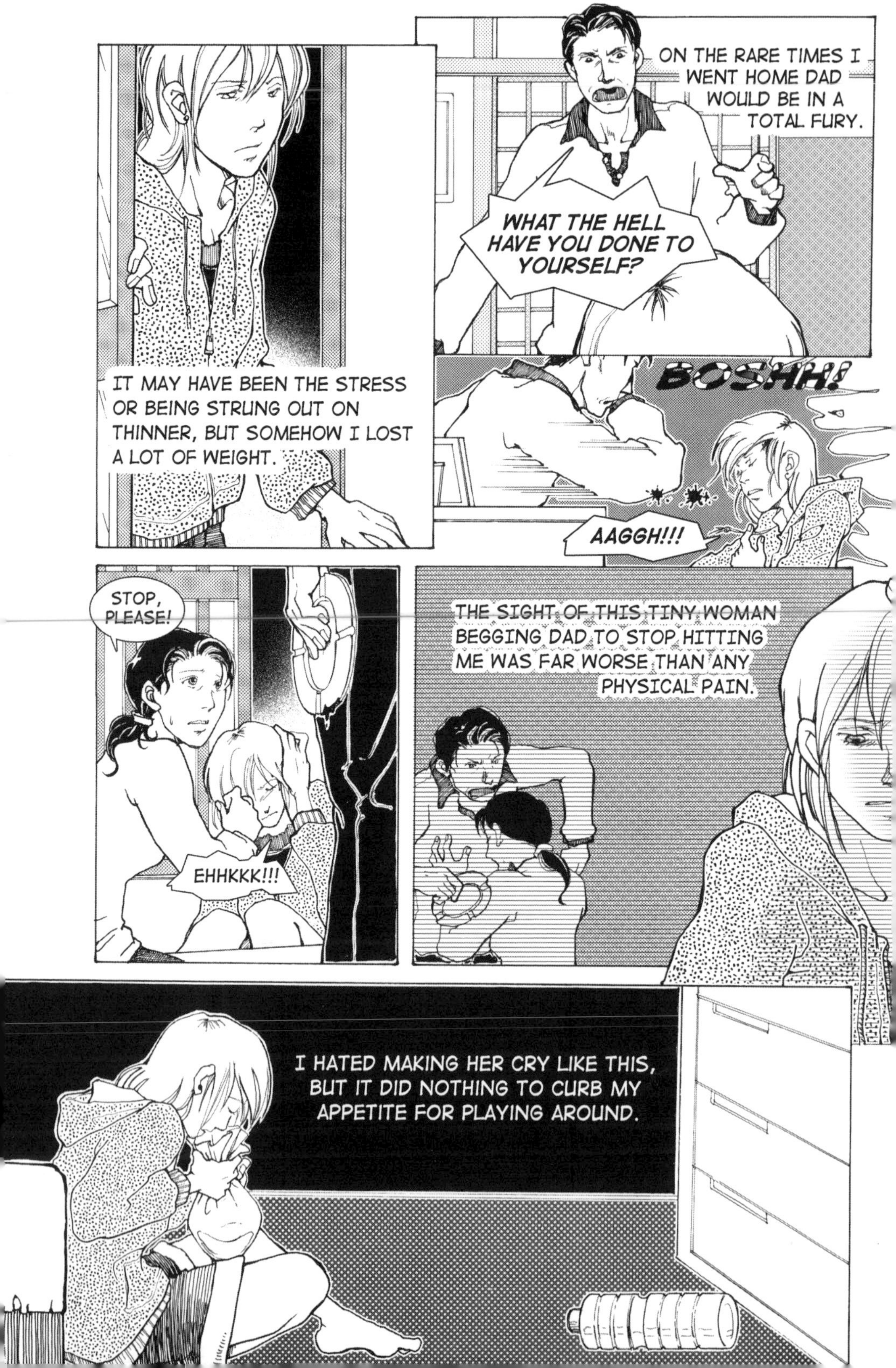
ON THE RARE TIMES I WENT HOME DAD WOULD BE IN A TOTAL FURY.
WHAT THE HELL HAVE YOU DONE TO YOURSELF?
IT MAY HAVE BEEN THE STRESS OR BEING STRUNG OUT ON THINNER, BUT SOMEHOW I LOST A LOT OF WEIGHT.
BOSHH!
AAGGH!!!
STOP, PLEASE!
EHHKKK!!!
THE SIGHT OF THIS TINY WOMAN BEGGING DAD TO STOP HITTING ME WAS FAR WORSE THAN ANY PHYSICAL PAIN.
I HATED MAKING HER CRY LIKE THIS, BUT IT DID NOTHING TO CURB MY APPETITE FOR PLAYING AROUND.

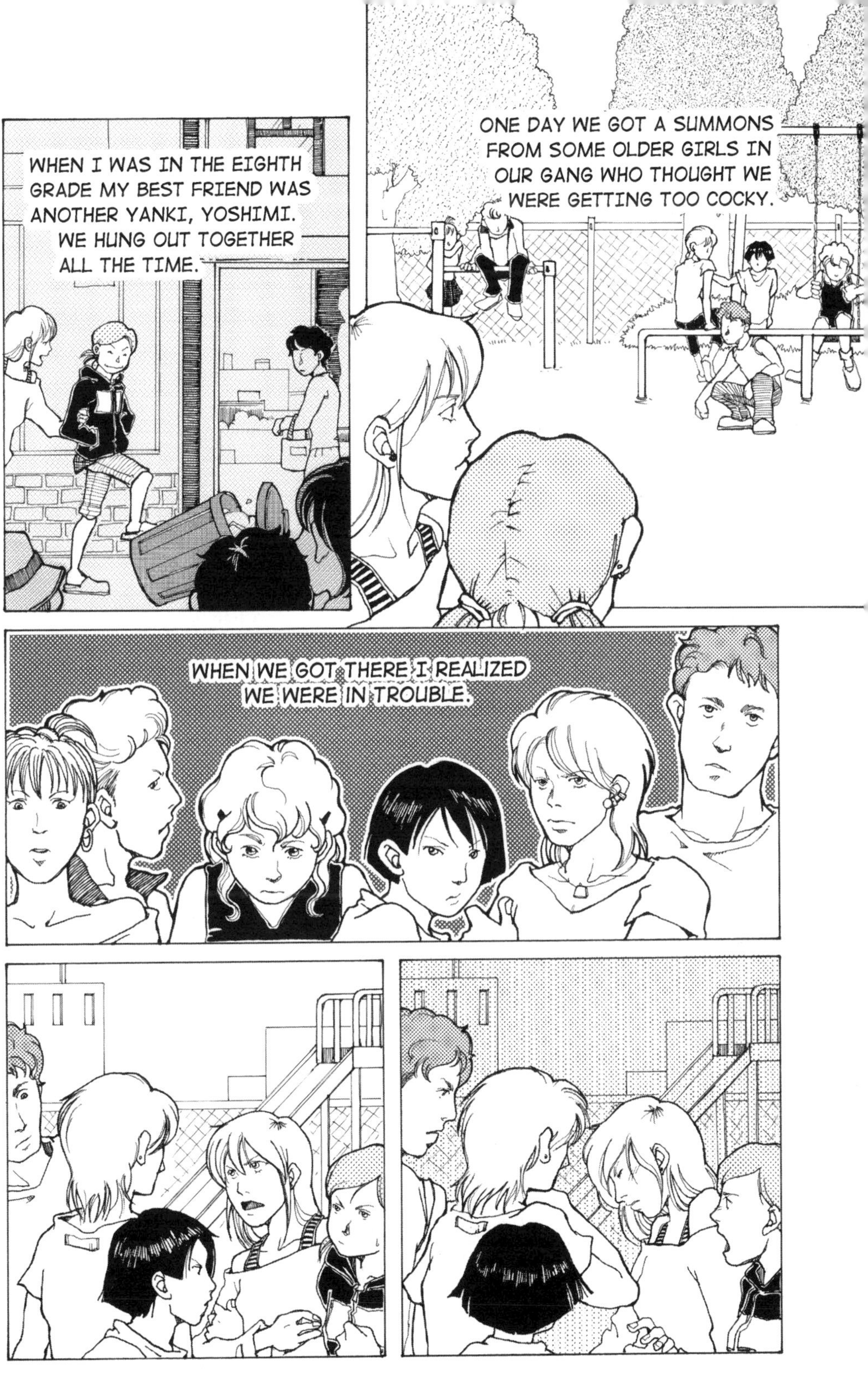
WHEN I WAS IN THE EIGHTH GRADE MY BEST FRIEND WAS ANOTHER YANKI, YOSHIMI. WE HUNG OUT TOGETHER ALL THE TIME.
ONE DAY WE GOT A SUMMONS FROM SOME OLDER GIRLS IN OUR GANG WHO THOUGHT WE WERE GETTING TOO COCKY.
WHEN WE GOT THERE I REALIZED WE WERE IN TROUBLE.

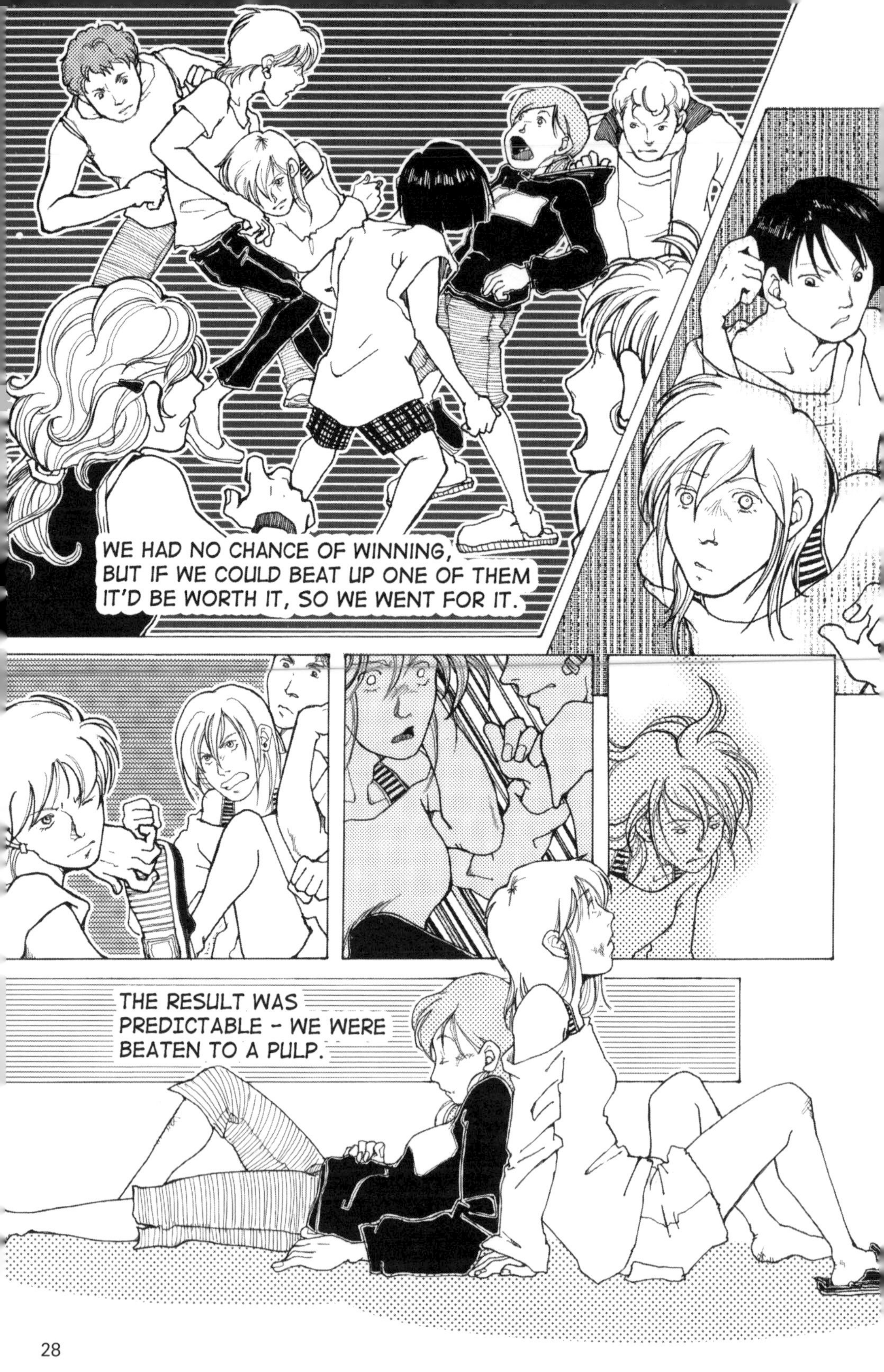
WE HAD NO CHANCE OF WINNING, BUT IF WE COULD BEAT UP ONE OF THEM IT'D BE WORTH IT, SO WE WENT FOR IT.
THE RESULT WAS PREDICTABLE - WE WERE BEATEN TO A PULP.

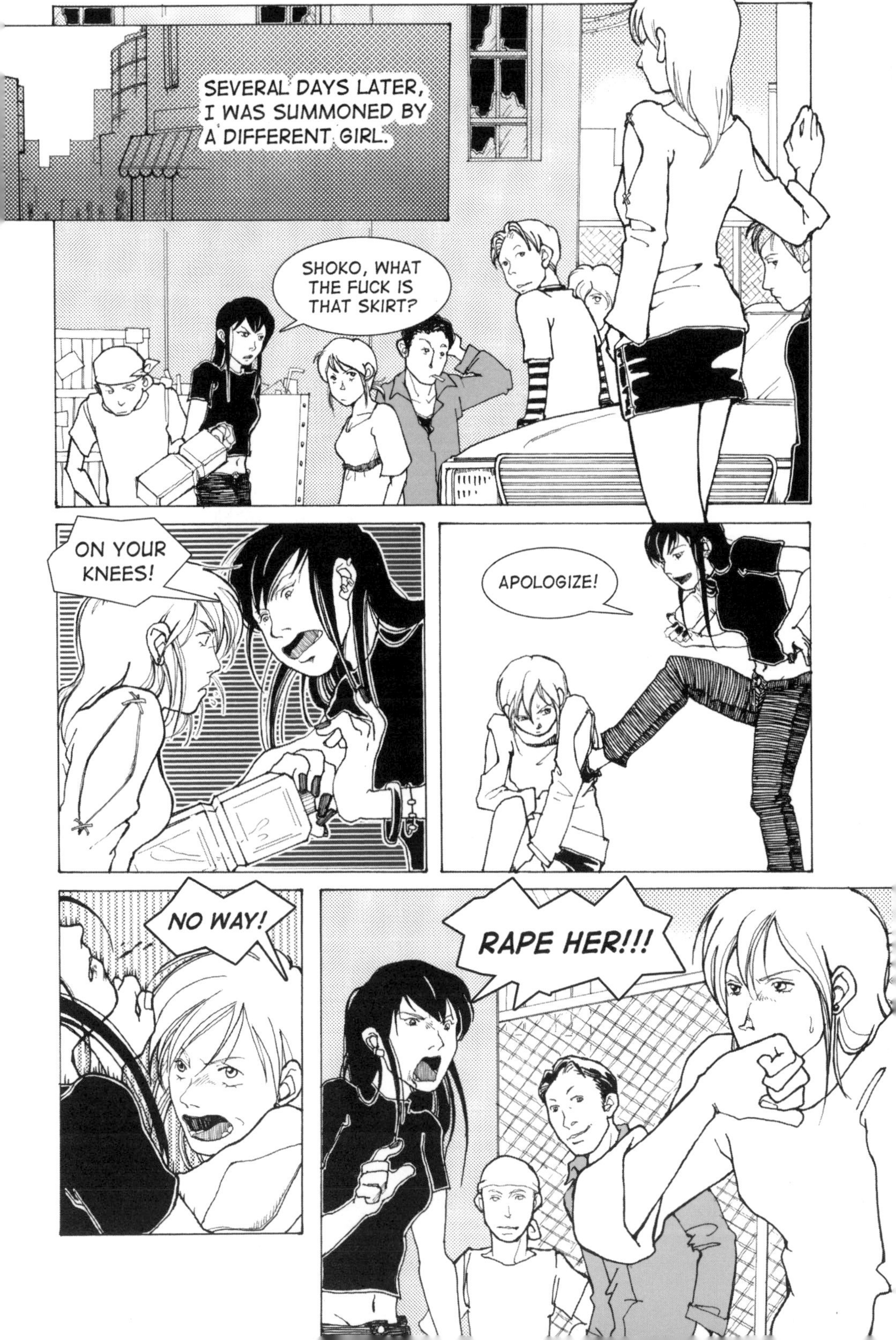
SEVERAL DAYS LATER, I WAS SUMMONED BY A DIFFERENT GIRL.
SHOKO, WHAT THE FUCK IS THAT SKIRT?
ON YOUR KNEES!
APOLOGIZE!
NO WAY!
RAPE HER!!!

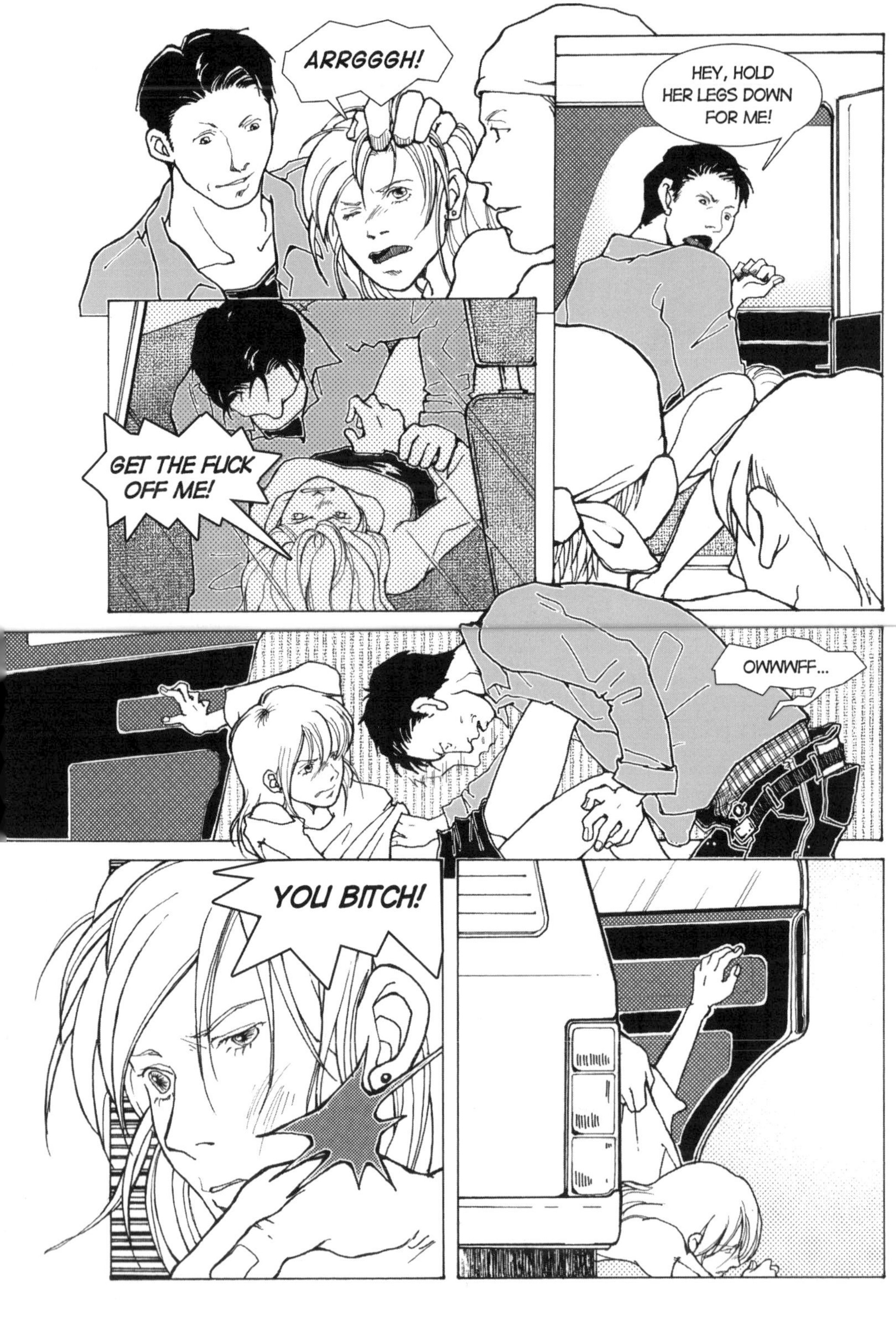
ARRGGGH!
HEY, HOLD HER LEGS DOWN FOR ME!
GET THE FUCK OFF ME!
OWWWFF...
YOU BITCH!

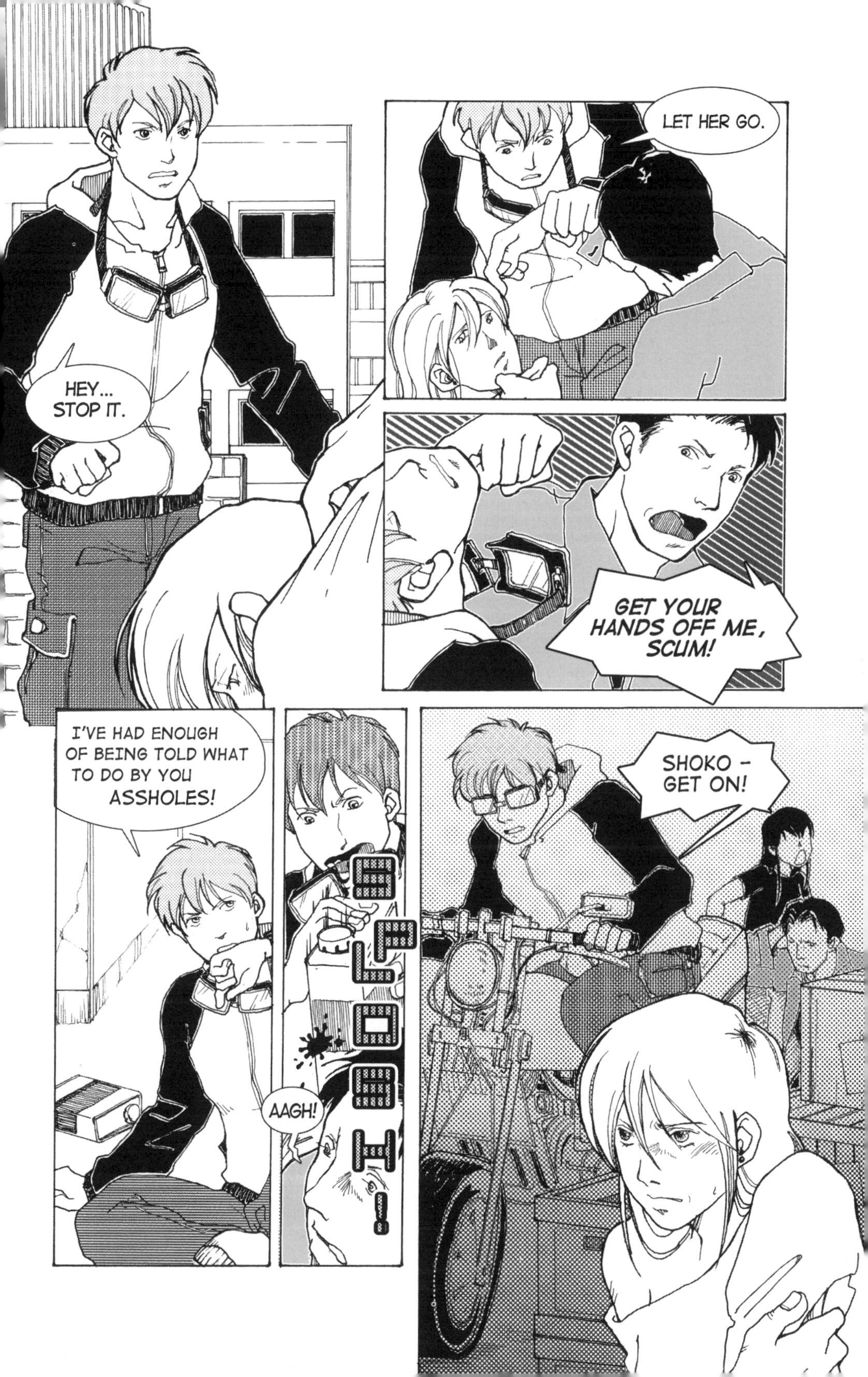
HEY... STOP IT.
LET HER GO.
GET YOUR HANDS OFF ME, SCUM!
I'VE HAD ENOUGH OF BEING TOLD WHAT TO DO BY YOU ASSHOLES!
SPLOOSH!
AAGH!
SHOKO - GET ON!

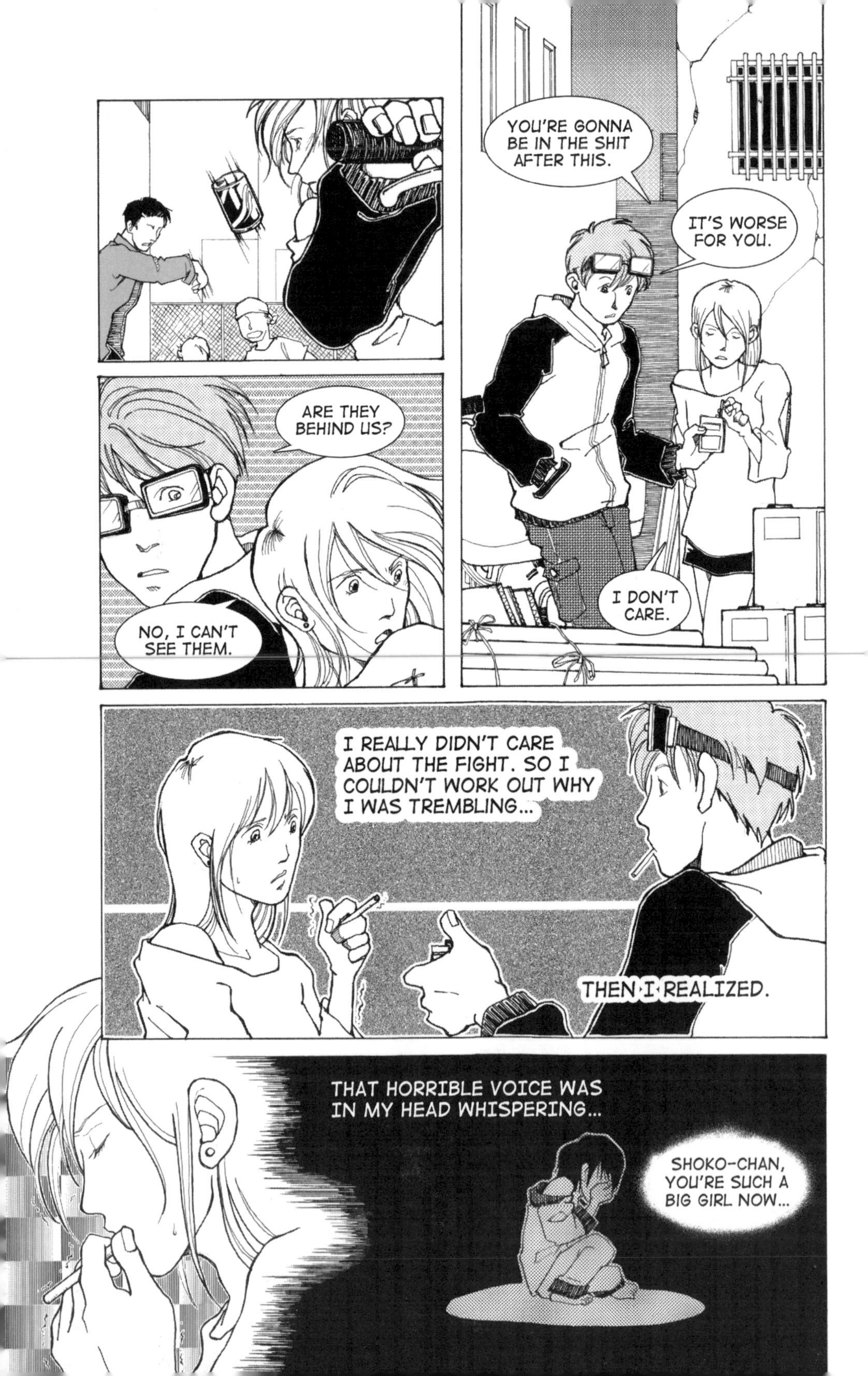
ARE THEY BEHIND US?
NO, I CAN'T SEE THEM.
YOU'RE GONNA BE IN THE SHIT AFTER THIS.
IT'S WORSE FOR YOU.
I DON'T CARE.
I REALLY DIDN'T CARE ABOUT THE FIGHT. SO I COULDN'T WORK OUT WHY I WAS TREMBLING...
THEN I REALIZED.
THAT HORRIBLE VOICE WAS IN MY HEAD WHISPERING...
SHOKO-CHAN, YOU'RE SUCH A BIG GIRL NOW...

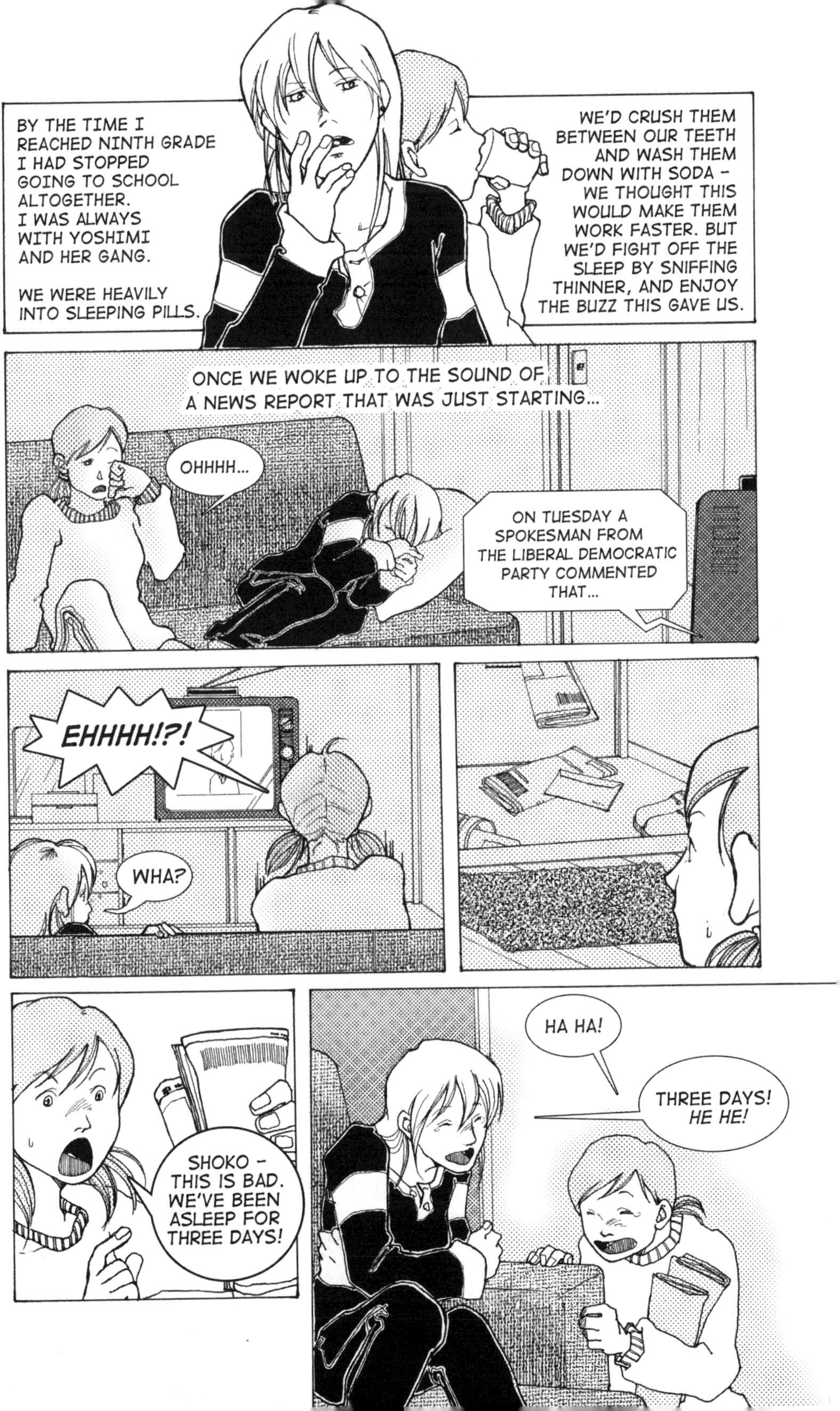
BY THE TIME I REACHED NINTH GRADE I HAD STOPPED GOING TO SCHOOL ALTOGETHER. I WAS ALWAYS WITH YOSHIMI AND HER GANG.
WE WERE HEAVILY INTO SLEEPING PILLS.
WE'D CRUSH THEM BETWEEN OUR TEETH AND WASH THEM DOWN WITH SODA - WE THOUGHT THIS WOULD MAKE THEM WORK FASTER. BUT WE'D FIGHT OFF THE SLEEP BY SNIFFING THINNER, AND ENJOY THE BUZZ THIS GAVE US.
ONCE WE WOKE UP TO THE SOUND OF A NEWS REPORT THAT WAS JUST STARTING...
OHHHH...
ON TUESDAY A SPOKESMAN FROM THE LIBERAL DEMOCRATIC PARTY COMMENTED THAT...
EHHHH!?!
WHA?
SHOKO - THIS IS BAD. WE'VE BEEN ASLEEP FOR THREE DAYS!
HA HA!
THREE DAYS! HE HE!

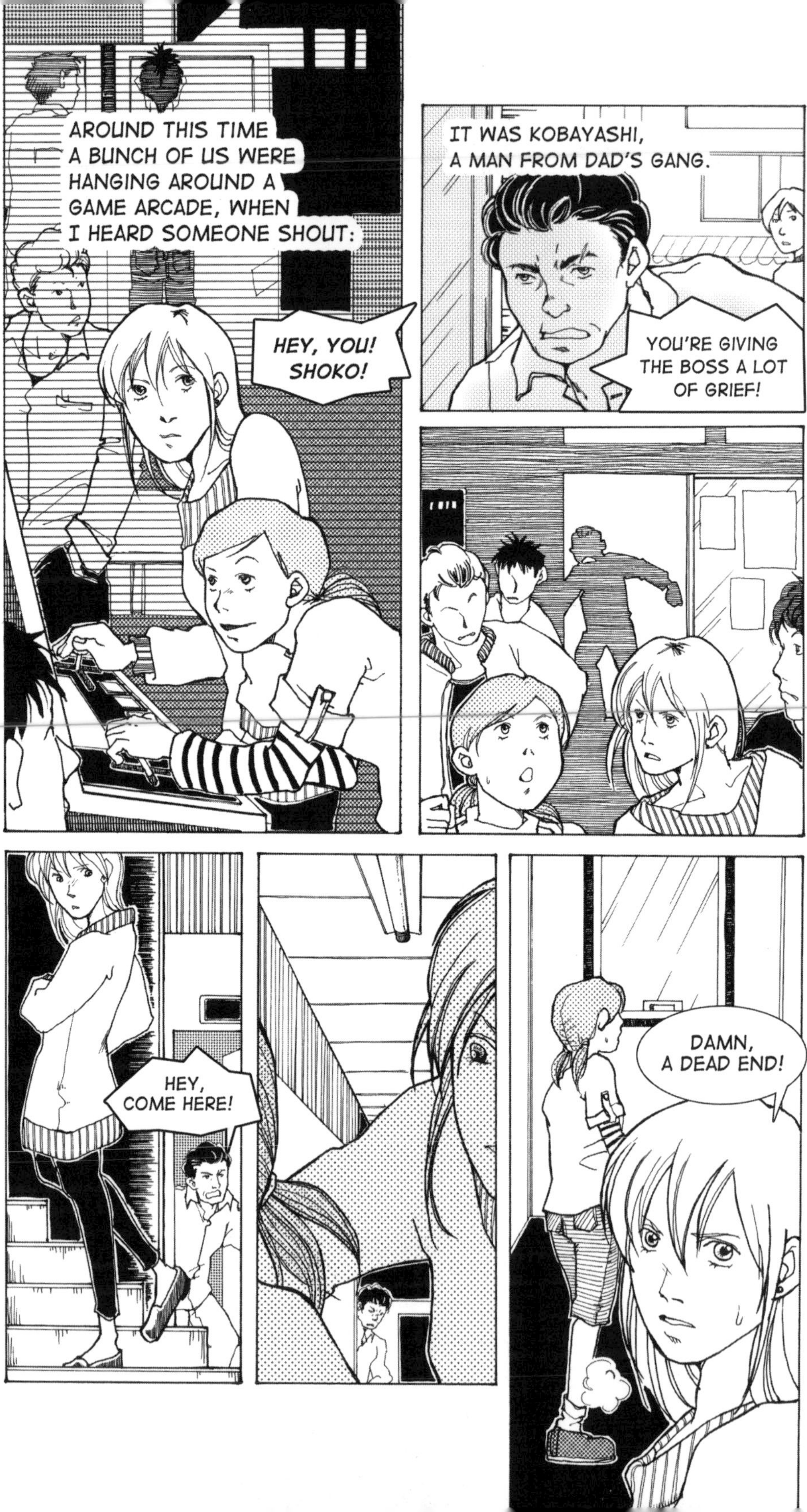
AROUND THIS TIME A BUNCH OF US WERE HANGING AROUND A GAME ARCADE, WHEN I HEARD SOMEONE SHOUT:
HEY, YOU! SHOKO!
IT WAS KOBAYASHI, A MAN FROM DAD'S GANG.
YOU'RE GIVING THE BOSS A LOT OF GRIEF!
HEY, COME HERE!
DAMN, A DEAD END!

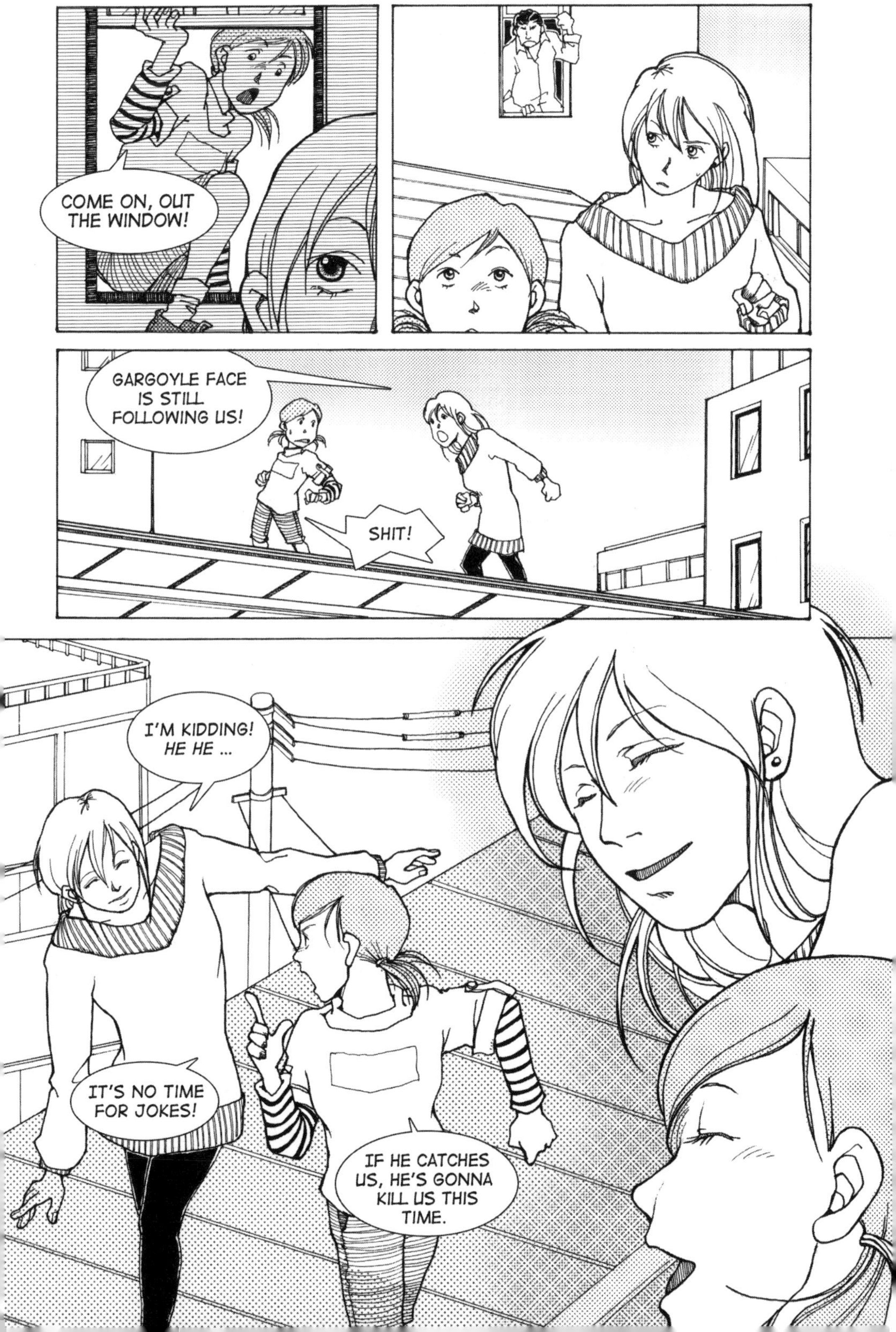
COME ON, OUT THE WINDOW!
GARGOYLE FACE IS STILL FOLLOWING US!
SHIT!
I'M KIDDING! HE HE ...
IT'S NO TIME FOR JOKES!
IF HE CATCHES US, HE'S GONNA KILL US THIS TIME.

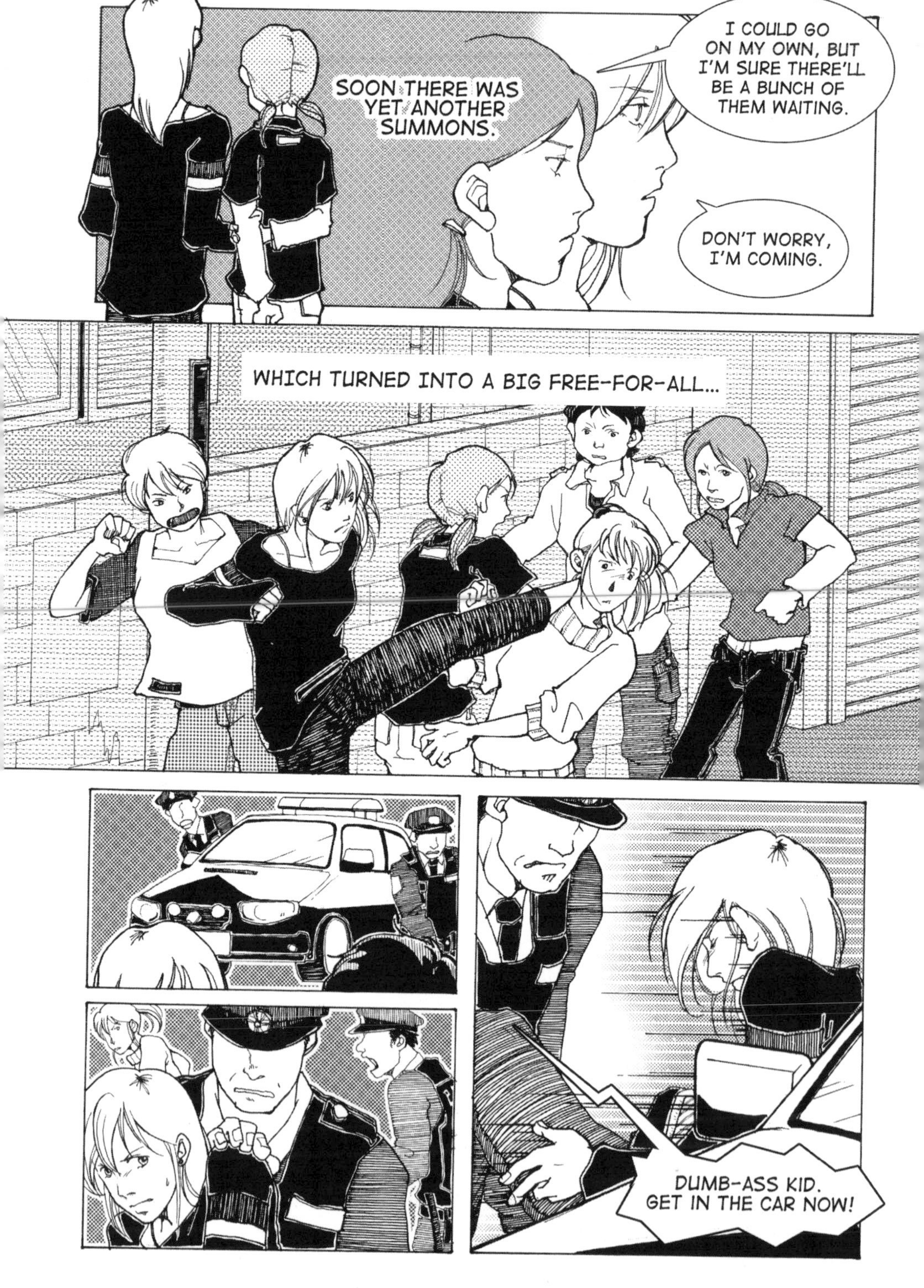
SOON THERE WAS YET ANOTHER SUMMONS.
I COULD GO ON MY OWN, BUT I'M SURE THERE'LL BE A BUNCH OF THEM WAITING.
DON'T WORRY, I'M COMING.
WHICH TURNED INTO A BIG FREE-FOR-ALL...
DUMB-ASS KID. GET IN THE CAR NOW!

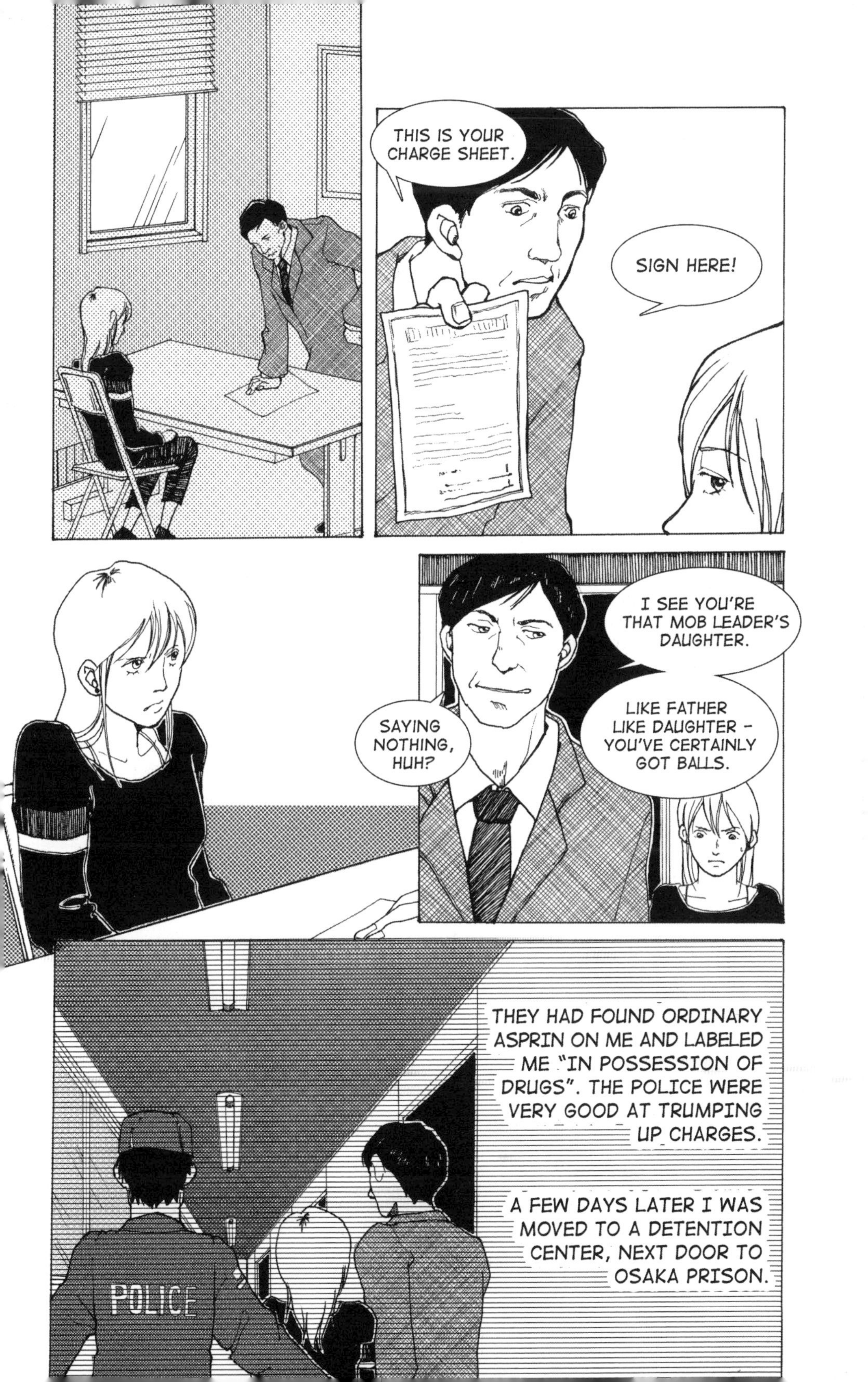
THIS IS YOUR CHARGE SHEET.
SIGN HERE!
I SEE YOU'RE THAT MOB LEADER'S DAUGHTER.
LIKE FATHER LIKE DAUGHTER - YOU'VE CERTAINLY GOT BALLS.
SAYING NOTHING, HUH?
THEY HAD FOUND ORDINARY ASPRIN ON ME AND LABELED ME "IN POSSESSION OF DRUGS". THE POLICE WERE VERY GOOD AT TRUMPING UP CHARGES.
A FEW DAYS LATER I WAS MOVED TO A DETENTION CENTER, NEXT DOOR TO OSAKA PRISON.
POLICE

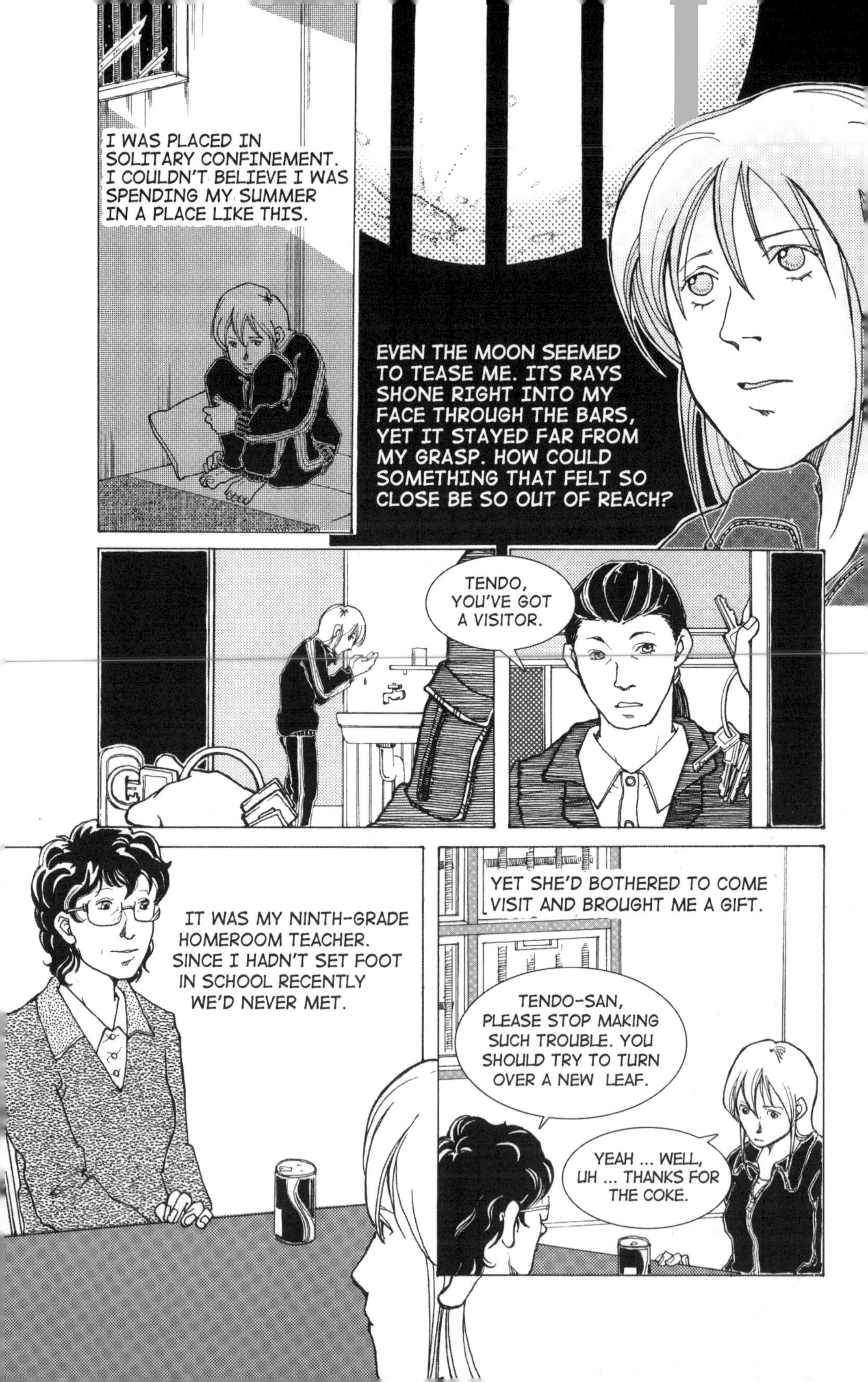
I WAS PLACED IN SOLITARY CONFINEMENT. I COULDN'T BELIEVE I WAS SPENDING MY SUMMER IN A PLACE LIKE THIS.
EVEN THE MOON SEEMED TO TEASE ME. ITS RAYS SHONE RIGHT INTO MY FACE THROUGH THE BARS, YET IT STAYED FAR FROM MY GRASP. HOW COULD SOMETHING THAT FELT SO CLOSE BE SO OUT OF REACH?
TENDO, YOU'VE GOT A VISITOR.
IT WAS MY NINTH-GRADE HOMEROOM TEACHER. SINCE I HADN'T SET FOOT IN SCHOOL RECENTLY WE'D NEVER MET.
YET SHE'D BOTHERED TO COME VISIT AND BROUGHT ME A GIFT.
TENDO-SAN, PLEASE STOP MAKING SUCH TROUBLE. YOU SHOULD TRY TO TURN OVER A NEW LEAF.
YEAH ... WELL, UH ... THANKS FOR THE COKE.

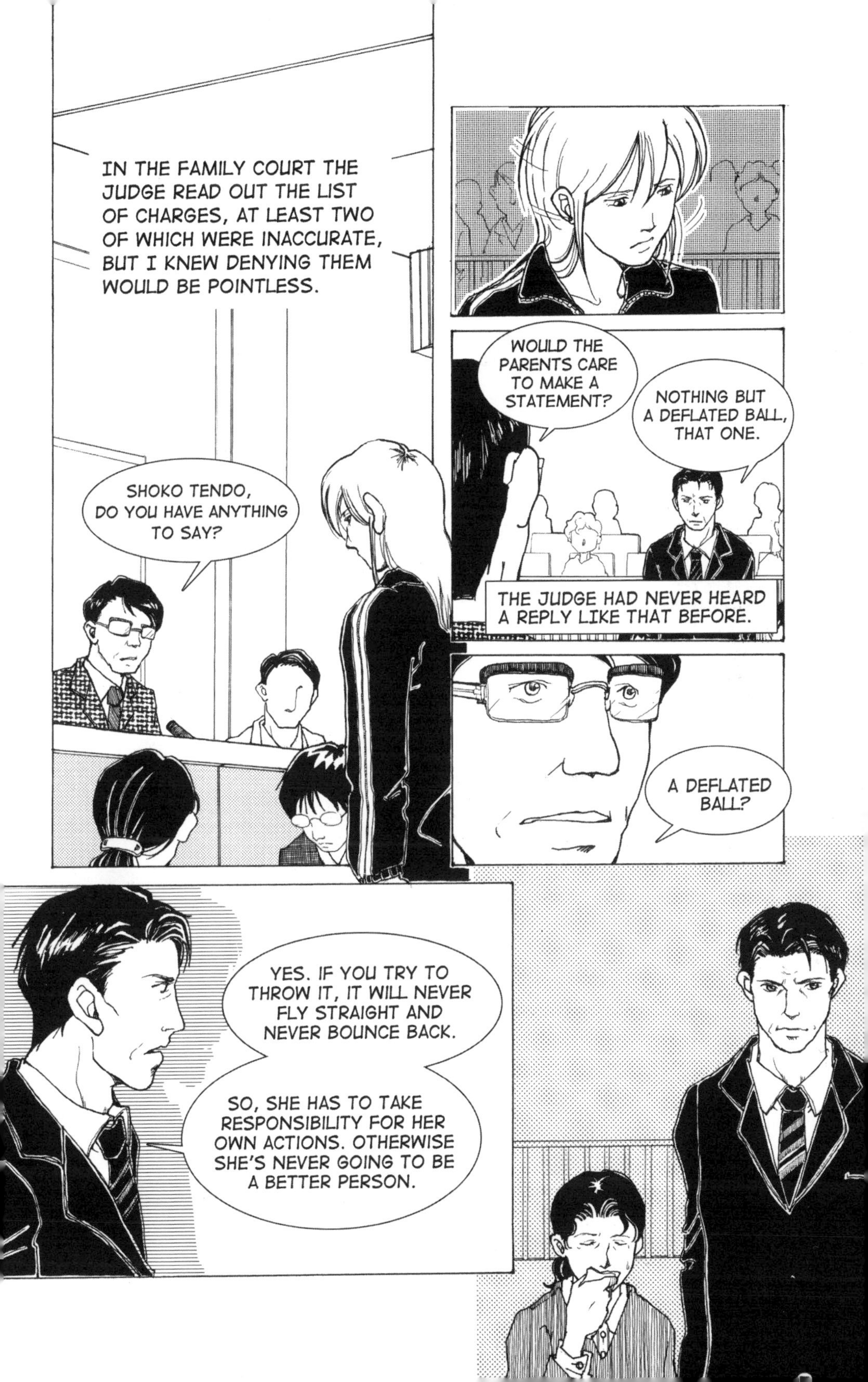
IN THE FAMILY COURT THE JUDGE READ OUT THE LIST OF CHARGES, AT LEAST TWO OF WHICH WERE INACCURATE, BUT I KNEW DENYING THEM WOULD BE POINTLESS.
SHOKO TENDO, DO YOU HAVE ANYTHING TO SAY?
WOULD THE PARENTS CARE TO MAKE A STATEMENT?
NOTHING BUT A DEFLATED BALL, THAT ONE.
THE JUDGE HAD NEVER HEARD A REPLY LIKE THAT BEFORE.
A DEFLATED BALL?
YES. IF YOU TRY TO THROW IT, IT WILL NEVER FLY STRAIGHT AND NEVER BOUNCE BACK.
SO, SHE HAS TO TAKE RESPONSIBILITY FOR HER OWN ACTIONS. OTHERWISE SHE'S NEVER GOING TO BE A BETTER PERSON.

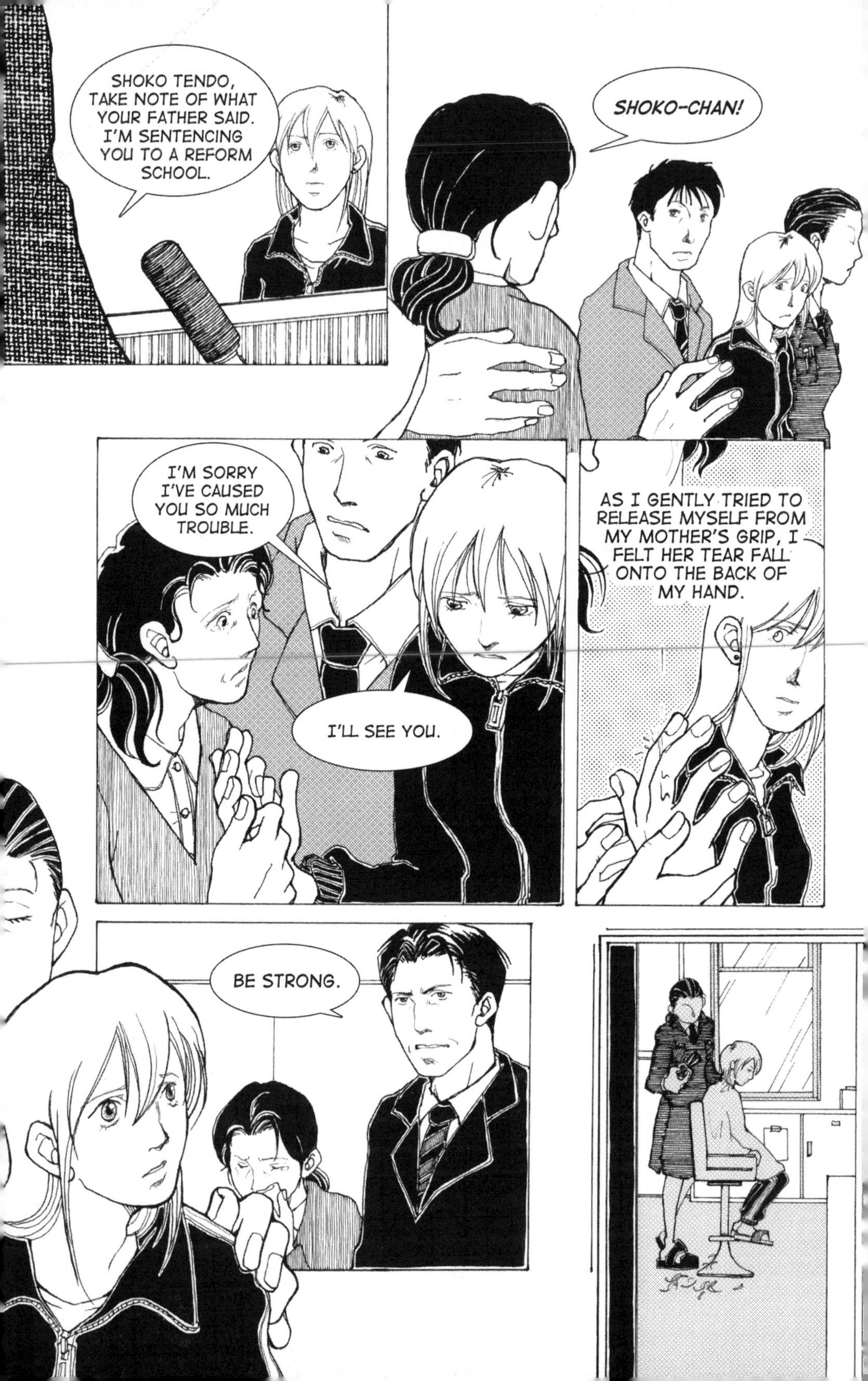
SHOKO TENDO, TAKE NOTE OF WHAT YOUR FATHER SAID. I'M SENTENCING YOU TO A REFORM SCHOOL.
SHOKO-CHAN!
I'M SORRY I'VE CAUSED YOU SO MUCH TROUBLE.
I'LL SEE YOU.
AS I GENTLY TRIED TO RELEASE MYSELF FROM MY MOTHER'S GRIP, I FELT HER TEAR FALL ONTO THE BACK OF MY HAND.
BE STRONG.

CHAPTER 3

Speed

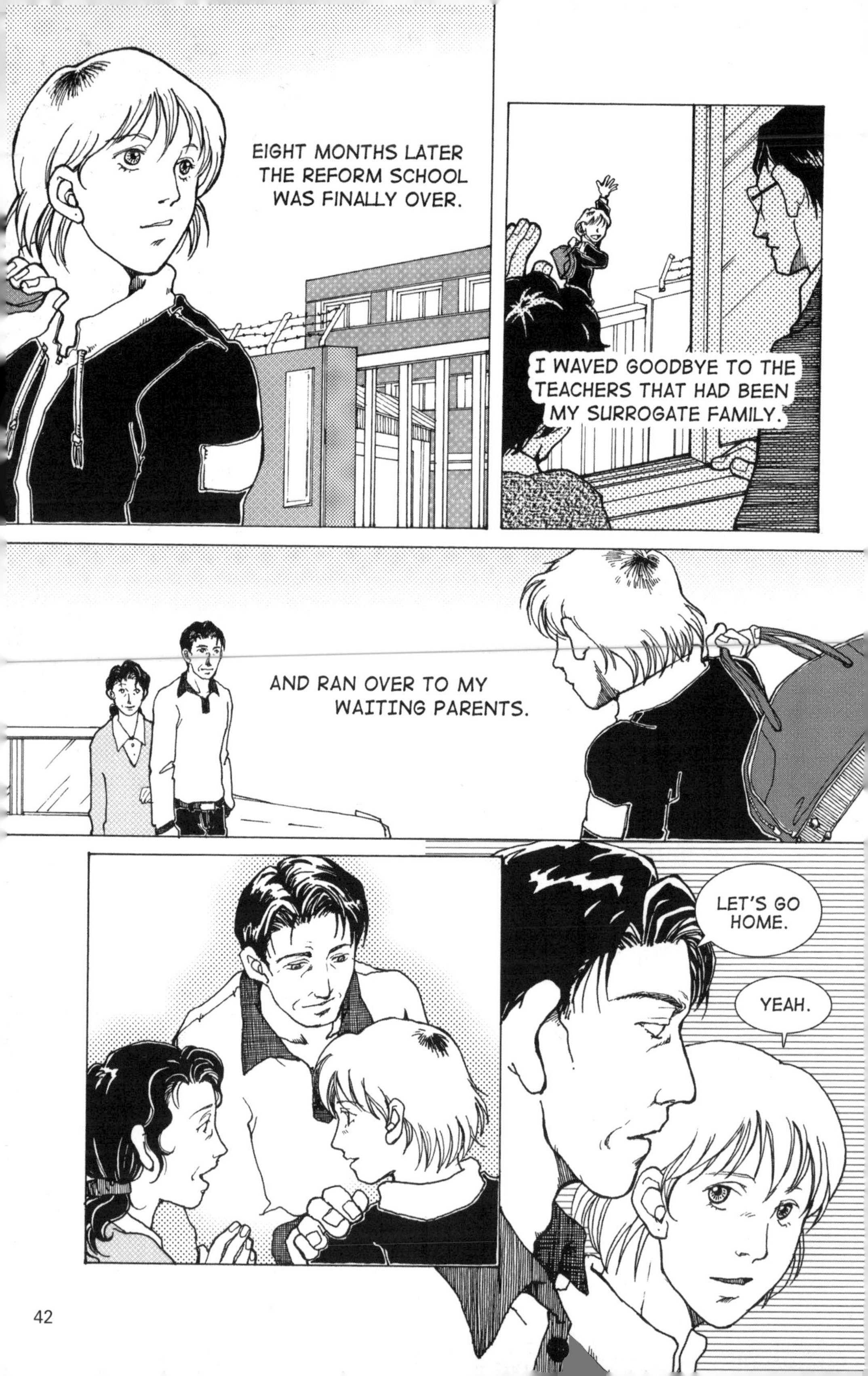
EIGHT MONTHS LATER THE REFORM SCHOOL WAS FINALLY OVER.
I WAVED GOODBYE TO THE TEACHERS THAT HAD BEEN MY SURROGATE FAMILY.
AND RAN OVER TO MY WAITING PARENTS.
LET'S GO HOME.
YEAH.

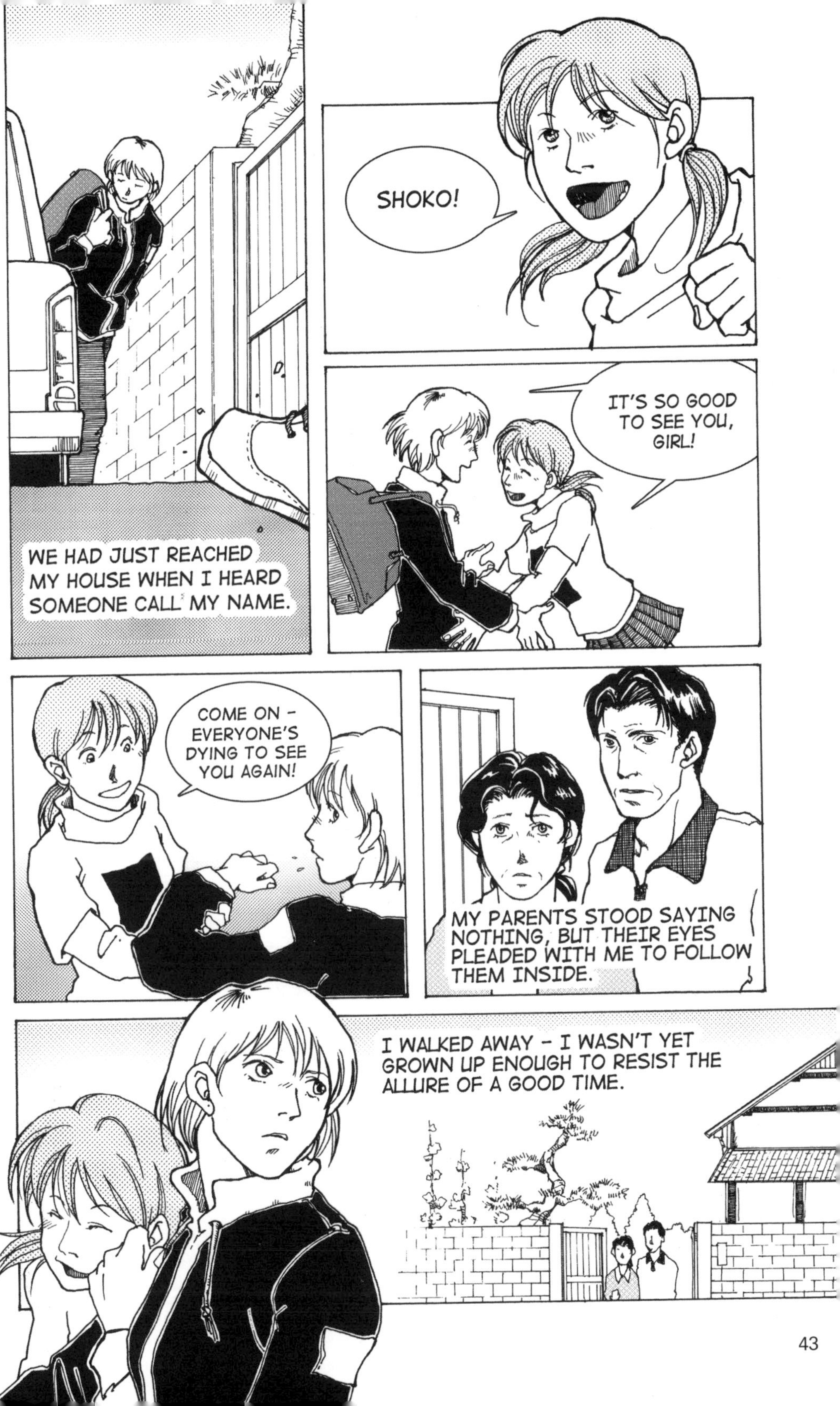

WE HAD JUST REACHED MY HOUSE WHEN I HEARD SOMEONE CALL MY NAME.
SHOKO!
IT'S SO GOOD TO SEE YOU, GIRL!
COME ON - EVERYONE'S DYING TO SEE YOU AGAIN!
MY PARENTS STOOD SAYING NOTHING, BUT THEIR EYES PLEADED WITH ME TO FOLLOW THEM INSIDE.
I WALKED AWAY - I WASN'T YET GROWN UP ENOUGH TO RESIST THE ALLURE OF A GOOD TIME.

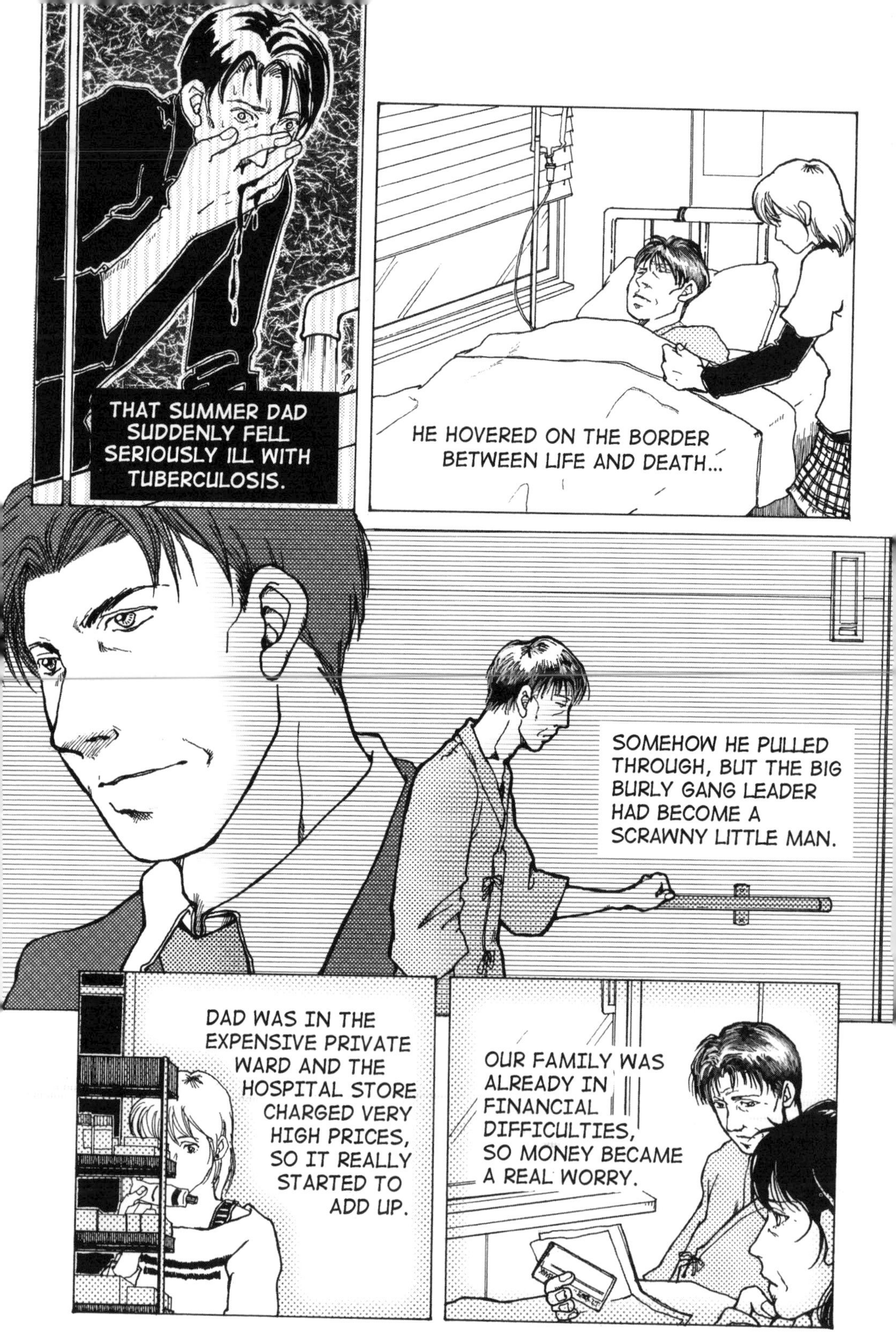
THAT SUMMER DAD SUDDENLY FELL SERIOUSLY ILL WITH TUBERCULOSIS.
HE HOVERED ON THE BORDER BETWEEN LIFE AND DEATH...
SOMEHOW HE PULLED THROUGH, BUT THE BIG BURLY GANG LEADER HAD BECOME A SCRAWNY LITTLE MAN.
DAD WAS IN THE EXPENSIVE PRIVATE WARD AND THE HOSPITAL STORE CHARGED VERY HIGH PRICES, SO IT REALLY STARTED TO ADD UP.
OUR FAMILY WAS ALREADY IN FINANCIAL DIFFICULTIES, SO MONEY BECAME A REAL WORRY.

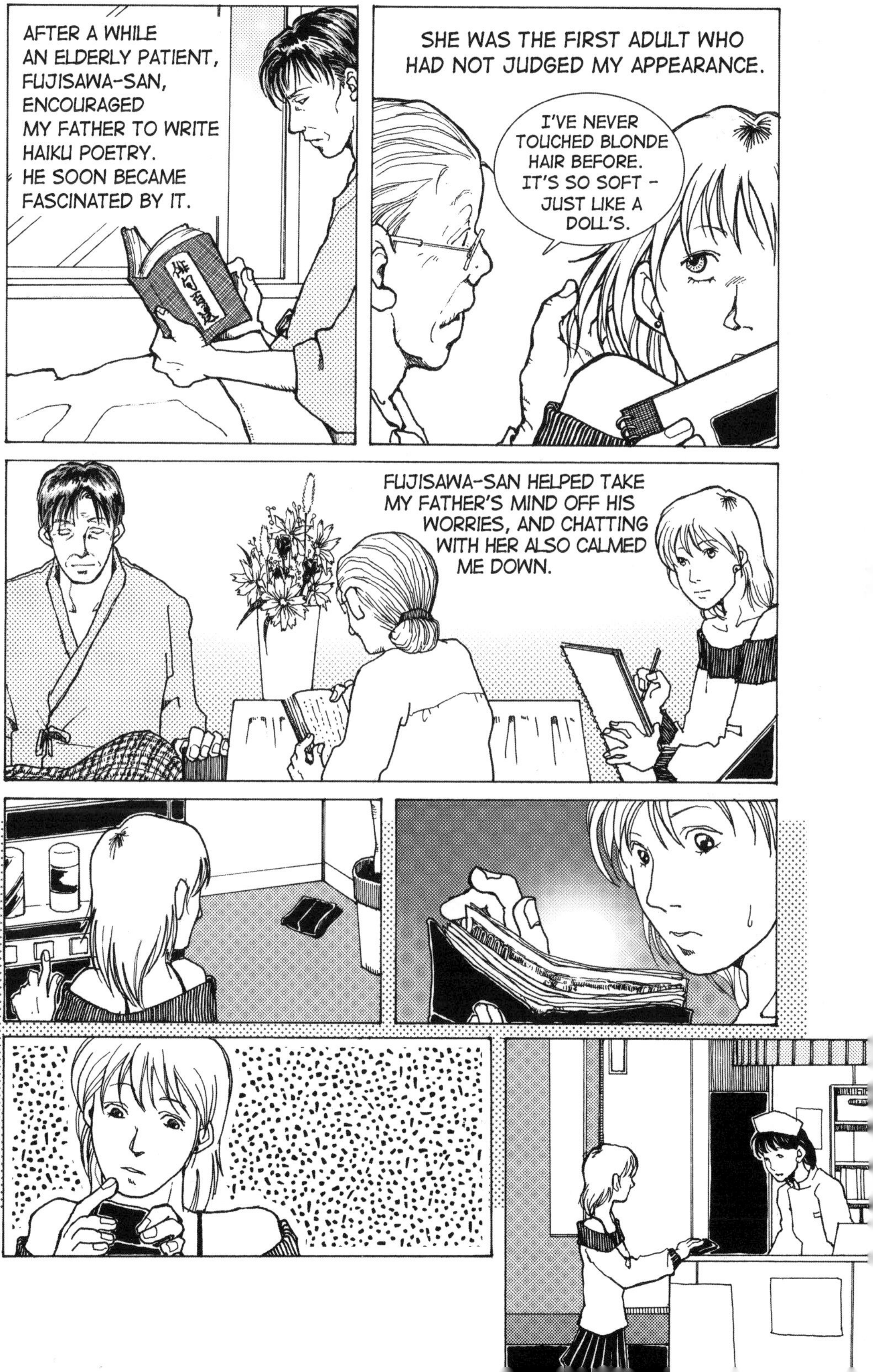
AFTER A WHILE AN ELDERLY PATIENT, FUJISAWA-SAN, ENCOURAGED MY FATHER TO WRITE HAIKU POETRY. HE SOON BECAME FASCINATED BY IT.
SHE WAS THE FIRST ADULT WHO HAD NOT JUDGED MY APPEARANCE.
I'VE NEVER TOUCHED BLONDE HAIR BEFORE. IT'S SO SOFT - JUST LIKE A DOLL'S.
FUJISAWA-SAN HELPED TAKE MY FATHER'S MIND OFF HIS WORRIES, AND CHATTING WITH HER ALSO CALMED ME DOWN.

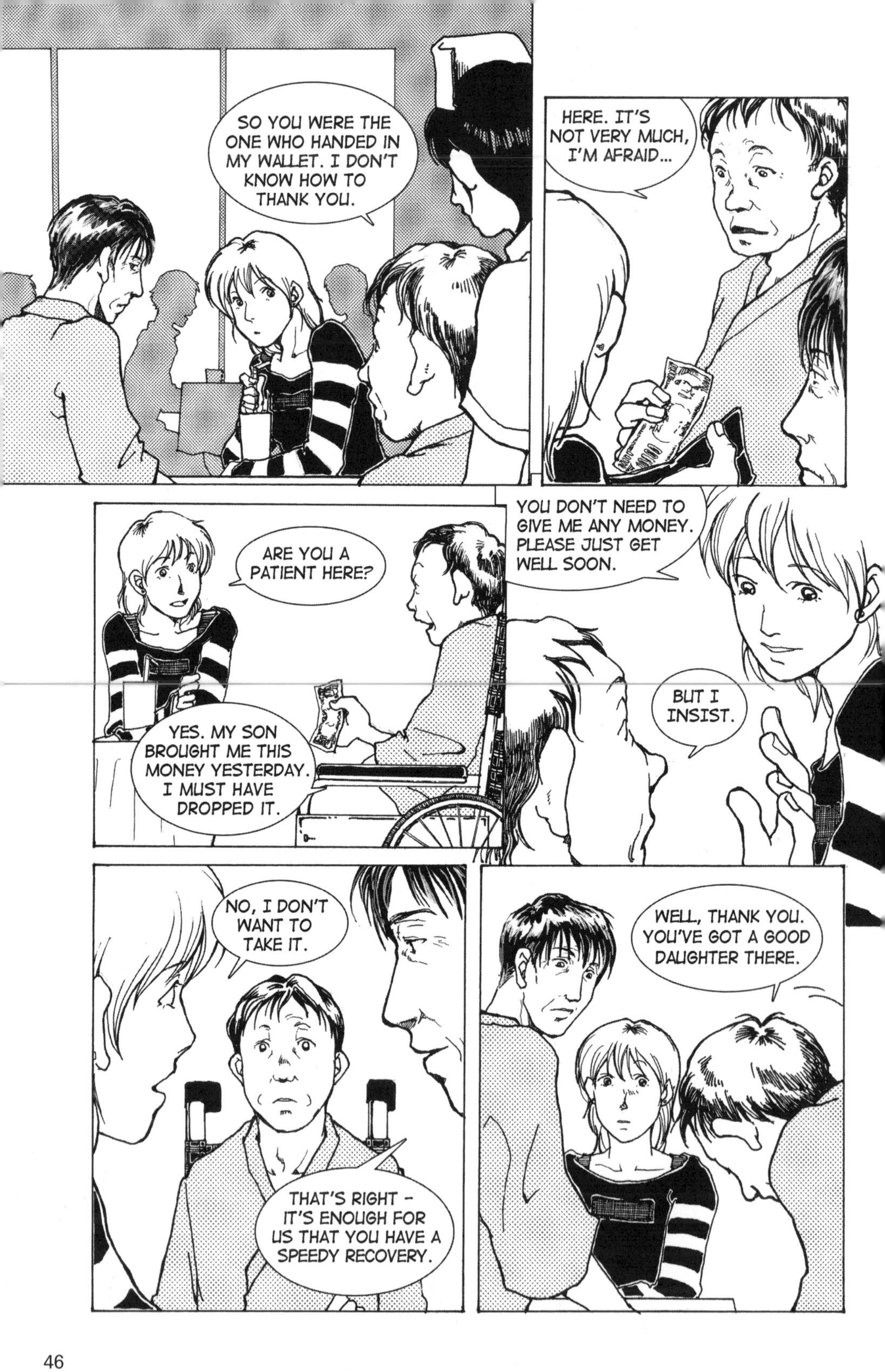
SO YOU WERE THE ONE WHO HANDED IN MY WALLET. I DON'T KNOW HOW TO THANK YOU.
HERE. IT'S NOT VERY MUCH, I'M AFRAID...
ARE YOU A PATIENT HERE?
YES. MY SON BROUGHT ME THIS MONEY YESTERDAY. I MUST HAVE DROPPED IT.
YOU DON'T NEED TO GIVE ME ANY MONEY. PLEASE JUST GET WELL SOON.
BUT I INSIST.
NO, I DON'T WANT TO TAKE IT.
THAT'S RIGHT - IT'S ENOUGH FOR US THAT YOU HAVE A SPEEDY RECOVERY.
WELL, THANK YOU. YOU'VE GOT A GOOD DAUGHTER THERE.

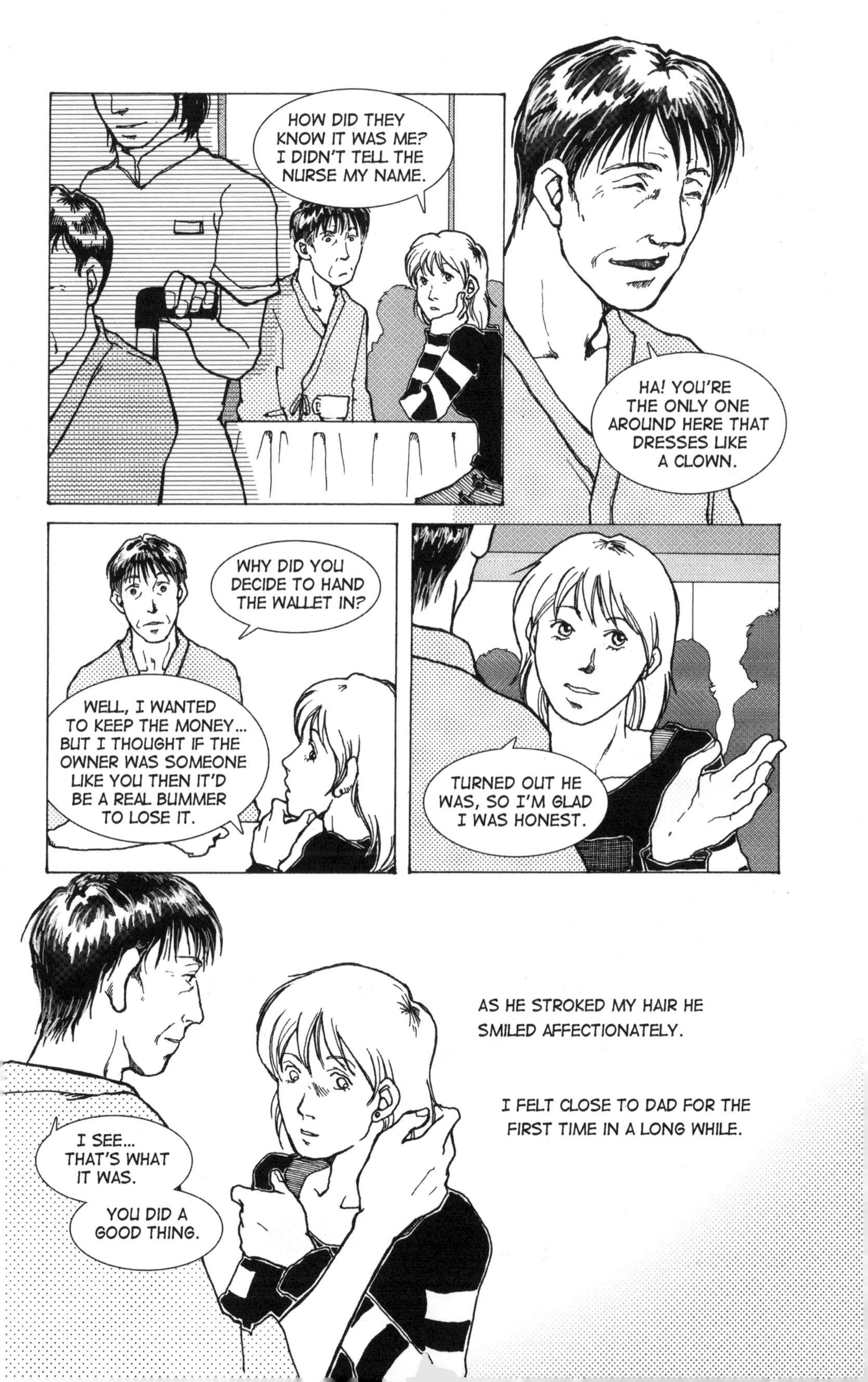
HOW DID THEY KNOW IT WAS ME? I DIDN'T TELL THE NURSE MY NAME.
HA! YOU'RE THE ONLY ONE AROUND HERE THAT DRESSES LIKE A CLOWN.
WHY DID YOU DECIDE TO HAND THE WALLET IN?
WELL, I WANTED TO KEEP THE MONEY... BUT I THOUGHT IF THE OWNER WAS SOMEONE LIKE YOU THEN IT'D BE A REAL BUMMER TO LOSE IT.
TURNED OUT HE WAS, SO I'M GLAD I WAS HONEST.
I SEE... THAT'S WHAT IT WAS.
YOU DID A GOOD THING.
AS HE STROKED MY HAIR HE SMILED AFFECTIONATELY.
I FELT CLOSE TO DAD FOR THE FIRST TIME IN A LONG WHILE.

DAD HAD BEEN THE GUARANTOR FOR AN ACQUAINTANCE'S LOAN, BUT THE MAN SKIPPED TOWN, LEAVING HUGE DEBTS. DAD WAS FORCED TO TURN TO ALL KINDS OF SHADY MONEYLENDERS.

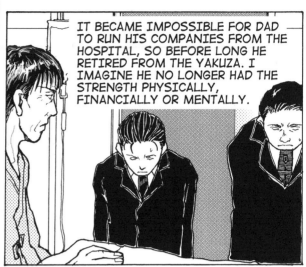

IT BECAME IMPOSSIBLE FOR DAD TO RUN HIS COMPANIES FROM THE HOSPITAL, SO BEFORE LONG HE RETIRED FROM THE YAKUZA. I IMAGINE HE NO LONGER HAD THE STRENGTH PHYSICALLY, FINANCIALLY OR MENTALLY.

OUR FAMILY WAS NOW PLUNGED INTO DEBTOR'S HELL. WE WERE PURSUED BY COLLECTORS DEMANDING ASTRONOMICAL LOAN CHARGE INCREASES OF 10% EVERY DAY, AND 50% EVERY TEN DAYS!

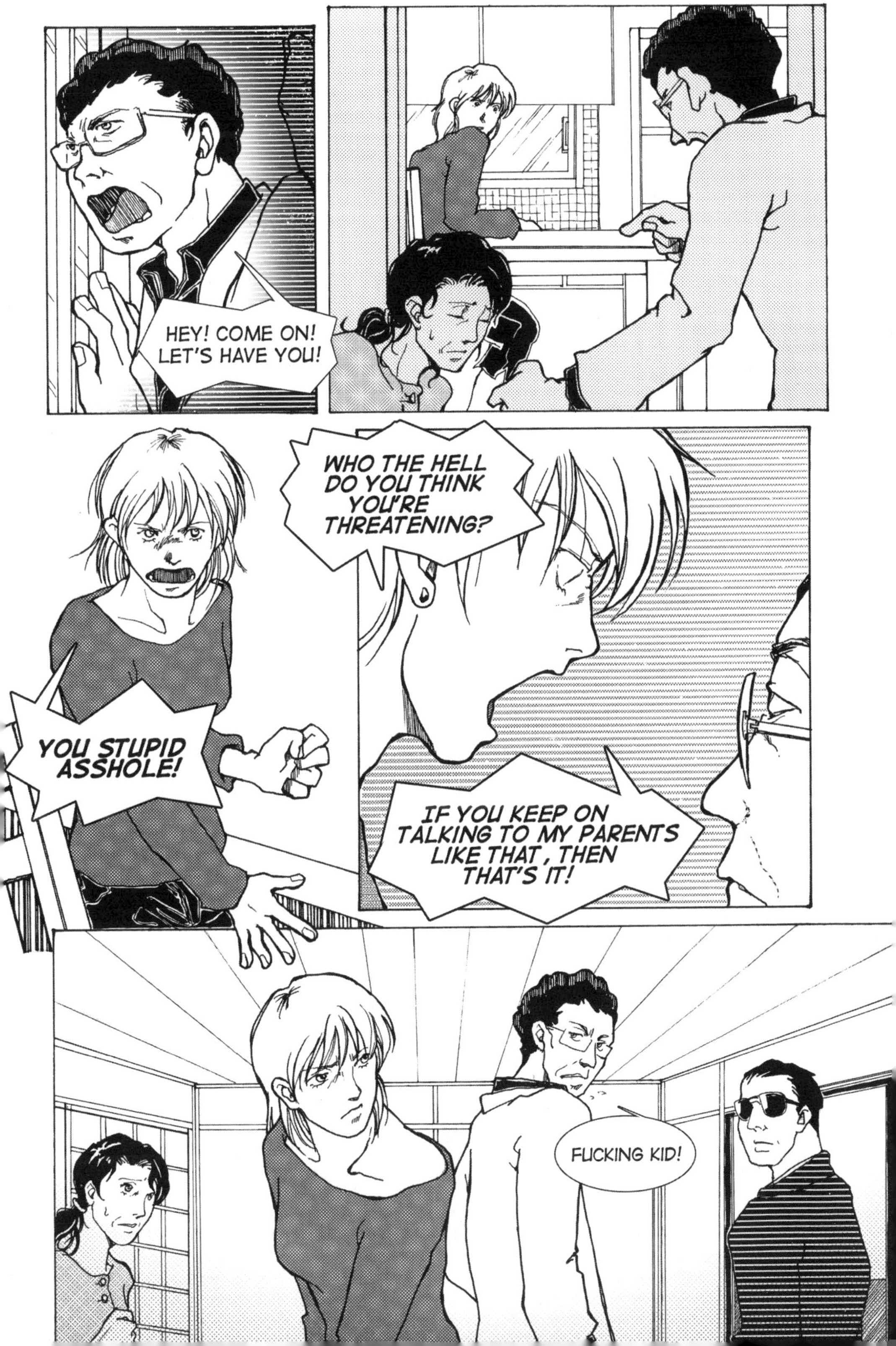
HEY! COME ON! LET'S HAVE YOU!
WHO THE HELL DO YOU THINK YOU'RE THREATENING?
YOU STUPID ASSHOLE!
IF YOU KEEP ON TALKING TO MY PARENTS LIKE THAT, THEN THAT'S IT!
FUCKING KID!

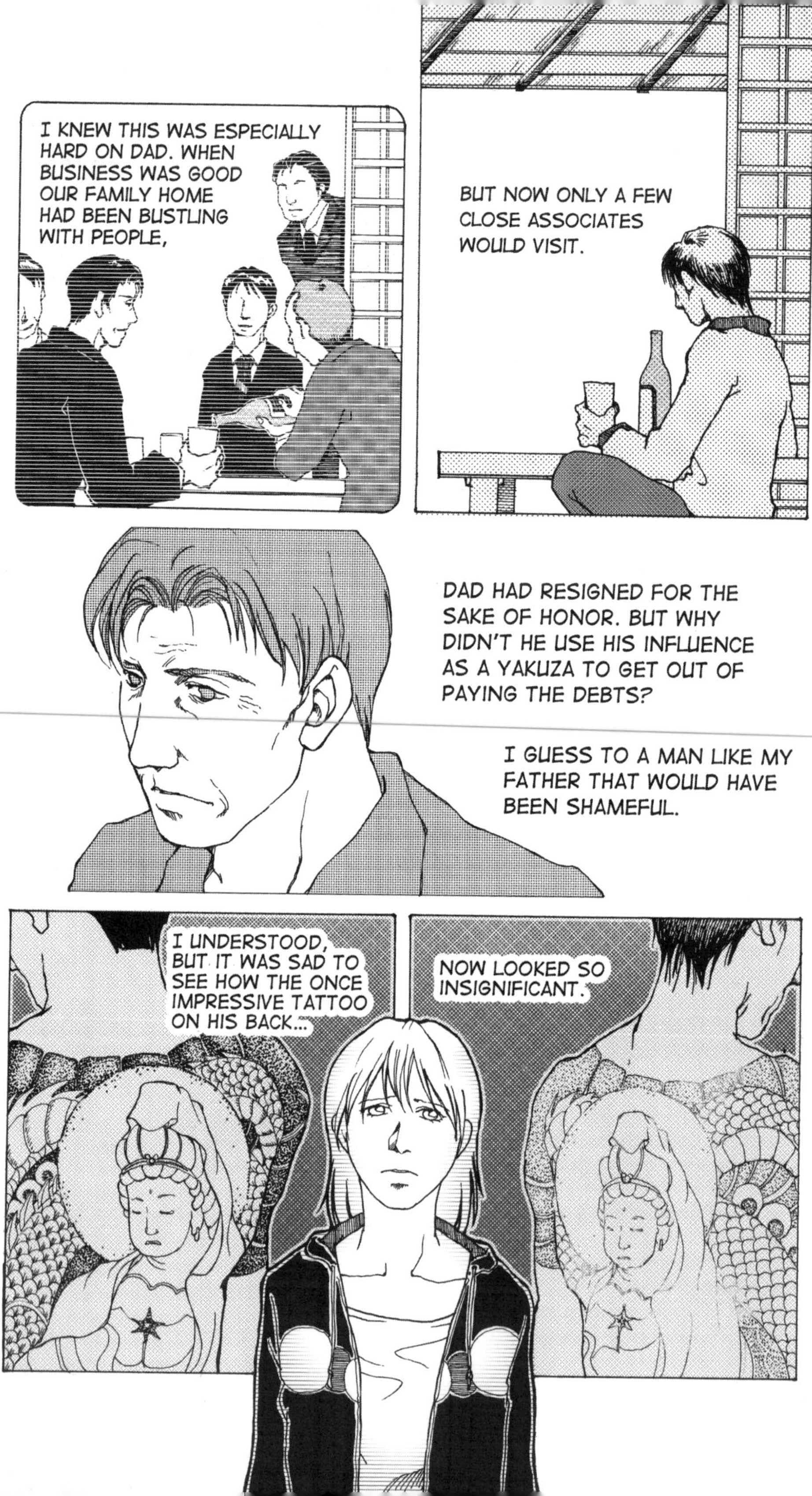
I KNEW THIS WAS ESPECIALLY HARD ON DAD. WHEN BUSINESS WAS GOOD OUR FAMILY HOME HAD BEEN BUSTLING WITH PEOPLE,
BUT NOW ONLY A FEW CLOSE ASSOCIATES WOULD VISIT.
DAD HAD RESIGNED FOR THE SAKE OF HONOR. BUT WHY DIDN'T HE USE HIS INFLUENCE AS A YAKUZA TO GET OUT OF PAYING THE DEBTS?
I GUESS TO A MAN LIKE MY FATHER THAT WOULD HAVE BEEN SHAMEFUL.
I UNDERSTOOD, BUT IT WAS SAD TO SEE HOW THE ONCE IMPRESSIVE TATTOO ON HIS BACK...
NOW LOOKED SO INSIGNIFICANT.

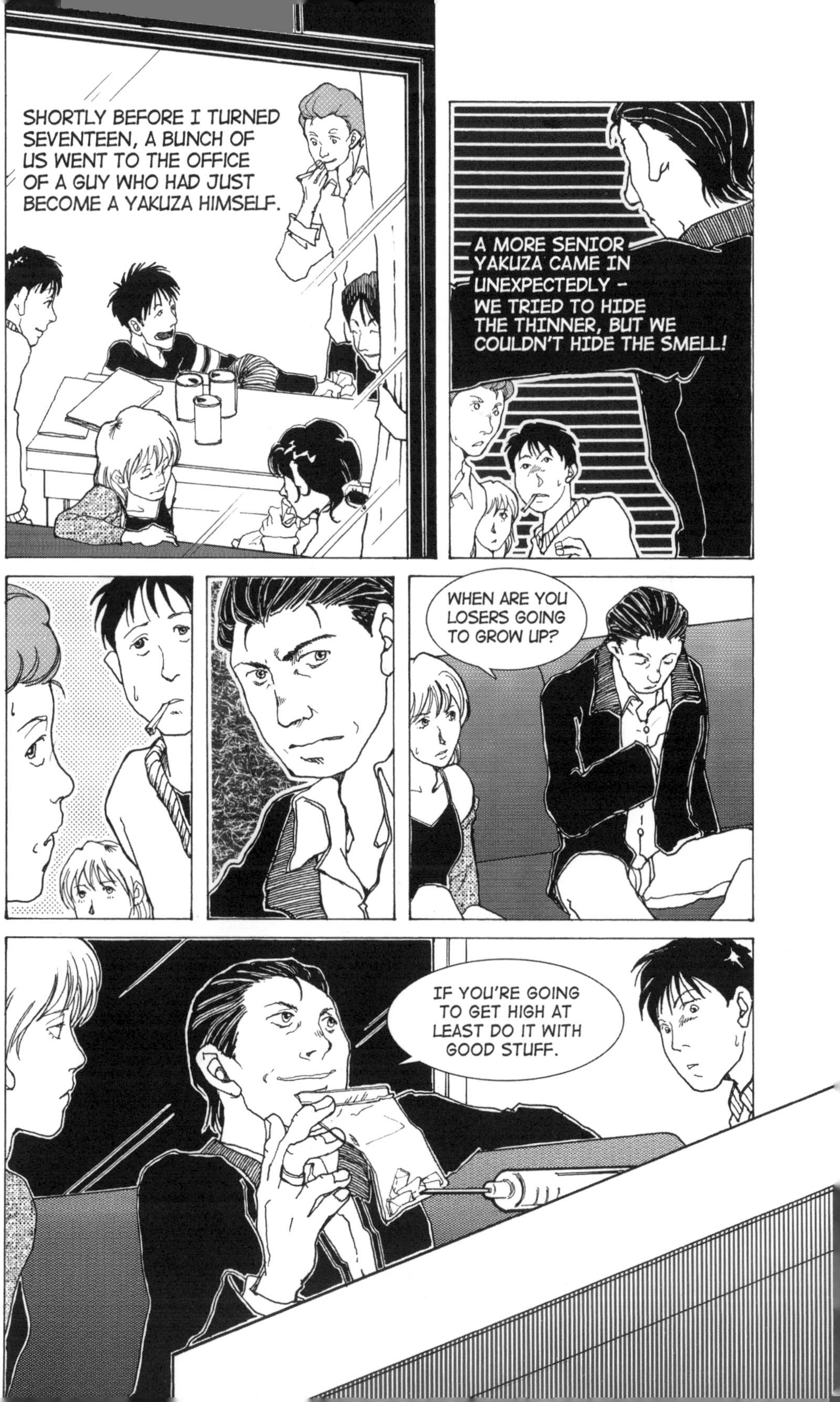
SHORTLY BEFORE I TURNED SEVENTEEN, A BUNCH OF US WENT TO THE OFFICE OF A GUY WHO HAD JUST BECOME A YAKUZA HIMSELF.
A MORE SENIOR YAKUZA CAME IN UNEXPECTEDLY - WE TRIED TO HIDE THE THINNER, BUT WE COULDN'T HIDE THE SMELL!
WHEN ARE YOU LOSERS GOING TO GROW UP?
IF YOU'RE GOING TO GET HIGH AT LEAST DO IT WITH GOOD STUFF.

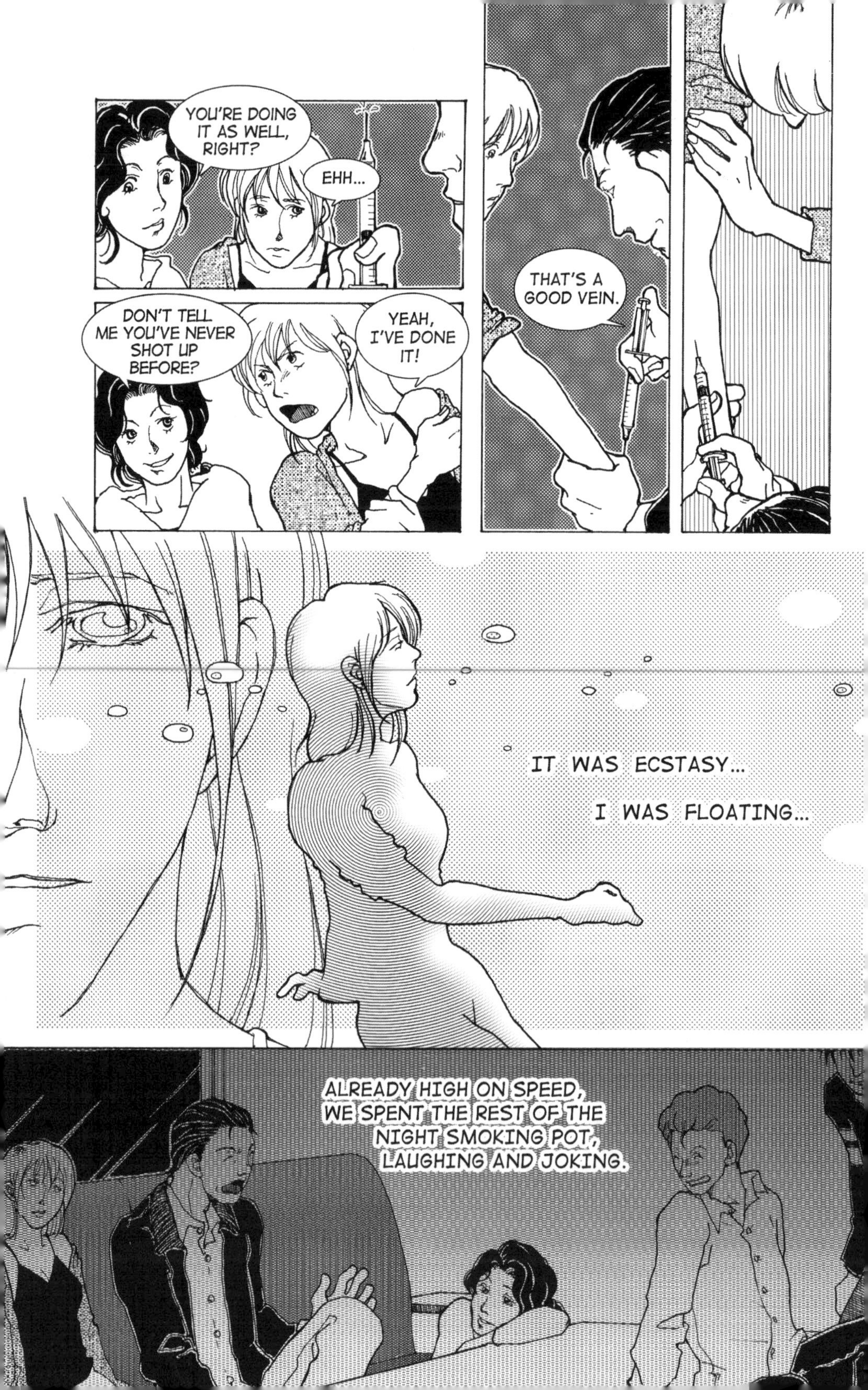
YOU'RE DOING IT AS WELL, RIGHT?
EHH...
DON'T TELL ME YOU'VE NEVER SHOT UP BEFORE?
YEAH, I'VE DONE IT!
THAT'S A GOOD VEIN.
IT WAS ECSTASY...
I WAS FLOATING...
ALREADY HIGH ON SPEED, WE SPENT THE REST OF THE NIGHT SMOKING POT, LAUGHING AND JOKING.

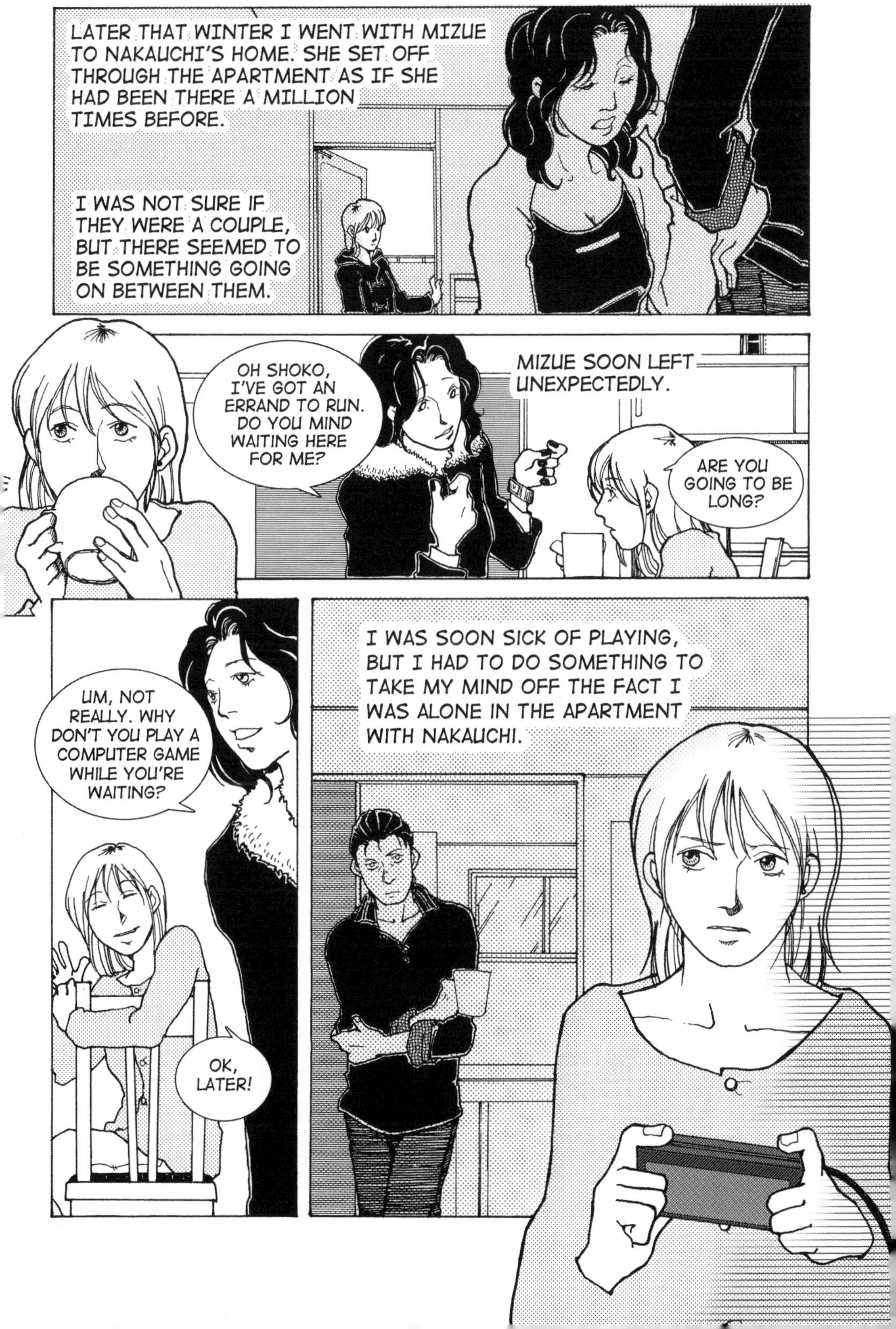
LATER THAT WINTER I WENT WITH MIZUE TO NAKAUCHI'S HOME. SHE SET OFF THROUGH THE APARTMENT AS IF SHE HAD BEEN THERE A MILLION TIMES BEFORE.
I WAS NOT SURE IF THEY WERE A COUPLE, BUT THERE SEEMED TO BE SOMETHING GOING ON BETWEEN THEM.
OH SHOKO, I'VE GOT AN ERRAND TO RUN. DO YOU MIND WAITING HERE FOR ME?
MIZUE SOON LEFT UNEXPECTEDLY.
ARE YOU GOING TO BE LONG?
UM, NOT REALLY. WHY DON'T YOU PLAY A COMPUTER GAME WHILE YOU'RE WAITING?
OK, LATER!
I WAS SOON SICK OF PLAYING, BUT I HAD TO DO SOMETHING TO TAKE MY MIND OFF THE FACT I WAS ALONE IN THE APARTMENT WITH NAKAUCHI.

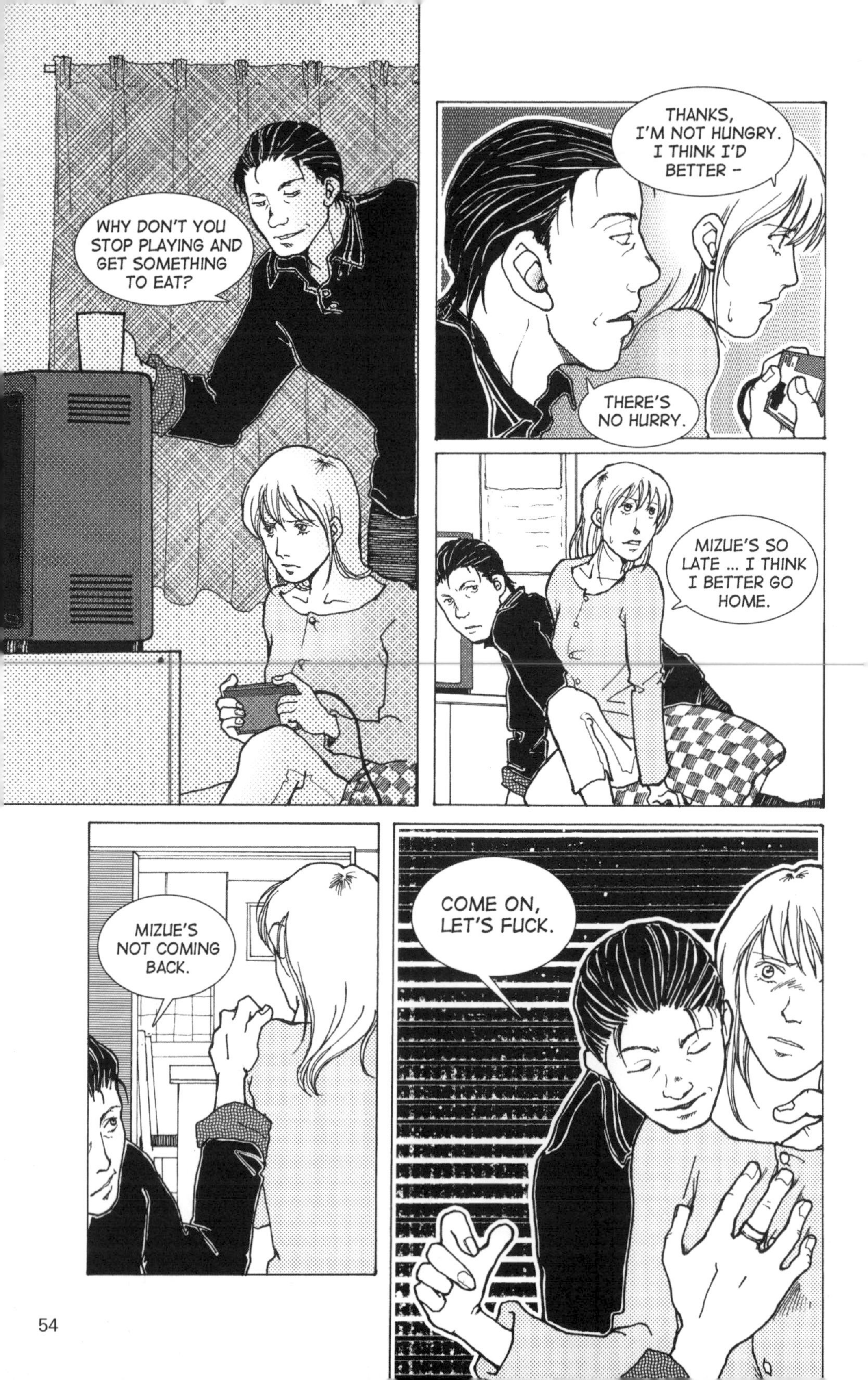
WHY DON'T YOU STOP PLAYING AND GET SOMETHING TO EAT?
THANKS, I'M NOT HUNGRY. I THINK I'D BETTER –
THERE'S NO HURRY.
MIZUE'S SO LATE ... I THINK I BETTER GO HOME.
MIZUE'S NOT COMING BACK.
COME ON, LET'S FUCK.

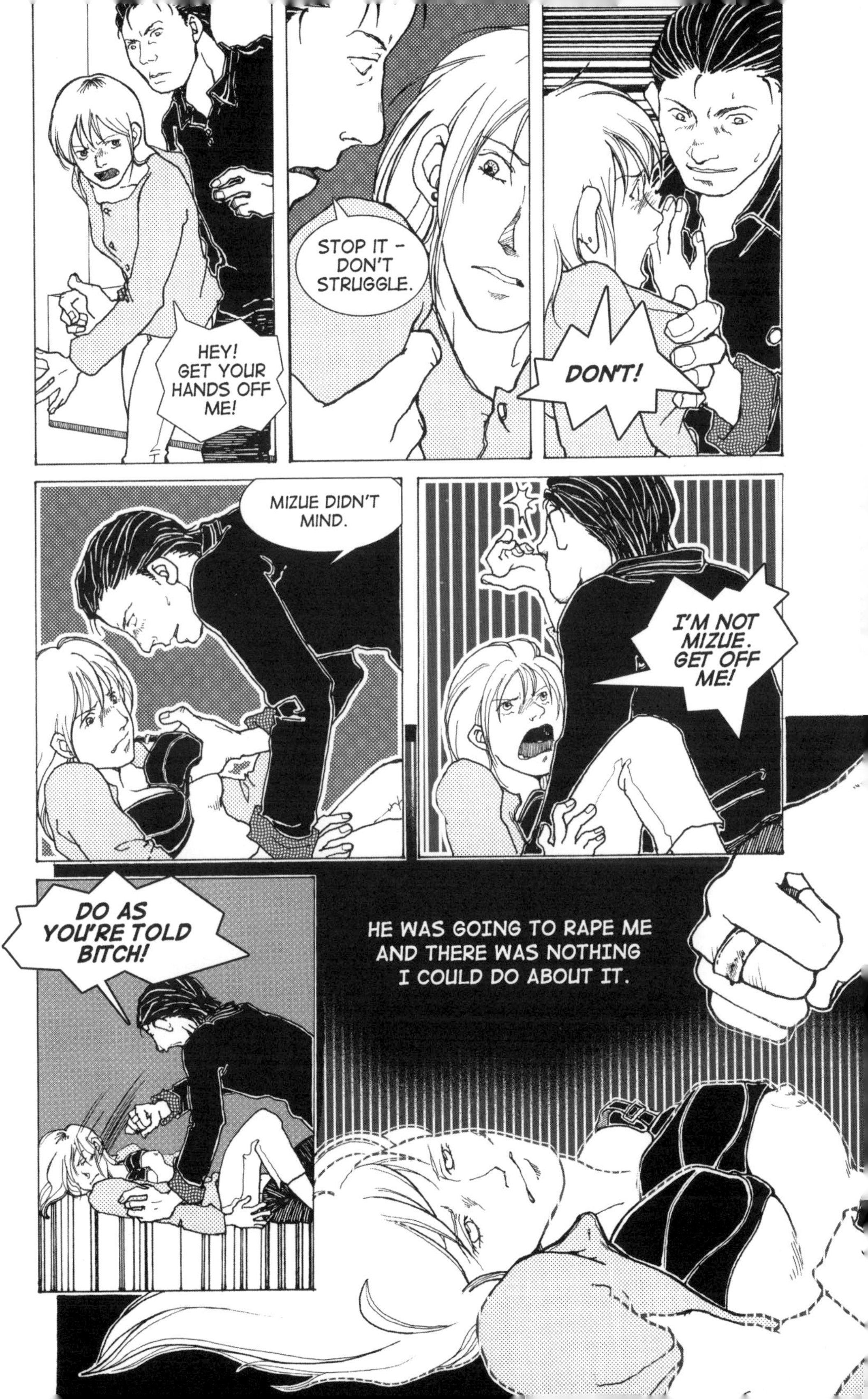
HEY! GET YOUR HANDS OFF ME!
STOP IT - DON'T STRUGGLE.
DON'T!
MIZUE DIDN'T MIND.
I'M NOT MIZUE. GET OFF ME!
DO AS YOU'RE TOLD BITCH!
HE WAS GOING TO RAPE ME AND THERE WAS NOTHING I COULD DO ABOUT IT.

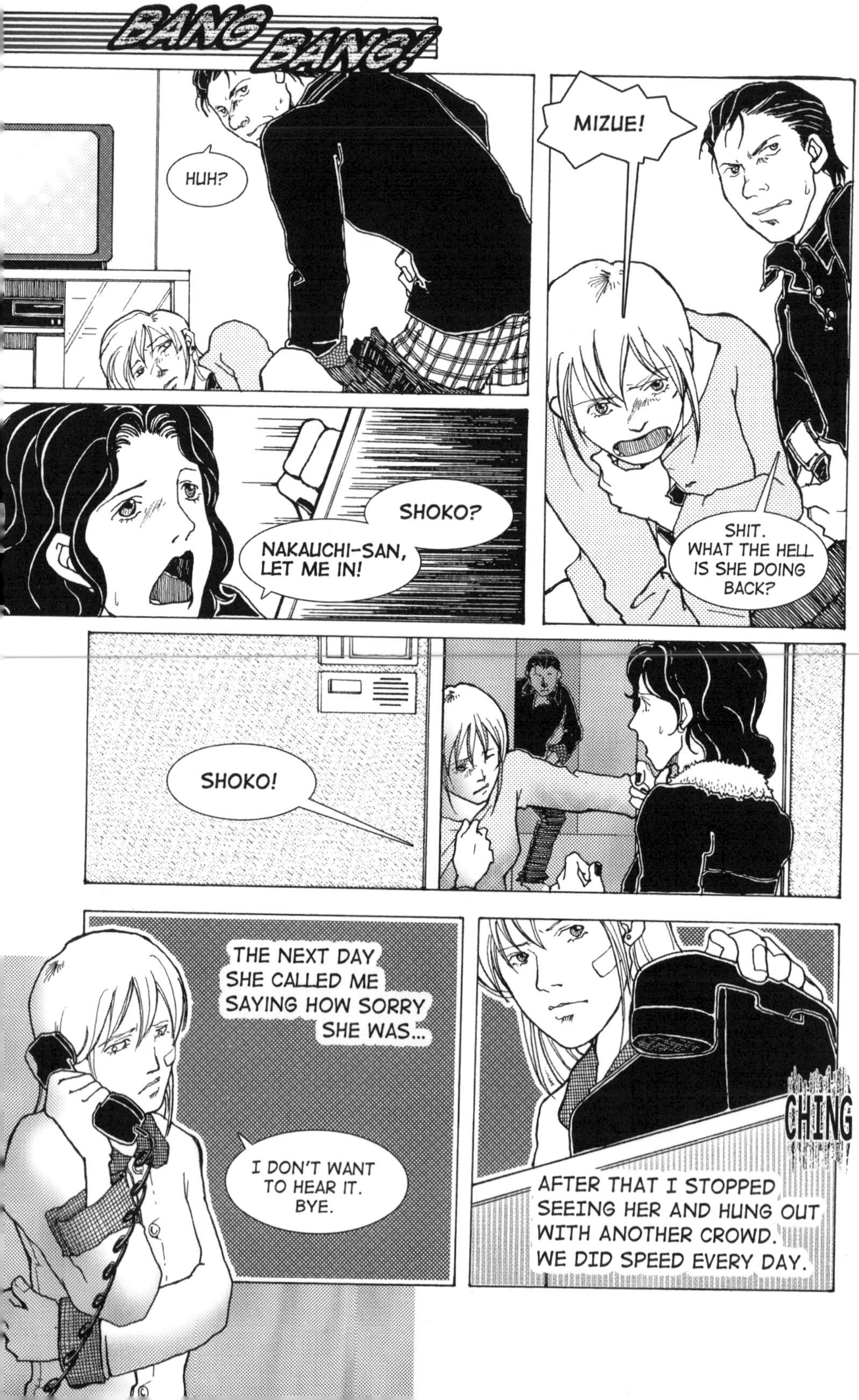
BANG BANG!
HUH?
MIZUE!
SHIT. WHAT THE HELL IS SHE DOING BACK?
SHOKO?
NAKAUCHI-SAN, LET ME IN!
SHOKO!
THE NEXT DAY SHE CALLED ME SAYING HOW SORRY SHE WAS...
I DON'T WANT TO HEAR IT. BYE.
CHING
AFTER THAT I STOPPED SEEING HER AND HUNG OUT WITH ANOTHER CROWD. WE DID SPEED EVERY DAY.

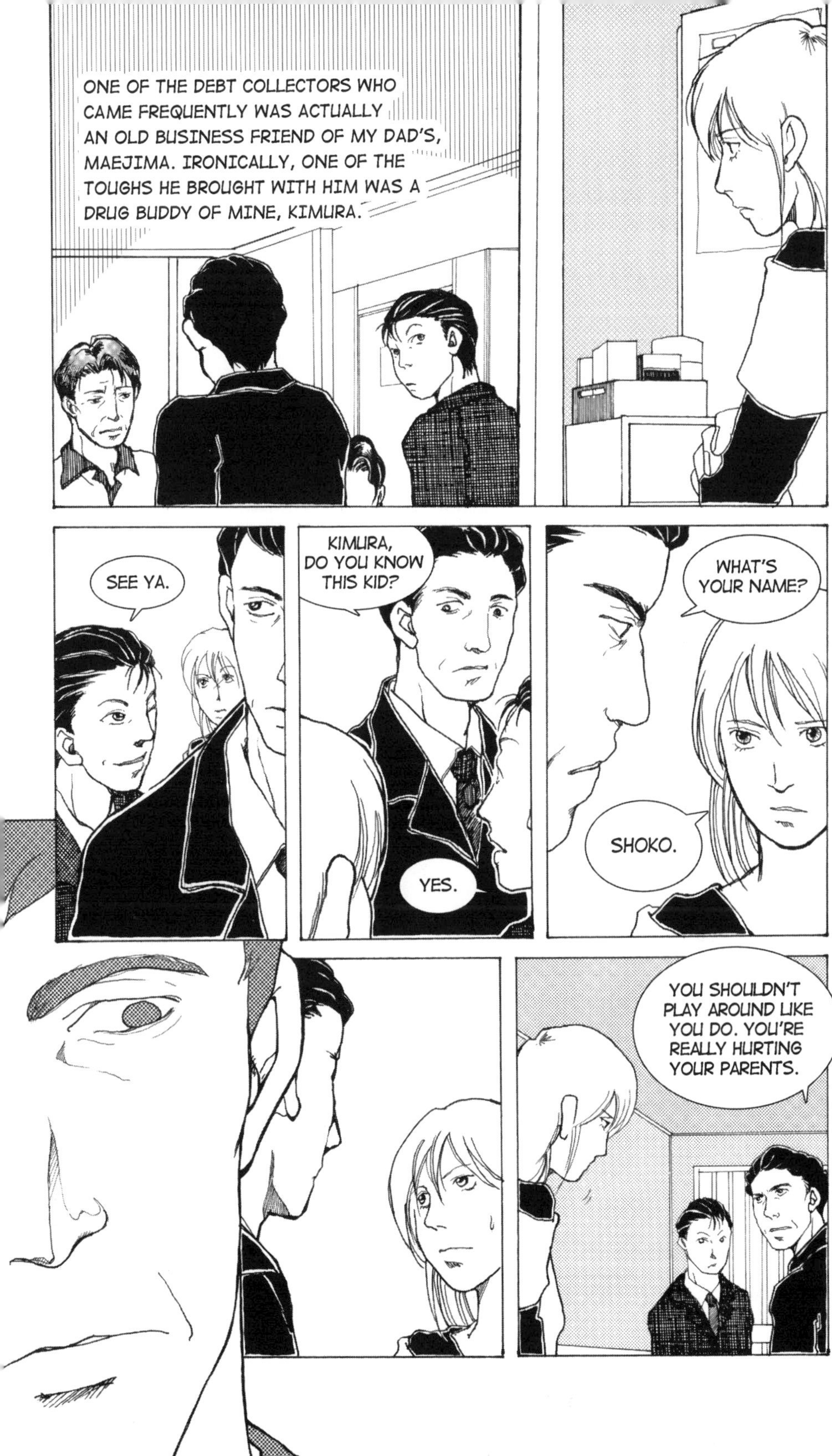
ONE OF THE DEBT COLLECTORS WHO CAME FREQUENTLY WAS ACTUALLY AN OLD BUSINESS FRIEND OF MY DAD'S, MAEJIMA. IRONICALLY, ONE OF THE TOUGHS HE BROUGHT WITH HIM WAS A DRUG BUDDY OF MINE, KIMURA.
SEE YA.
KIMURA, DO YOU KNOW THIS KID?
YES.
WHAT'S YOUR NAME?
SHOKO.
YOU SHOULDN'T PLAY AROUND LIKE YOU DO. YOU'RE REALLY HURTING YOUR PARENTS.

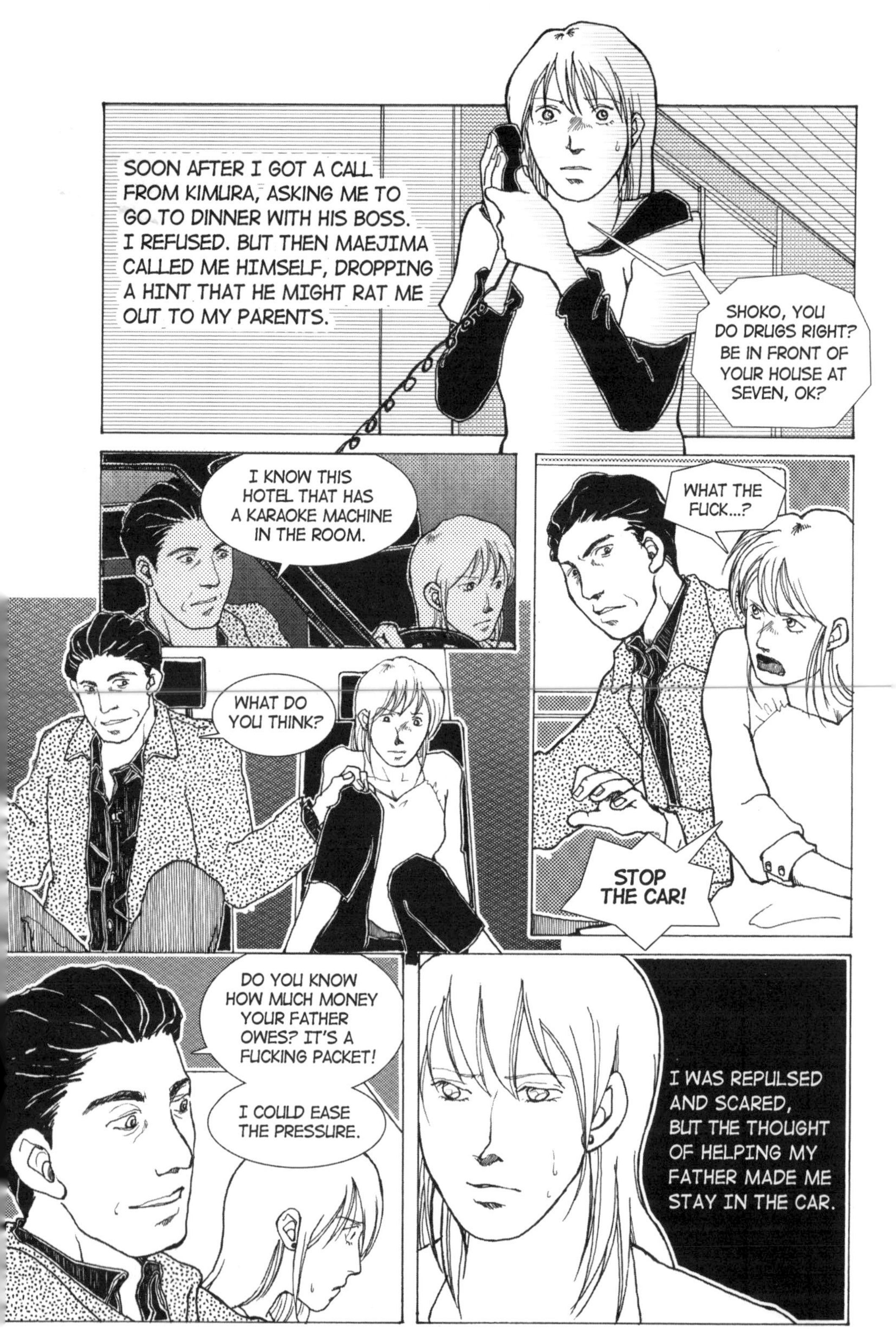
SOON AFTER I GOT A CALL FROM KIMURA, ASKING ME TO GO TO DINNER WITH HIS BOSS. I REFUSED. BUT THEN MAEJIMA CALLED ME HIMSELF, DROPPING A HINT THAT HE MIGHT RAT ME OUT TO MY PARENTS.
SHOKO, YOU DO DRUGS RIGHT? BE IN FRONT OF YOUR HOUSE AT SEVEN, OK?
I KNOW THIS HOTEL THAT HAS A KARAOKE MACHINE IN THE ROOM.
WHAT DO YOU THINK?
WHAT THE FUCK...?
STOP THE CAR!
DO YOU KNOW HOW MUCH MONEY YOUR FATHER OWES? IT'S A FUCKING PACKET!
I COULD EASE THE PRESSURE.
I WAS REPULSED AND SCARED, BUT THE THOUGHT OF HELPING MY FATHER MADE ME STAY IN THE CAR.

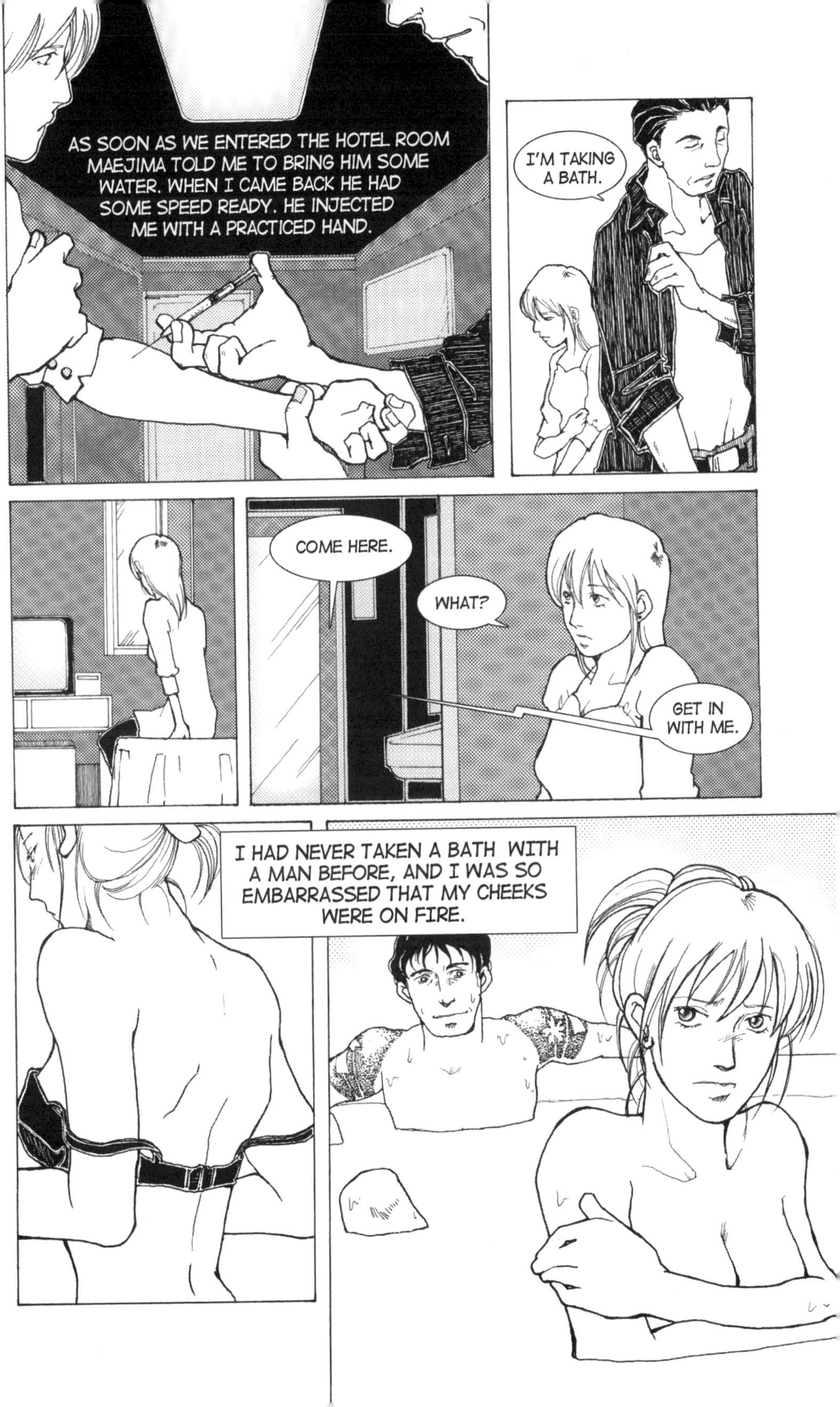
AS SOON AS WE ENTERED THE HOTEL ROOM MAEJIMA TOLD ME TO BRING HIM SOME WATER. WHEN I CAME BACK HE HAD SOME SPEED READY. HE INJECTED ME WITH A PRACTICED HAND.
I'M TAKING A BATH.
COME HERE.
WHAT?
GET IN WITH ME.
I HAD NEVER TAKEN A BATH WITH A MAN BEFORE, AND I WAS SO EMBARRASSED THAT MY CHEEKS WERE ON FIRE.

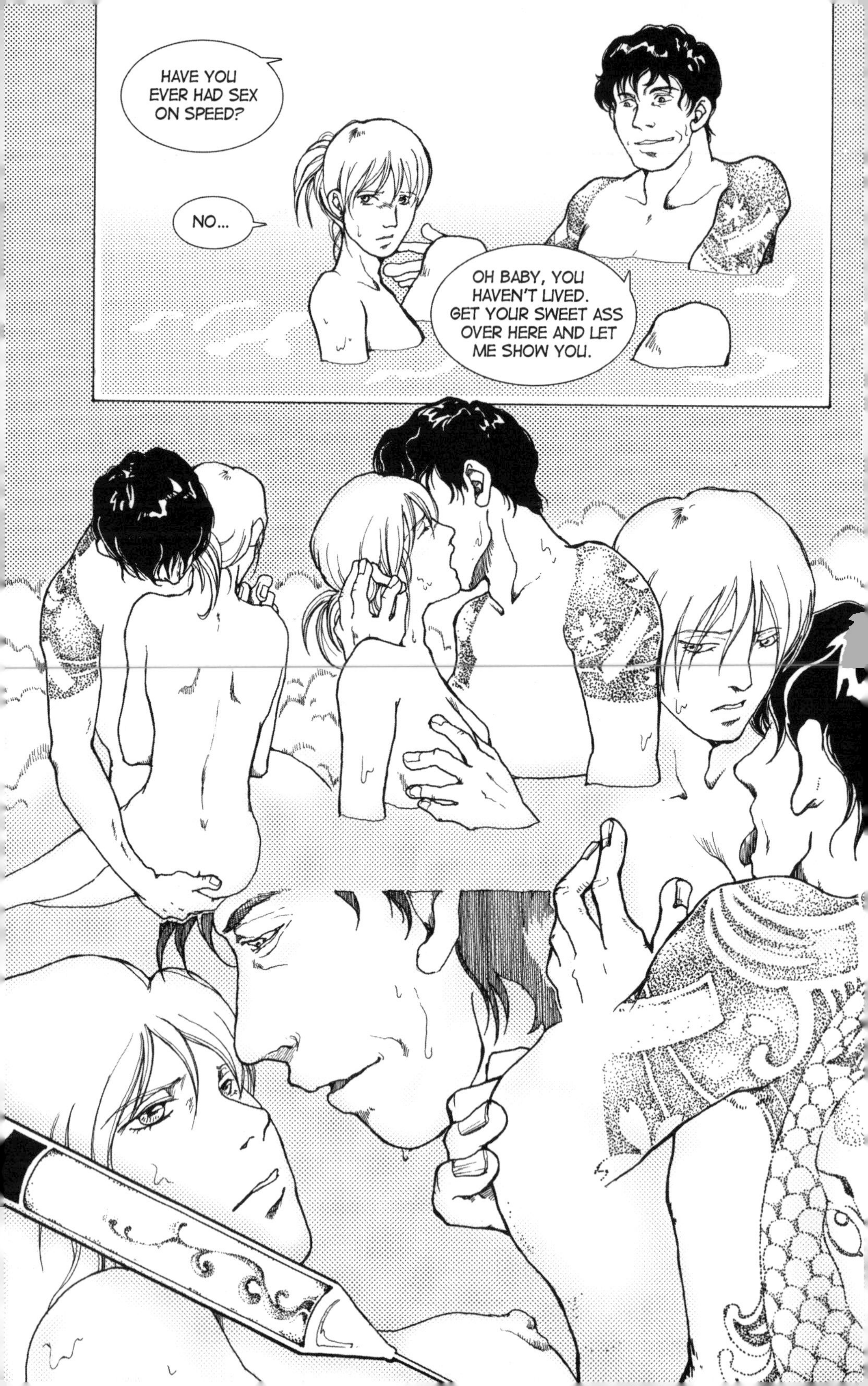
HAVE YOU EVER HAD SEX ON SPEED?
NO...
OH BABY, YOU HAVEN'T LIVED. GET YOUR SWEET ASS OVER HERE AND LET ME SHOW YOU.

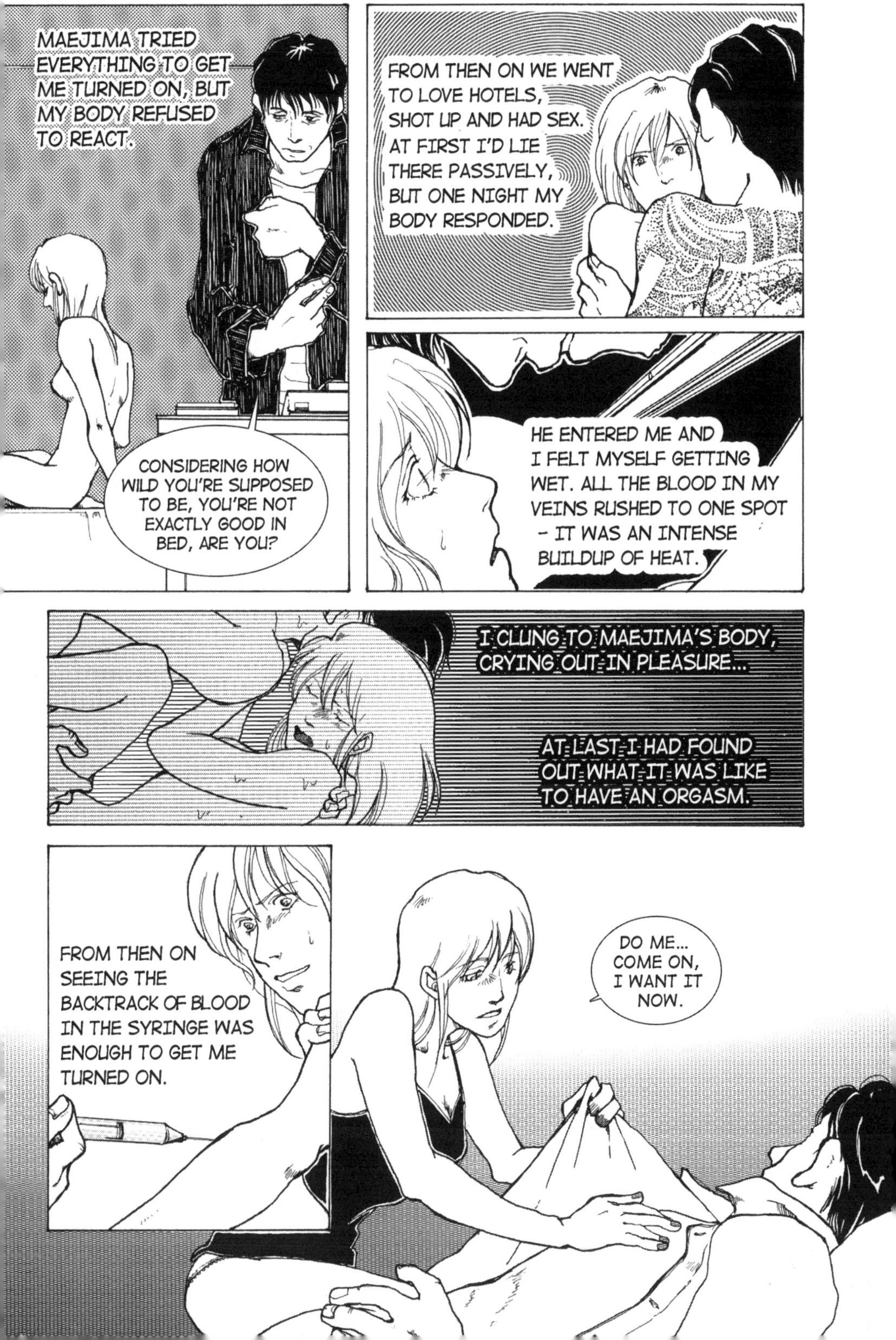

MAEJIMA TRIED EVERYTHING TO GET ME TURNED ON, BUT MY BODY REFUSED TO REACT.
CONSIDERING HOW WILD YOU'RE SUPPOSED TO BE, YOU'RE NOT EXACTLY GOOD IN BED, ARE YOU?
FROM THEN ON WE WENT TO LOVE HOTELS, SHOT UP AND HAD SEX. AT FIRST I'D LIE THERE PASSIVELY, BUT ONE NIGHT MY BODY RESPONDED.
HE ENTERED ME AND I FELT MYSELF GETTING WET. ALL THE BLOOD IN MY VEINS RUSHED TO ONE SPOT - IT WAS AN INTENSE BUILDUP OF HEAT.
I CLUNG TO MAEJIMA'S BODY, CRYING OUT IN PLEASURE...
AT LAST I HAD FOUND OUT WHAT IT WAS LIKE TO HAVE AN ORGASM.
FROM THEN ON SEEING THE BACKTRACK OF BLOOD IN THE SYRINGE WAS ENOUGH TO GET ME TURNED ON.
DO ME... COME ON, I WANT IT NOW.

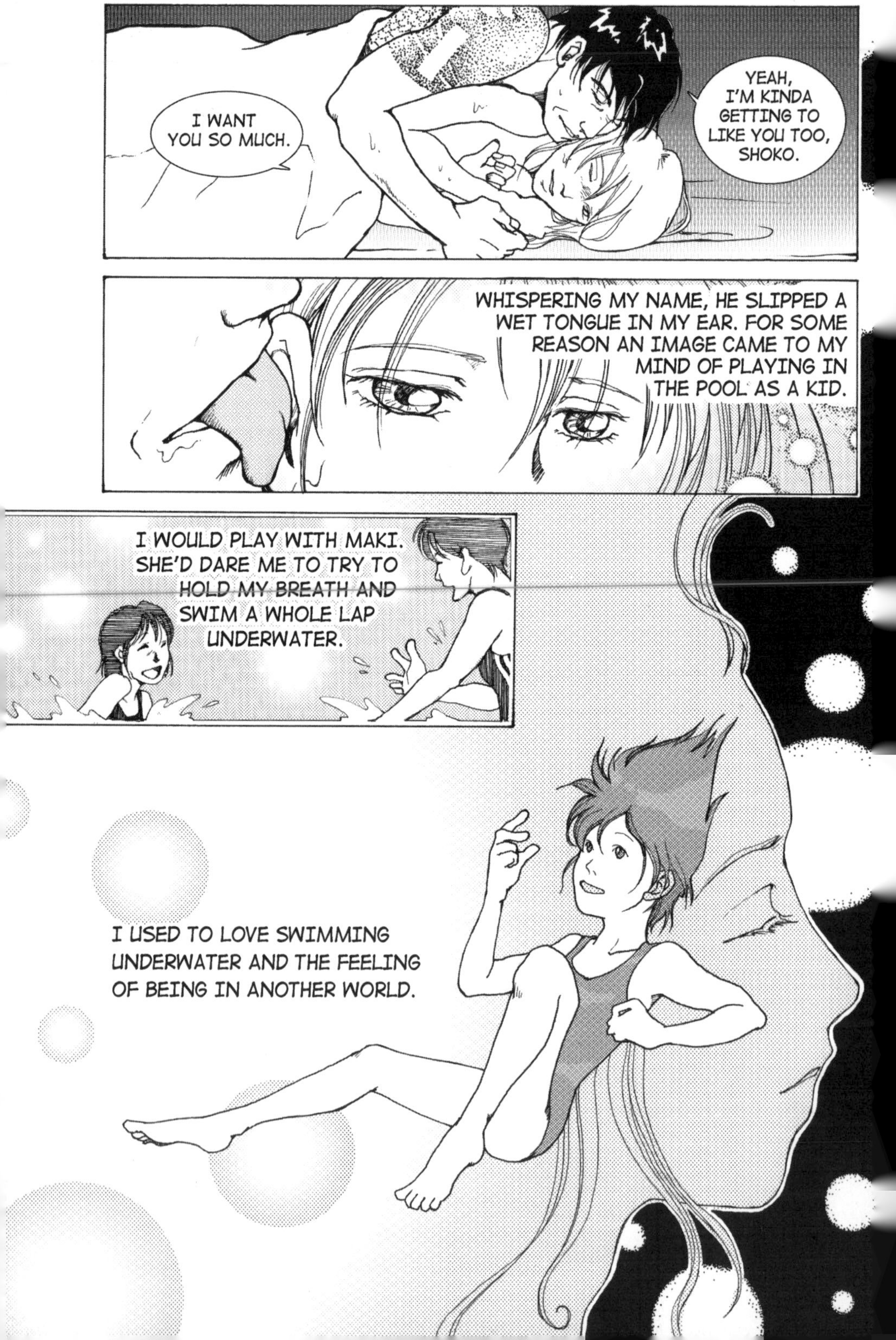
YEAH, I'M KINDA GETTING TO LIKE YOU TOO, SHOKO.
I WANT YOU SO MUCH.
WHISPERING MY NAME, HE SLIPPED A WET TONGUE IN MY EAR. FOR SOME REASON AN IMAGE CAME TO MY MIND OF PLAYING IN THE POOL AS A KID.
I WOULD PLAY WITH MAKI. SHE'D DARE ME TO TRY TO HOLD MY BREATH AND SWIM A WHOLE LAP UNDERWATER.
I USED TO LOVE SWIMMING UNDERWATER AND THE FEELING OF BEING IN ANOTHER WORLD.

CHAPTER 4

Lovers

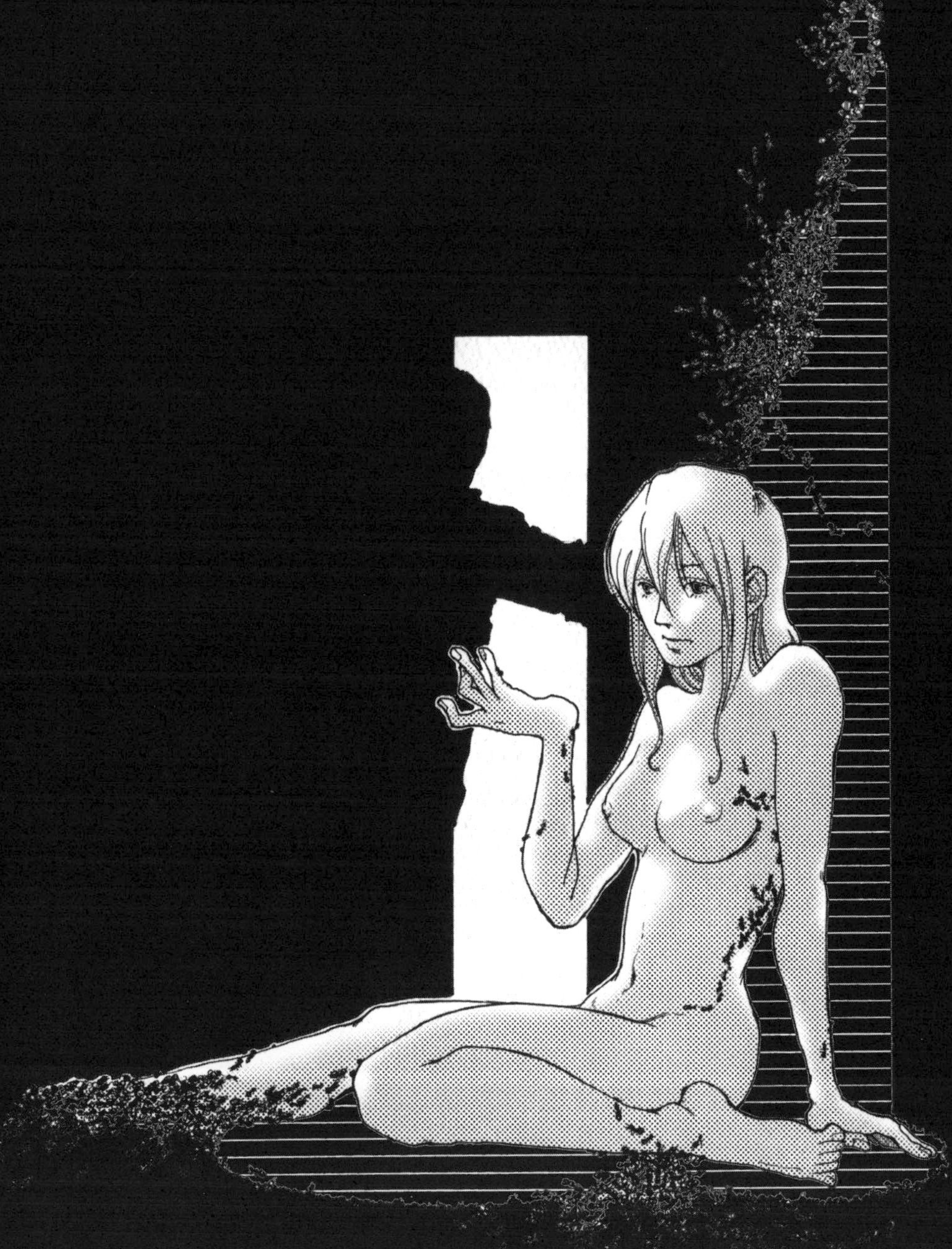

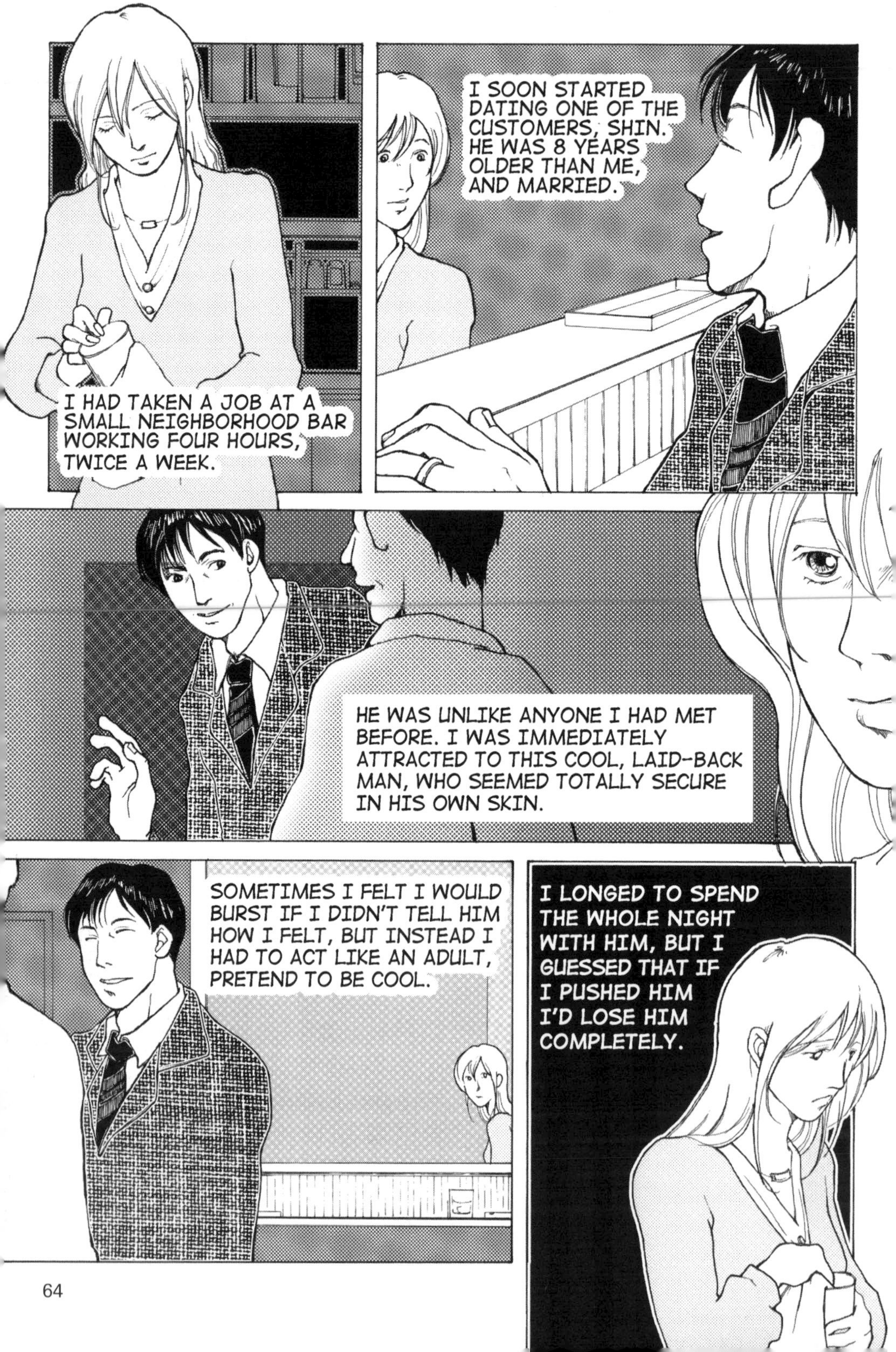
I HAD TAKEN A JOB AT A SMALL NEIGHBORHOOD BAR WORKING FOUR HOURS, TWICE A WEEK.
I SOON STARTED DATING ONE OF THE CUSTOMERS, SHIN. HE WAS 8 YEARS OLDER THAN ME, AND MARRIED.
HE WAS UNLIKE ANYONE I HAD MET BEFORE. I WAS IMMEDIATELY ATTRACTED TO THIS COOL, LAID-BACK MAN, WHO SEEMED TOTALLY SECURE IN HIS OWN SKIN.
SOMETIMES I FELT I WOULD BURST IF I DIDN'T TELL HIM HOW I FELT, BUT INSTEAD I HAD TO ACT LIKE AN ADULT, PRETEND TO BE COOL.
I LONGED TO SPEND THE WHOLE NIGHT WITH HIM, BUT I GUESSED THAT IF I PUSHED HIM I'D LOSE HIM COMPLETELY.

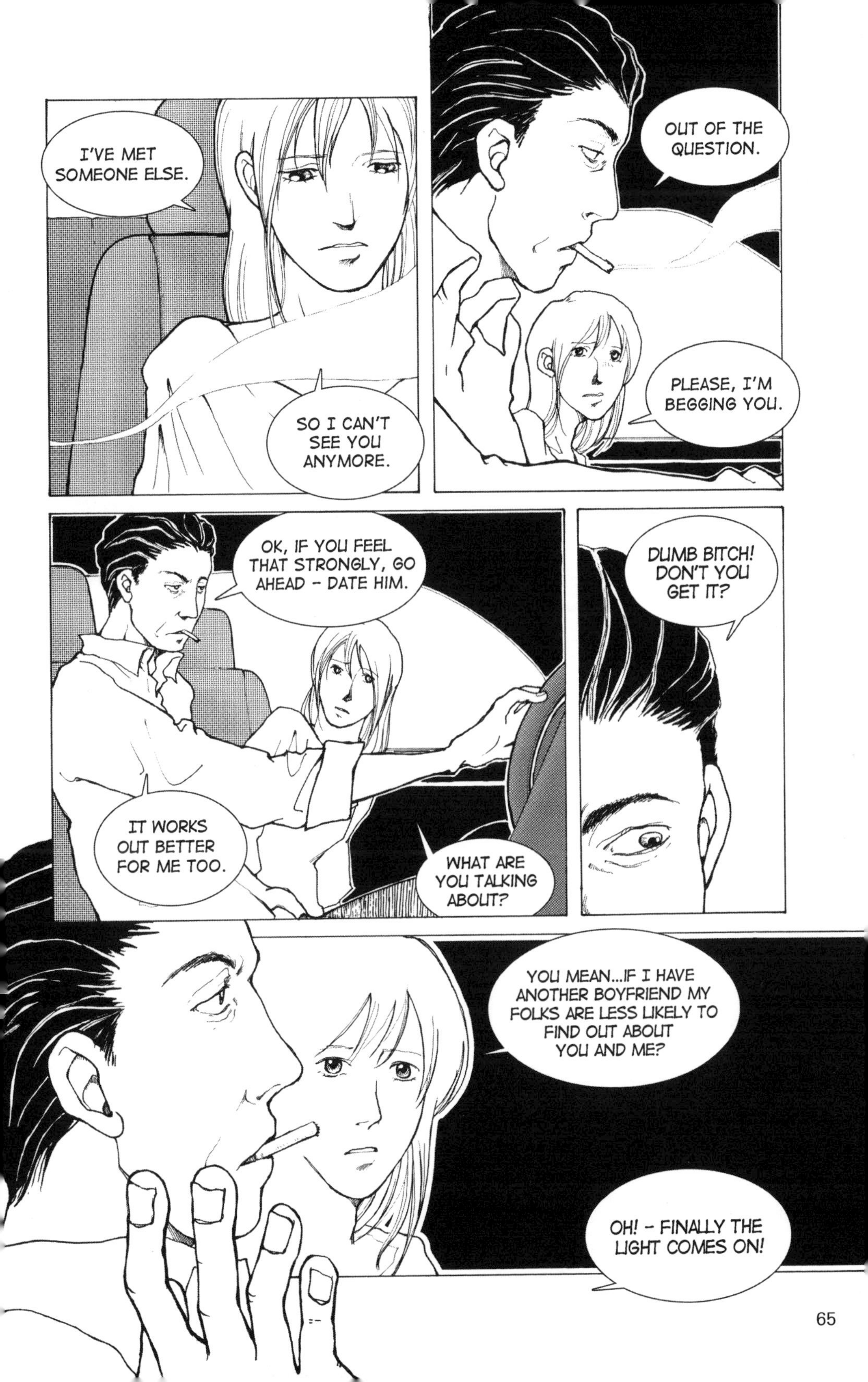
I'VE MET SOMEONE ELSE.
SO I CAN'T SEE YOU ANYMORE.
OUT OF THE QUESTION.
PLEASE, I'M BEGGING YOU.
OK, IF YOU FEEL THAT STRONGLY, GO AHEAD - DATE HIM.
IT WORKS OUT BETTER FOR ME TOO.
WHAT ARE YOU TALKING ABOUT?
DUMB BITCH! DON'T YOU GET IT?
YOU MEAN...IF I HAVE ANOTHER BOYFRIEND MY FOLKS ARE LESS LIKELY TO FIND OUT ABOUT YOU AND ME?
OH! - FINALLY THE LIGHT COMES ON!

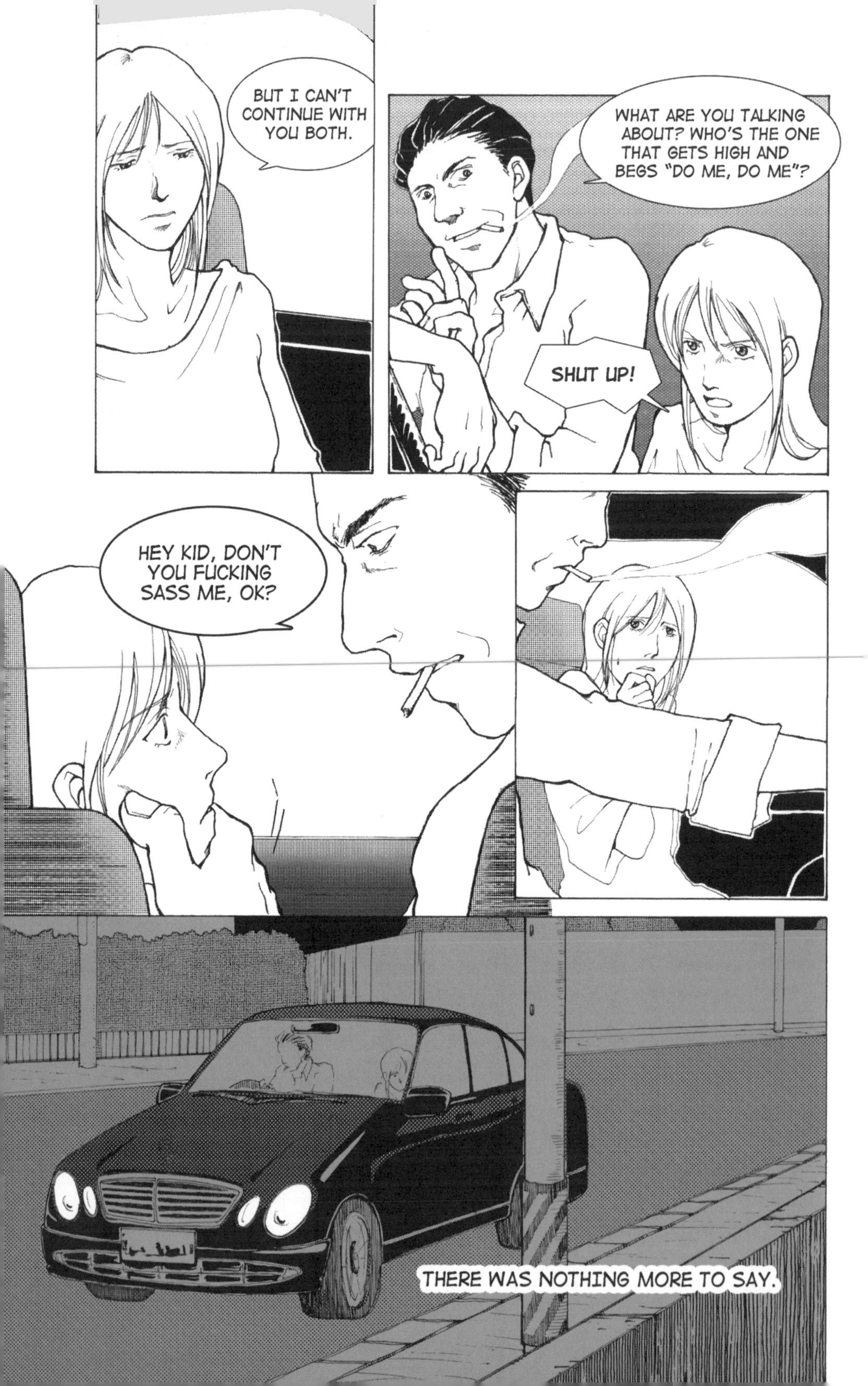
BUT I CAN'T CONTINUE WITH YOU BOTH.
WHAT ARE YOU TALKING ABOUT? WHO'S THE ONE THAT GETS HIGH AND BEGS "DO ME, DO ME"?
SHUT UP!
HEY KID, DON'T YOU FUCKING SASS ME, OK?
THERE WAS NOTHING MORE TO SAY.

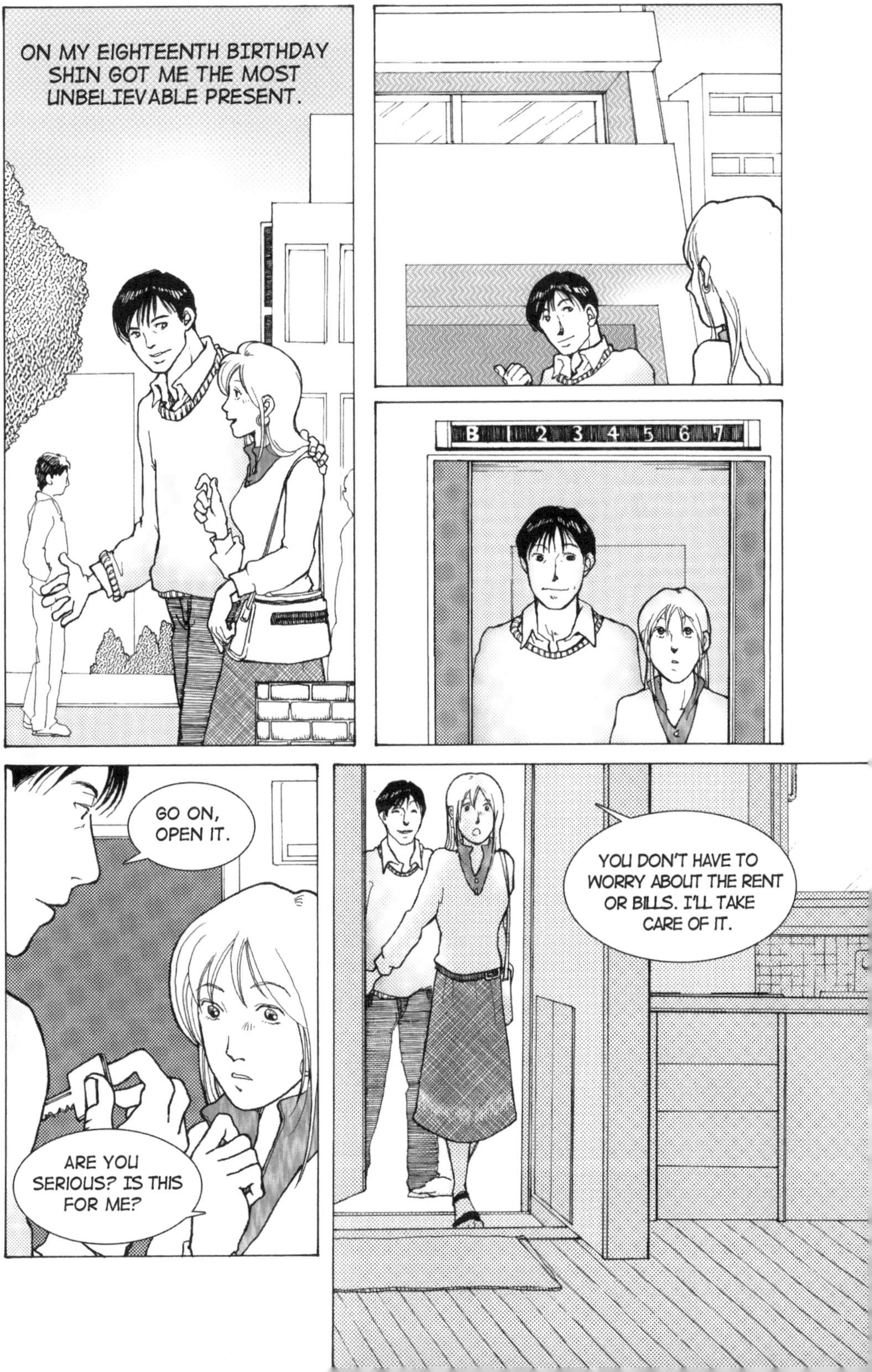
ON MY EIGHTEENTH BIRTHDAY SHIN GOT ME THE MOST UNBELIEVABLE PRESENT.
B 1 2 3 4 5 6 7
GO ON, OPEN IT.
ARE YOU SERIOUS? IS THIS FOR ME?
YOU DON'T HAVE TO WORRY ABOUT THE RENT OR BILLS. I'LL TAKE CARE OF IT.

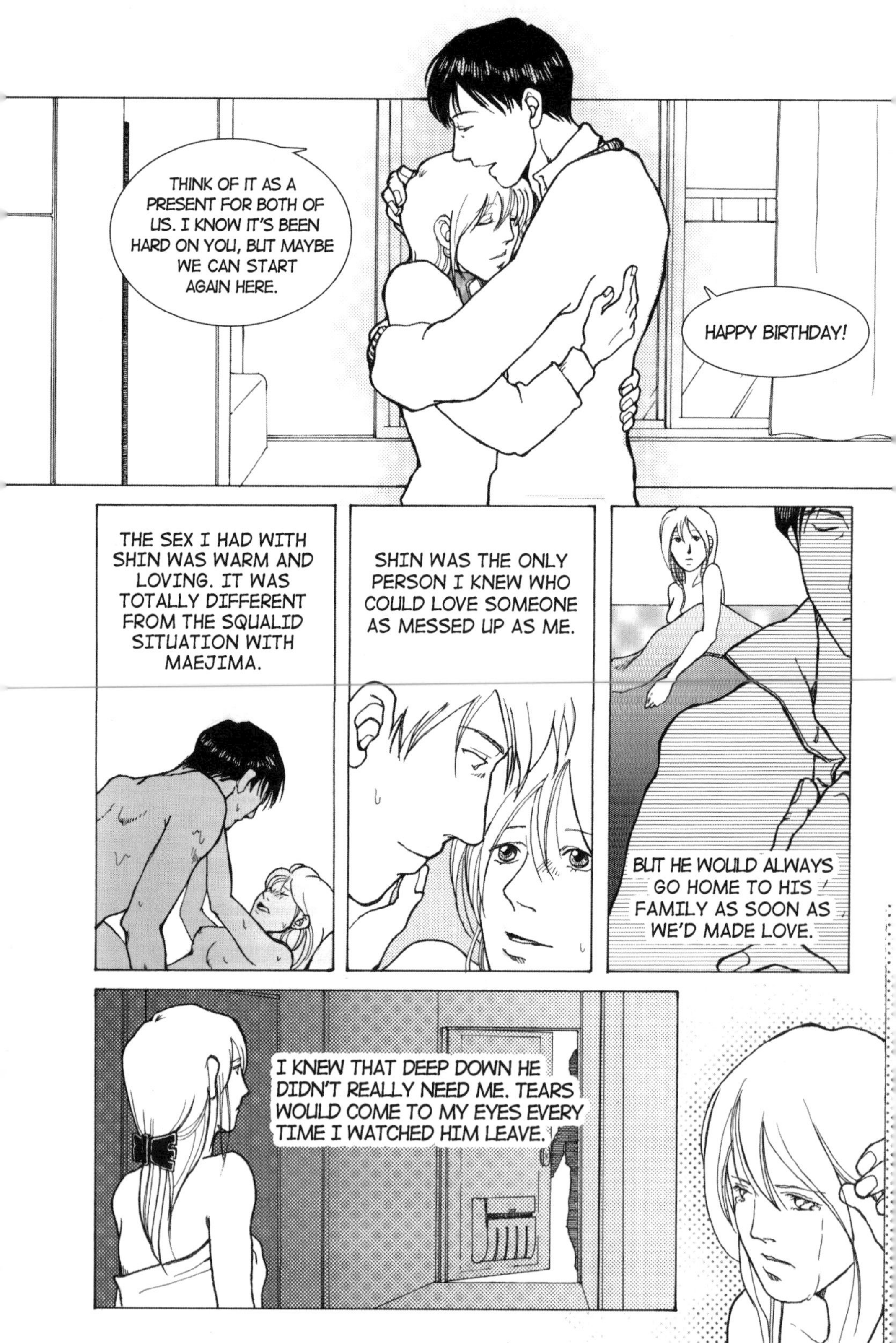
THINK OF IT AS A PRESENT FOR BOTH OF US. I KNOW IT'S BEEN HARD ON YOU, BUT MAYBE WE CAN START AGAIN HERE.
HAPPY BIRTHDAY!
THE SEX I HAD WITH SHIN WAS WARM AND LOVING. IT WAS TOTALLY DIFFERENT FROM THE SQUALID SITUATION WITH MAEJIMA.
SHIN WAS THE ONLY PERSON I KNEW WHO COULD LOVE SOMEONE AS MESSED UP AS ME.
BUT HE WOULD ALWAYS GO HOME TO HIS FAMILY AS SOON AS WE'D MADE LOVE.
I KNEW THAT DEEP DOWN HE DIDN'T REALLY NEED ME. TEARS WOULD COME TO MY EYES EVERY TIME I WATCHED HIM LEAVE.

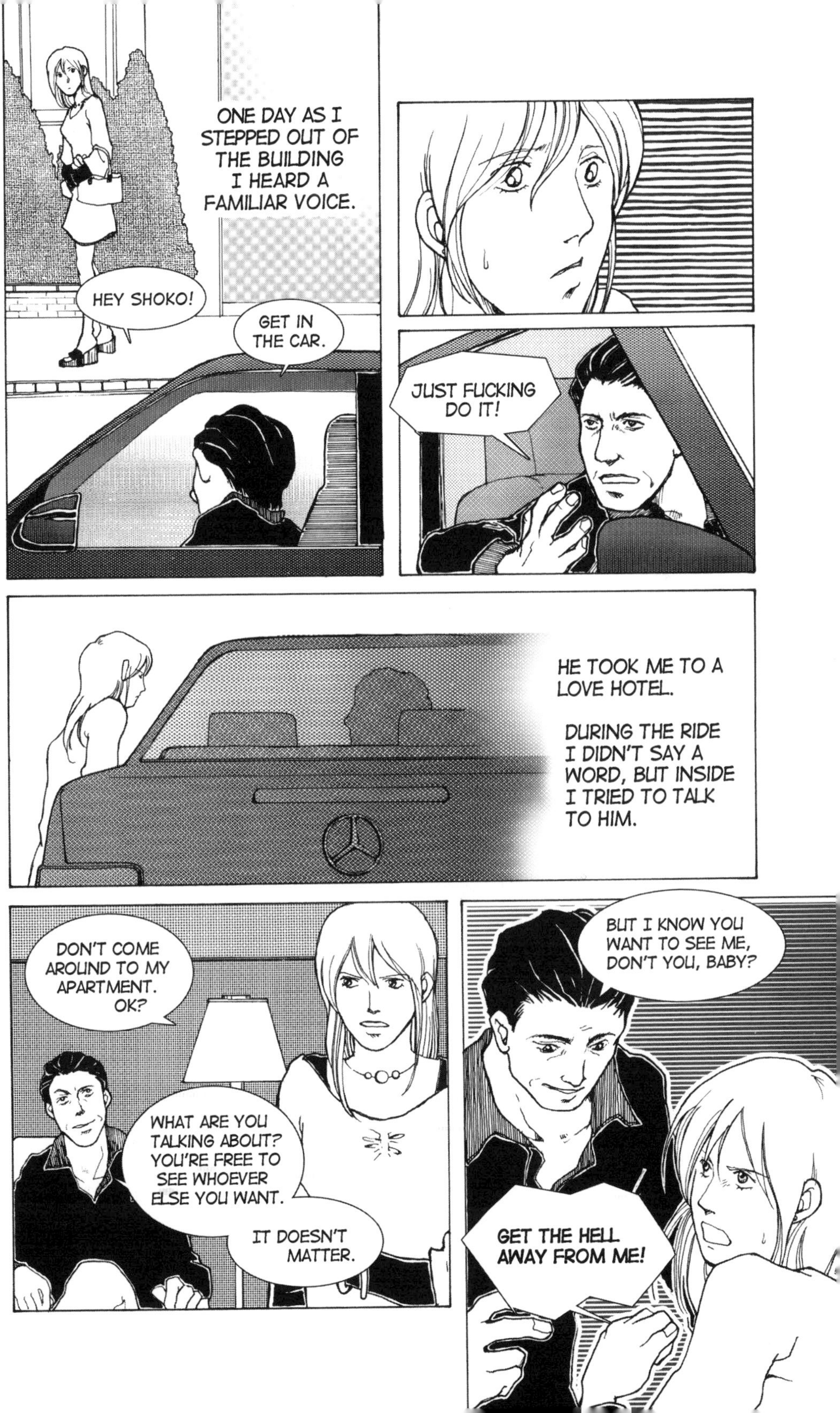
ONE DAY AS I STEPPED OUT OF THE BUILDING I HEARD A FAMILIAR VOICE.
HEY SHOKO!
GET IN THE CAR.
JUST FUCKING DO IT!
HE TOOK ME TO A LOVE HOTEL.
DURING THE RIDE I DIDN'T SAY A WORD, BUT INSIDE I TRIED TO TALK TO HIM.
DON'T COME AROUND TO MY APARTMENT. OK?
WHAT ARE YOU TALKING ABOUT? YOU'RE FREE TO SEE WHOEVER ELSE YOU WANT.
IT DOESN'T MATTER.
BUT I KNOW YOU WANT TO SEE ME, DON'T YOU, BABY?
GET THE HELL AWAY FROM ME!

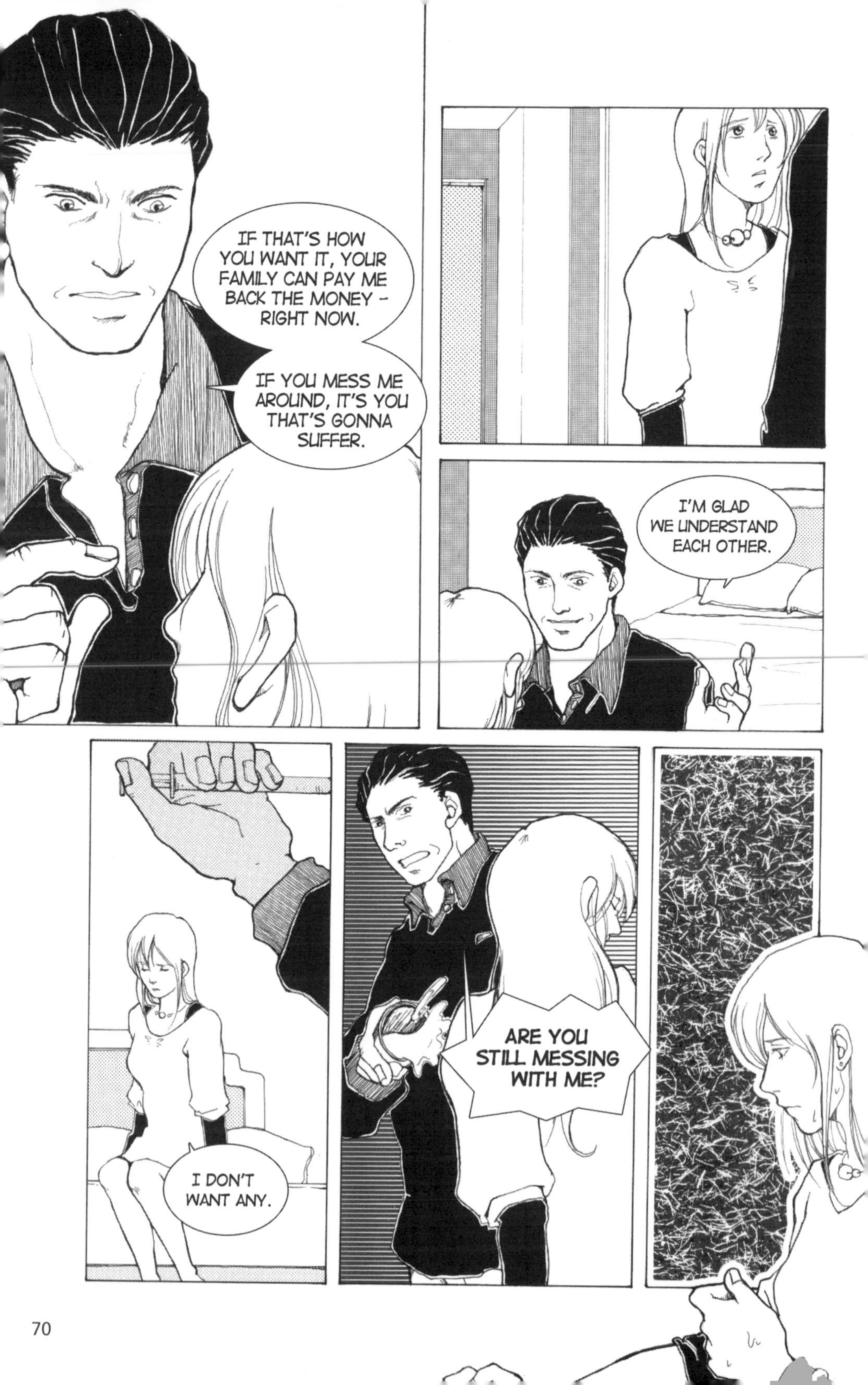
IF THAT'S HOW YOU WANT IT, YOUR FAMILY CAN PAY ME BACK THE MONEY - RIGHT NOW.
IF YOU MESS ME AROUND, IT'S YOU THAT'S GONNA SUFFER.
I'M GLAD WE UNDERSTAND EACH OTHER.
I DON'T WANT ANY.
ARE YOU STILL MESSING WITH ME?

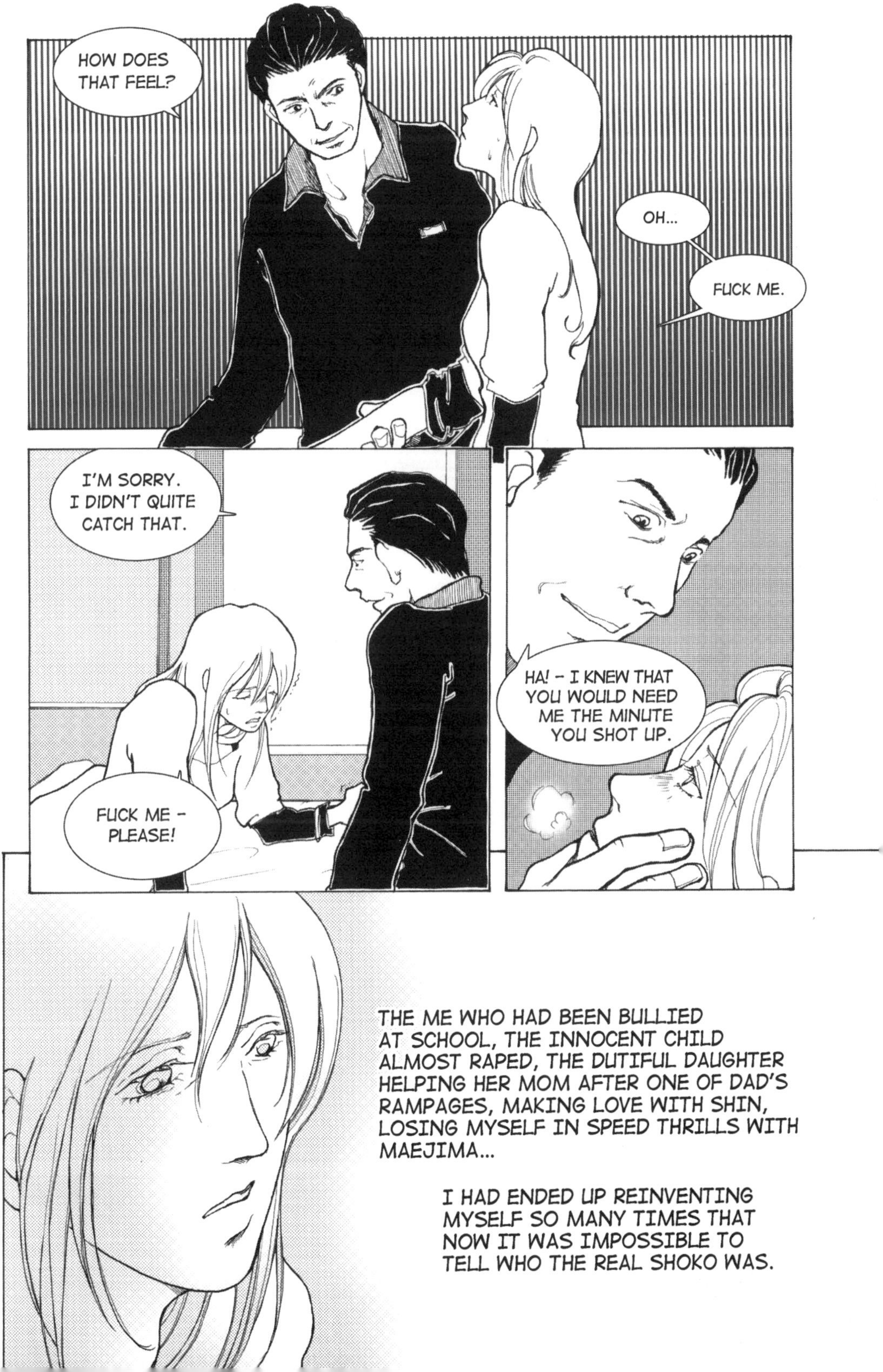
HOW DOES THAT FEEL?
OH...
FUCK ME.
I'M SORRY. I DIDN'T QUITE CATCH THAT.
FUCK ME - PLEASE!
HA! - I KNEW THAT YOU WOULD NEED ME THE MINUTE YOU SHOT UP.
THE ME WHO HAD BEEN BULLIED AT SCHOOL, THE INNOCENT CHILD ALMOST RAPED, THE DUTIFUL DAUGHTER HELPING HER MOM AFTER ONE OF DAD'S RAMPAGES, MAKING LOVE WITH SHIN, LOSING MYSELF IN SPEED THRILLS WITH MAEJIMA...
I HAD ENDED UP REINVENTING MYSELF SO MANY TIMES THAT NOW IT WAS IMPOSSIBLE TO TELL WHO THE REAL SHOKO WAS.

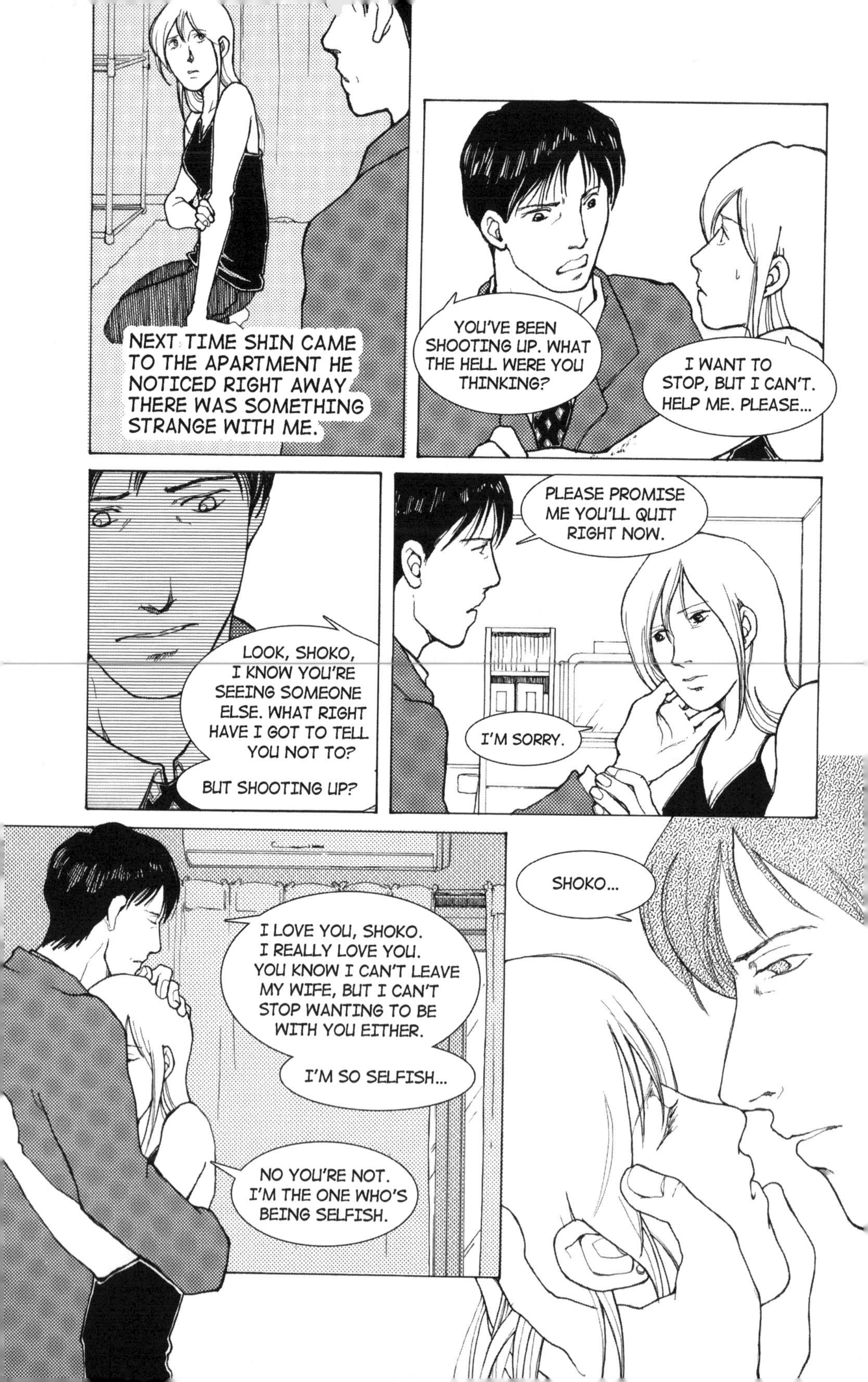
NEXT TIME SHIN CAME TO THE APARTMENT HE NOTICED RIGHT AWAY THERE WAS SOMETHING STRANGE WITH ME.
YOU'VE BEEN SHOOTING UP. WHAT THE HELL WERE YOU THINKING?
I WANT TO STOP, BUT I CAN'T. HELP ME. PLEASE...
LOOK, SHOKO, I KNOW YOU'RE SEEING SOMEONE ELSE. WHAT RIGHT HAVE I GOT TO TELL YOU NOT TO?
BUT SHOOTING UP?
PLEASE PROMISE ME YOU'LL QUIT RIGHT NOW.
I'M SORRY.
I LOVE YOU, SHOKO. I REALLY LOVE YOU. YOU KNOW I CAN'T LEAVE MY WIFE, BUT I CAN'T STOP WANTING TO BE WITH YOU EITHER.
I'M SO SELFISH...
NO YOU'RE NOT. I'M THE ONE WHO'S BEING SELFISH.
SHOKO...

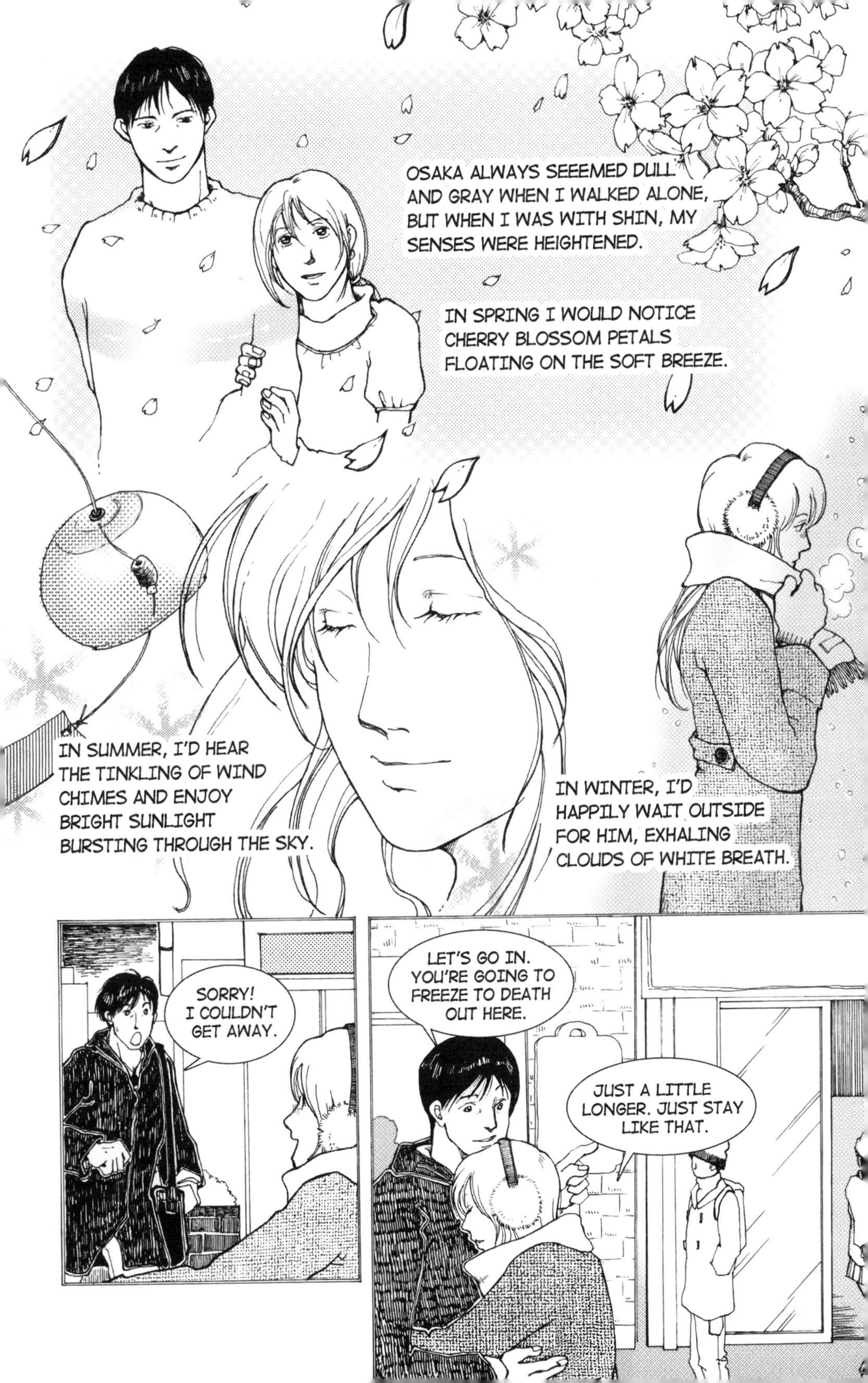
OSAKA ALWAYS SEEEMED DULL AND GRAY WHEN I WALKED ALONE, BUT WHEN I WAS WITH SHIN, MY SENSES WERE HEIGHTENED.
IN SPRING I WOULD NOTICE CHERRY BLOSSOM PETALS FLOATING ON THE SOFT BREEZE.
IN SUMMER, I'D HEAR THE TINKLING OF WIND CHIMES AND ENJOY BRIGHT SUNLIGHT BURSTING THROUGH THE SKY.
IN WINTER, I'D HAPPILY WAIT OUTSIDE FOR HIM, EXHALING CLOUDS OF WHITE BREATH.
SORRY! I COULDN'T GET AWAY.
LET'S GO IN. YOU'RE GOING TO FREEZE TO DEATH OUT HERE.
JUST A LITTLE LONGER. JUST STAY LIKE THAT.

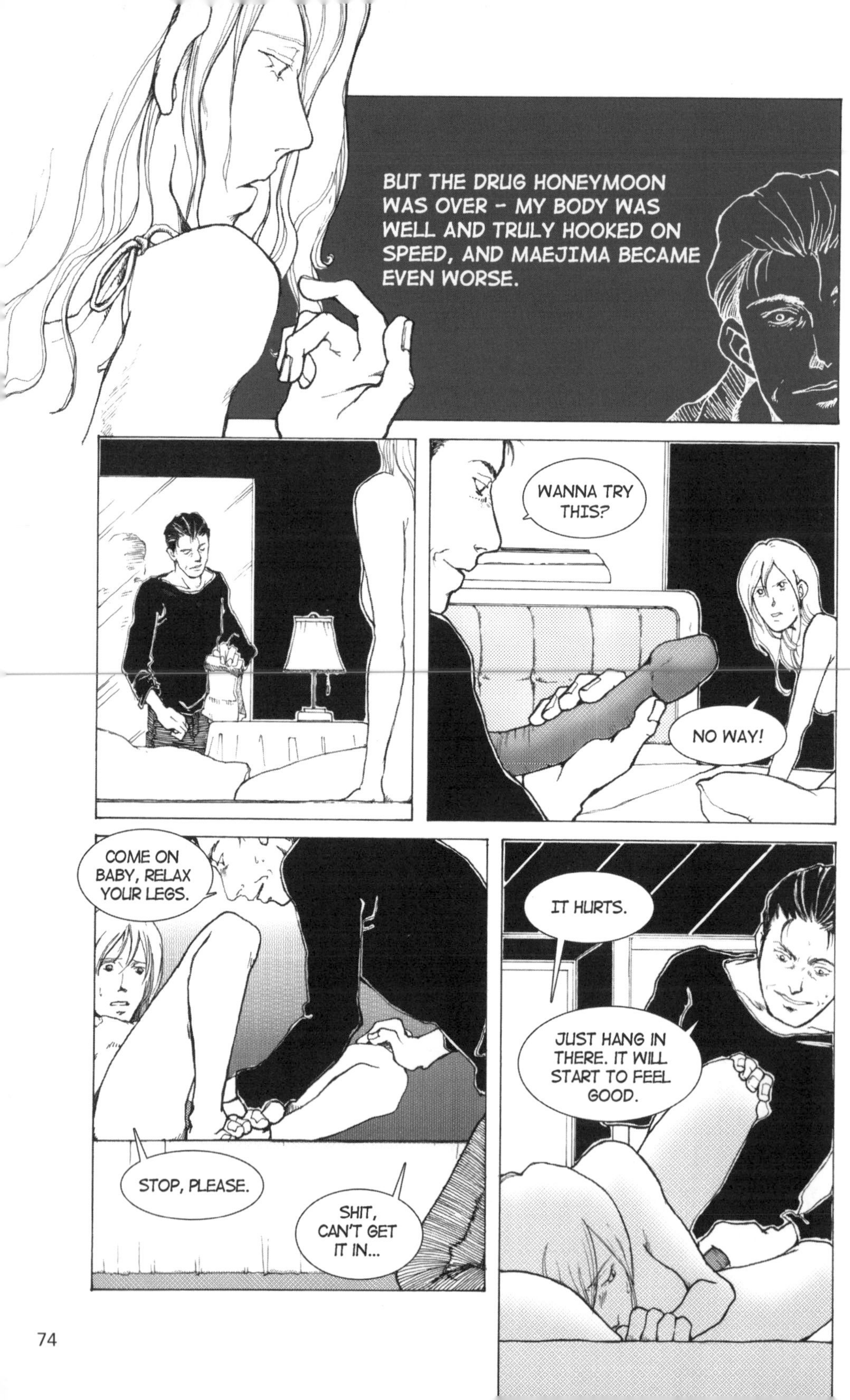
BUT THE DRUG HONEYMOON WAS OVER - MY BODY WAS WELL AND TRULY HOOKED ON SPEED, AND MAEJIMA BECAME EVEN WORSE.
WANNA TRY THIS?
NO WAY!
COME ON BABY, RELAX YOUR LEGS.
STOP, PLEASE.
SHIT, CAN'T GET IT IN...
IT HURTS.
JUST HANG IN THERE. IT WILL START TO FEEL GOOD.

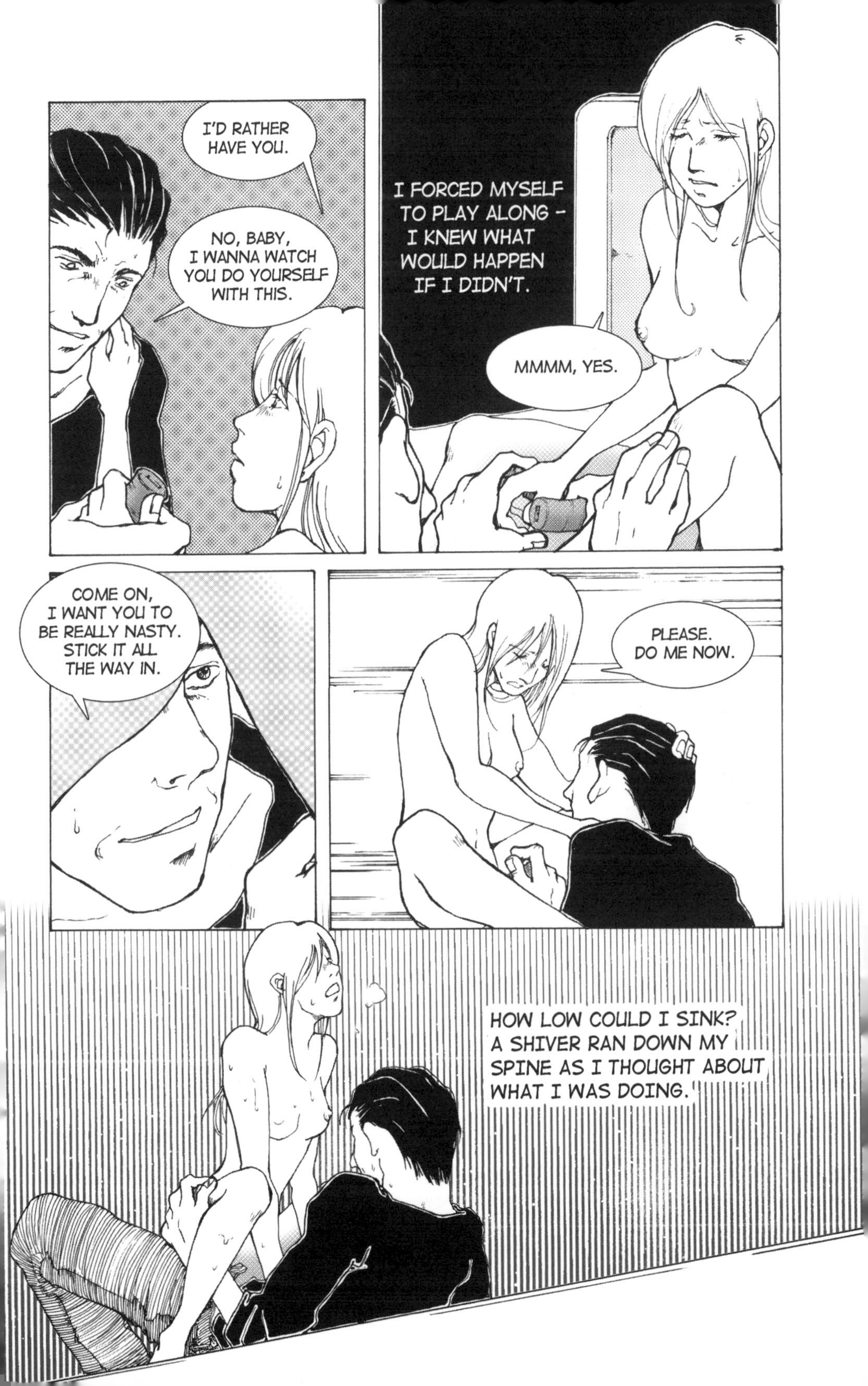
I'D RATHER HAVE YOU.
NO, BABY, I WANNA WATCH YOU DO YOURSELF WITH THIS.
I FORCED MYSELF TO PLAY ALONG - I KNEW WHAT WOULD HAPPEN IF I DIDN'T.
MMMM, YES.
COME ON, I WANT YOU TO BE REALLY NASTY. STICK IT ALL THE WAY IN.
PLEASE. DO ME NOW.
HOW LOW COULD I SINK? A SHIVER RAN DOWN MY SPINE AS I THOUGHT ABOUT WHAT I WAS DOING.

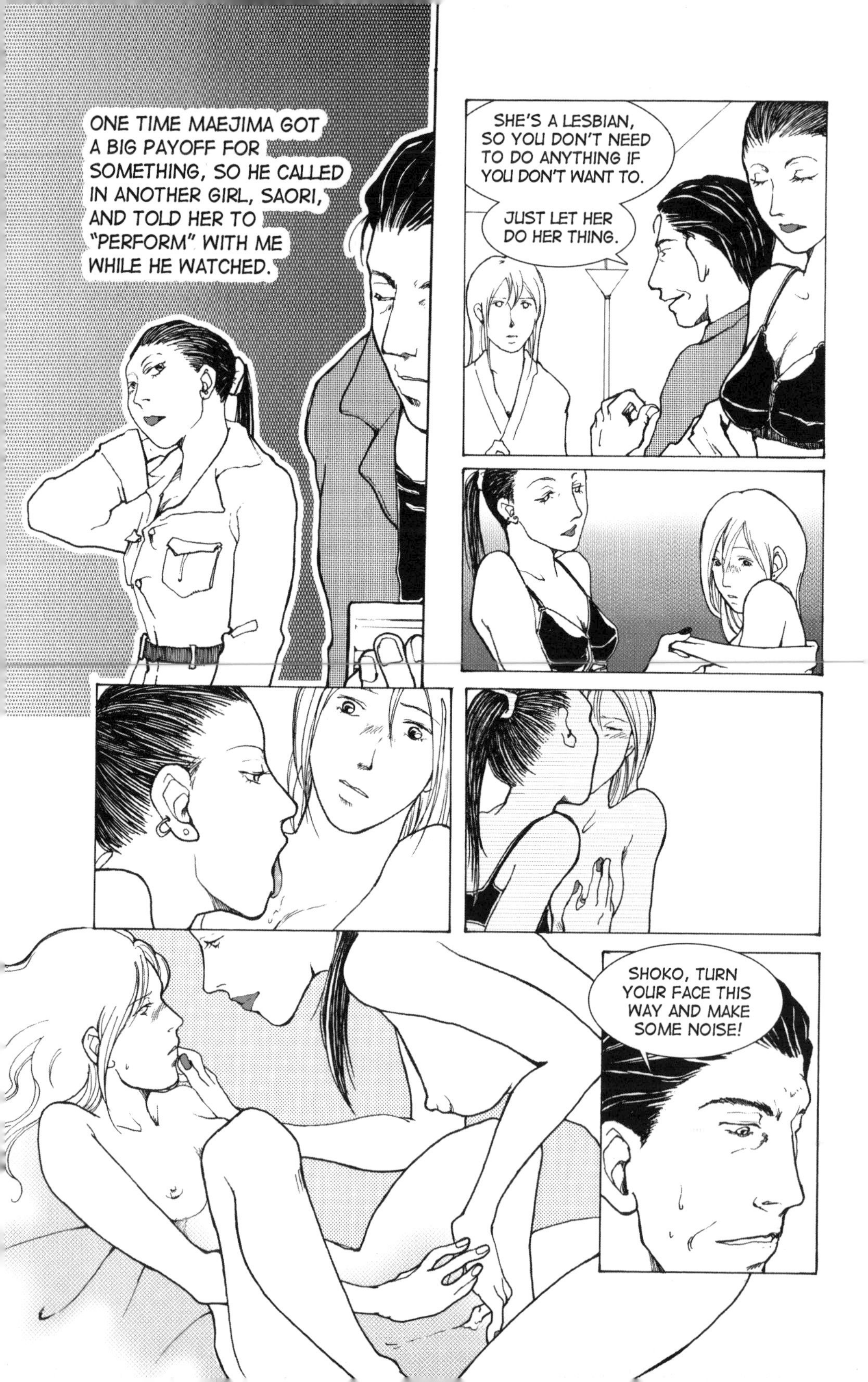
ONE TIME MAEJIMA GOT A BIG PAYOFF FOR SOMETHING, SO HE CALLED IN ANOTHER GIRL, SAORI, AND TOLD HER TO "PERFORM" WITH ME WHILE HE WATCHED.
SHE'S A LESBIAN, SO YOU DON'T NEED TO DO ANYTHING IF YOU DON'T WANT TO.
JUST LET HER DO HER THING.
SHOKO, TURN YOUR FACE THIS WAY AND MAKE SOME NOISE!

AH, NO, I'M GONNA... PLEASE!

COME HERE!

OK, YOU CAN GET OUT OF HERE.

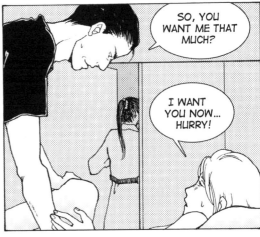

SO, YOU WANT ME THAT MUCH?

I WANT YOU NOW... HURRY!

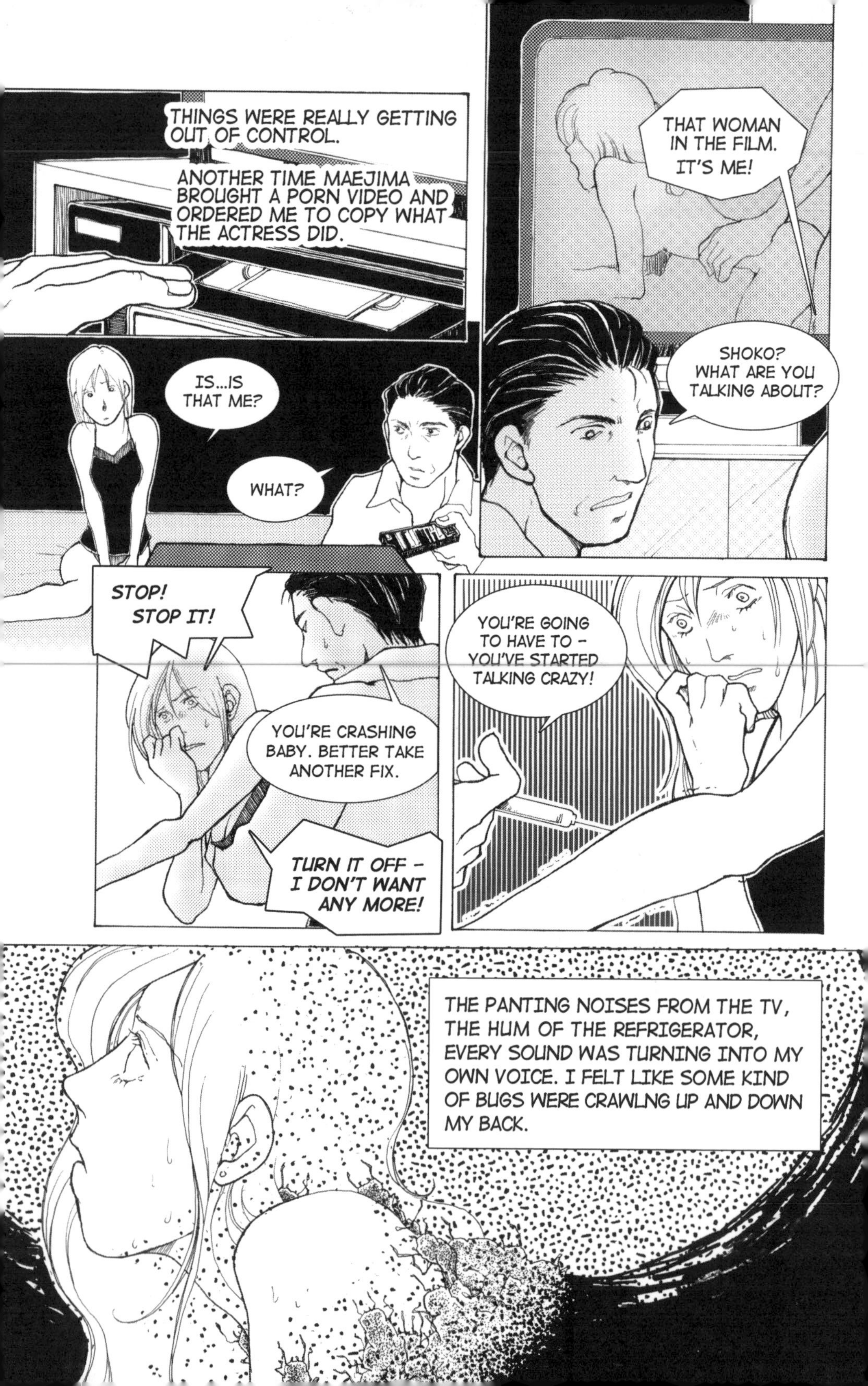
THINGS WERE REALLY GETTING OUT OF CONTROL.
ANOTHER TIME MAEJIMA BROUGHT A PORN VIDEO AND ORDERED ME TO COPY WHAT THE ACTRESS DID.
THAT WOMAN IN THE FILM. IT'S ME!
IS...IS THAT ME?
WHAT?
SHOKO? WHAT ARE YOU TALKING ABOUT?
STOP! STOP IT!
YOU'RE CRASHING BABY. BETTER TAKE ANOTHER FIX.
TURN IT OFF – I DON'T WANT ANY MORE!
YOU'RE GOING TO HAVE TO – YOU'VE STARTED TALKING CRAZY!
THE PANTING NOISES FROM THE TV, THE HUM OF THE REFRIGERATOR, EVERY SOUND WAS TURNING INTO MY OWN VOICE. I FELT LIKE SOME KIND OF BUGS WERE CRAWLNG UP AND DOWN MY BACK.

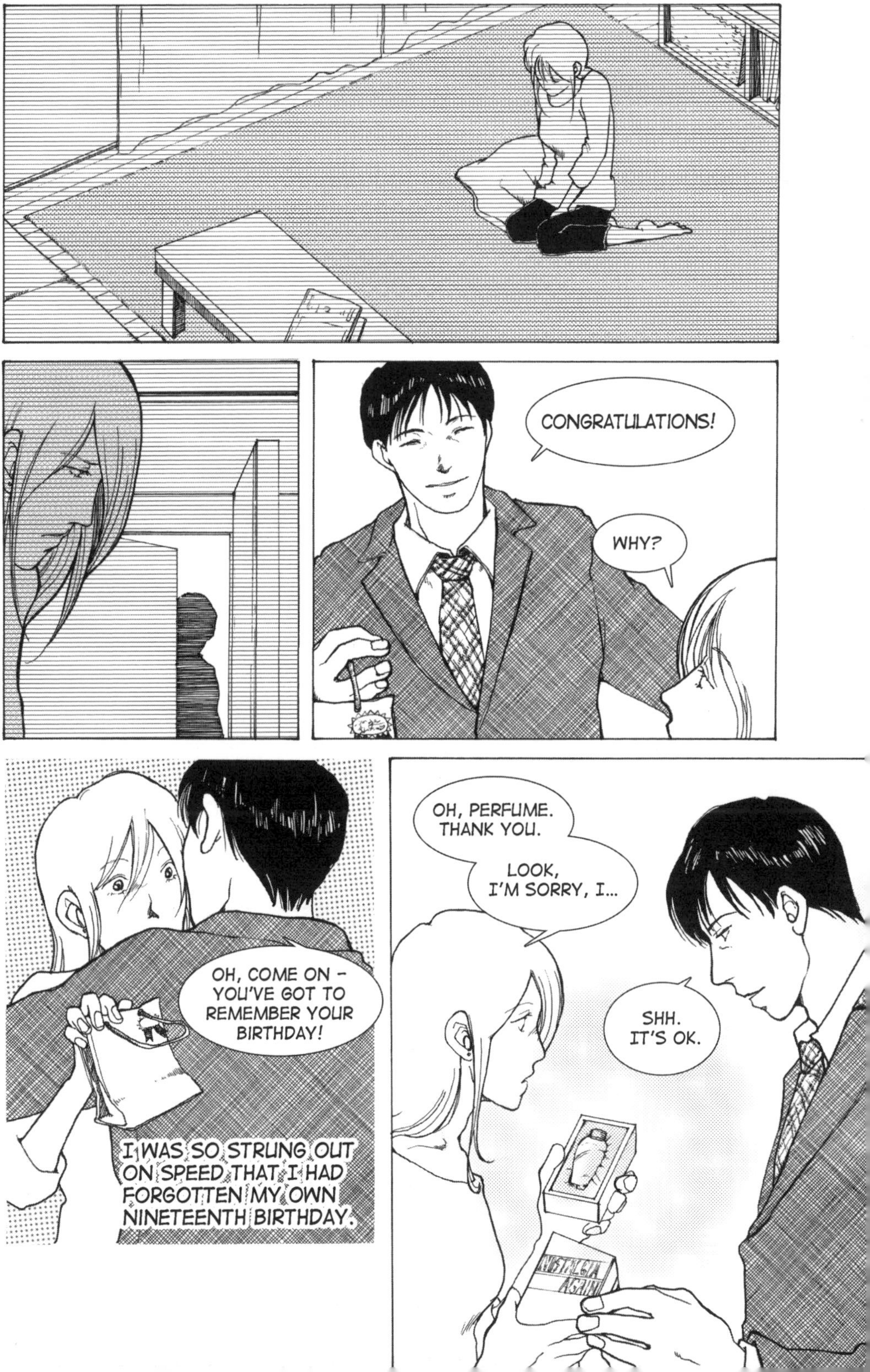
CONGRATULATIONS!
WHY?
OH, COME ON - YOU'VE GOT TO REMEMBER YOUR BIRTHDAY!
I WAS SO STRUNG OUT ON SPEED THAT I HAD FORGOTTEN MY OWN NINETEENTH BIRTHDAY.
OH, PERFUME. THANK YOU.
LOOK, I'M SORRY, I...
SHH. IT'S OK.

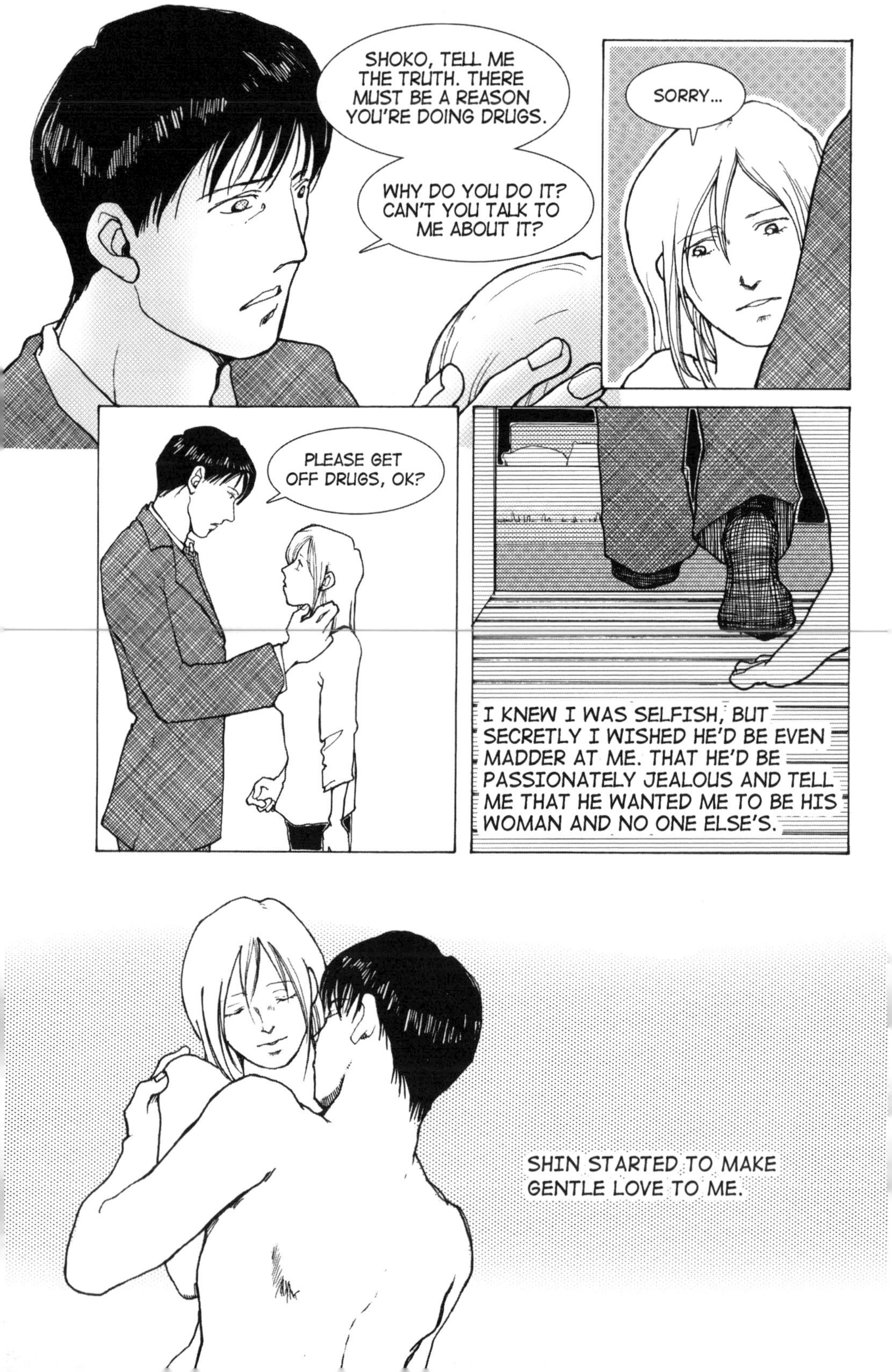
SHOKO, TELL ME THE TRUTH. THERE MUST BE A REASON YOU'RE DOING DRUGS.
WHY DO YOU DO IT? CAN'T YOU TALK TO ME ABOUT IT?
SORRY...
PLEASE GET OFF DRUGS, OK?
I KNEW I WAS SELFISH, BUT SECRETLY I WISHED HE'D BE EVEN MADDER AT ME. THAT HE'D BE PASSIONATELY JEALOUS AND TELL ME THAT HE WANTED ME TO BE HIS WOMAN AND NO ONE ELSE'S.
SHIN STARTED TO MAKE GENTLE LOVE TO ME.

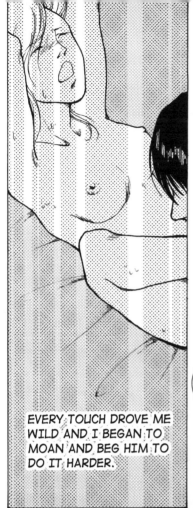

SHOKO! YOU'RE HIGH RIGHT NOW, AREN'T YOU?

I CAN TELL WHEN YOU ARE. YOUR REACTIONS AREN'T THE SAME AT ALL.

EVERY TOUCH DROVE ME WILD AND I BEGAN TO MOAN AND BEG HIM TO DO IT HARDER.

HIS WORDS MADE ME FEEL DIRTY. THE INNOCENT VERSION OF ME, THE GIRL WHO WALKED HAPPILY HAND IN HAND WITH SHIN – SHE NO LONGER EXISTED.

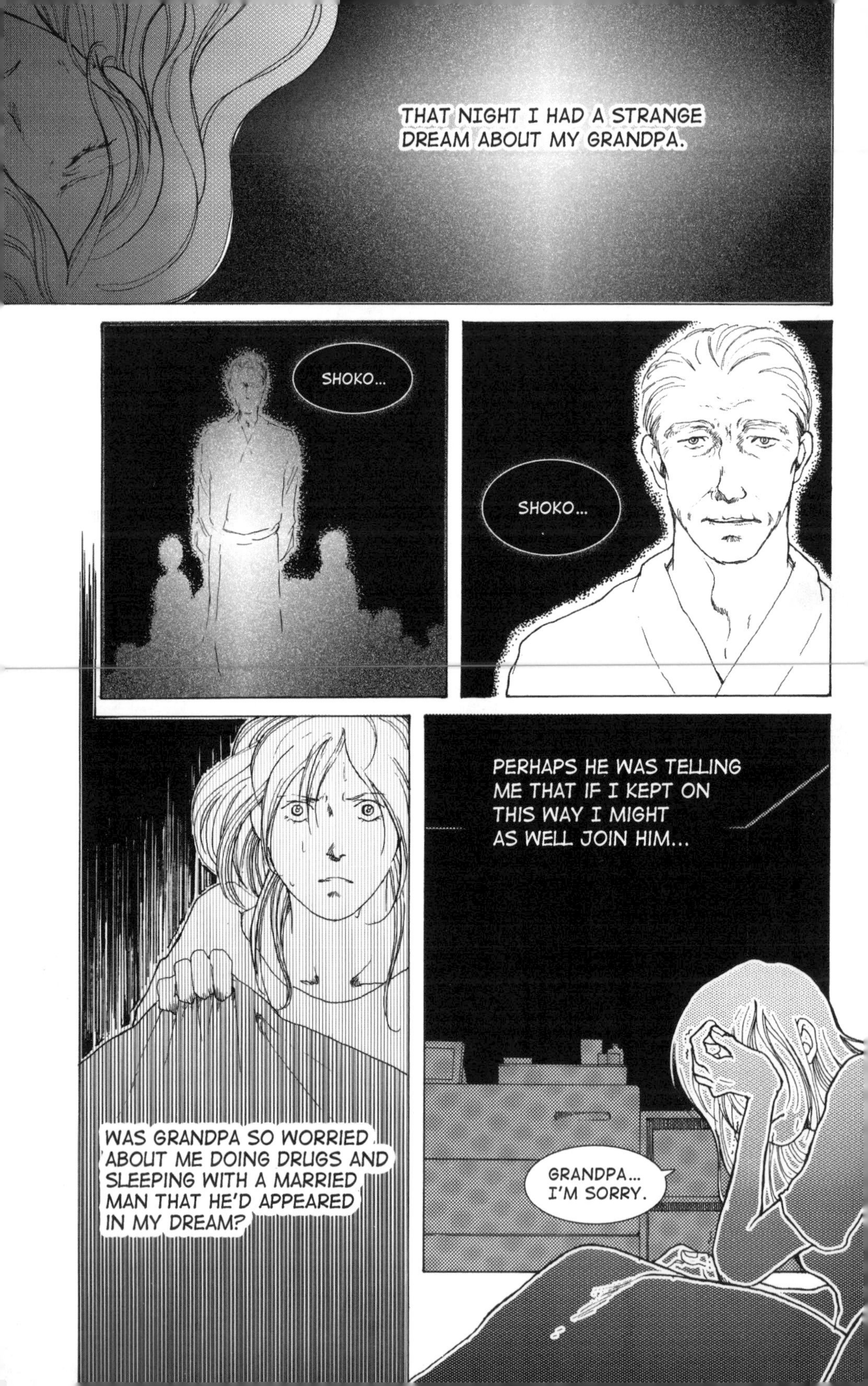
THAT NIGHT I HAD A STRANGE DREAM ABOUT MY GRANDPA.
SHOKO...
SHOKO...
WAS GRANDPA SO WORRIED ABOUT ME DOING DRUGS AND SLEEPING WITH A MARRIED MAN THAT HE'D APPEARED IN MY DREAM?
PERHAPS HE WAS TELLING ME THAT IF I KEPT ON THIS WAY I MIGHT AS WELL JOIN HIM...
GRANDPA... I'M SORRY.

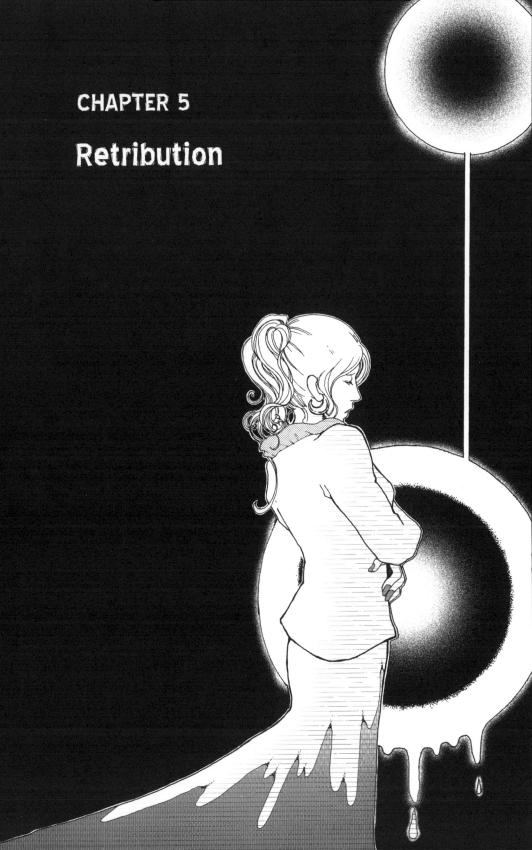

CHAPTER 5

Retribution

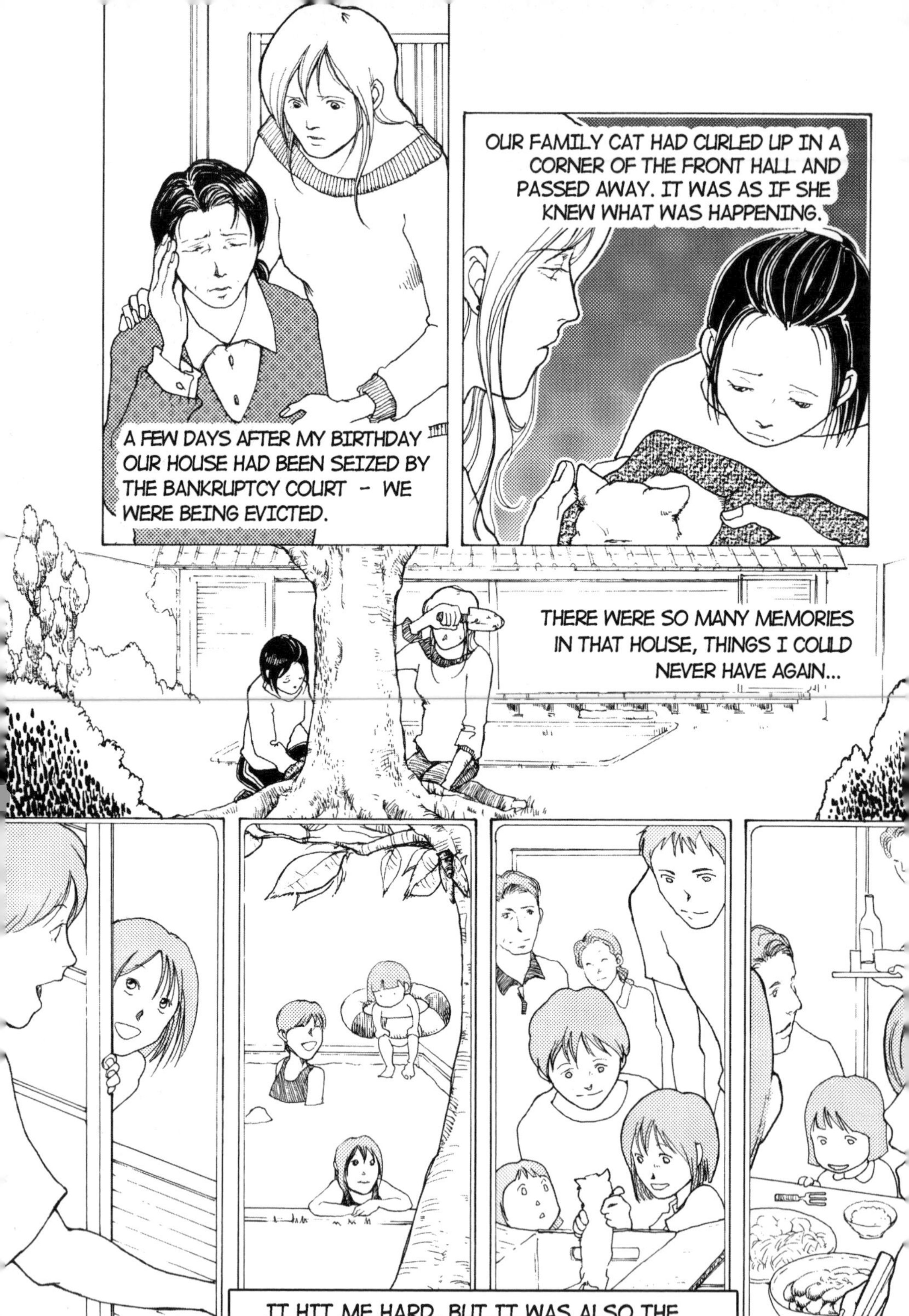
A FEW DAYS AFTER MY BIRTHDAY OUR HOUSE HAD BEEN SEIZED BY THE BANKRUPTCY COURT - WE WERE BEING EVICTED.
OUR FAMILY CAT HAD CURLED UP IN A CORNER OF THE FRONT HALL AND PASSED AWAY. IT WAS AS IF SHE KNEW WHAT WAS HAPPENING.
THERE WERE SO MANY MEMORIES IN THAT HOUSE, THINGS I COULD NEVER HAVE AGAIN...
IT HIT ME HARD, BUT IT WAS ALSO THE WAKE-UP CALL I NEEDED TO GIVE UP DRUGS.

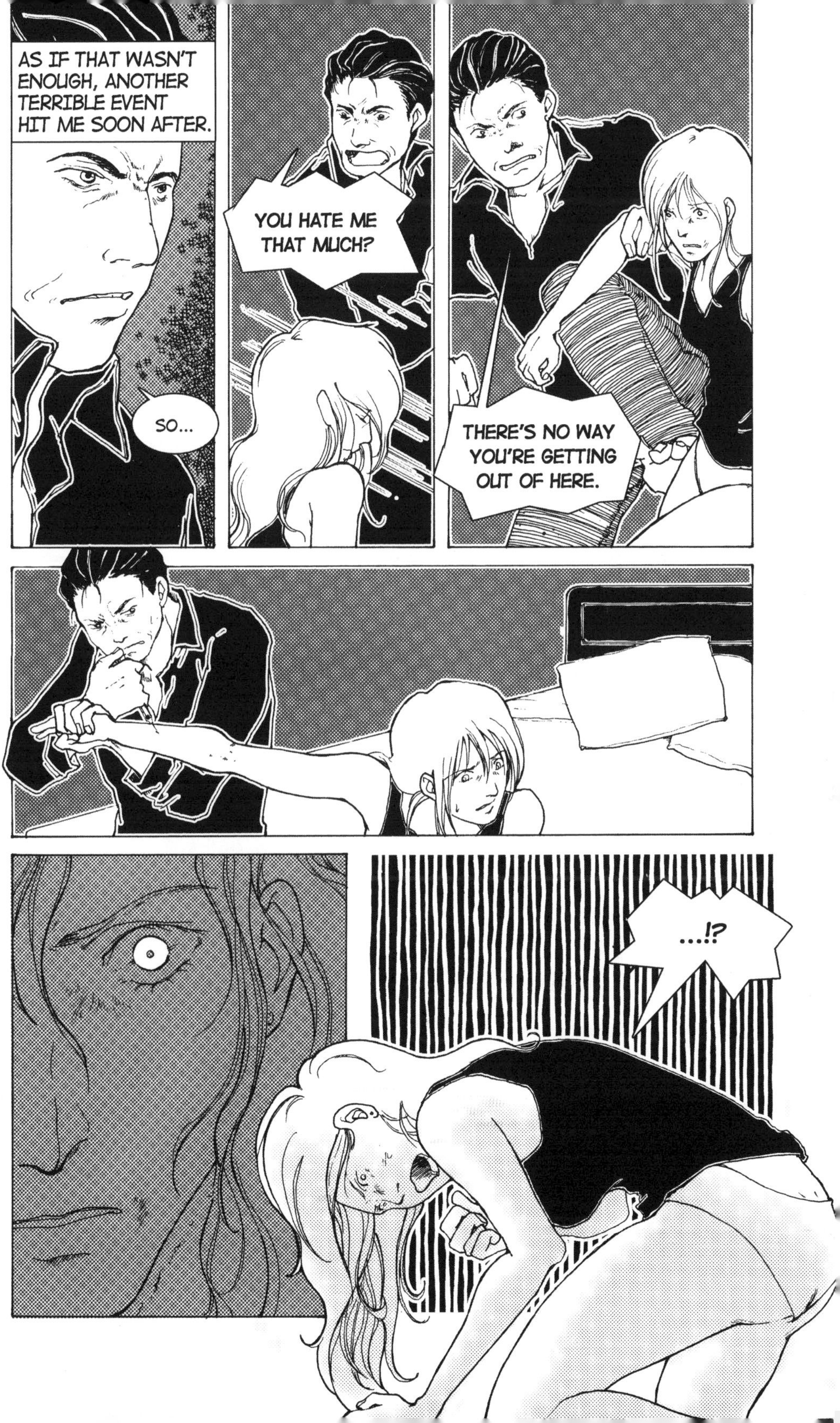
AS IF THAT WASN'T ENOUGH, ANOTHER TERRIBLE EVENT HIT ME SOON AFTER.
SO...
YOU HATE ME THAT MUCH?
THERE'S NO WAY YOU'RE GETTING OUT OF HERE.
...!?

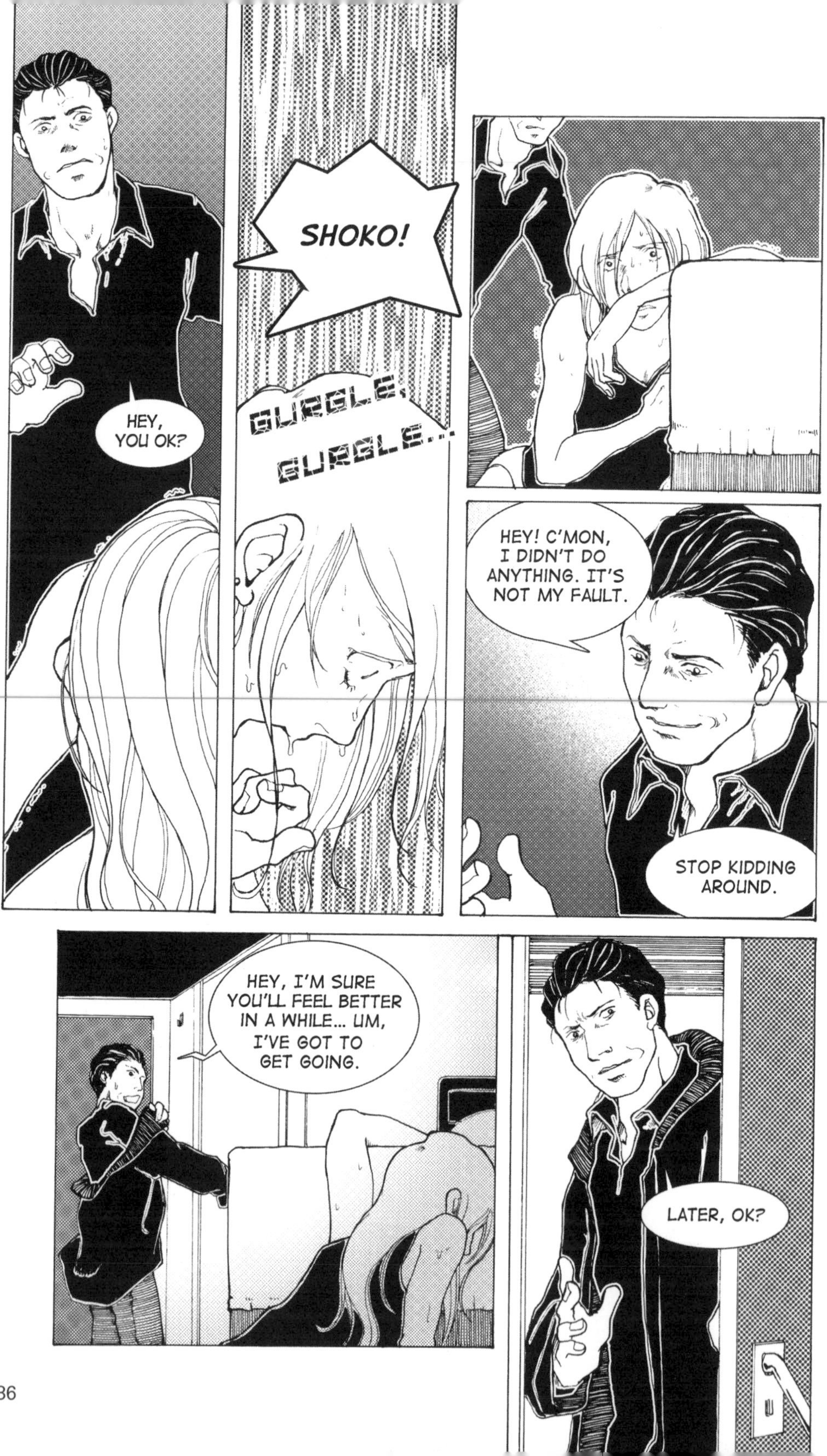
HEY, YOU OK?
SHOKO!
GURGLE, GURGLE...
HEY! C'MON, I DIDN'T DO ANYTHING. IT'S NOT MY FAULT.
STOP KIDDING AROUND.
HEY, I'M SURE YOU'LL FEEL BETTER IN A WHILE... UM, I'VE GOT TO GET GOING.
LATER, OK?

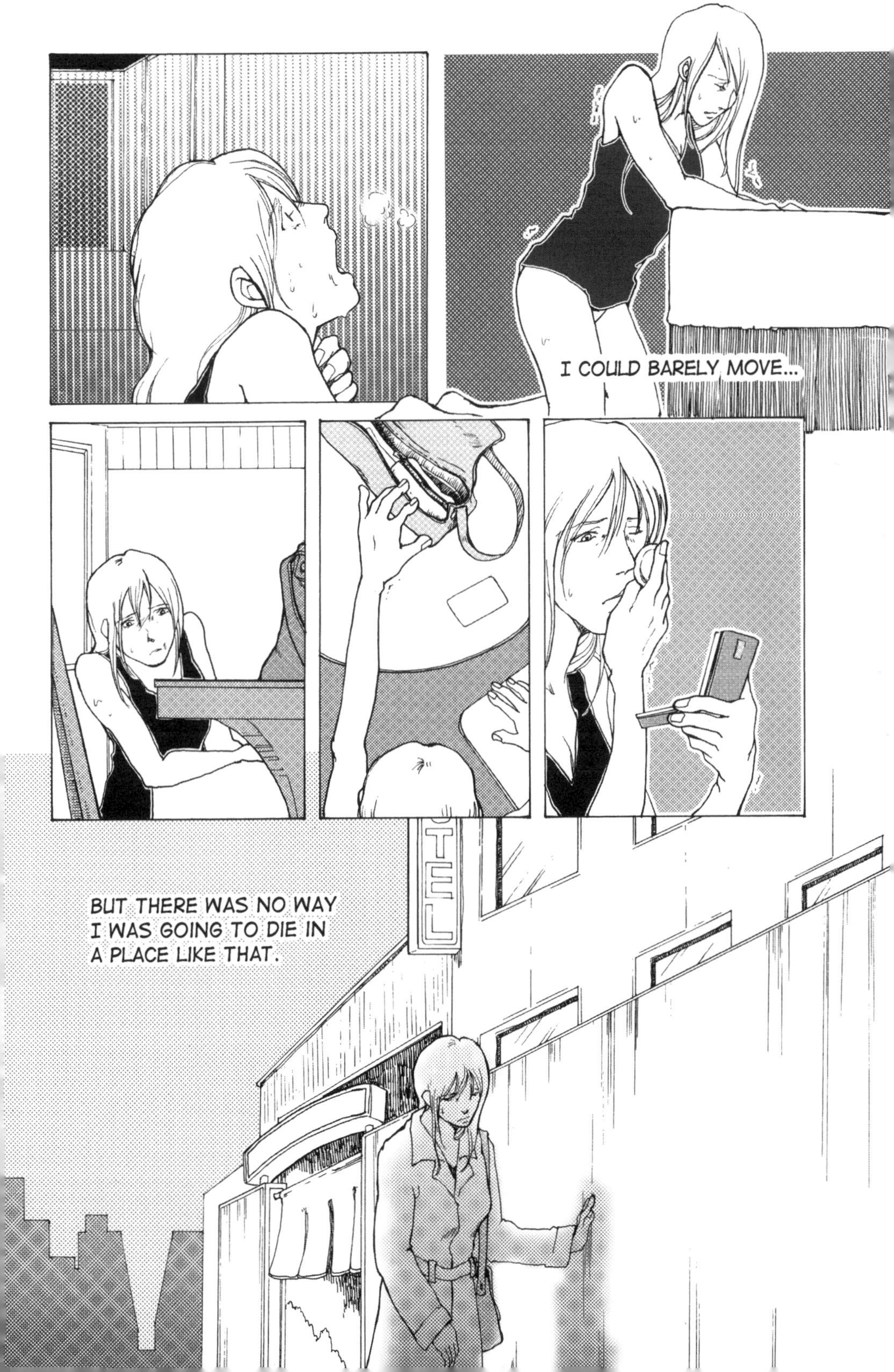
I COULD BARELY MOVE...
OTEL
BUT THERE WAS NO WAY
I WAS GOING TO DIE IN
A PLACE LIKE THAT.

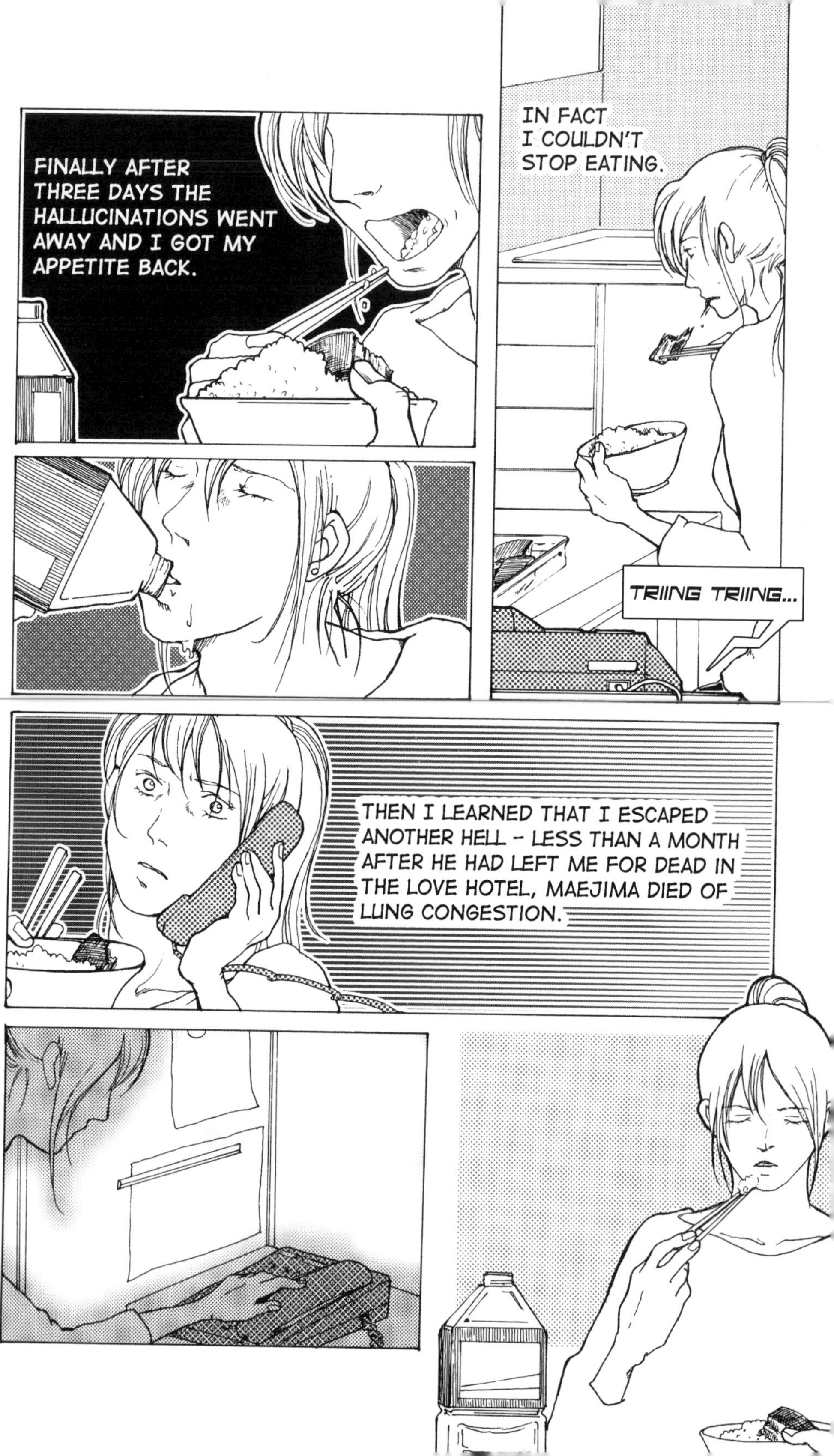
FINALLY AFTER THREE DAYS THE HALLUCINATIONS WENT AWAY AND I GOT MY APPETITE BACK.
IN FACT I COULDN'T STOP EATING.
TRIING TRIING...
THEN I LEARNED THAT I ESCAPED ANOTHER HELL - LESS THAN A MONTH AFTER HE HAD LEFT ME FOR DEAD IN THE LOVE HOTEL, MAEJIMA DIED OF LUNG CONGESTION.

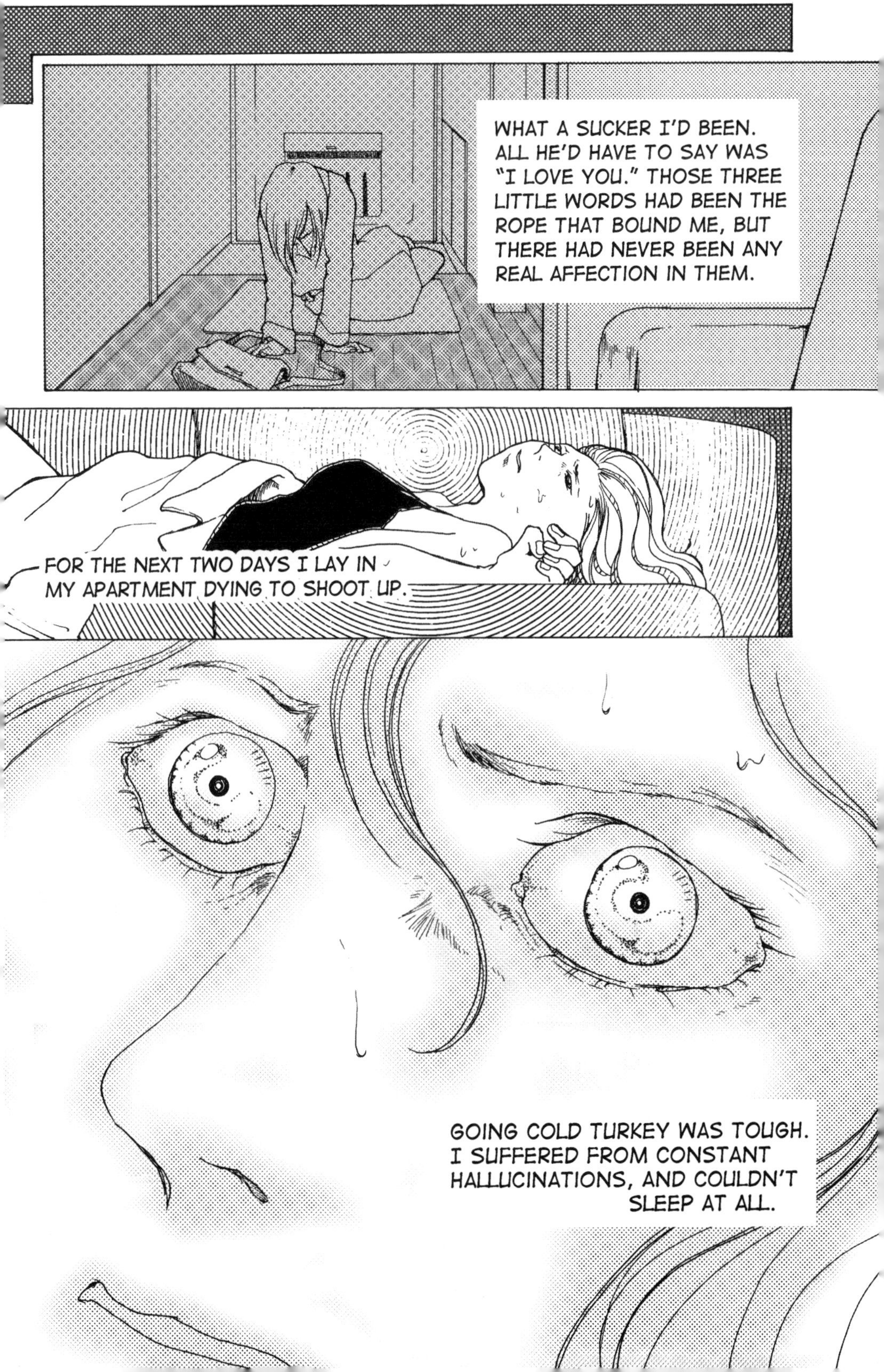
WHAT A SUCKER I'D BEEN. ALL HE'D HAVE TO SAY WAS "I LOVE YOU." THOSE THREE LITTLE WORDS HAD BEEN THE ROPE THAT BOUND ME, BUT THERE HAD NEVER BEEN ANY REAL AFFECTION IN THEM.
FOR THE NEXT TWO DAYS I LAY IN MY APARTMENT DYING TO SHOOT UP.
GOING COLD TURKEY WAS TOUGH. I SUFFERED FROM CONSTANT HALLUCINATIONS, AND COULDN'T SLEEP AT ALL.

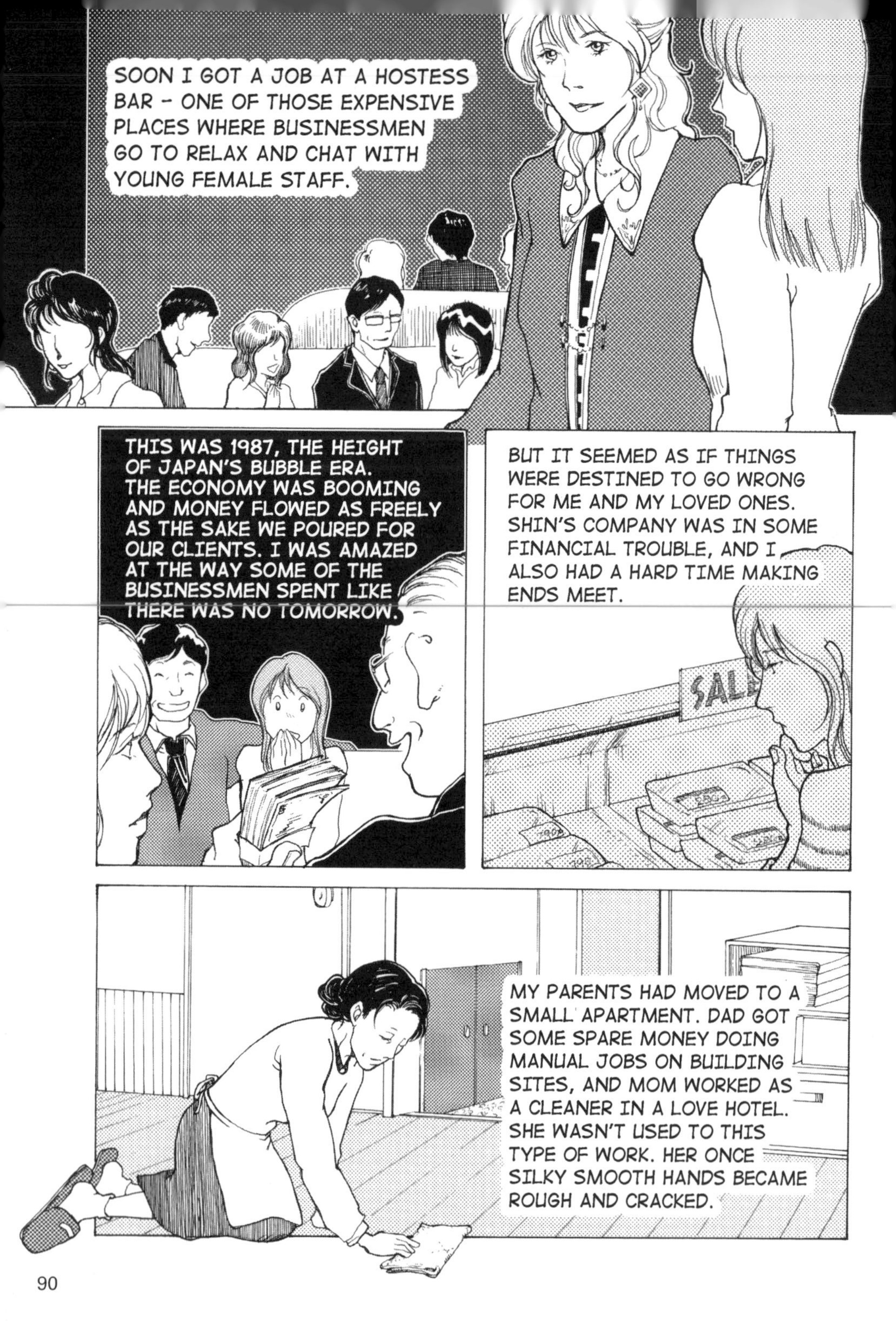
SOON I GOT A JOB AT A HOSTESS BAR - ONE OF THOSE EXPENSIVE PLACES WHERE BUSINESSMEN GO TO RELAX AND CHAT WITH YOUNG FEMALE STAFF.
THIS WAS 1987, THE HEIGHT OF JAPAN'S BUBBLE ERA. THE ECONOMY WAS BOOMING AND MONEY FLOWED AS FREELY AS THE SAKE WE POURED FOR OUR CLIENTS. I WAS AMAZED AT THE WAY SOME OF THE BUSINESSMEN SPENT LIKE THERE WAS NO TOMORROW.
BUT IT SEEMED AS IF THINGS WERE DESTINED TO GO WRONG FOR ME AND MY LOVED ONES. SHIN'S COMPANY WAS IN SOME FINANCIAL TROUBLE, AND I ALSO HAD A HARD TIME MAKING ENDS MEET.
MY PARENTS HAD MOVED TO A SMALL APARTMENT. DAD GOT SOME SPARE MONEY DOING MANUAL JOBS ON BUILDING SITES, AND MOM WORKED AS A CLEANER IN A LOVE HOTEL. SHE WASN'T USED TO THIS TYPE OF WORK. HER ONCE SILKY SMOOTH HANDS BECAME ROUGH AND CRACKED.

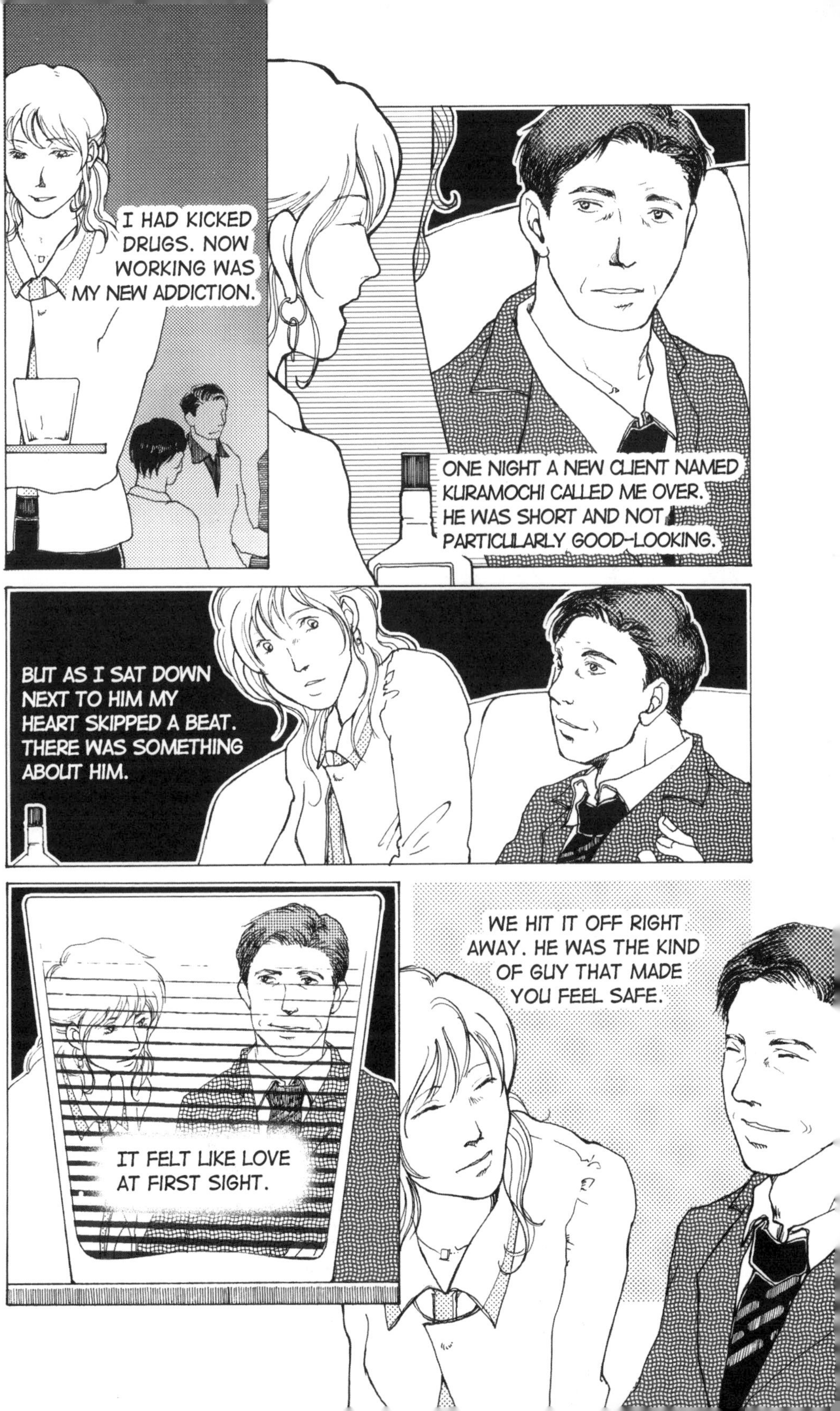
I HAD KICKED DRUGS. NOW WORKING WAS MY NEW ADDICTION.
ONE NIGHT A NEW CLIENT NAMED KURAMOCHI CALLED ME OVER. HE WAS SHORT AND NOT PARTICULARLY GOOD-LOOKING.
BUT AS I SAT DOWN NEXT TO HIM MY HEART SKIPPED A BEAT. THERE WAS SOMETHING ABOUT HIM.
IT FELT LIKE LOVE AT FIRST SIGHT.
WE HIT IT OFF RIGHT AWAY. HE WAS THE KIND OF GUY THAT MADE YOU FEEL SAFE.

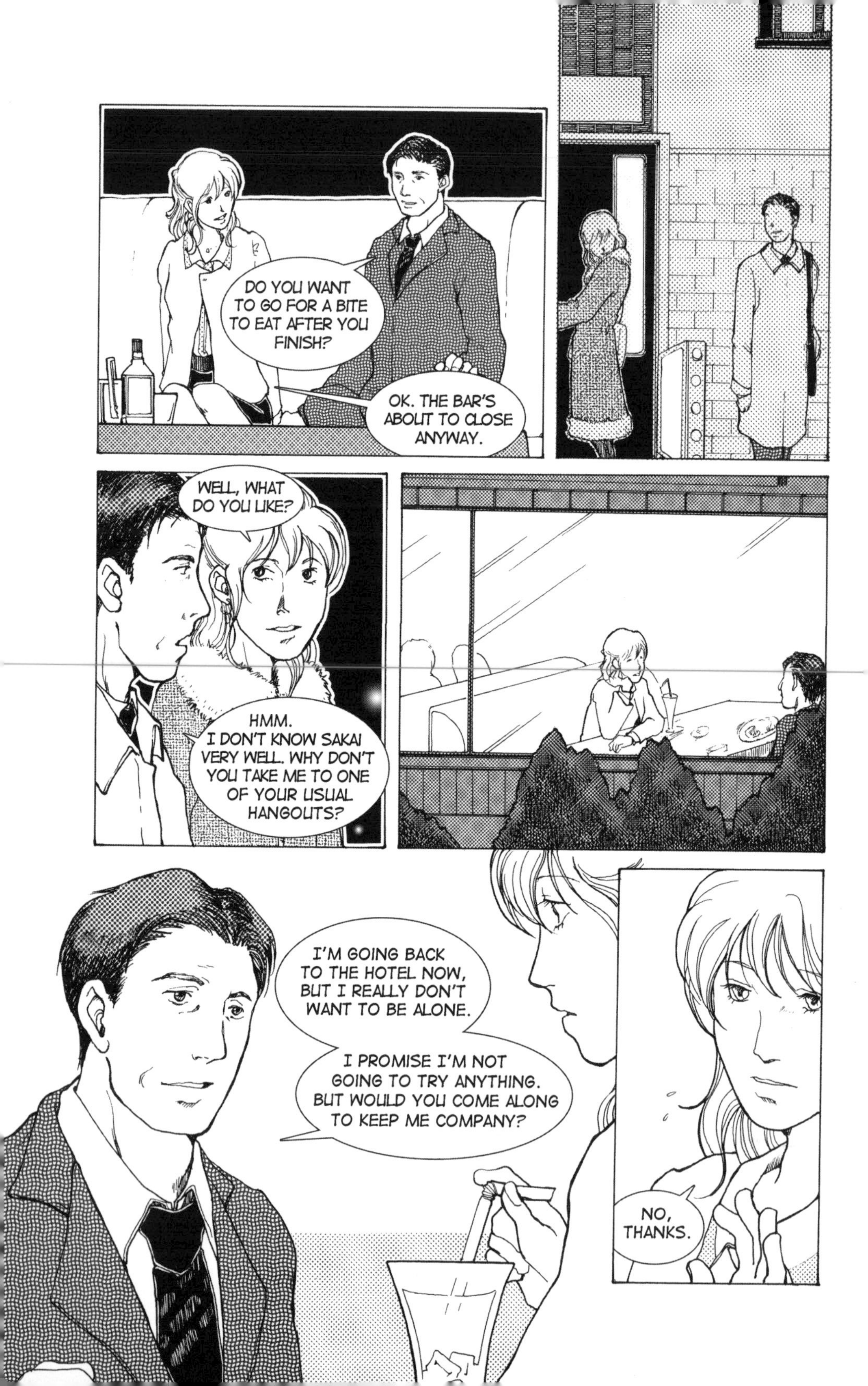
DO YOU WANT TO GO FOR A BITE TO EAT AFTER YOU FINISH?
OK. THE BAR'S ABOUT TO CLOSE ANYWAY.
WELL, WHAT DO YOU LIKE?
HMM. I DON'T KNOW SAKAI VERY WELL. WHY DON'T YOU TAKE ME TO ONE OF YOUR USUAL HANGOUTS?
I'M GOING BACK TO THE HOTEL NOW, BUT I REALLY DON'T WANT TO BE ALONE.
I PROMISE I'M NOT GOING TO TRY ANYTHING. BUT WOULD YOU COME ALONG TO KEEP ME COMPANY?
NO, THANKS.

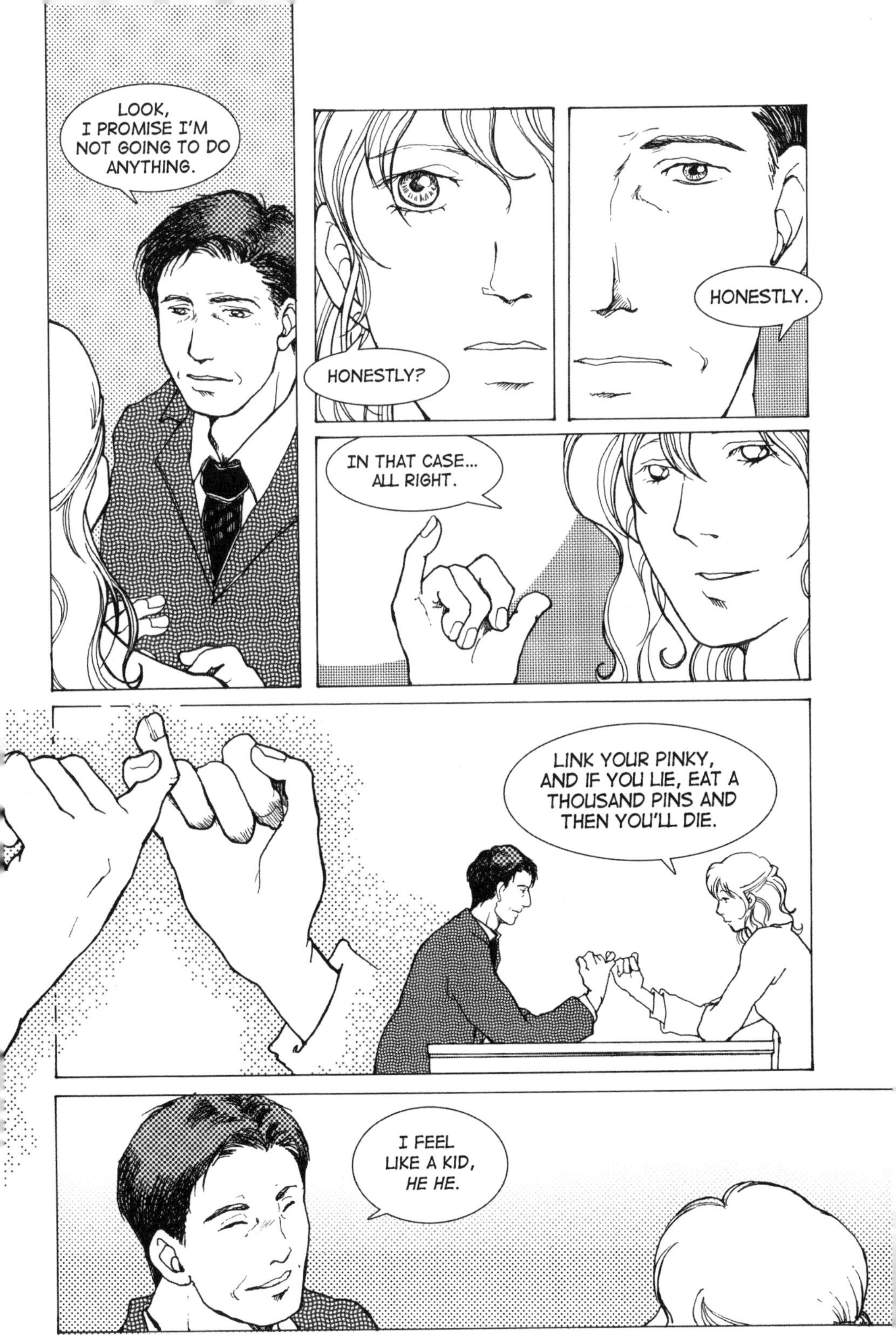
LOOK, I PROMISE I'M NOT GOING TO DO ANYTHING.
HONESTLY?
HONESTLY.
IN THAT CASE... ALL RIGHT.
LINK YOUR PINKY, AND IF YOU LIE, EAT A THOUSAND PINS AND THEN YOU'LL DIE.
I FEEL LIKE A KID, *HE HE*.

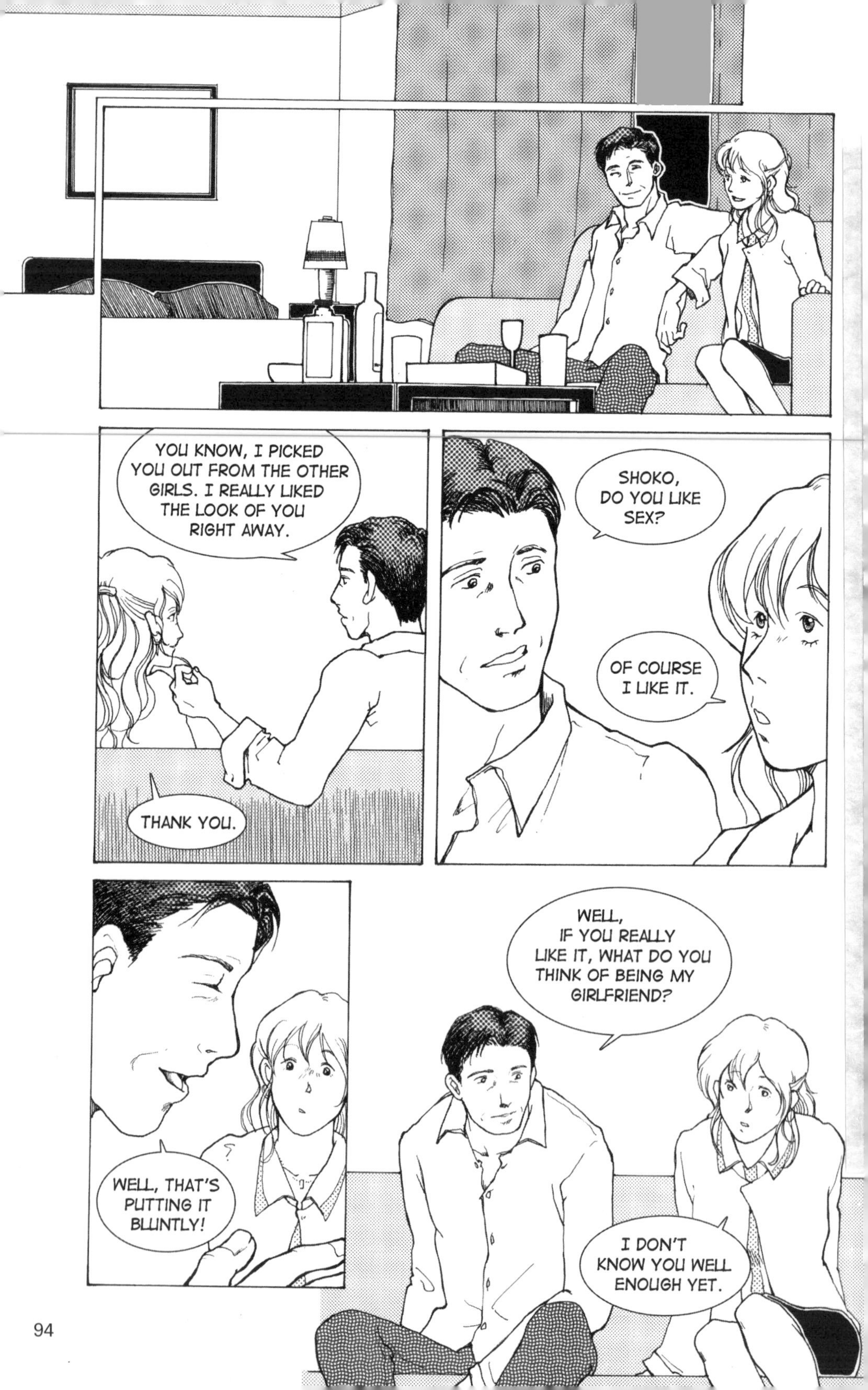
YOU KNOW, I PICKED YOU OUT FROM THE OTHER GIRLS. I REALLY LIKED THE LOOK OF YOU RIGHT AWAY.
THANK YOU.
SHOKO, DO YOU LIKE SEX?
OF COURSE I LIKE IT.
WELL, IF YOU REALLY LIKE IT, WHAT DO YOU THINK OF BEING MY GIRLFRIEND?
WELL, THAT'S PUTTING IT BLUNTLY!
I DON'T KNOW YOU WELL ENOUGH YET.

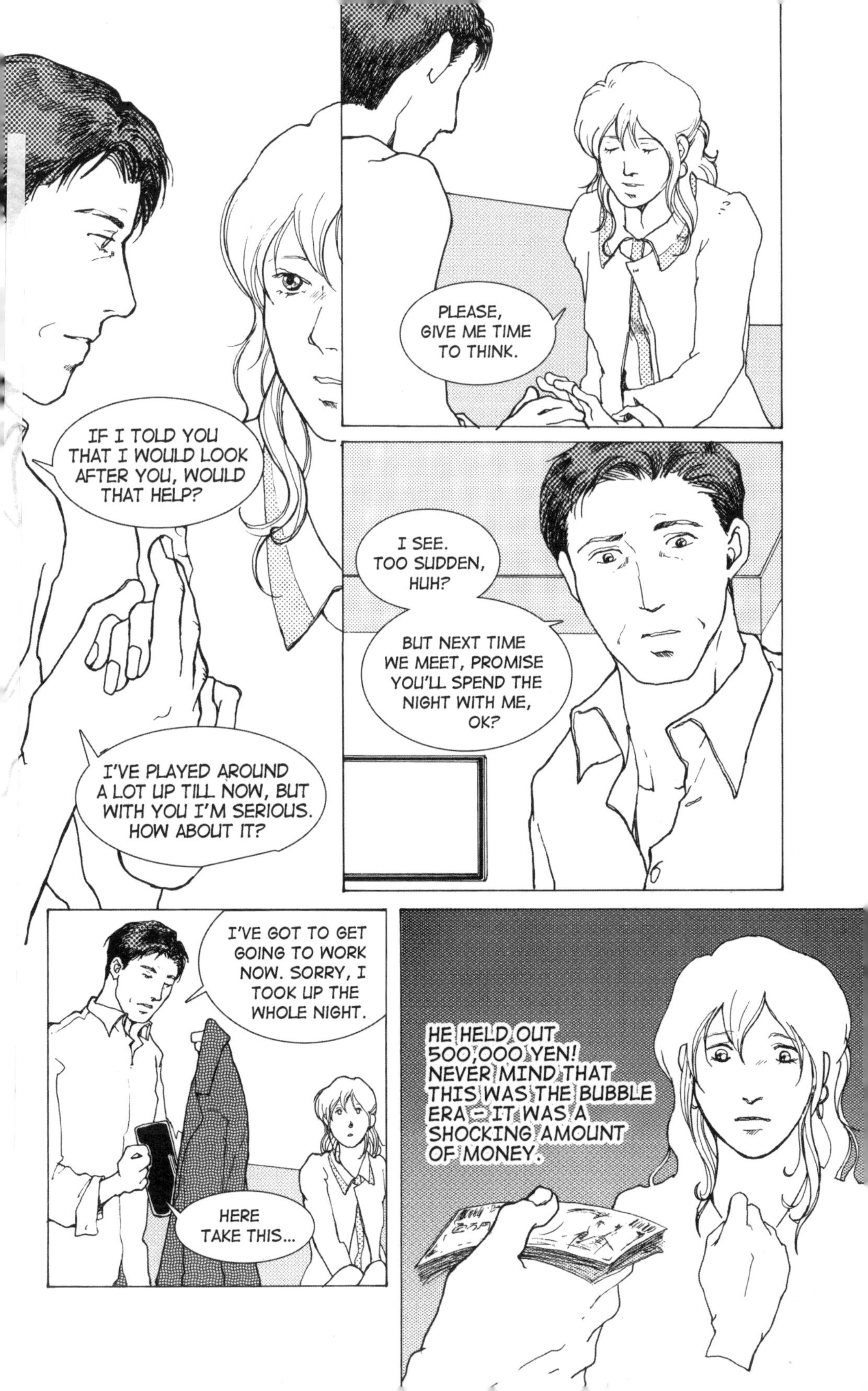
IF I TOLD YOU THAT I WOULD LOOK AFTER YOU, WOULD THAT HELP?
I'VE PLAYED AROUND A LOT UP TILL NOW, BUT WITH YOU I'M SERIOUS. HOW ABOUT IT?
PLEASE, GIVE ME TIME TO THINK.
I SEE. TOO SUDDEN, HUH?
BUT NEXT TIME WE MEET, PROMISE YOU'LL SPEND THE NIGHT WITH ME, OK?
I'VE GOT TO GET GOING TO WORK NOW. SORRY, I TOOK UP THE WHOLE NIGHT.
HERE TAKE THIS...
HE HELD OUT 500,000 YEN! NEVER MIND THAT THIS WAS THE BUBBLE ERA - IT WAS A SHOCKING AMOUNT OF MONEY.

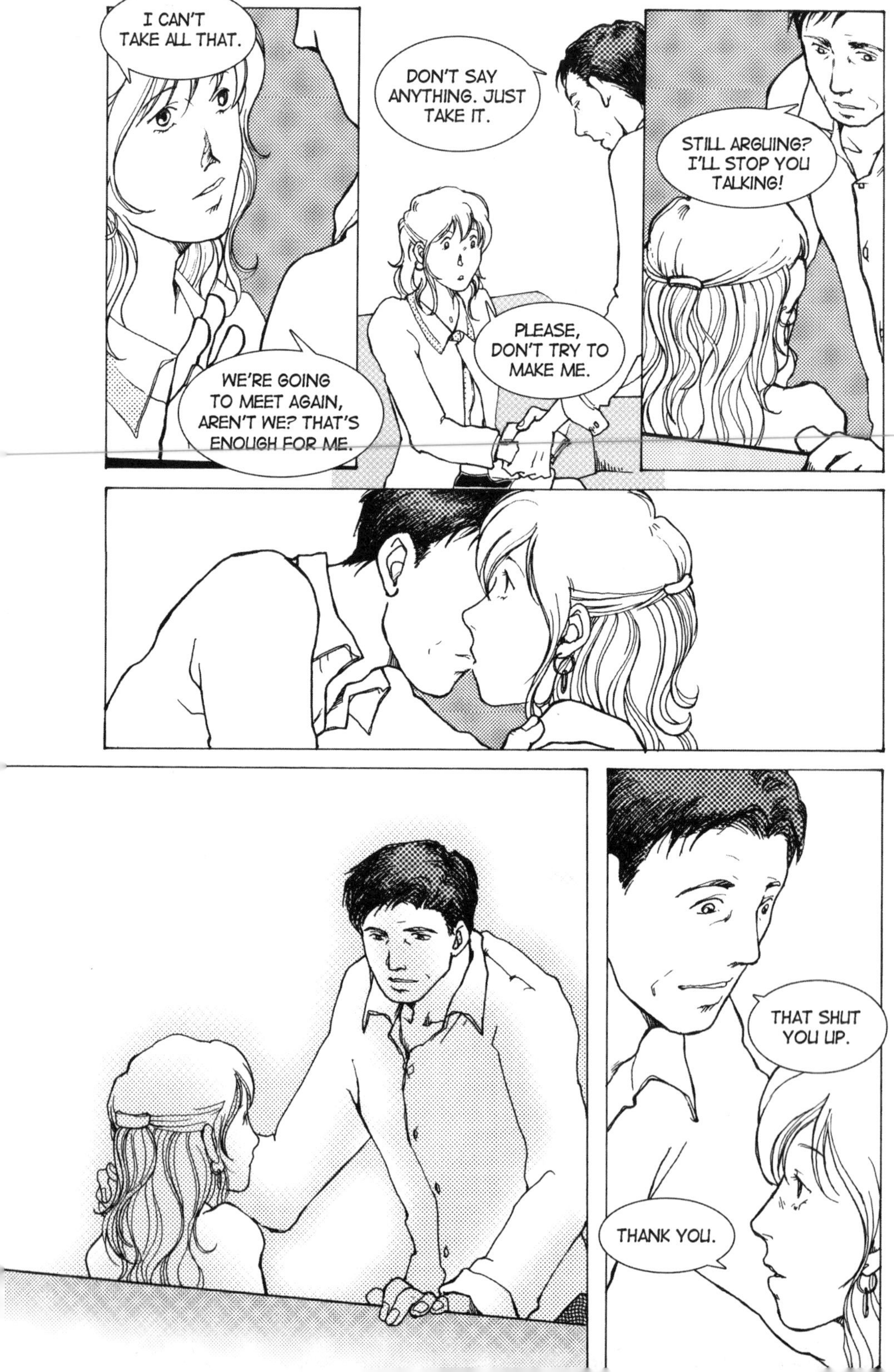
I CAN'T TAKE ALL THAT.
DON'T SAY ANYTHING. JUST TAKE IT.
WE'RE GOING TO MEET AGAIN, AREN'T WE? THAT'S ENOUGH FOR ME.
PLEASE, DON'T TRY TO MAKE ME.
STILL ARGUING? I'LL STOP YOU TALKING!
THAT SHUT YOU UP.
THANK YOU.

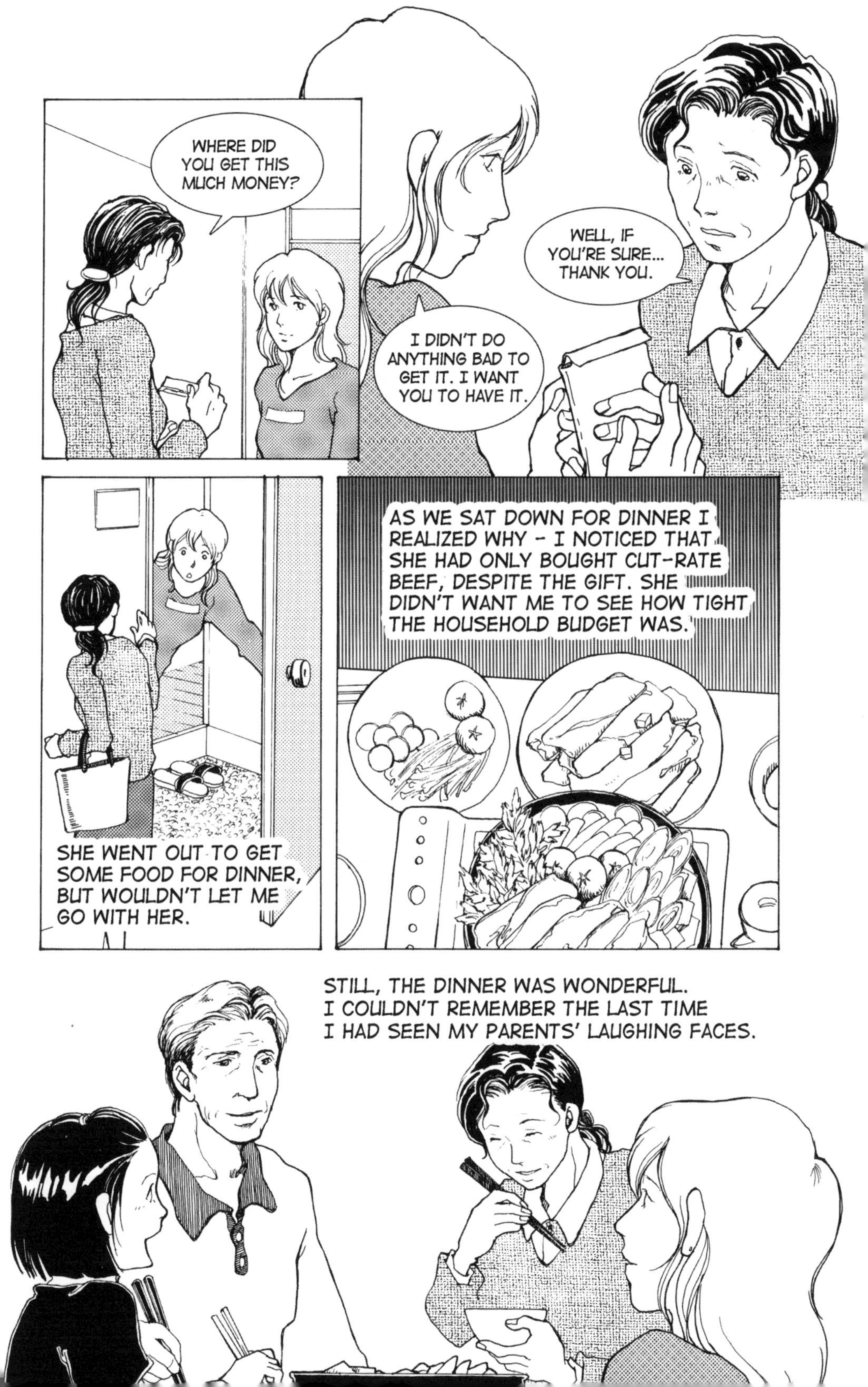
WHERE DID YOU GET THIS MUCH MONEY?
I DIDN'T DO ANYTHING BAD TO GET IT. I WANT YOU TO HAVE IT.
WELL, IF YOU'RE SURE... THANK YOU.
SHE WENT OUT TO GET SOME FOOD FOR DINNER, BUT WOULDN'T LET ME GO WITH HER.
AS WE SAT DOWN FOR DINNER I REALIZED WHY - I NOTICED THAT SHE HAD ONLY BOUGHT CUT-RATE BEEF, DESPITE THE GIFT. SHE DIDN'T WANT ME TO SEE HOW TIGHT THE HOUSEHOLD BUDGET WAS.
STILL, THE DINNER WAS WONDERFUL. I COULDN'T REMEMBER THE LAST TIME I HAD SEEN MY PARENTS' LAUGHING FACES.

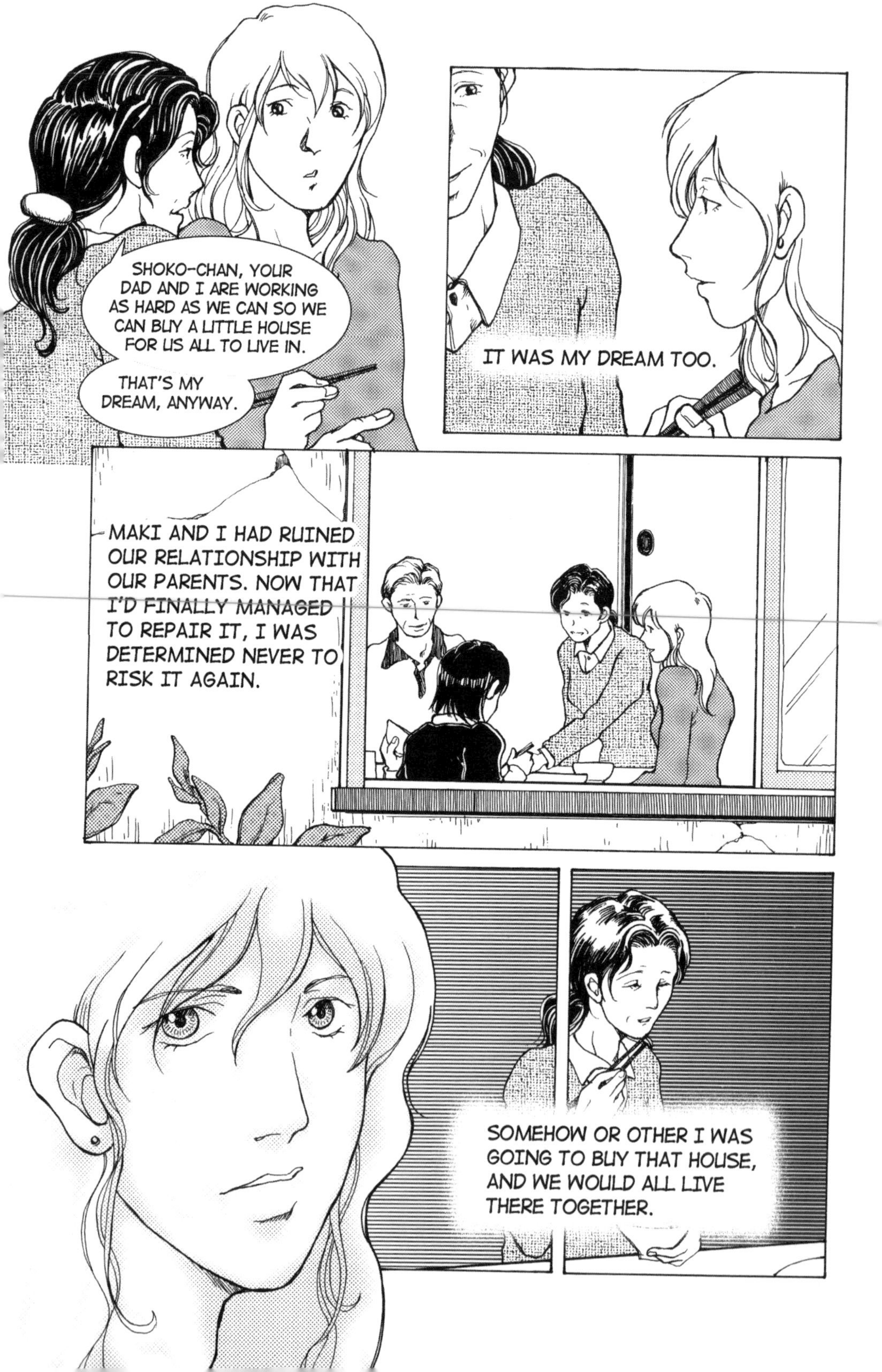
SHOKO-CHAN, YOUR DAD AND I ARE WORKING AS HARD AS WE CAN SO WE CAN BUY A LITTLE HOUSE FOR US ALL TO LIVE IN.
THAT'S MY DREAM, ANYWAY.
IT WAS MY DREAM TOO.
MAKI AND I HAD RUINED OUR RELATIONSHIP WITH OUR PARENTS. NOW THAT I'D FINALLY MANAGED TO REPAIR IT, I WAS DETERMINED NEVER TO RISK IT AGAIN.
SOMEHOW OR OTHER I WAS GOING TO BUY THAT HOUSE, AND WE WOULD ALL LIVE THERE TOGETHER.

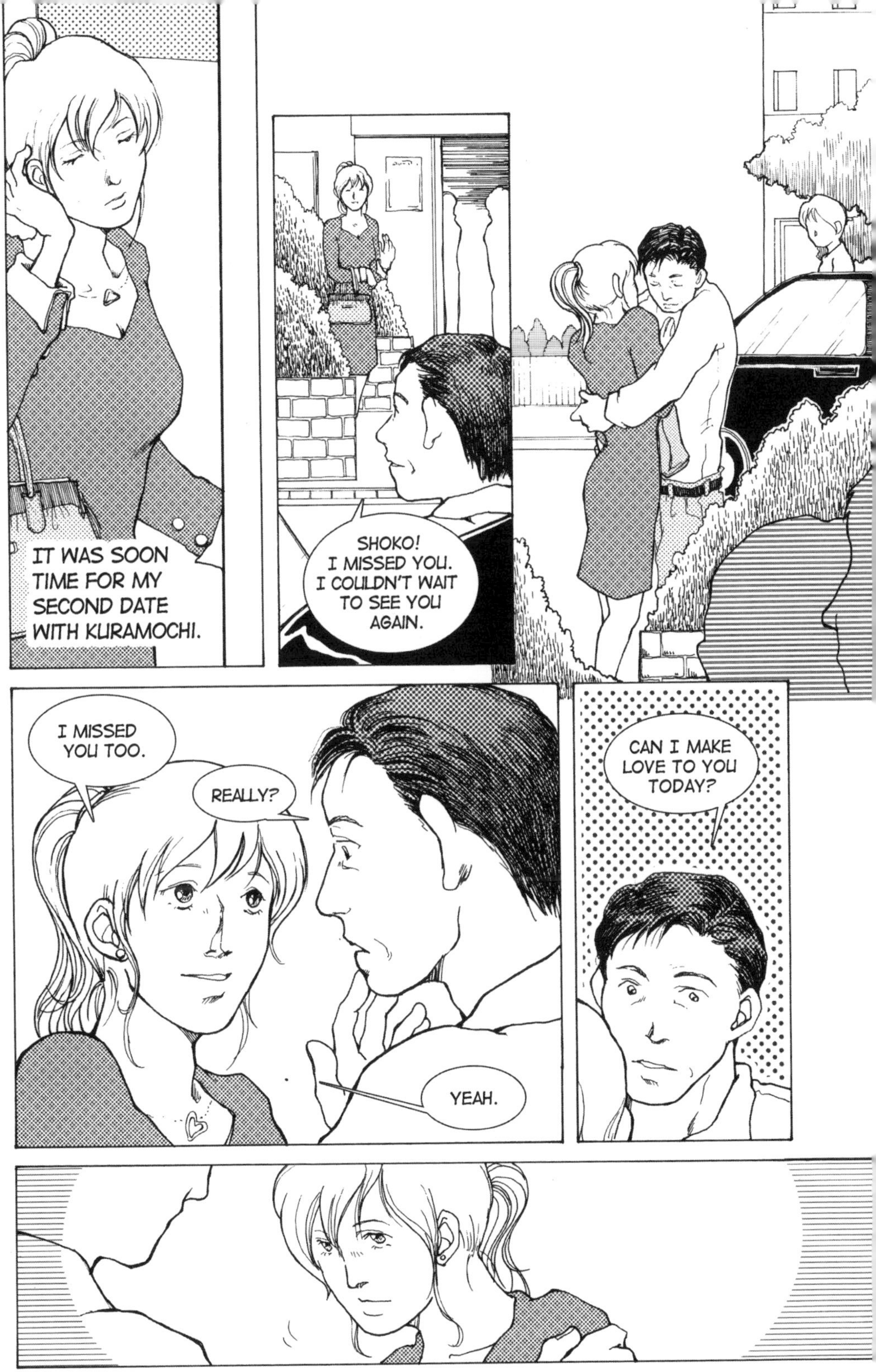
IT WAS SOON TIME FOR MY SECOND DATE WITH KURAMOCHI.
SHOKO! I MISSED YOU. I COULDN'T WAIT TO SEE YOU AGAIN.
I MISSED YOU TOO.
REALLY?
YEAH.
CAN I MAKE LOVE TO YOU TODAY?

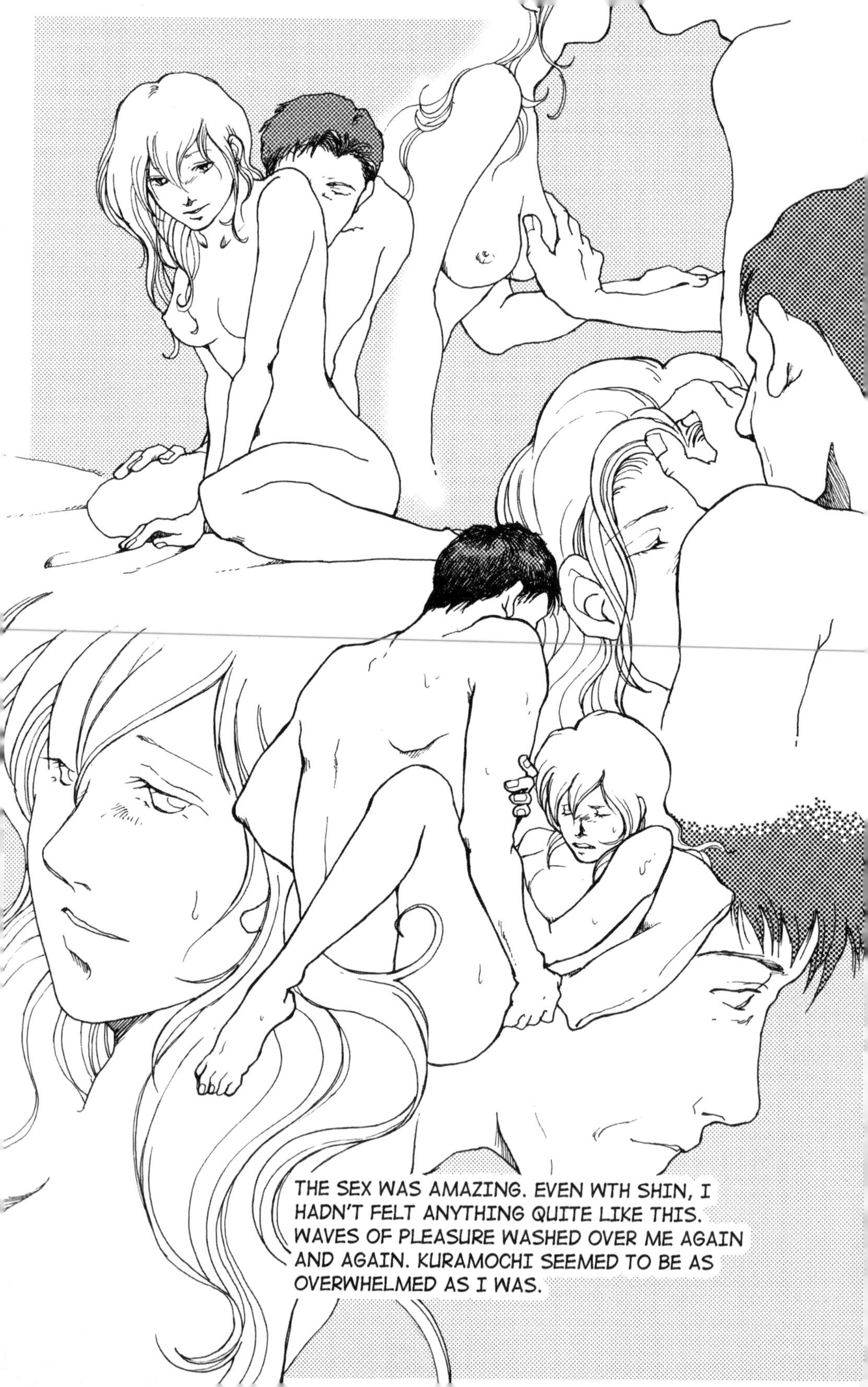
THE SEX WAS AMAZING. EVEN WTH SHIN, I HADN'T FELT ANYTHING QUITE LIKE THIS. WAVES OF PLEASURE WASHED OVER ME AGAIN AND AGAIN. KURAMOCHI SEEMED TO BE AS OVERWHELMED AS I WAS.

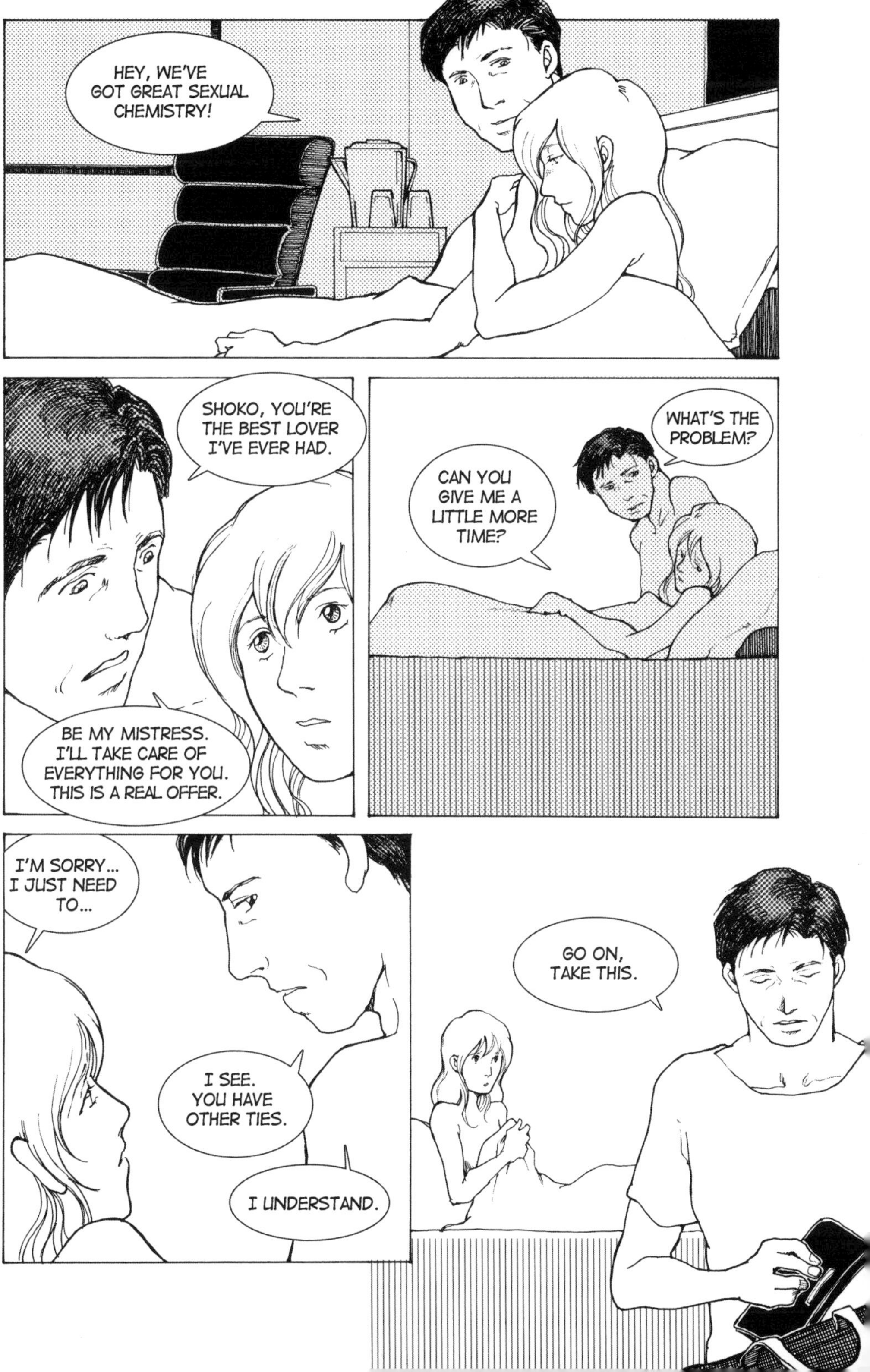
HEY, WE'VE GOT GREAT SEXUAL CHEMISTRY!
SHOKO, YOU'RE THE BEST LOVER I'VE EVER HAD.
BE MY MISTRESS. I'LL TAKE CARE OF EVERYTHING FOR YOU. THIS IS A REAL OFFER.
WHAT'S THE PROBLEM?
CAN YOU GIVE ME A LITTLE MORE TIME?
I'M SORRY... I JUST NEED TO...
I SEE. YOU HAVE OTHER TIES.
I UNDERSTAND.
GO ON, TAKE THIS.

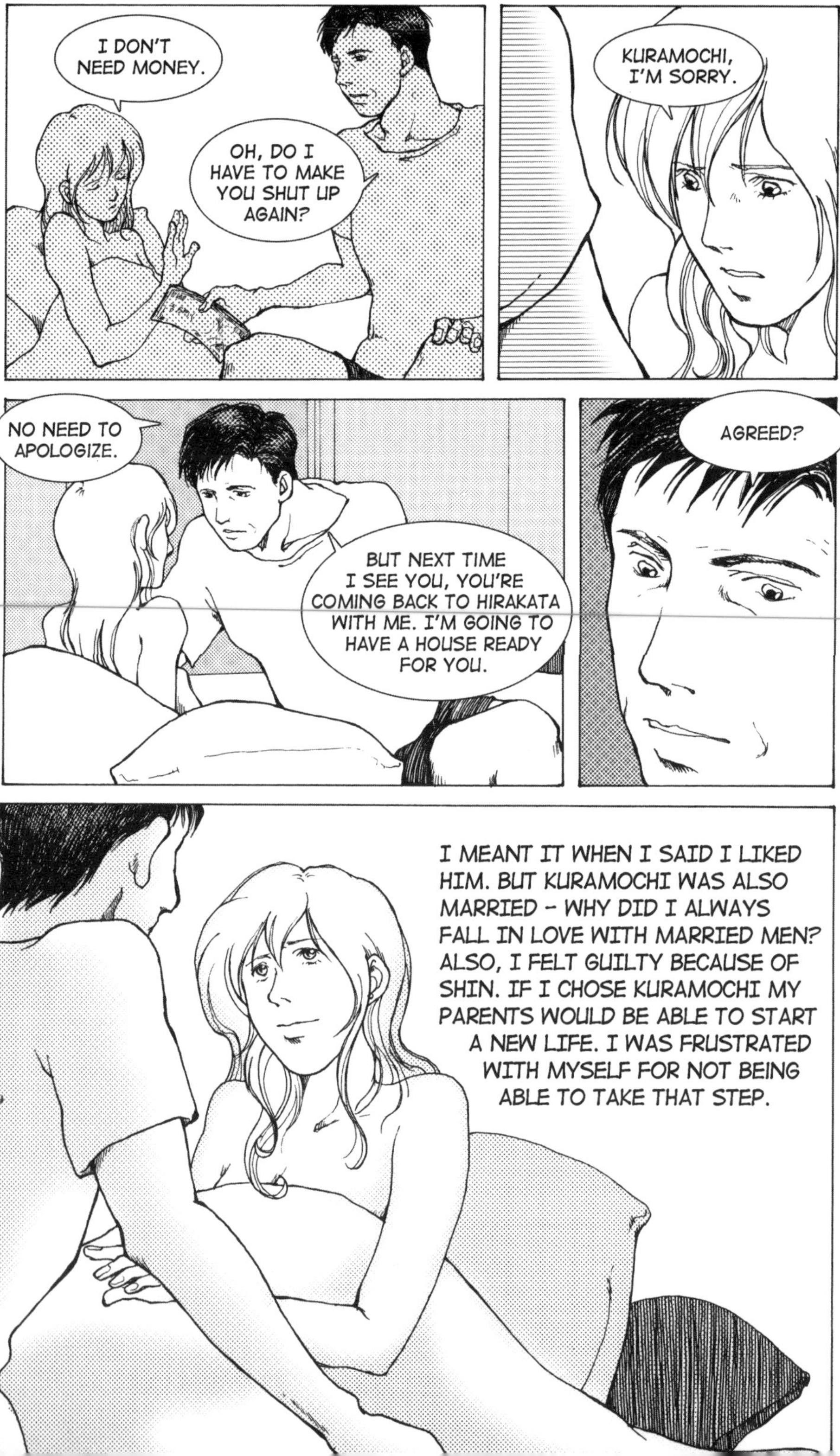
I DON'T NEED MONEY.
OH, DO I HAVE TO MAKE YOU SHUT UP AGAIN?
KURAMOCHI, I'M SORRY.
NO NEED TO APOLOGIZE.
BUT NEXT TIME I SEE YOU, YOU'RE COMING BACK TO HIRAKATA WITH ME. I'M GOING TO HAVE A HOUSE READY FOR YOU.
AGREED?
I MEANT IT WHEN I SAID I LIKED HIM. BUT KURAMOCHI WAS ALSO MARRIED - WHY DID I ALWAYS FALL IN LOVE WITH MARRIED MEN? ALSO, I FELT GUILTY BECAUSE OF SHIN. IF I CHOSE KURAMOCHI MY PARENTS WOULD BE ABLE TO START A NEW LIFE. I WAS FRUSTRATED WITH MYSELF FOR NOT BEING ABLE TO TAKE THAT STEP.

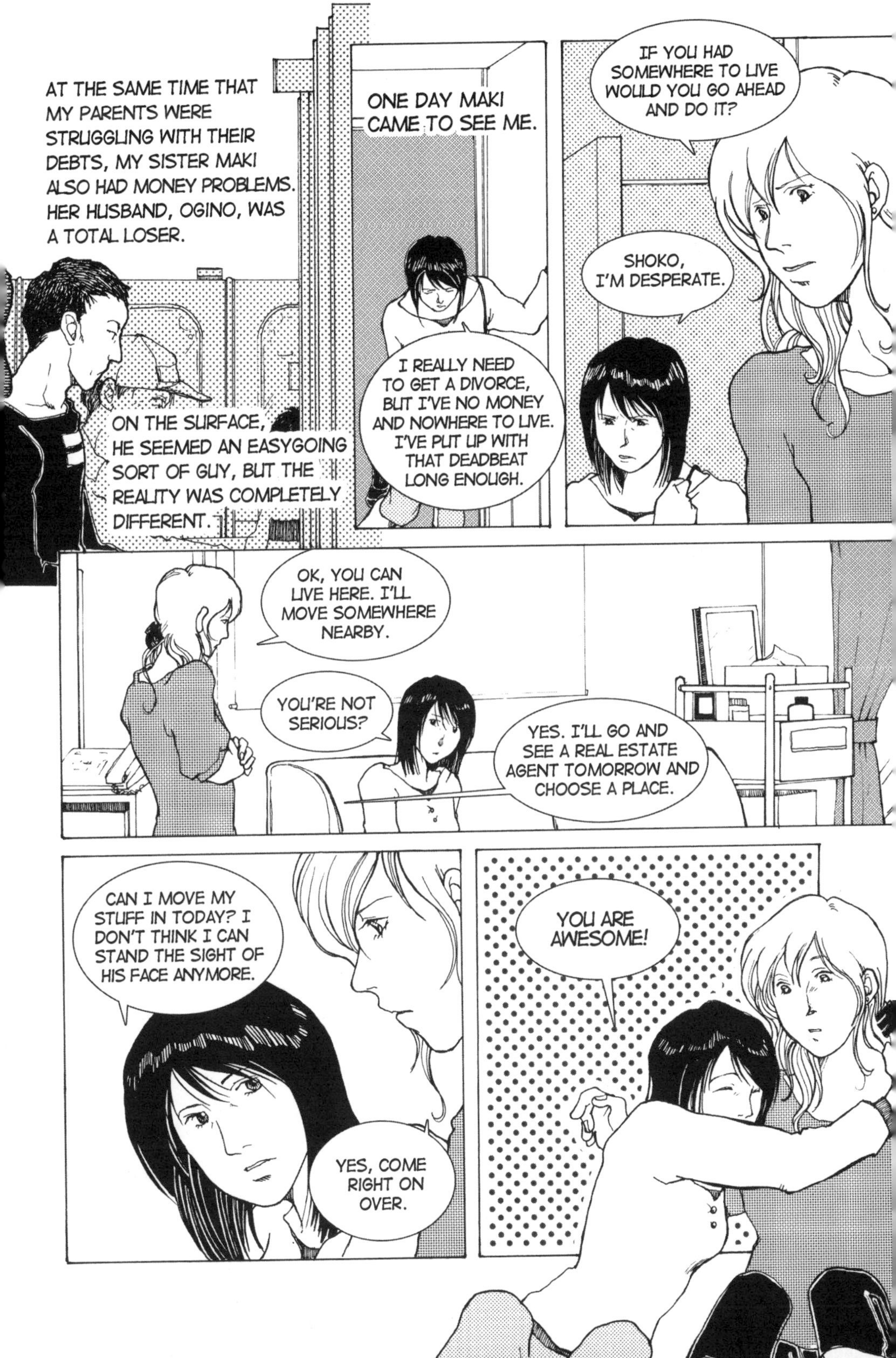
AT THE SAME TIME THAT MY PARENTS WERE STRUGGLING WITH THEIR DEBTS, MY SISTER MAKI ALSO HAD MONEY PROBLEMS. HER HUSBAND, OGINO, WAS A TOTAL LOSER.
ON THE SURFACE, HE SEEMED AN EASYGOING SORT OF GUY, BUT THE REALITY WAS COMPLETELY DIFFERENT.
ONE DAY MAKI CAME TO SEE ME.
I REALLY NEED TO GET A DIVORCE, BUT I'VE NO MONEY AND NOWHERE TO LIVE. I'VE PUT UP WITH THAT DEADBEAT LONG ENOUGH.
SHOKO, I'M DESPERATE.
IF YOU HAD SOMEWHERE TO LIVE WOULD YOU GO AHEAD AND DO IT?
OK, YOU CAN LIVE HERE. I'LL MOVE SOMEWHERE NEARBY.
YOU'RE NOT SERIOUS?
YES. I'LL GO AND SEE A REAL ESTATE AGENT TOMORROW AND CHOOSE A PLACE.
CAN I MOVE MY STUFF IN TODAY? I DON'T THINK I CAN STAND THE SIGHT OF HIS FACE ANYMORE.
YES, COME RIGHT ON OVER.
YOU ARE AWESOME!

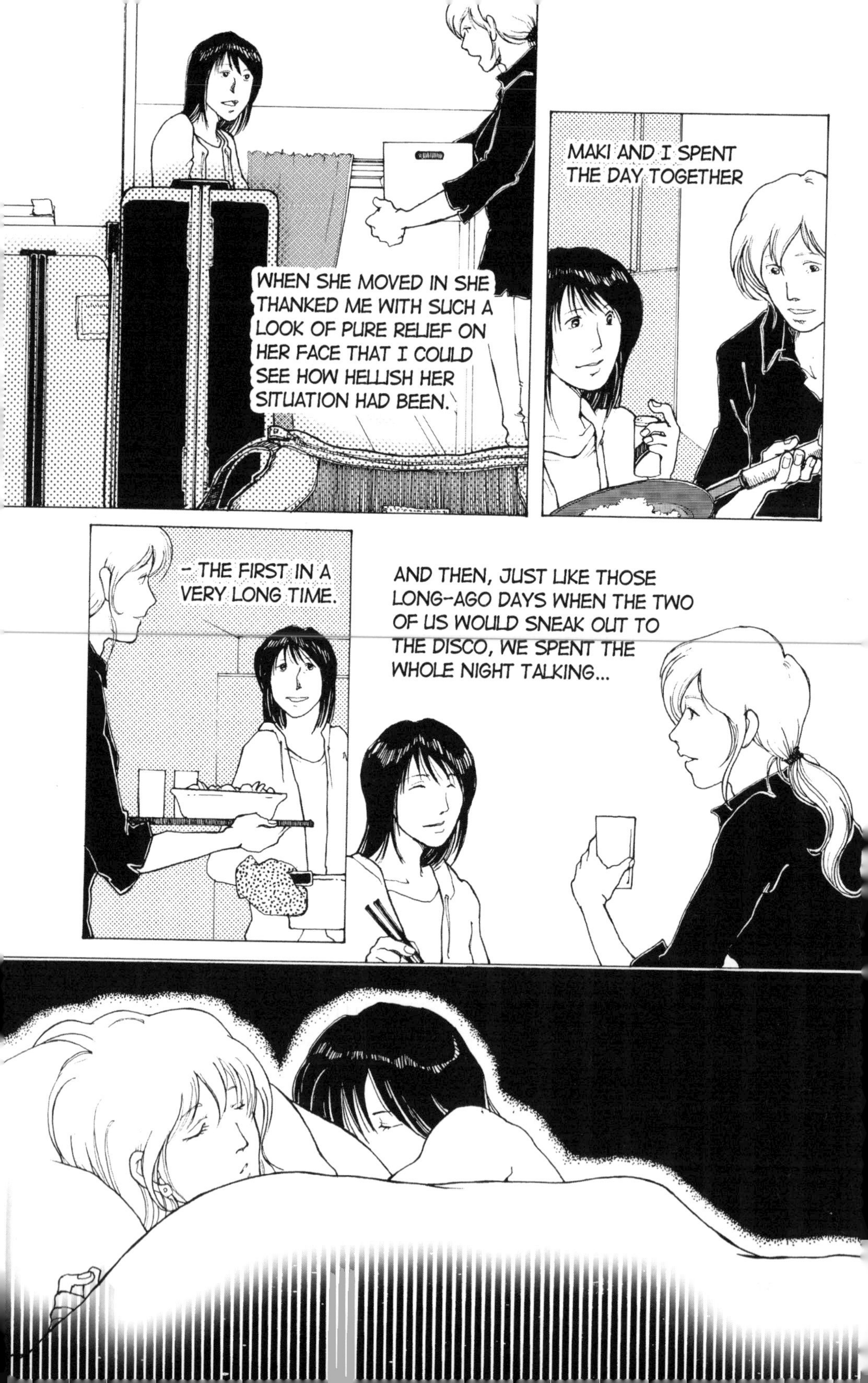
WHEN SHE MOVED IN SHE THANKED ME WITH SUCH A LOOK OF PURE RELIEF ON HER FACE THAT I COULD SEE HOW HELLISH HER SITUATION HAD BEEN.
MAKI AND I SPENT THE DAY TOGETHER
- THE FIRST IN A VERY LONG TIME.
AND THEN, JUST LIKE THOSE LONG-AGO DAYS WHEN THE TWO OF US WOULD SNEAK OUT TO THE DISCO, WE SPENT THE WHOLE NIGHT TALKING...

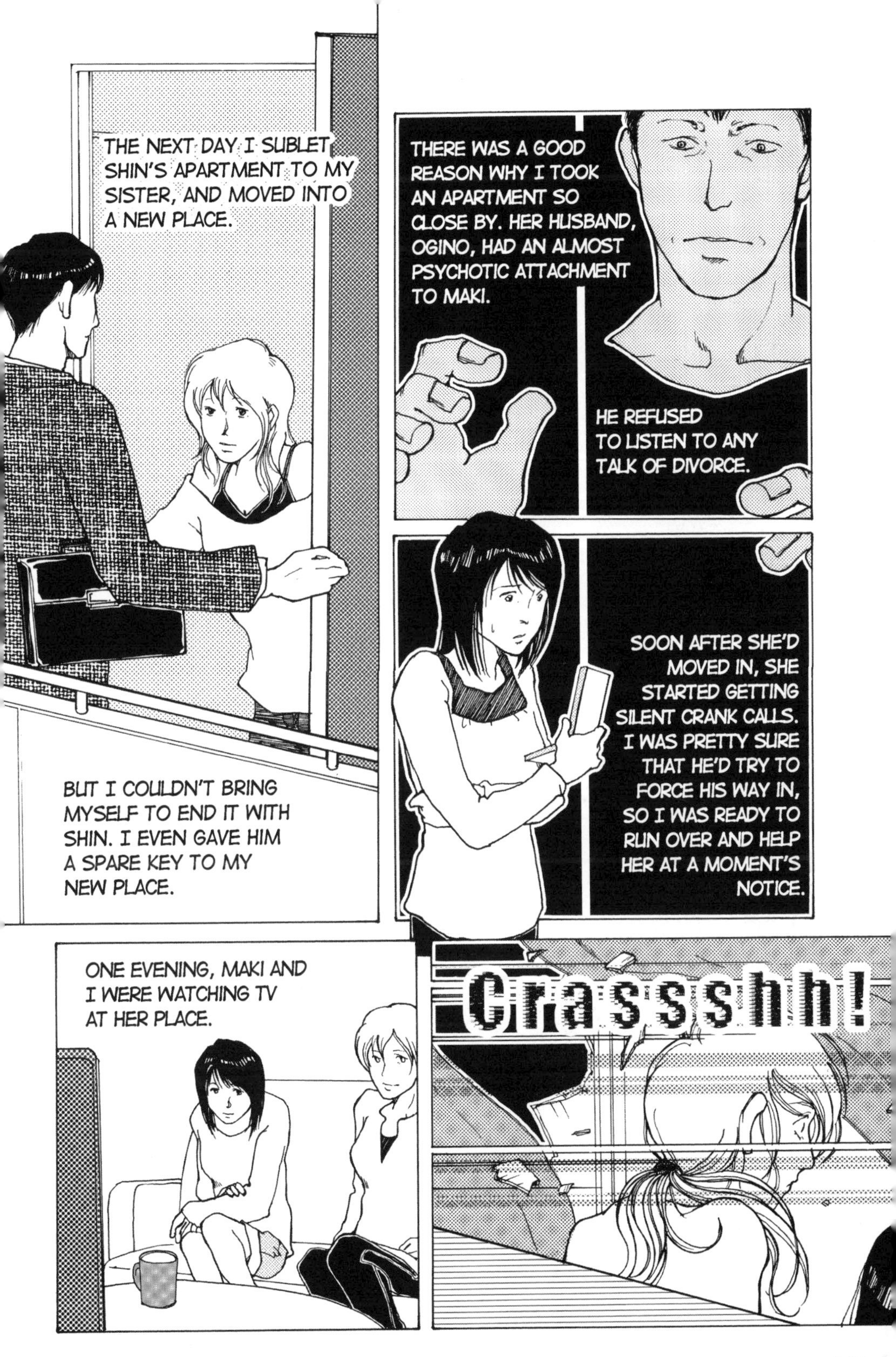
THE NEXT DAY I SUBLET SHIN'S APARTMENT TO MY SISTER, AND MOVED INTO A NEW PLACE.
BUT I COULDN'T BRING MYSELF TO END IT WITH SHIN. I EVEN GAVE HIM A SPARE KEY TO MY NEW PLACE.
THERE WAS A GOOD REASON WHY I TOOK AN APARTMENT SO CLOSE BY. HER HUSBAND, OGINO, HAD AN ALMOST PSYCHOTIC ATTACHMENT TO MAKI.
HE REFUSED TO LISTEN TO ANY TALK OF DIVORCE.
SOON AFTER SHE'D MOVED IN, SHE STARTED GETTING SILENT CRANK CALLS. I WAS PRETTY SURE THAT HE'D TRY TO FORCE HIS WAY IN, SO I WAS READY TO RUN OVER AND HELP HER AT A MOMENT'S NOTICE.
ONE EVENING, MAKI AND I WERE WATCHING TV AT HER PLACE.
Crassshh!

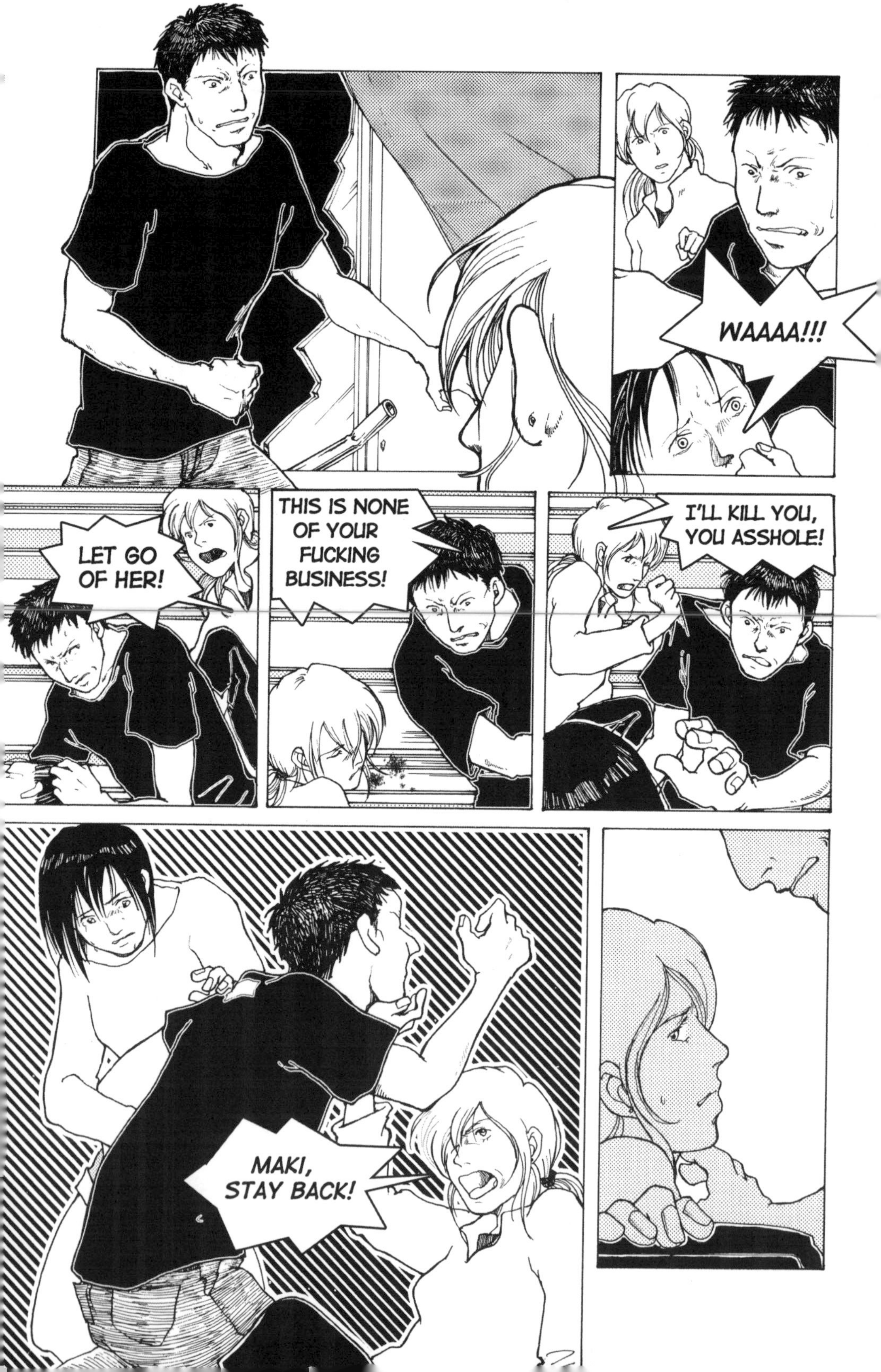
WAAAA!!!
LET GO OF HER!
THIS IS NONE OF YOUR FUCKING BUSINESS!
I'LL KILL YOU, YOU ASSHOLE!
MAKI, STAY BACK!

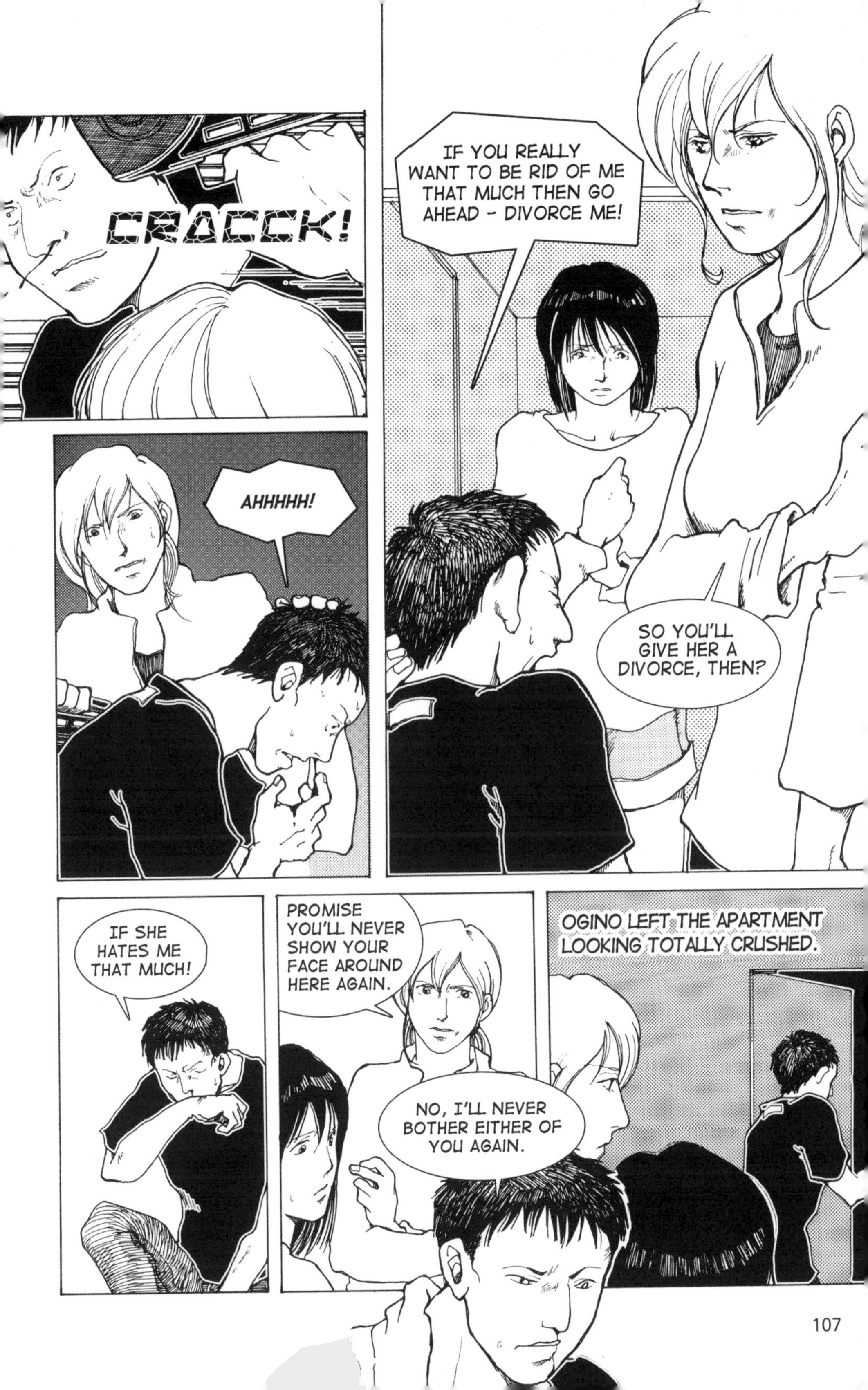
CRACCK!
AHHHHH!
IF YOU REALLY WANT TO BE RID OF ME THAT MUCH THEN GO AHEAD - DIVORCE ME!
SO YOU'LL GIVE HER A DIVORCE, THEN?
IF SHE HATES ME THAT MUCH!
PROMISE YOU'LL NEVER SHOW YOUR FACE AROUND HERE AGAIN.
NO, I'LL NEVER BOTHER EITHER OF YOU AGAIN.
OGINO LEFT THE APARTMENT LOOKING TOTALLY CRUSHED.

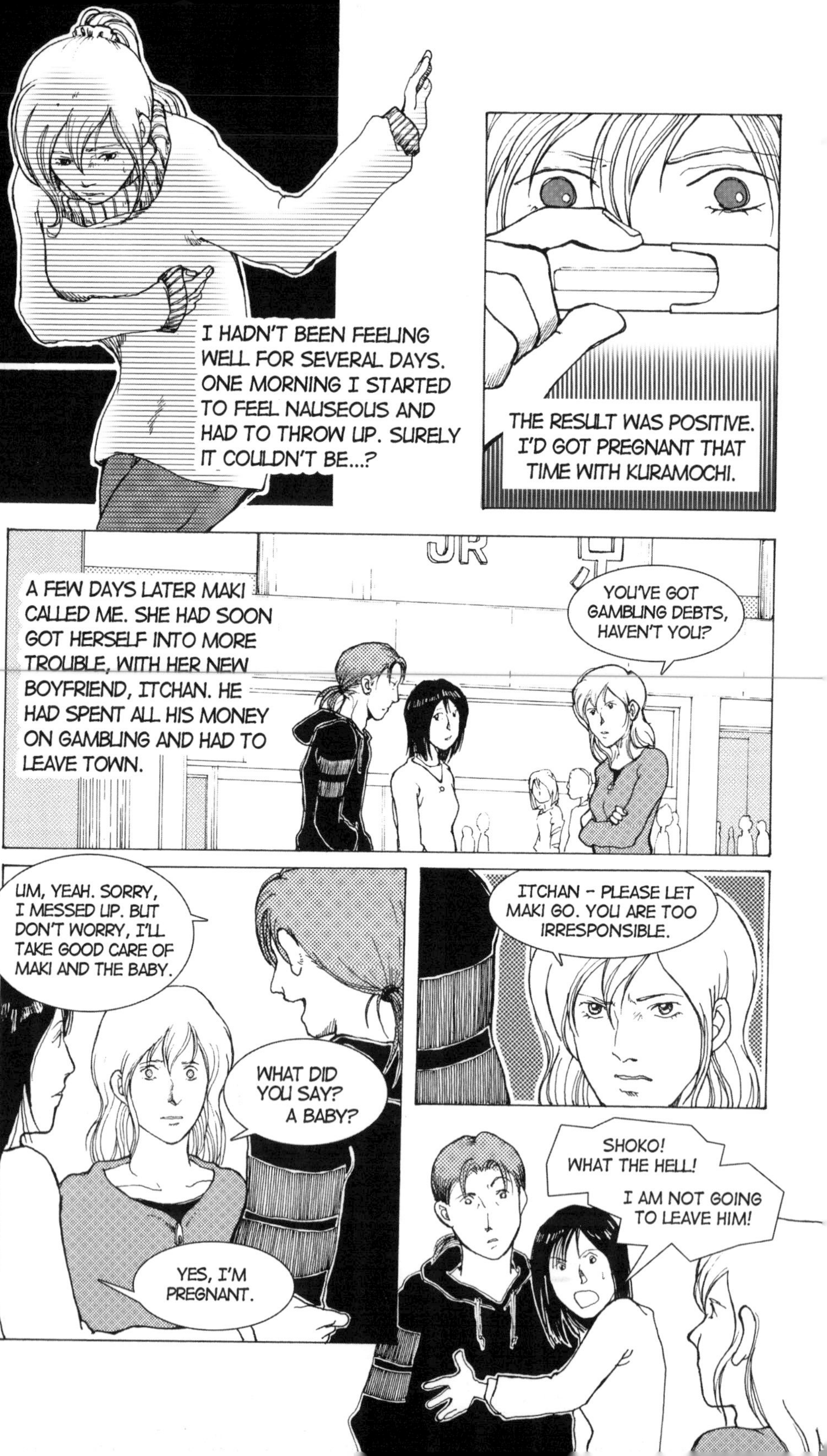
I HADN'T BEEN FEELING WELL FOR SEVERAL DAYS. ONE MORNING I STARTED TO FEEL NAUSEOUS AND HAD TO THROW UP. SURELY IT COULDN'T BE...?
THE RESULT WAS POSITIVE. I'D GOT PREGNANT THAT TIME WITH KURAMOCHI.
JR
A FEW DAYS LATER MAKI CALLED ME. SHE HAD SOON GOT HERSELF INTO MORE TROUBLE, WITH HER NEW BOYFRIEND, ITCHAN. HE HAD SPENT ALL HIS MONEY ON GAMBLING AND HAD TO LEAVE TOWN.
YOU'VE GOT GAMBLING DEBTS, HAVEN'T YOU?
UM, YEAH. SORRY, I MESSED UP. BUT DON'T WORRY, I'LL TAKE GOOD CARE OF MAKI AND THE BABY.
ITCHAN - PLEASE LET MAKI GO. YOU ARE TOO IRRESPONSIBLE.
WHAT DID YOU SAY? A BABY?
YES, I'M PREGNANT.
SHOKO! WHAT THE HELL!
I AM NOT GOING TO LEAVE HIM!

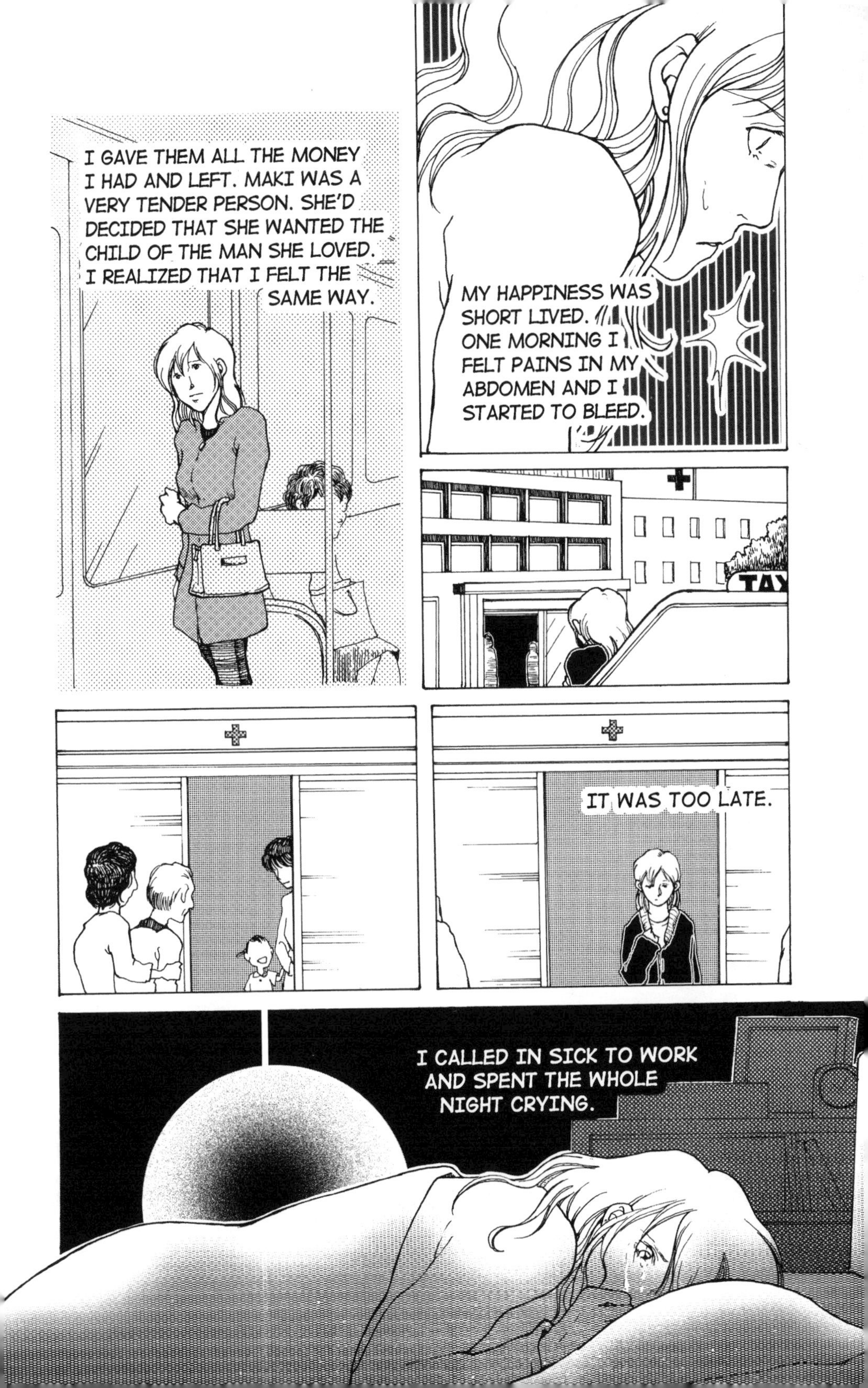
MY HAPPINESS WAS SHORT LIVED. ONE MORNING I FELT PAINS IN MY ABDOMEN AND I STARTED TO BLEED.
I GAVE THEM ALL THE MONEY I HAD AND LEFT. MAKI WAS A VERY TENDER PERSON. SHE'D DECIDED THAT SHE WANTED THE CHILD OF THE MAN SHE LOVED. I REALIZED THAT I FELT THE SAME WAY.
TAX
IT WAS TOO LATE.
I CALLED IN SICK TO WORK AND SPENT THE WHOLE NIGHT CRYING.

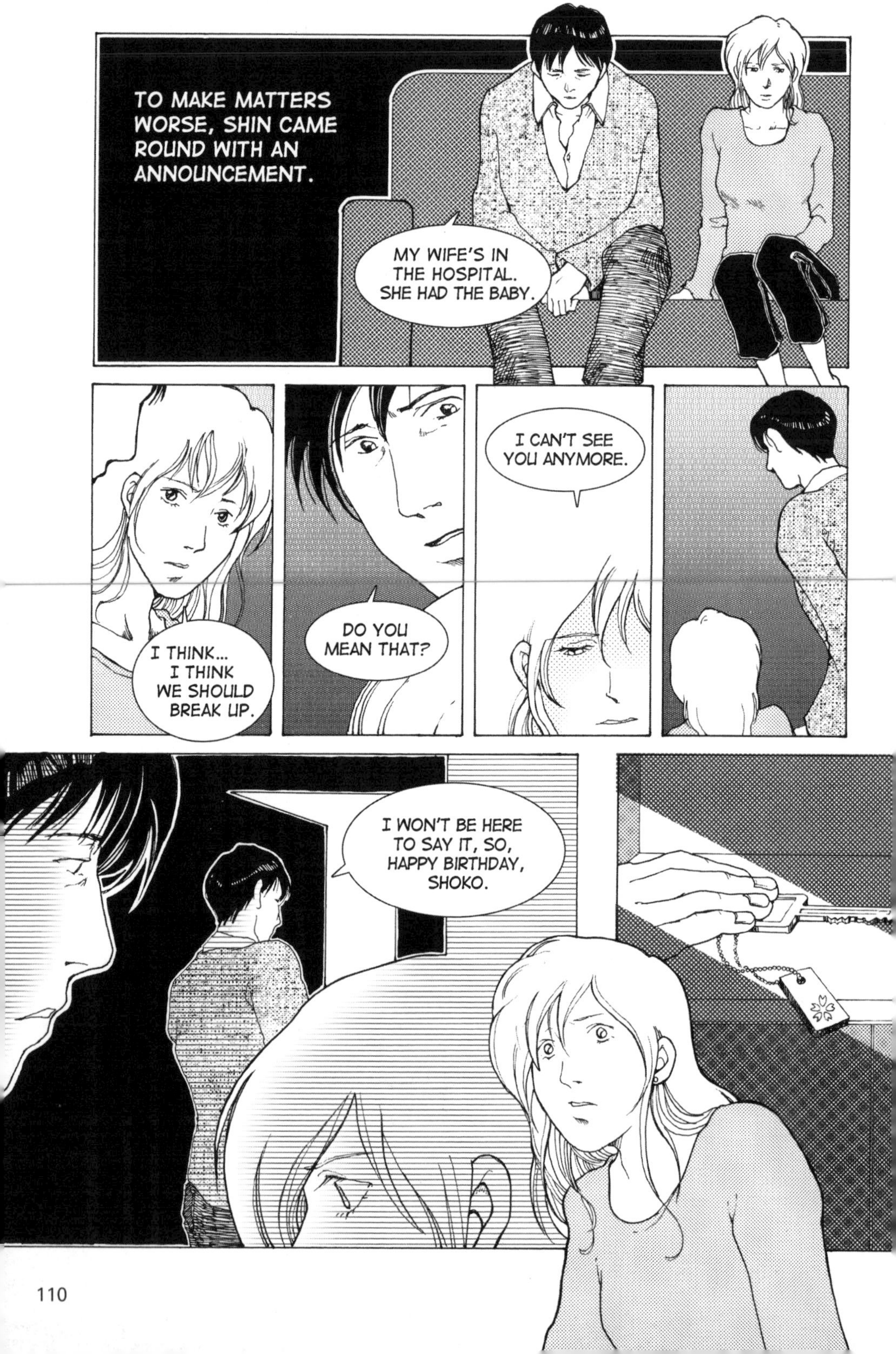

TO MAKE MATTERS WORSE, SHIN CAME ROUND WITH AN ANNOUNCEMENT.
MY WIFE'S IN THE HOSPITAL. SHE HAD THE BABY.
I THINK... I THINK WE SHOULD BREAK UP.
DO YOU MEAN THAT?
I CAN'T SEE YOU ANYMORE.
I WON'T BE HERE TO SAY IT, SO, HAPPY BIRTHDAY, SHOKO.

CHAPTER 6

Tattoo

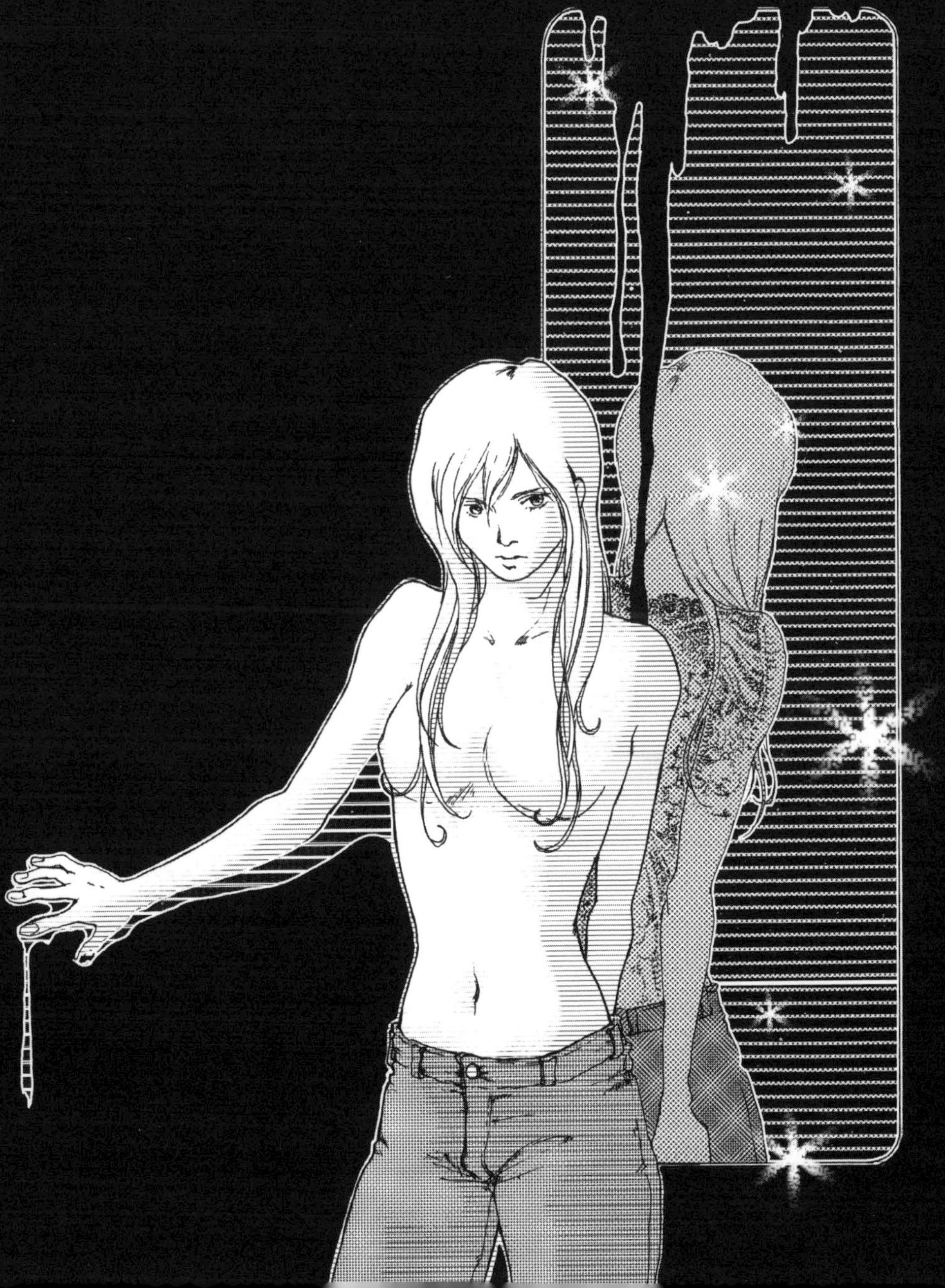

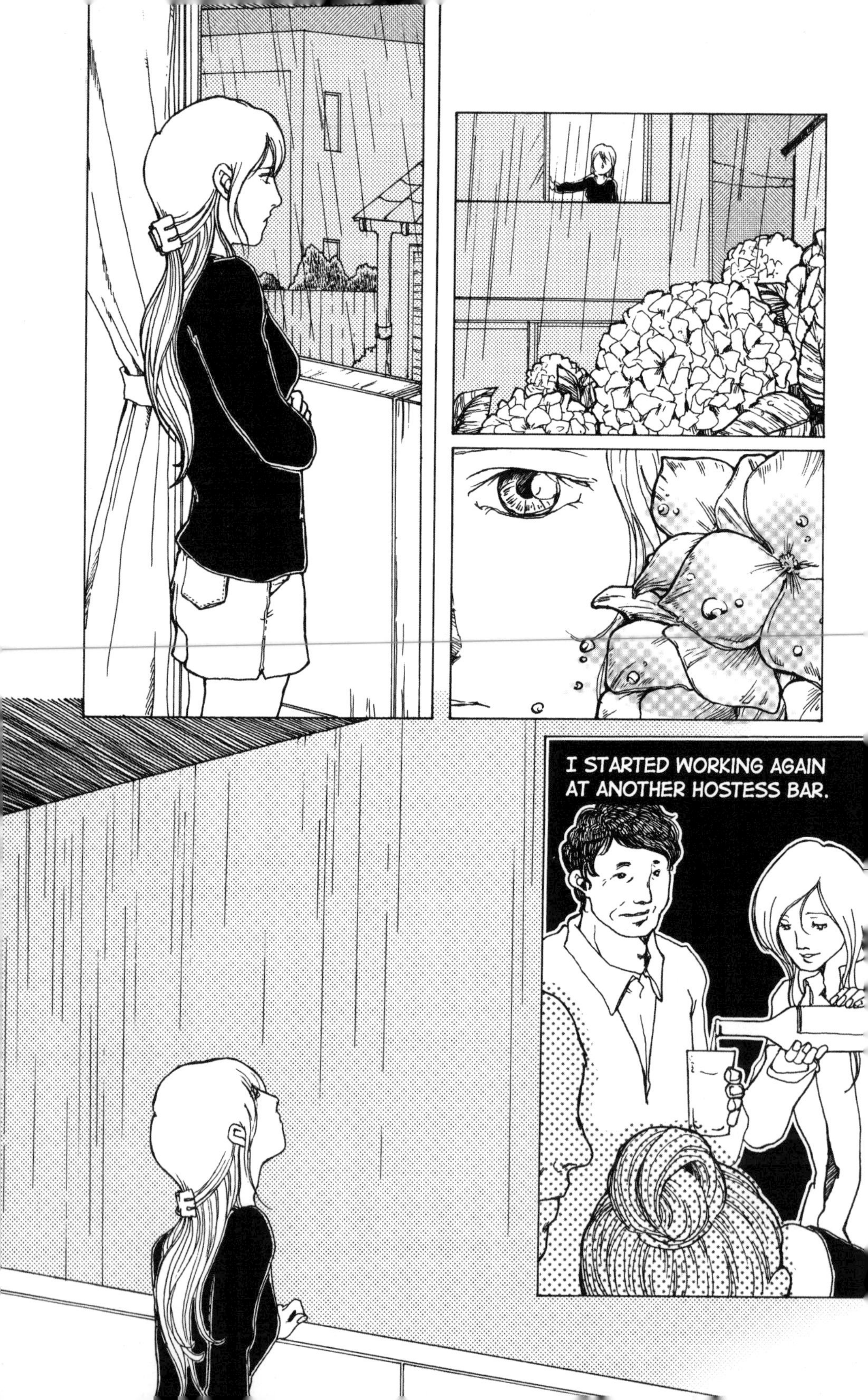
I STARTED WORKING AGAIN AT ANOTHER HOSTESS BAR.

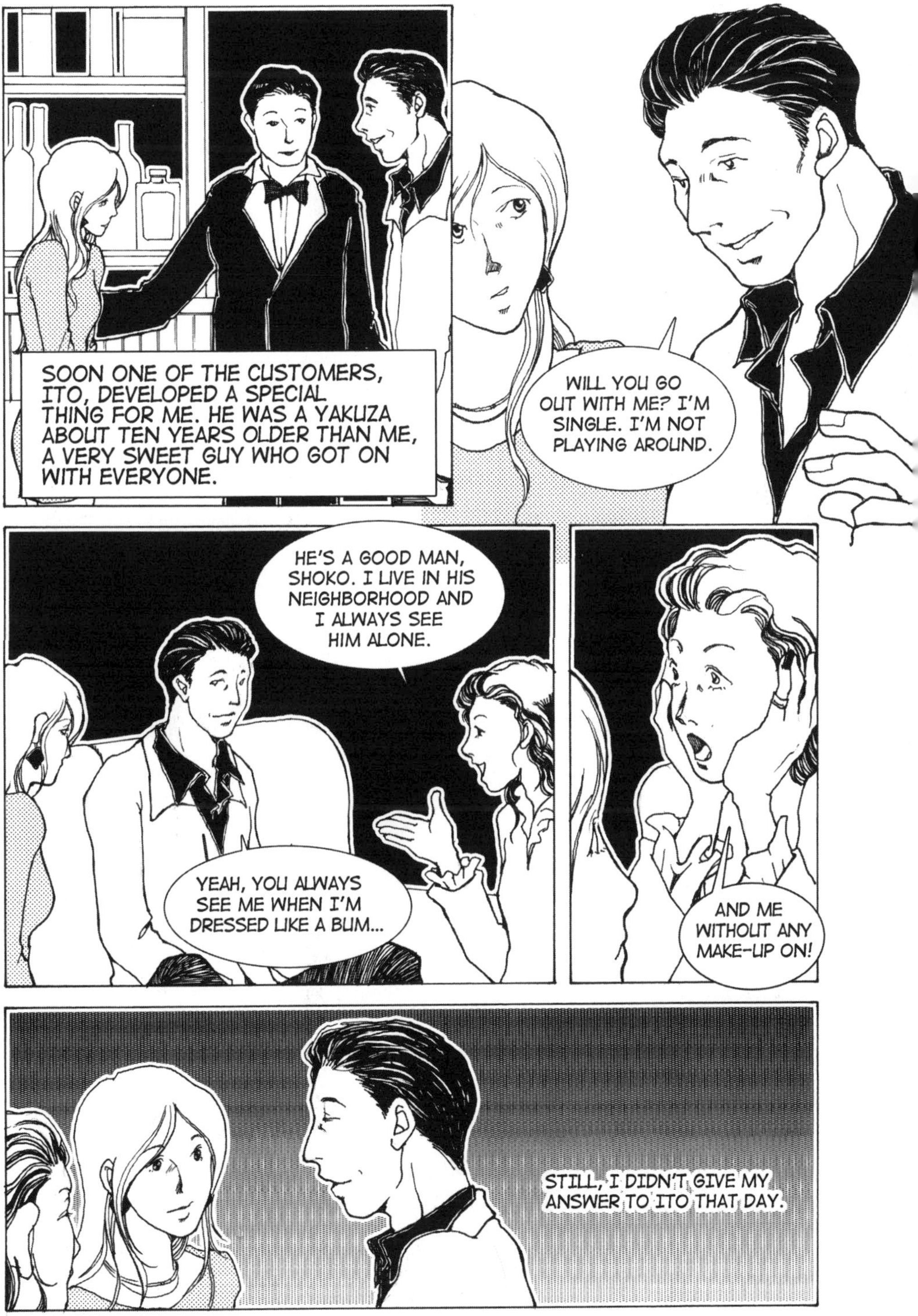
SOON ONE OF THE CUSTOMERS, ITO, DEVELOPED A SPECIAL THING FOR ME. HE WAS A YAKUZA ABOUT TEN YEARS OLDER THAN ME, A VERY SWEET GUY WHO GOT ON WITH EVERYONE.
WILL YOU GO OUT WITH ME? I'M SINGLE. I'M NOT PLAYING AROUND.
HE'S A GOOD MAN, SHOKO. I LIVE IN HIS NEIGHBORHOOD AND I ALWAYS SEE HIM ALONE.
YEAH, YOU ALWAYS SEE ME WHEN I'M DRESSED LIKE A BUM...
AND ME WITHOUT ANY MAKE-UP ON!
STILL, I DIDN'T GIVE MY ANSWER TO ITO THAT DAY.

A FEW DAYS LATER I HAD THE FLU AND TOOK THE NIGHT OFF. I WAS ASLEEP WHEN THE SOUND OF THE DOORBELL WOKE ME UP.

ding dong!

YES?

SHOKO, IT'S ME, ITO.

ITO-SAN, WHAT ARE YOU DOING HERE?

I HEARD YOU WERE ILL — SO HERE'S A GET-WELL PRESENT.

HAVE YOU EATEN?

NOT REALLY.

OK, I'LL MAKE YOU SOMETHING.

NO, BUT...

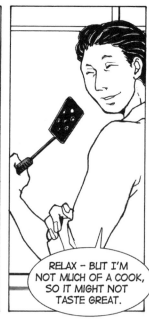

RELAX — BUT I'M NOT MUCH OF A COOK, SO IT MIGHT NOT TASTE GREAT.

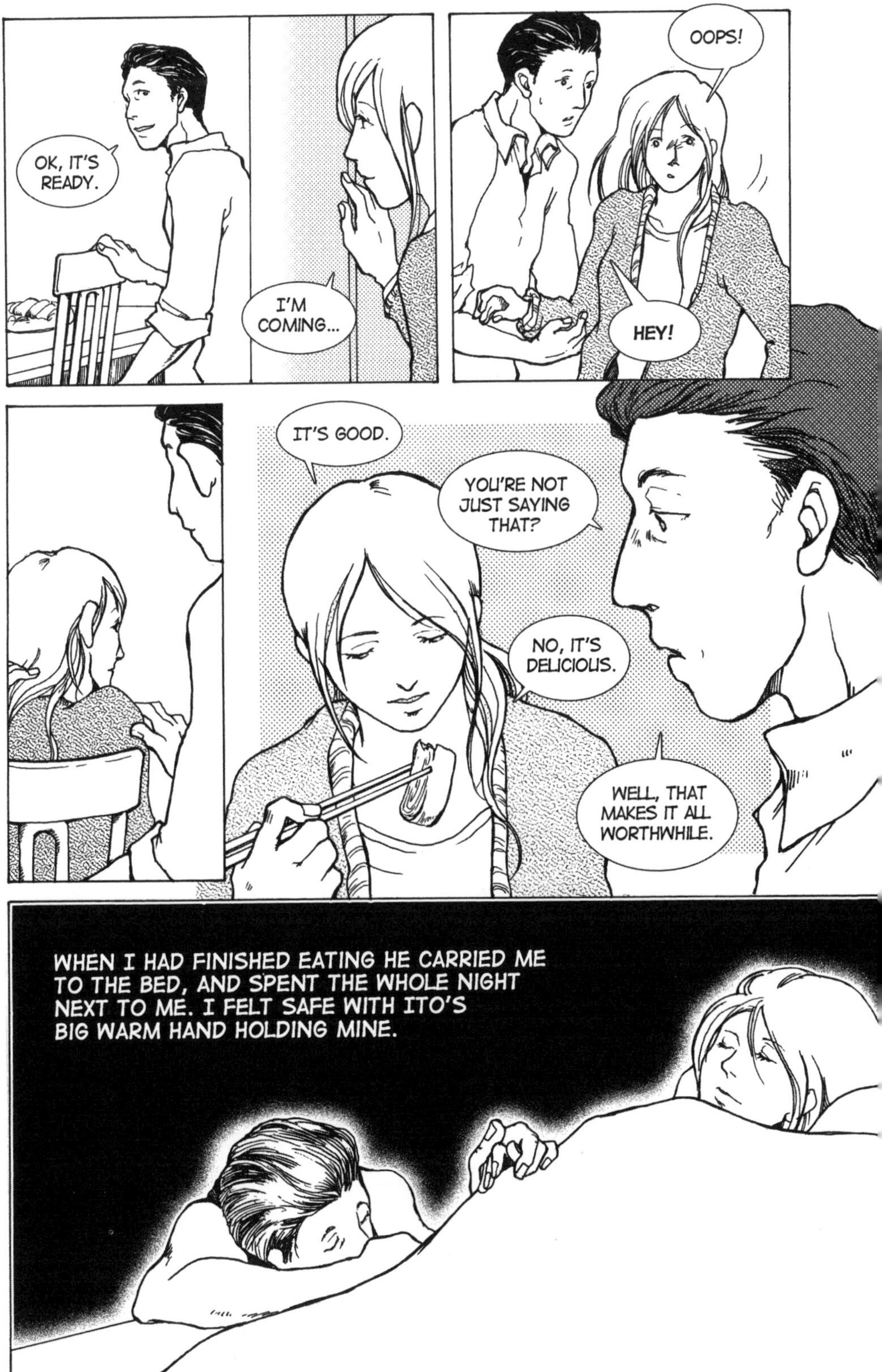
OK, IT'S READY.
I'M COMING...
OOPS!
HEY!
IT'S GOOD.
YOU'RE NOT JUST SAYING THAT?
NO, IT'S DELICIOUS.
WELL, THAT MAKES IT ALL WORTHWHILE.
WHEN I HAD FINISHED EATING HE CARRIED ME TO THE BED, AND SPENT THE WHOLE NIGHT NEXT TO ME. I FELT SAFE WITH ITO'S BIG WARM HAND HOLDING MINE.

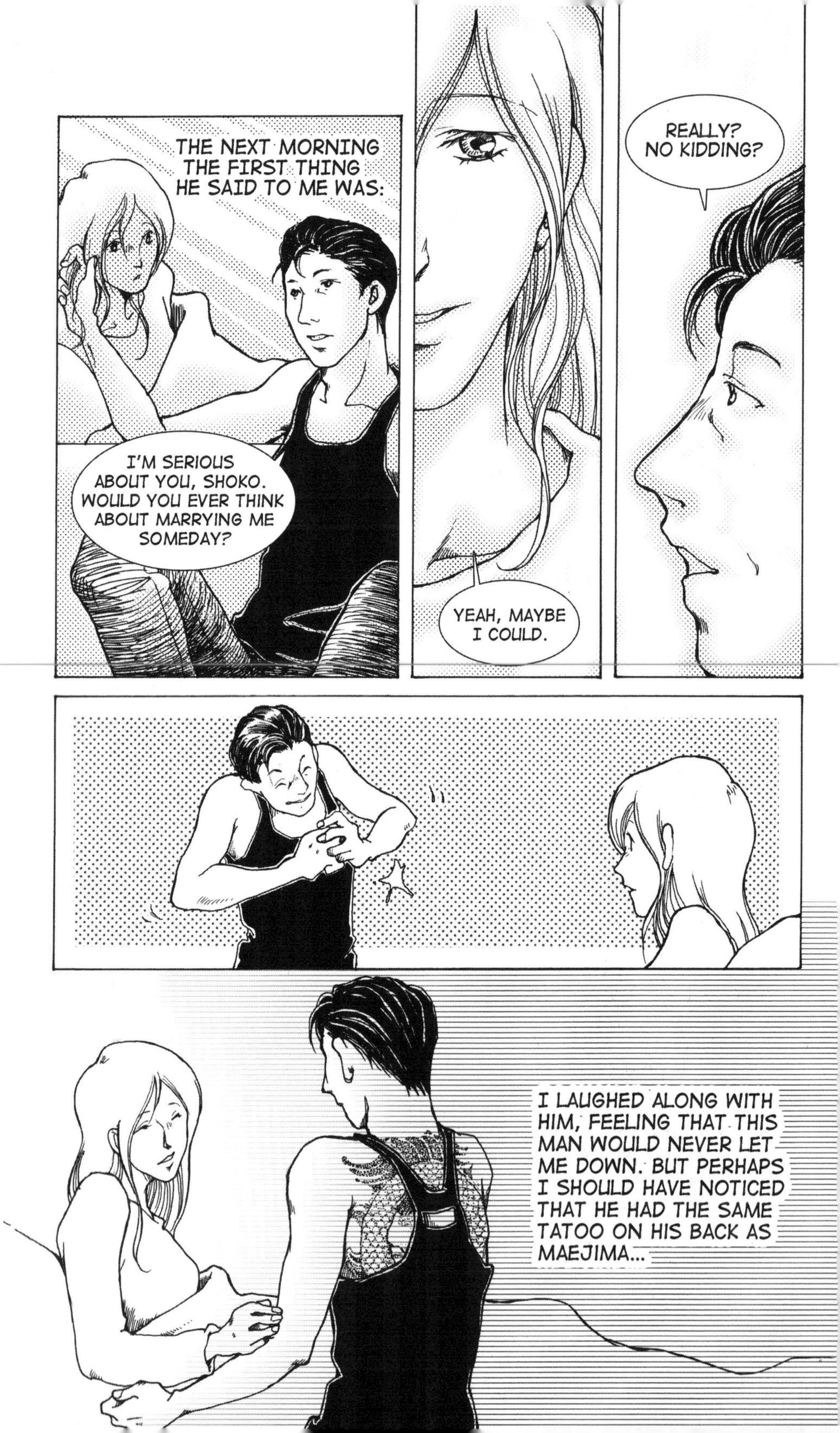
THE NEXT MORNING THE FIRST THING HE SAID TO ME WAS:
I'M SERIOUS ABOUT YOU, SHOKO. WOULD YOU EVER THINK ABOUT MARRYING ME SOMEDAY?
YEAH, MAYBE I COULD.
REALLY? NO KIDDING?
I LAUGHED ALONG WITH HIM, FEELING THAT THIS MAN WOULD NEVER LET ME DOWN. BUT PERHAPS I SHOULD HAVE NOTICED THAT HE HAD THE SAME TATOO ON HIS BACK AS MAEJIMA...

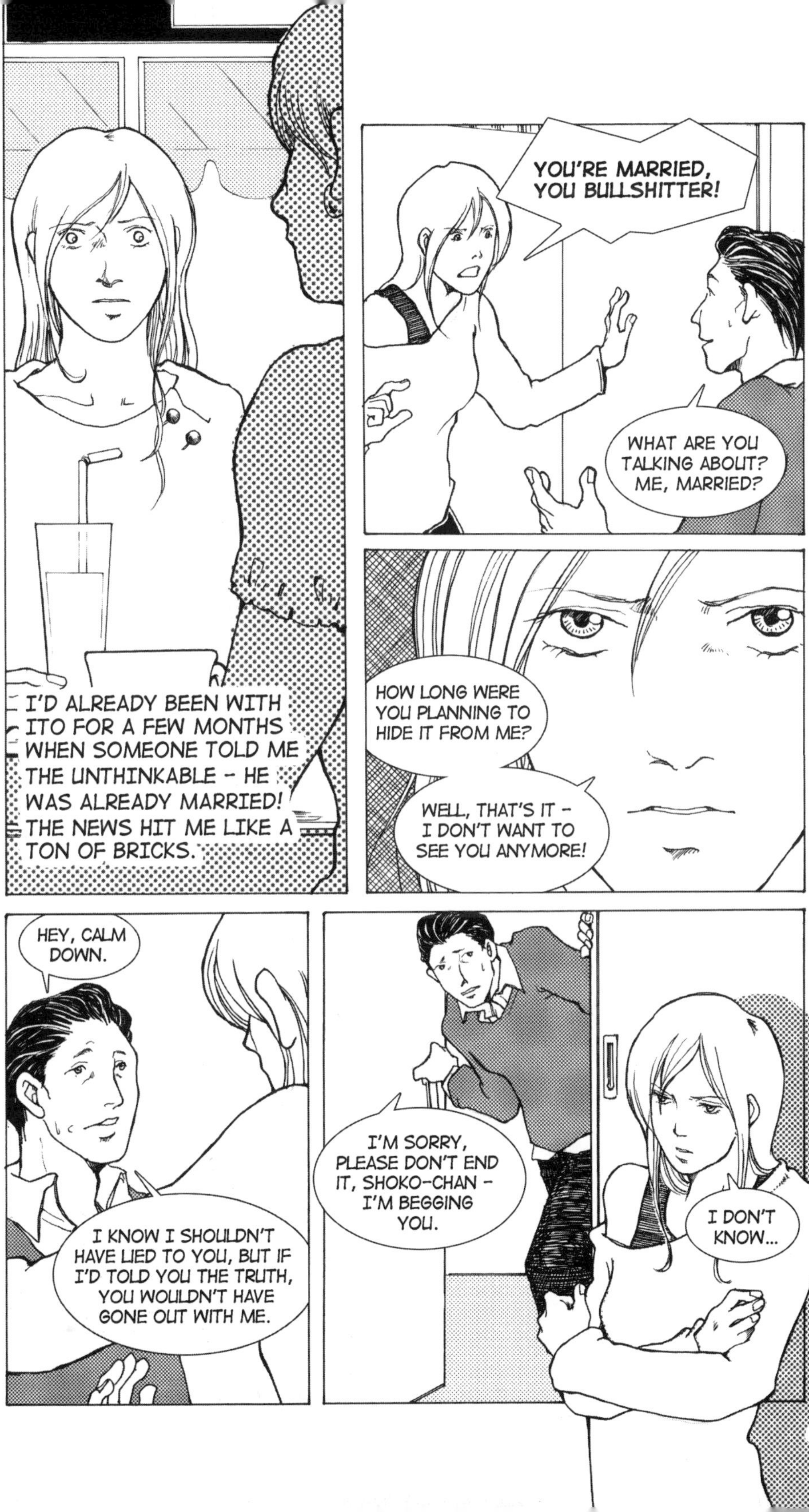
I'D ALREADY BEEN WITH ITO FOR A FEW MONTHS WHEN SOMEONE TOLD ME THE UNTHINKABLE - HE WAS ALREADY MARRIED! THE NEWS HIT ME LIKE A TON OF BRICKS.
YOU'RE MARRIED, YOU BULLSHITTER!
WHAT ARE YOU TALKING ABOUT? ME, MARRIED?
HOW LONG WERE YOU PLANNING TO HIDE IT FROM ME?
WELL, THAT'S IT - I DON'T WANT TO SEE YOU ANYMORE!
HEY, CALM DOWN.
I KNOW I SHOULDN'T HAVE LIED TO YOU, BUT IF I'D TOLD YOU THE TRUTH, YOU WOULDN'T HAVE GONE OUT WITH ME.
I'M SORRY, PLEASE DON'T END IT, SHOKO-CHAN - I'M BEGGING YOU.
I DON'T KNOW...

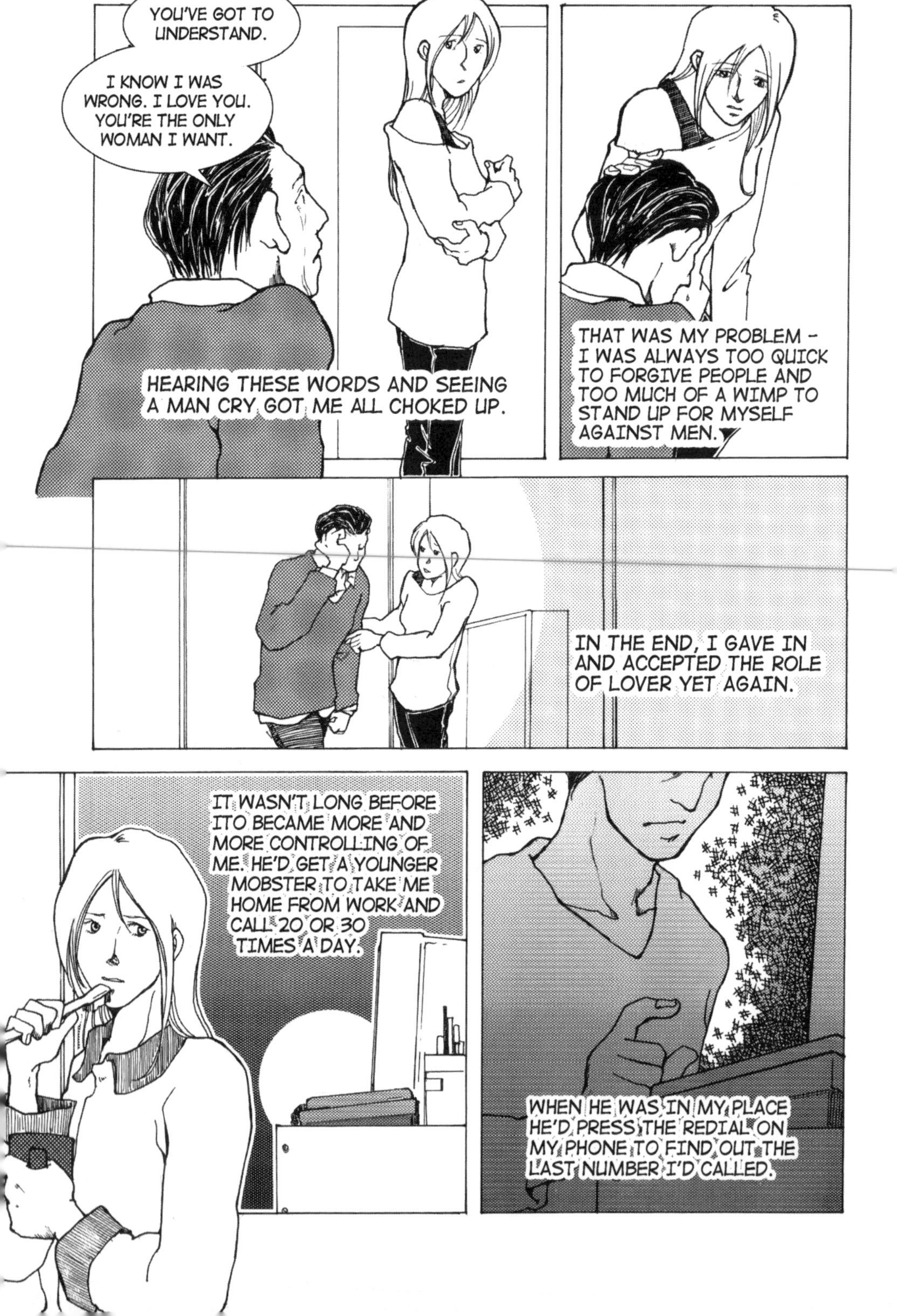
YOU'VE GOT TO UNDERSTAND.
I KNOW I WAS WRONG. I LOVE YOU. YOU'RE THE ONLY WOMAN I WANT.
HEARING THESE WORDS AND SEEING A MAN CRY GOT ME ALL CHOKED UP.
THAT WAS MY PROBLEM - I WAS ALWAYS TOO QUICK TO FORGIVE PEOPLE AND TOO MUCH OF A WIMP TO STAND UP FOR MYSELF AGAINST MEN.
IN THE END, I GAVE IN AND ACCEPTED THE ROLE OF LOVER YET AGAIN.
IT WASN'T LONG BEFORE ITO BECAME MORE AND MORE CONTROLLING OF ME. HE'D GET A YOUNGER MOBSTER TO TAKE ME HOME FROM WORK AND CALL 20 OR 30 TIMES A DAY.
WHEN HE WAS IN MY PLACE HE'D PRESS THE REDIAL ON MY PHONE TO FIND OUT THE LAST NUMBER I'D CALLED.

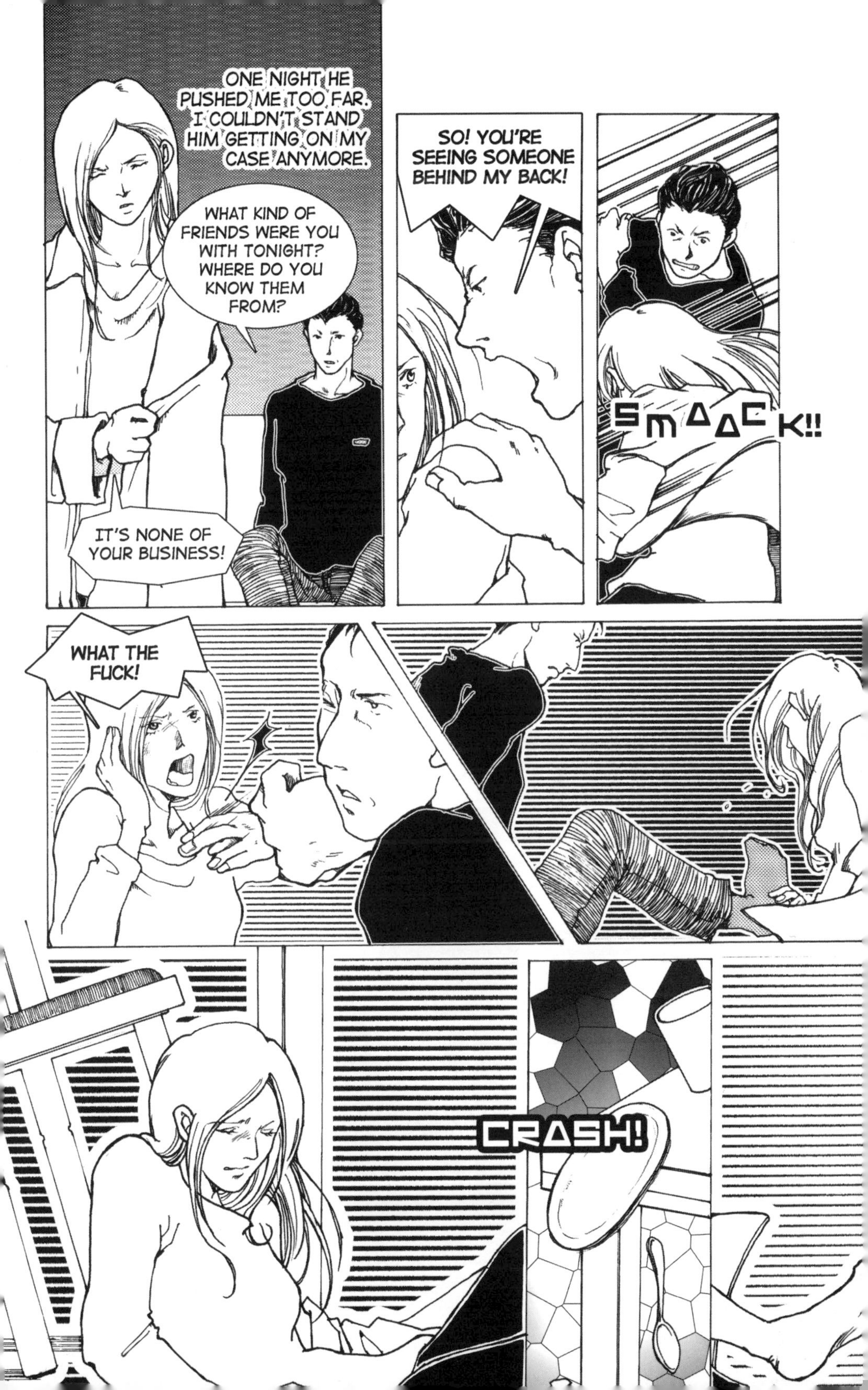
ONE NIGHT HE PUSHED ME TOO FAR. I COULDN'T STAND HIM GETTING ON MY CASE ANYMORE.
WHAT KIND OF FRIENDS WERE YOU WITH TONIGHT? WHERE DO YOU KNOW THEM FROM?
IT'S NONE OF YOUR BUSINESS!
SO! YOU'RE SEEING SOMEONE BEHIND MY BACK!
SMAACK!!
WHAT THE FUCK!
CRASH!

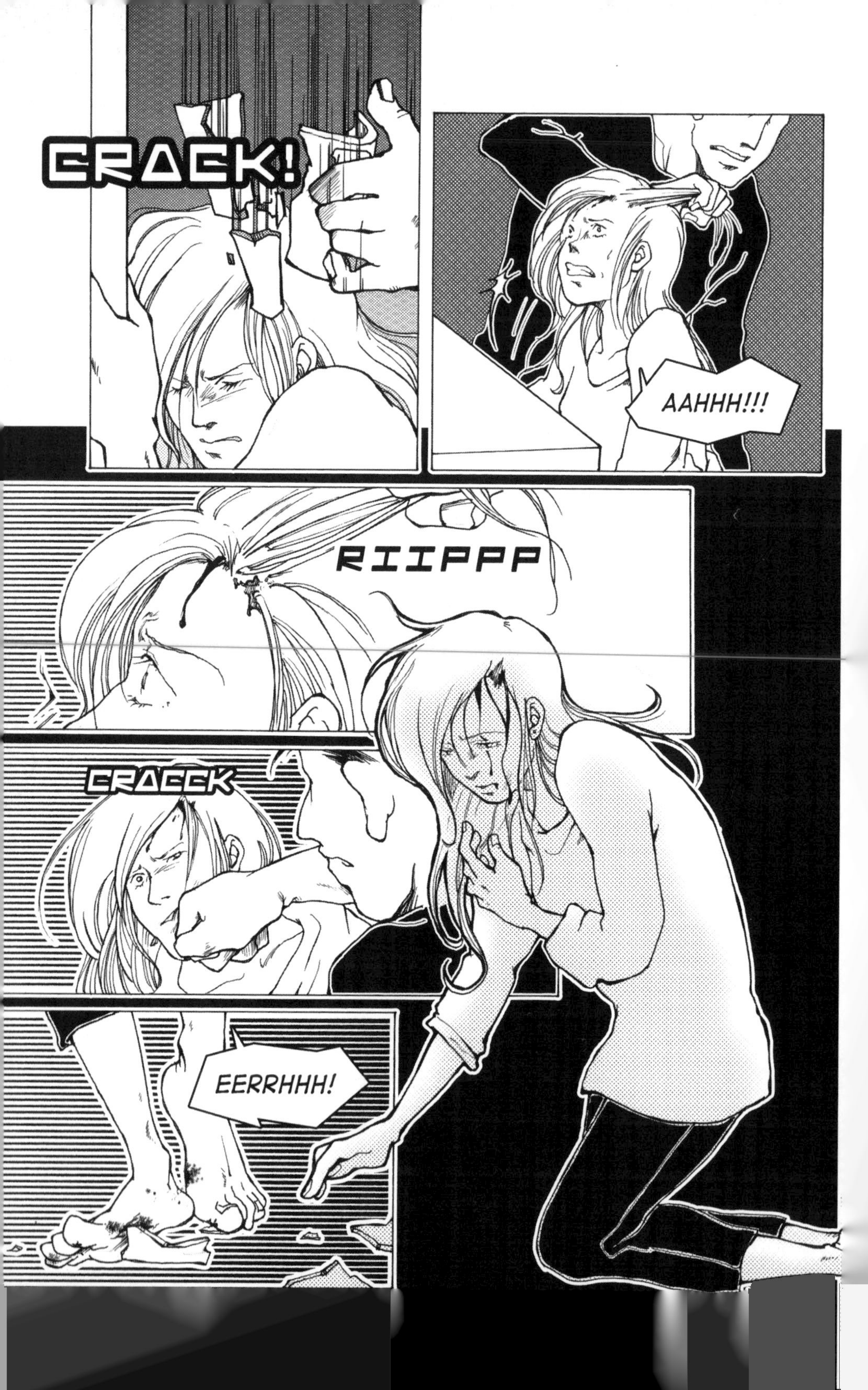
CRACK!
AAHHH!!!
RIIPPP
CRACCK
EERRHHH!

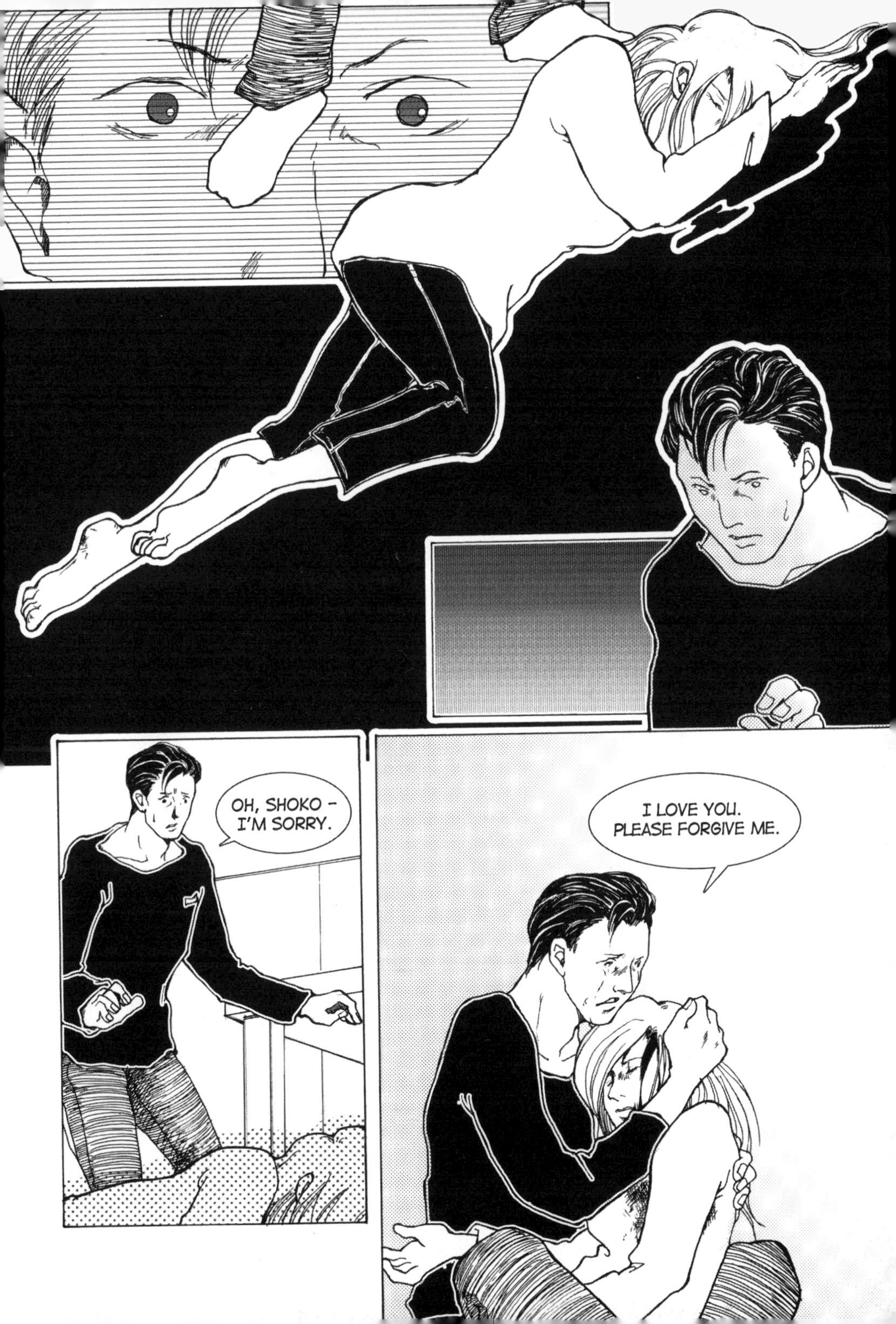
OH, SHOKO -
I'M SORRY.
I LOVE YOU.
PLEASE FORGIVE ME.

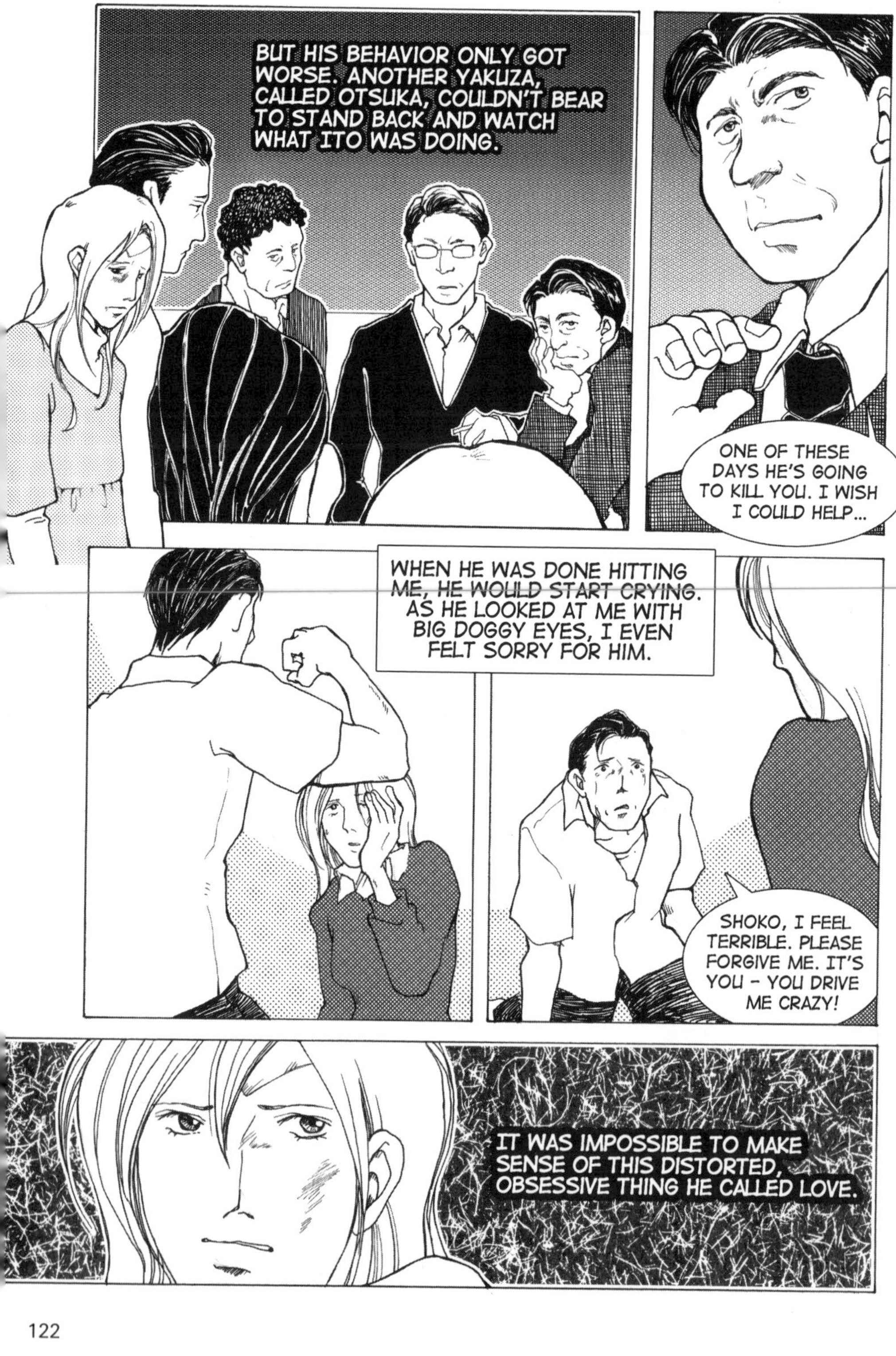
BUT HIS BEHAVIOR ONLY GOT WORSE. ANOTHER YAKUZA, CALLED OTSUKA, COULDN'T BEAR TO STAND BACK AND WATCH WHAT ITO WAS DOING.
ONE OF THESE DAYS HE'S GOING TO KILL YOU. I WISH I COULD HELP...
WHEN HE WAS DONE HITTING ME, HE WOULD START CRYING. AS HE LOOKED AT ME WITH BIG DOGGY EYES, I EVEN FELT SORRY FOR HIM.
SHOKO, I FEEL TERRIBLE. PLEASE FORGIVE ME. IT'S YOU - YOU DRIVE ME CRAZY!
IT WAS IMPOSSIBLE TO MAKE SENSE OF THIS DISTORTED, OBSESSIVE THING HE CALLED LOVE.

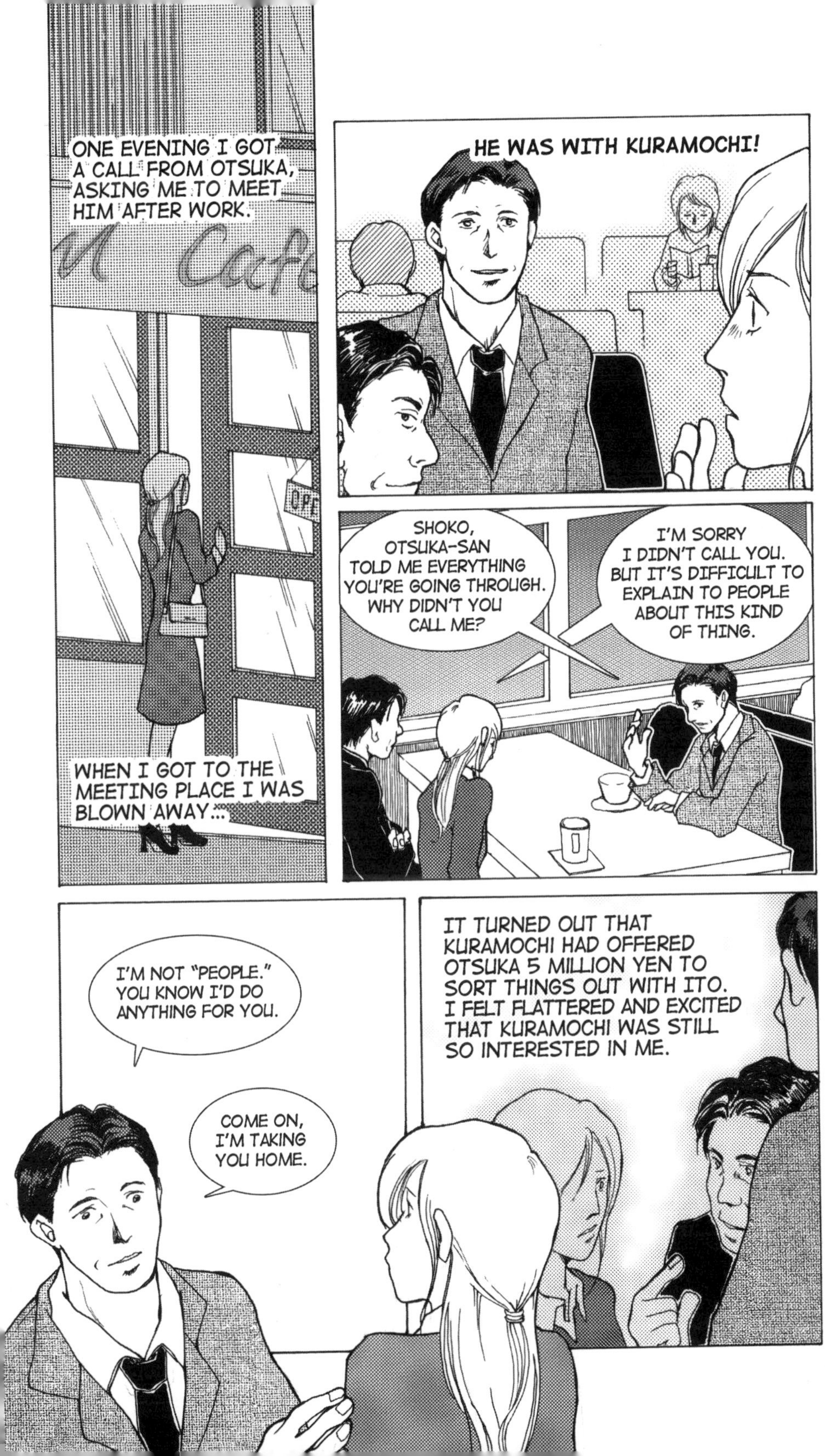

ONE EVENING I GOT A CALL FROM OTSUKA, ASKING ME TO MEET HIM AFTER WORK.
WHEN I GOT TO THE MEETING PLACE I WAS BLOWN AWAY...
HE WAS WITH KURAMOCHI!
SHOKO, OTSUKA-SAN TOLD ME EVERYTHING YOU'RE GOING THROUGH. WHY DIDN'T YOU CALL ME?
I'M SORRY I DIDN'T CALL YOU. BUT IT'S DIFFICULT TO EXPLAIN TO PEOPLE ABOUT THIS KIND OF THING.
I'M NOT "PEOPLE." YOU KNOW I'D DO ANYTHING FOR YOU.
COME ON, I'M TAKING YOU HOME.
IT TURNED OUT THAT KURAMOCHI HAD OFFERED OTSUKA 5 MILLION YEN TO SORT THINGS OUT WITH ITO. I FELT FLATTERED AND EXCITED THAT KURAMOCHI WAS STILL SO INTERESTED IN ME.

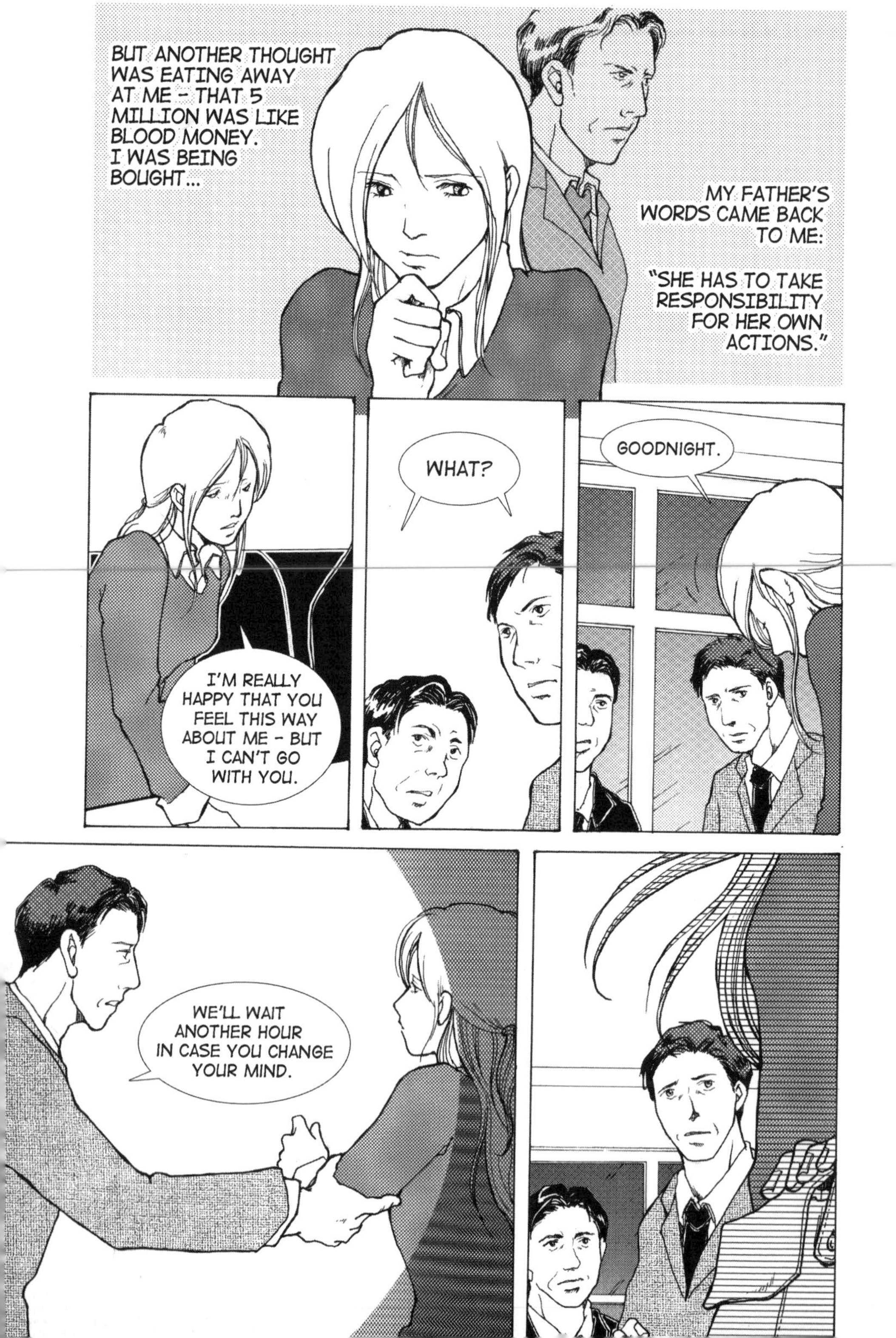
BUT ANOTHER THOUGHT WAS EATING AWAY AT ME - THAT 5 MILLION WAS LIKE BLOOD MONEY. I WAS BEING BOUGHT...
MY FATHER'S WORDS CAME BACK TO ME:
"SHE HAS TO TAKE RESPONSIBILITY FOR HER OWN ACTIONS."
I'M REALLY HAPPY THAT YOU FEEL THIS WAY ABOUT ME - BUT I CAN'T GO WITH YOU.
WHAT?
GOODNIGHT.
WE'LL WAIT ANOTHER HOUR IN CASE YOU CHANGE YOUR MIND.

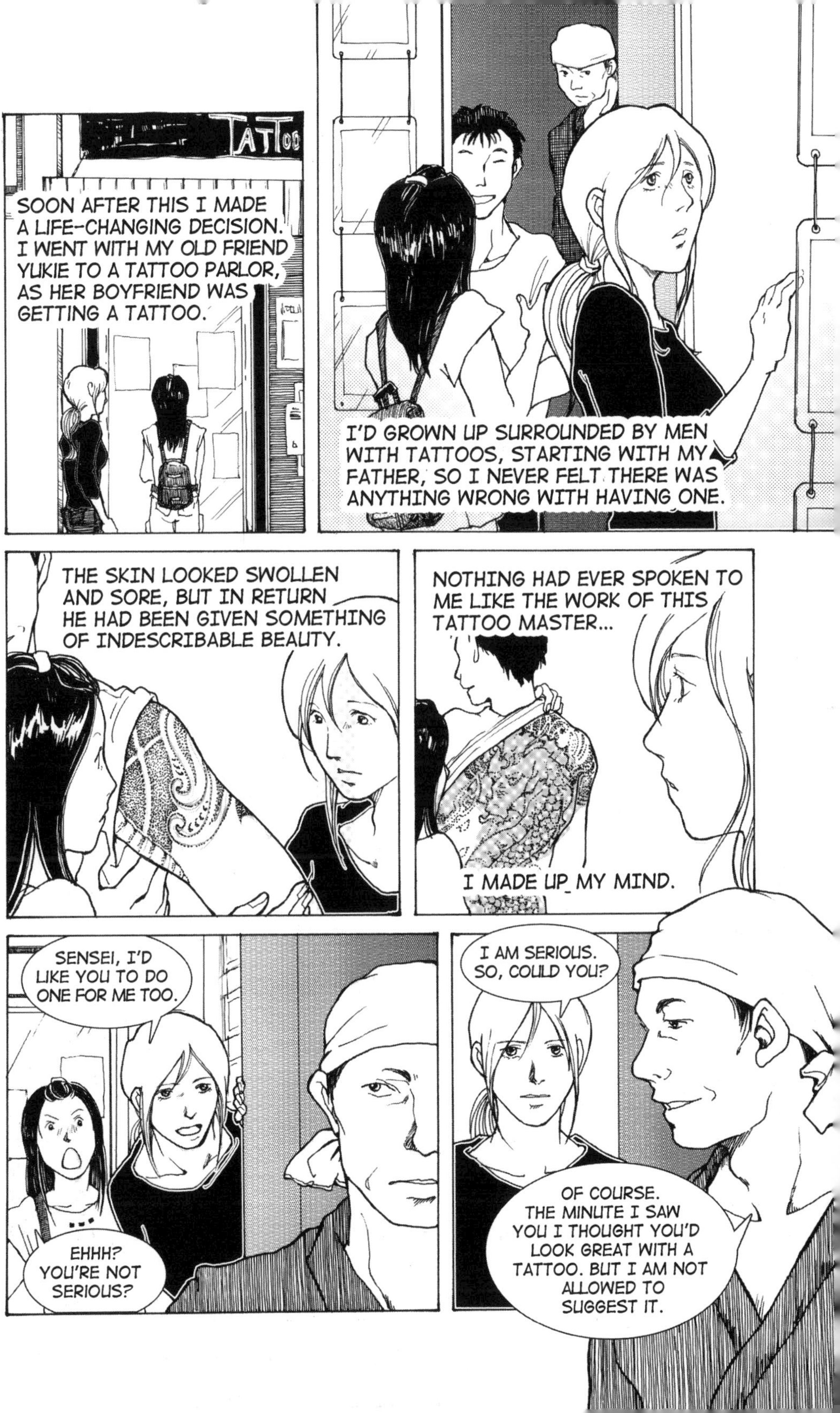
TATTOO
SOON AFTER THIS I MADE A LIFE-CHANGING DECISION. I WENT WITH MY OLD FRIEND YUKIE TO A TATTOO PARLOR, AS HER BOYFRIEND WAS GETTING A TATTOO.
I'D GROWN UP SURROUNDED BY MEN WITH TATTOOS, STARTING WITH MY FATHER, SO I NEVER FELT THERE WAS ANYTHING WRONG WITH HAVING ONE.
THE SKIN LOOKED SWOLLEN AND SORE, BUT IN RETURN HE HAD BEEN GIVEN SOMETHING OF INDESCRIBABLE BEAUTY.
NOTHING HAD EVER SPOKEN TO ME LIKE THE WORK OF THIS TATTOO MASTER...
I MADE UP MY MIND.
SENSEI, I'D LIKE YOU TO DO ONE FOR ME TOO.
EHHH? YOU'RE NOT SERIOUS?
I AM SERIOUS. SO, COULD YOU?
OF COURSE. THE MINUTE I SAW YOU I THOUGHT YOU'D LOOK GREAT WITH A TATTOO. BUT I AM NOT ALLOWED TO SUGGEST IT.

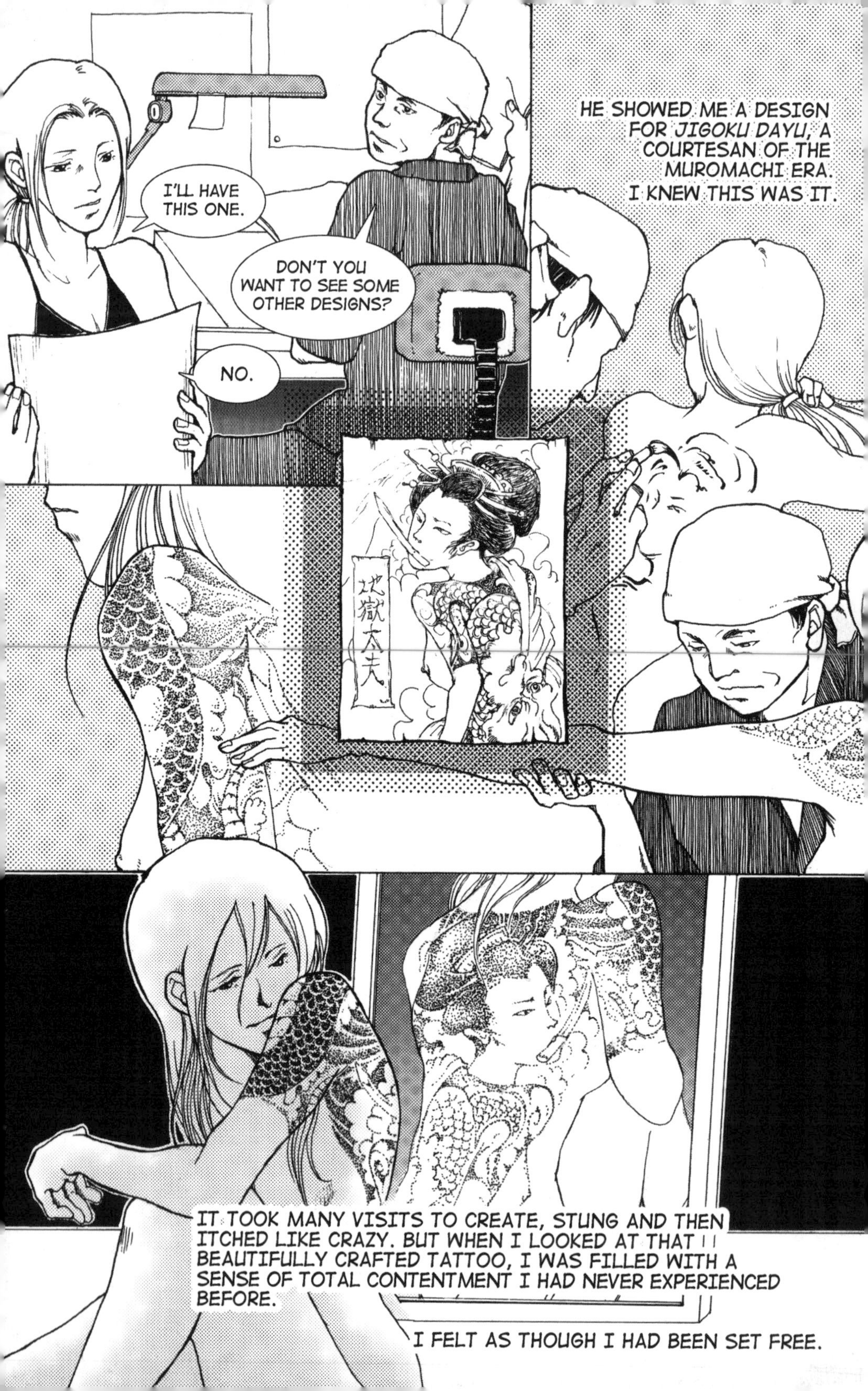
I'LL HAVE THIS ONE.
DON'T YOU WANT TO SEE SOME OTHER DESIGNS?
NO.
HE SHOWED ME A DESIGN FOR *JIGOKU DAYU*, A COURTESAN OF THE MUROMACHI ERA. I KNEW THIS WAS IT.
地獄太夫
IT TOOK MANY VISITS TO CREATE, STUNG AND THEN ITCHED LIKE CRAZY. BUT WHEN I LOOKED AT THAT BEAUTIFULLY CRAFTED TATTOO, I WAS FILLED WITH A SENSE OF TOTAL CONTENTMENT I HAD NEVER EXPERIENCED BEFORE.
I FELT AS THOUGH I HAD BEEN SET FREE.

CHAPTER 7

Clean Break

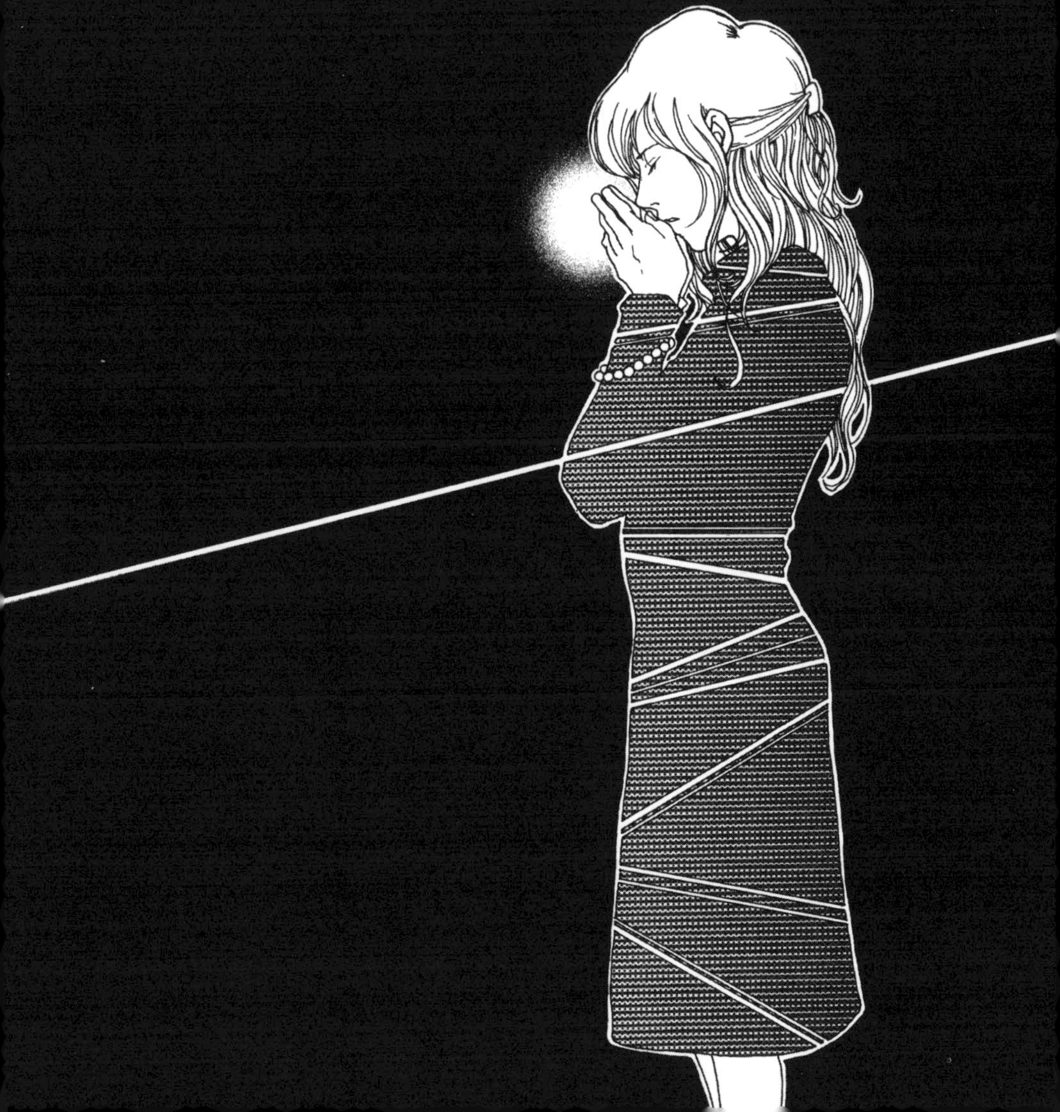

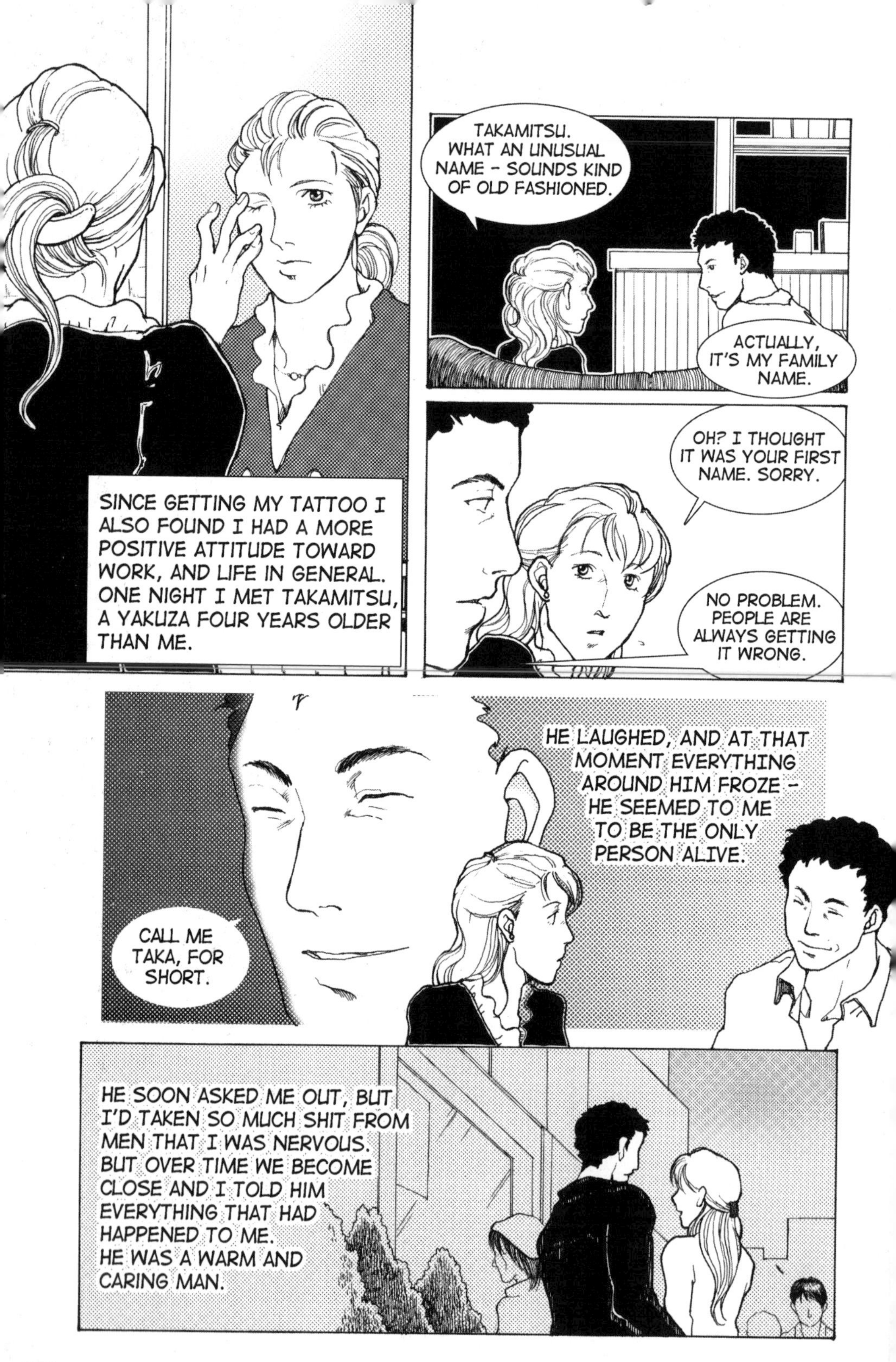
SINCE GETTING MY TATTOO I ALSO FOUND I HAD A MORE POSITIVE ATTITUDE TOWARD WORK, AND LIFE IN GENERAL. ONE NIGHT I MET TAKAMITSU, A YAKUZA FOUR YEARS OLDER THAN ME.
TAKAMITSU. WHAT AN UNUSUAL NAME - SOUNDS KIND OF OLD FASHIONED.
ACTUALLY, IT'S MY FAMILY NAME.
OH? I THOUGHT IT WAS YOUR FIRST NAME. SORRY.
NO PROBLEM. PEOPLE ARE ALWAYS GETTING IT WRONG.
HE LAUGHED, AND AT THAT MOMENT EVERYTHING AROUND HIM FROZE - HE SEEMED TO ME TO BE THE ONLY PERSON ALIVE.
CALL ME TAKA, FOR SHORT.
HE SOON ASKED ME OUT, BUT I'D TAKEN SO MUCH SHIT FROM MEN THAT I WAS NERVOUS. BUT OVER TIME WE BECOME CLOSE AND I TOLD HIM EVERYTHING THAT HAD HAPPENED TO ME. HE WAS A WARM AND CARING MAN.

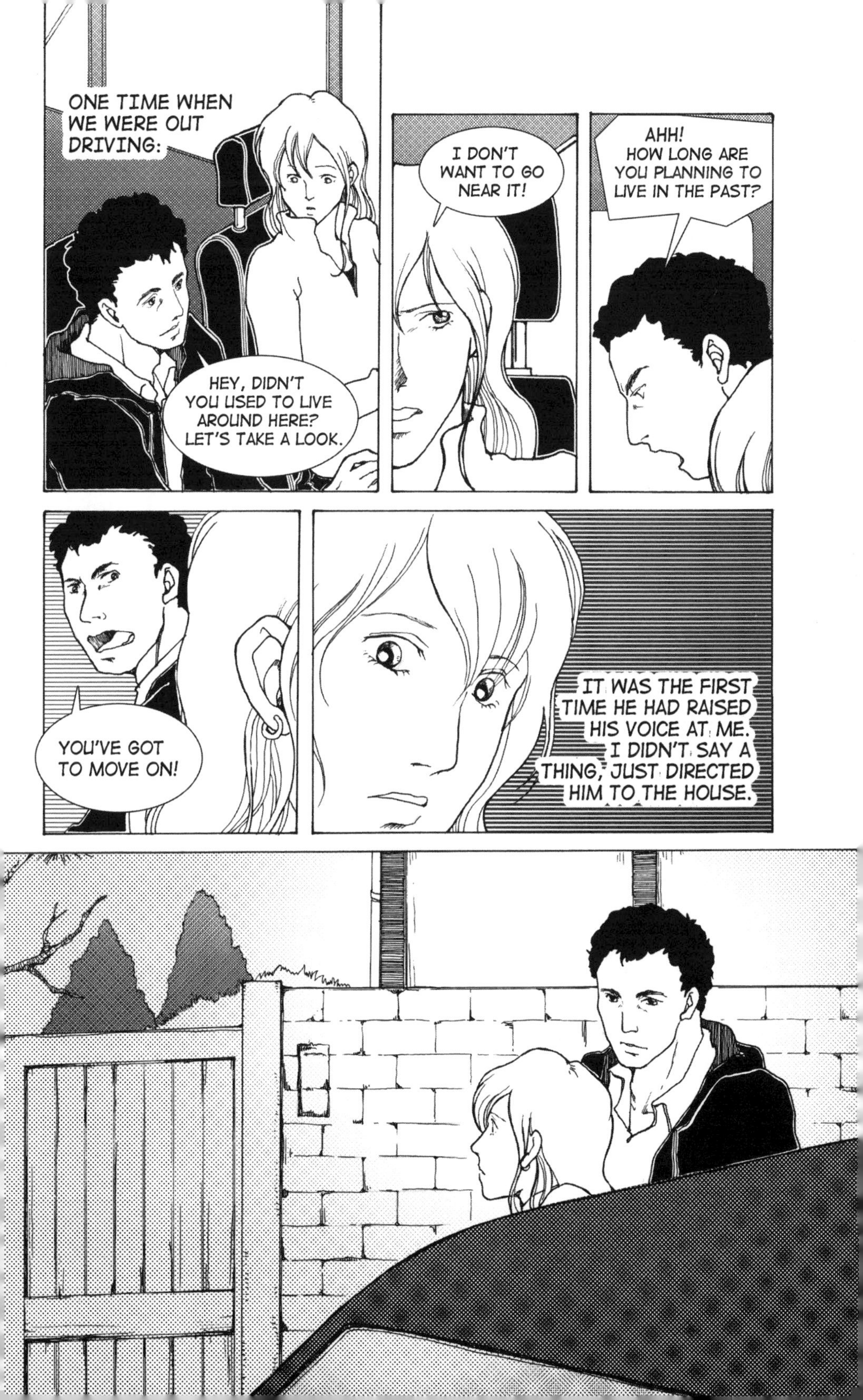
ONE TIME WHEN WE WERE OUT DRIVING:
HEY, DIDN'T YOU USED TO LIVE AROUND HERE? LET'S TAKE A LOOK.
I DON'T WANT TO GO NEAR IT!
AHH! HOW LONG ARE YOU PLANNING TO LIVE IN THE PAST?
YOU'VE GOT TO MOVE ON!
IT WAS THE FIRST TIME HE HAD RAISED HIS VOICE AT ME. I DIDN'T SAY A THING, JUST DIRECTED HIM TO THE HOUSE.

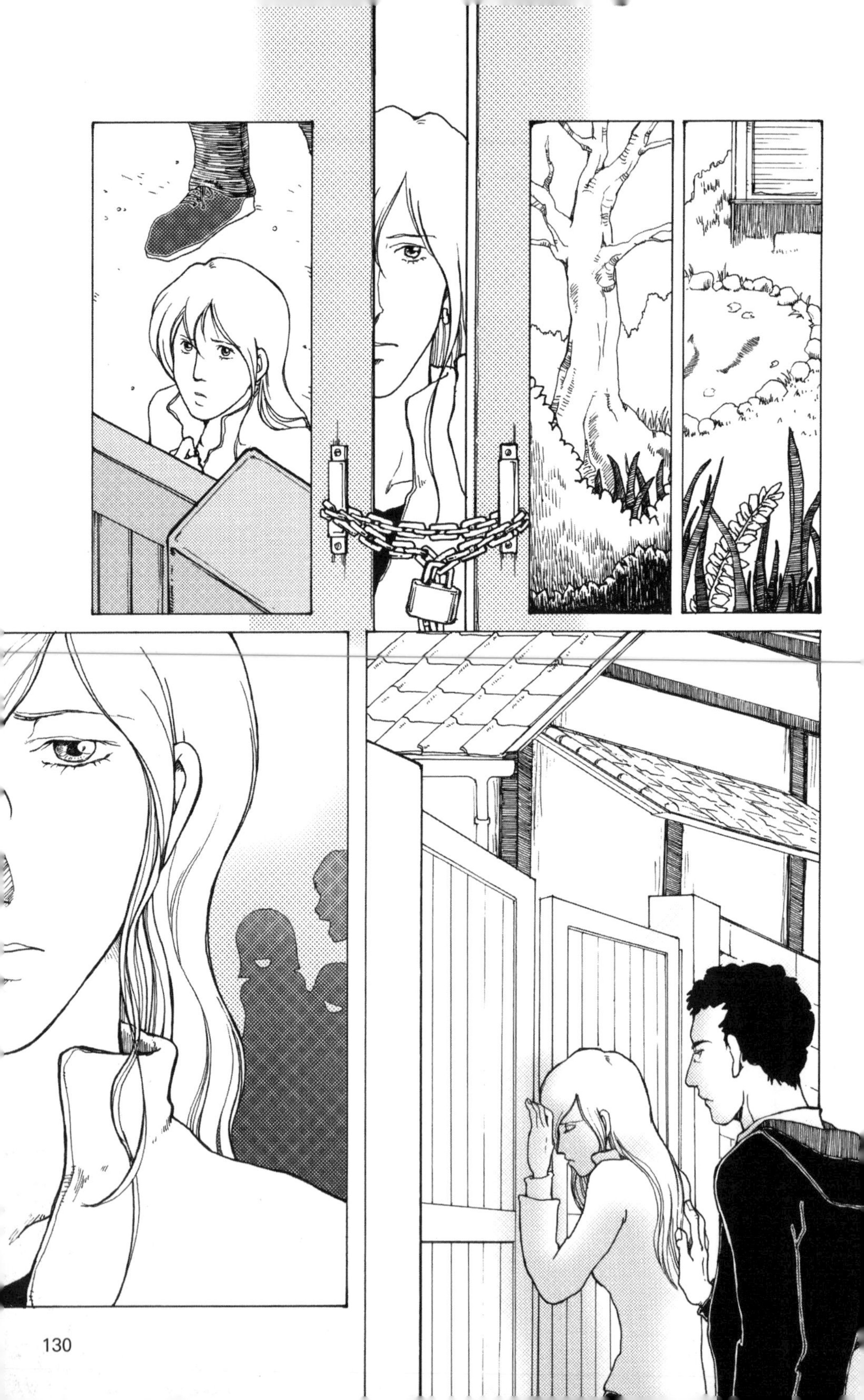

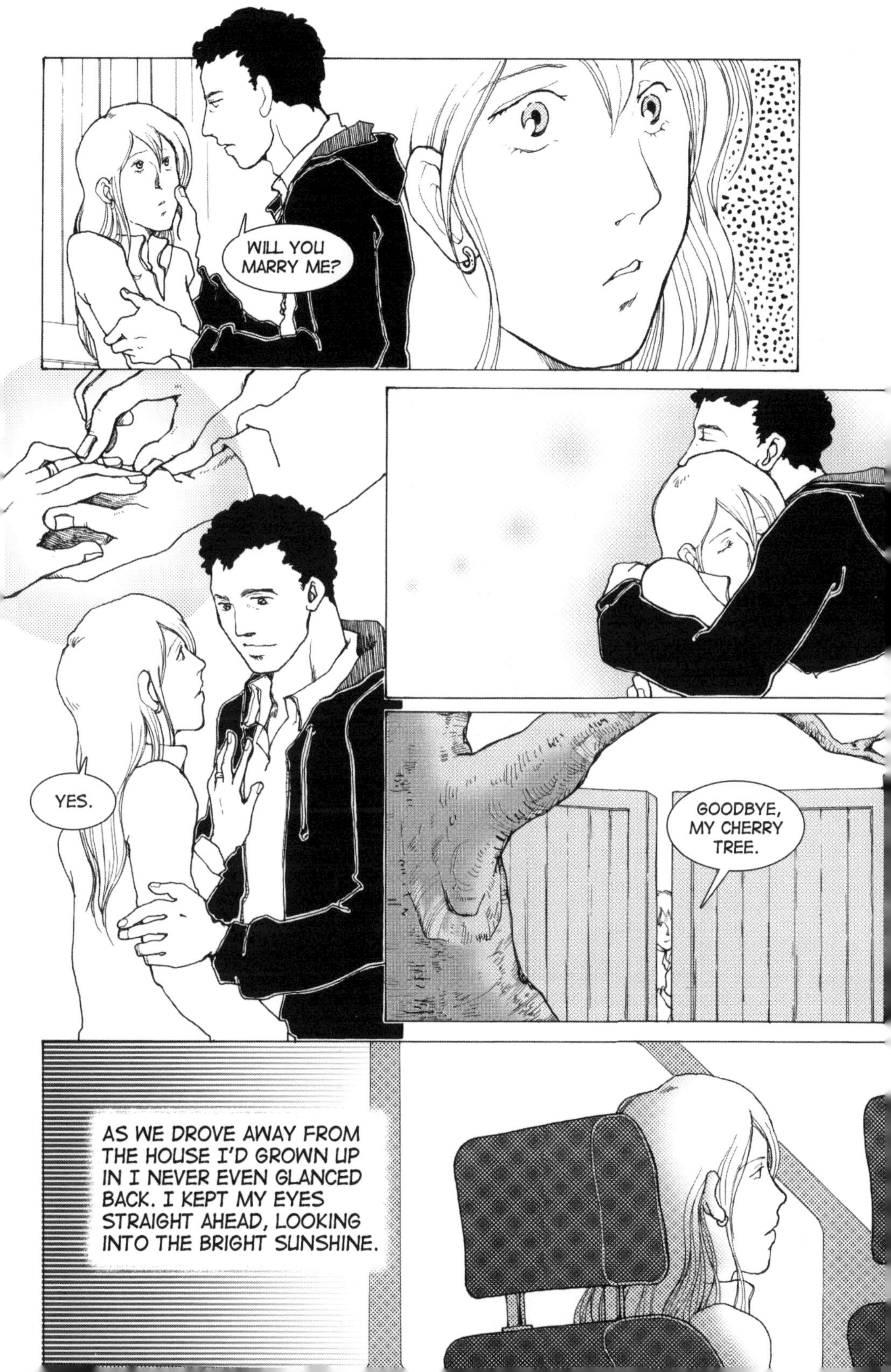
WILL YOU MARRY ME?
YES.
GOODBYE, MY CHERRY TREE.
AS WE DROVE AWAY FROM THE HOUSE I'D GROWN UP IN I NEVER EVEN GLANCED BACK. I KEPT MY EYES STRAIGHT AHEAD, LOOKING INTO THE BRIGHT SUNSHINE.

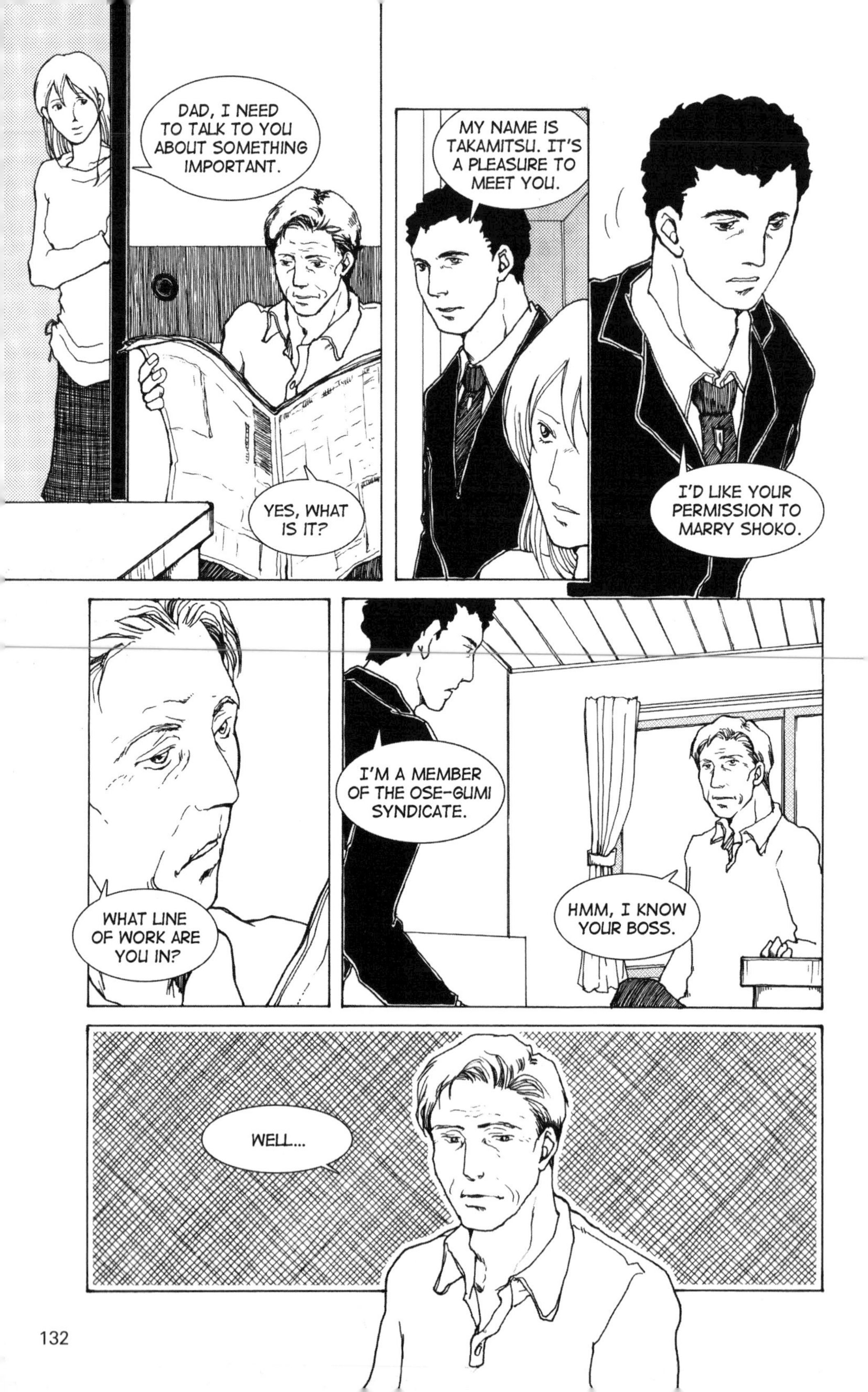
DAD, I NEED TO TALK TO YOU ABOUT SOMETHING IMPORTANT.
YES, WHAT IS IT?
MY NAME IS TAKAMITSU. IT'S A PLEASURE TO MEET YOU.
I'D LIKE YOUR PERMISSION TO MARRY SHOKO.
WHAT LINE OF WORK ARE YOU IN?
I'M A MEMBER OF THE OSE-GUMI SYNDICATE.
HMM, I KNOW YOUR BOSS.
WELL...

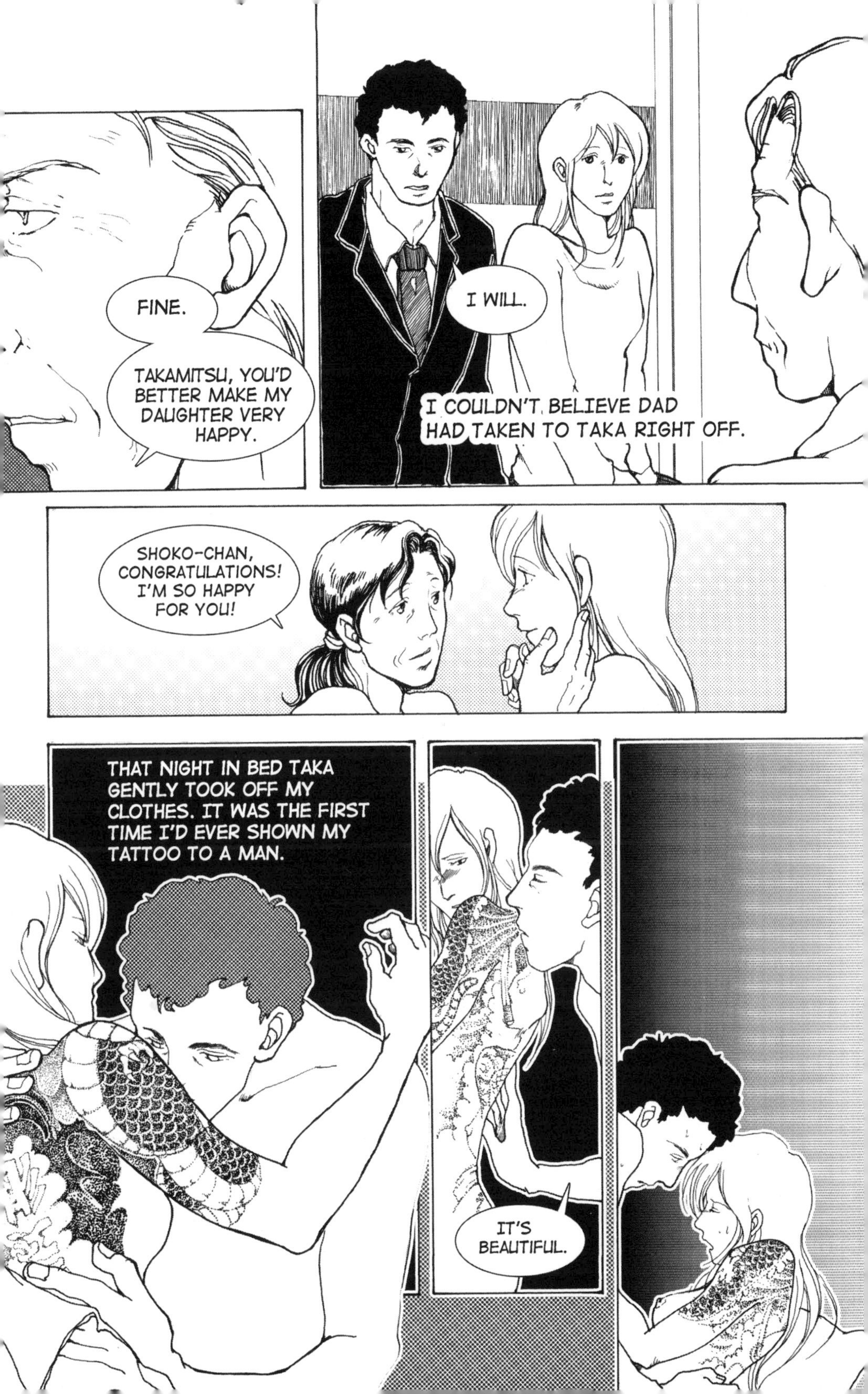
FINE.
TAKAMITSU, YOU'D BETTER MAKE MY DAUGHTER VERY HAPPY.
I WILL.
I COULDN'T BELIEVE DAD HAD TAKEN TO TAKA RIGHT OFF.
SHOKO-CHAN, CONGRATULATIONS! I'M SO HAPPY FOR YOU!
THAT NIGHT IN BED TAKA GENTLY TOOK OFF MY CLOTHES. IT WAS THE FIRST TIME I'D EVER SHOWN MY TATTOO TO A MAN.
IT'S BEAUTIFUL.

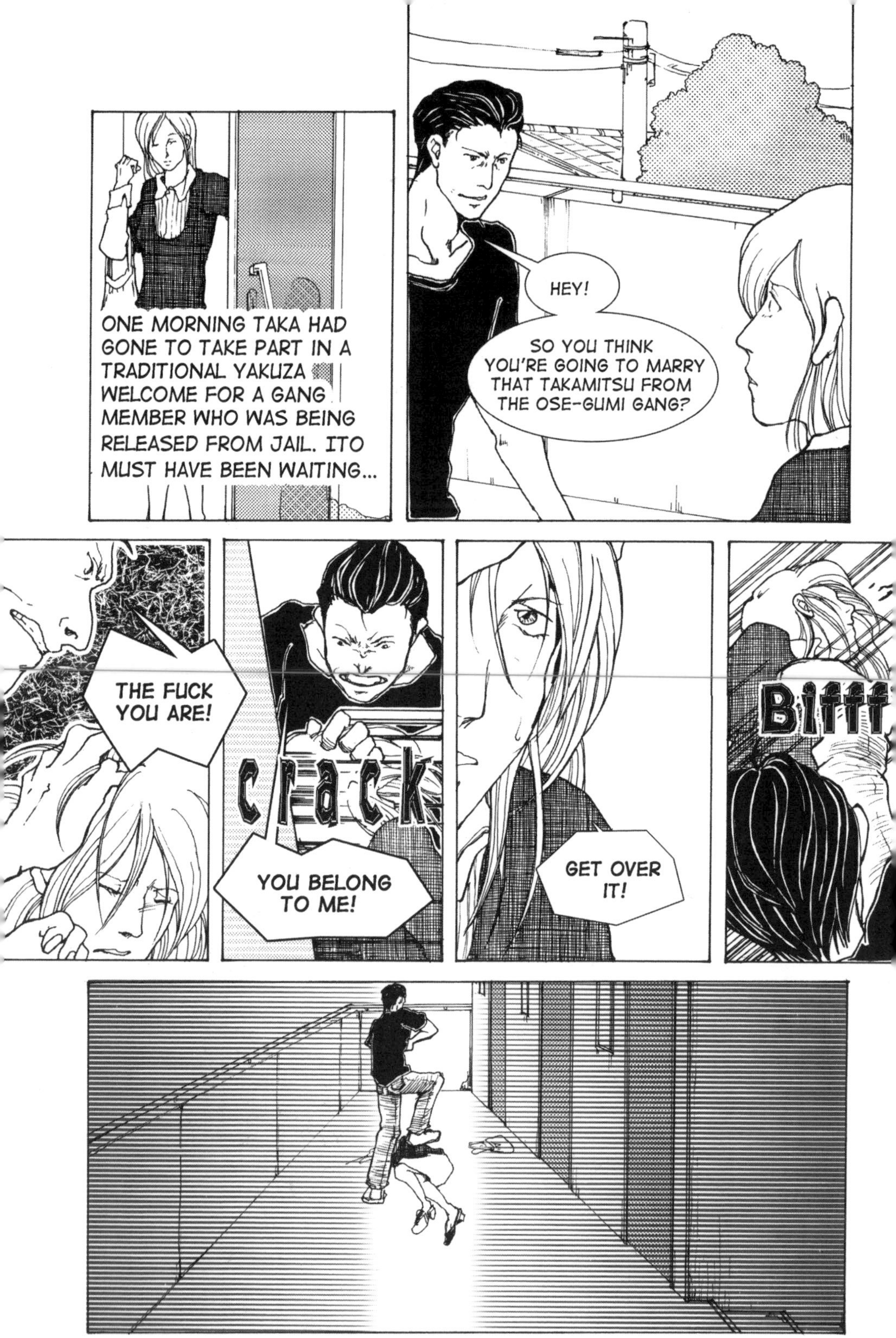
ONE MORNING TAKA HAD GONE TO TAKE PART IN A TRADITIONAL YAKUZA WELCOME FOR A GANG MEMBER WHO WAS BEING RELEASED FROM JAIL. ITO MUST HAVE BEEN WAITING...
HEY!
SO YOU THINK YOU'RE GOING TO MARRY THAT TAKAMITSU FROM THE OSE-GUMI GANG?
GET OVER IT!
Bifff
crack
YOU BELONG TO ME!
THE FUCK YOU ARE!

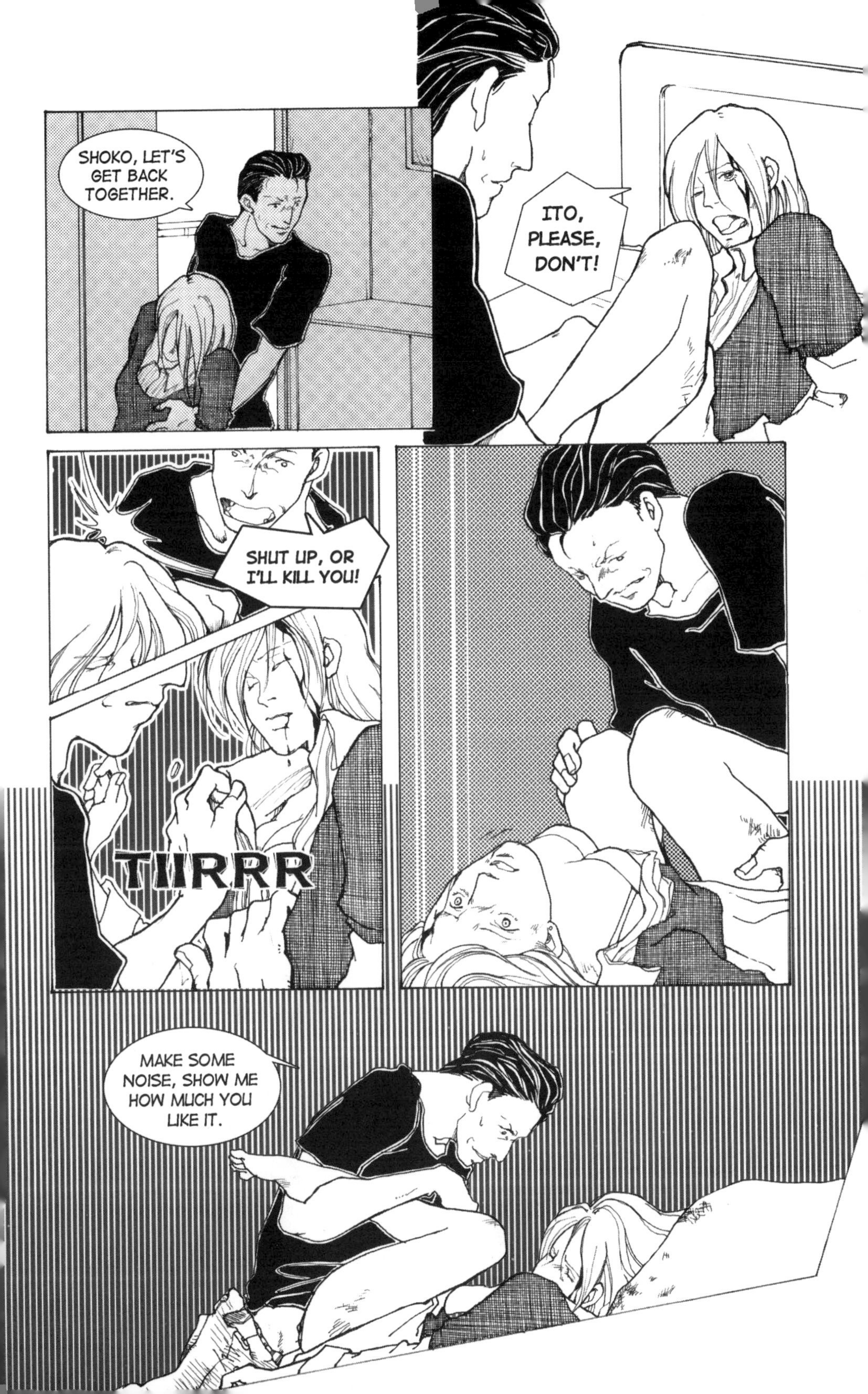
SHOKO, LET'S GET BACK TOGETHER.
ITO, PLEASE, DON'T!
SHUT UP, OR I'LL KILL YOU!
TIIRRR
MAKE SOME NOISE, SHOW ME HOW MUCH YOU LIKE IT.

FEELS GOOD, DOESN'T IT? I'M SO MUCH BETTER THAN TAKA, AREN'T I?

I BIT MY LIP AS HARD AS I COULD. I WAS TELLING MYSELF "THIS IS NOTHING. IT'S JUST SEX. IT DOESN'T MEAN ANYTHING."

ITO'S HAND ONCE HELD ME THE WHOLE NIGHT LONG WHEN I WAS SICK. NOW IT WAS REPULSIVE TO ME.

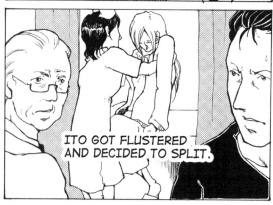

AFTERWARD HE TOOK ME TO THE HOSPITAL. THE DOCTOR COULD SEE WHAT HAD HAPPENED.

ITO GOT FLUSTERED AND DECIDED TO SPLIT.

BUT BEFORE HE LEFT, HE FLASHED ME A WARNING LOOK.

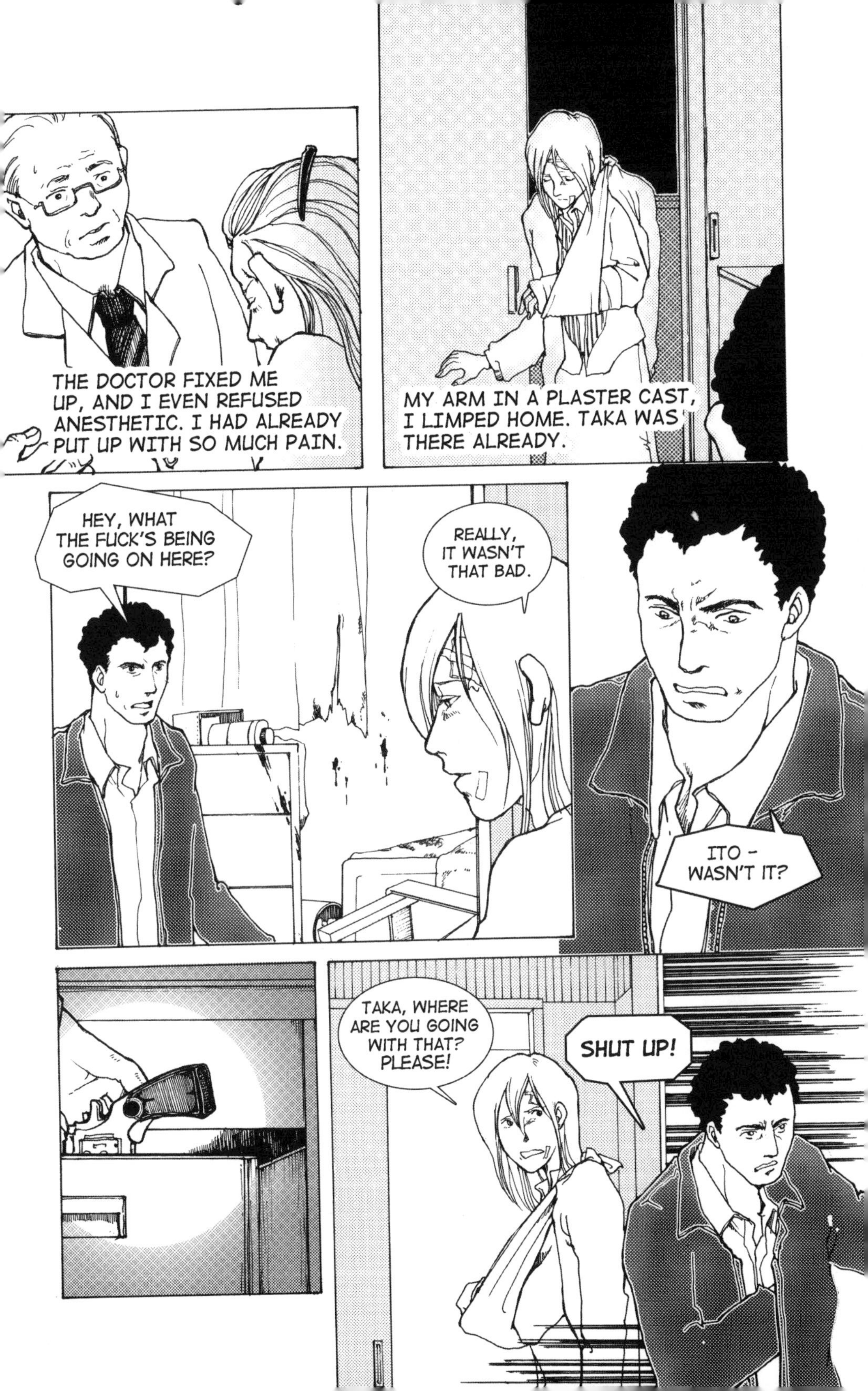

THE DOCTOR FIXED ME UP, AND I EVEN REFUSED ANESTHETIC. I HAD ALREADY PUT UP WITH SO MUCH PAIN.
MY ARM IN A PLASTER CAST, I LIMPED HOME. TAKA WAS THERE ALREADY.
HEY, WHAT THE FUCK'S BEING GOING ON HERE?
REALLY, IT WASN'T THAT BAD.
ITO - WASN'T IT?
TAKA, WHERE ARE YOU GOING WITH THAT? PLEASE!
SHUT UP!

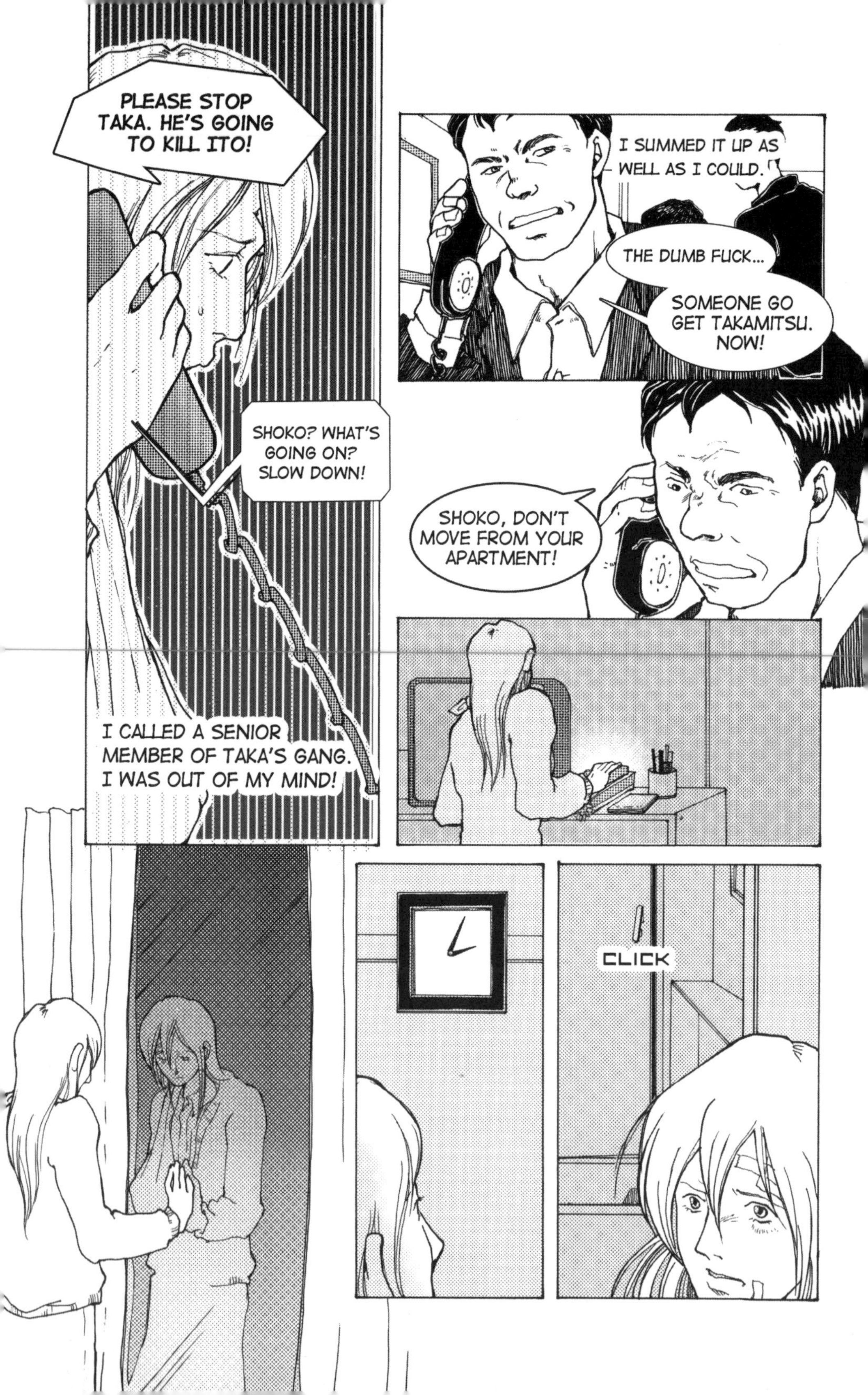
PLEASE STOP TAKA. HE'S GOING TO KILL ITO!
I SUMMED IT UP AS WELL AS I COULD.
THE DUMB FUCK...
SOMEONE GO GET TAKAMITSU. NOW!
SHOKO? WHAT'S GOING ON? SLOW DOWN!
SHOKO, DON'T MOVE FROM YOUR APARTMENT!
I CALLED A SENIOR MEMBER OF TAKA'S GANG. I WAS OUT OF MY MIND!
CLICK

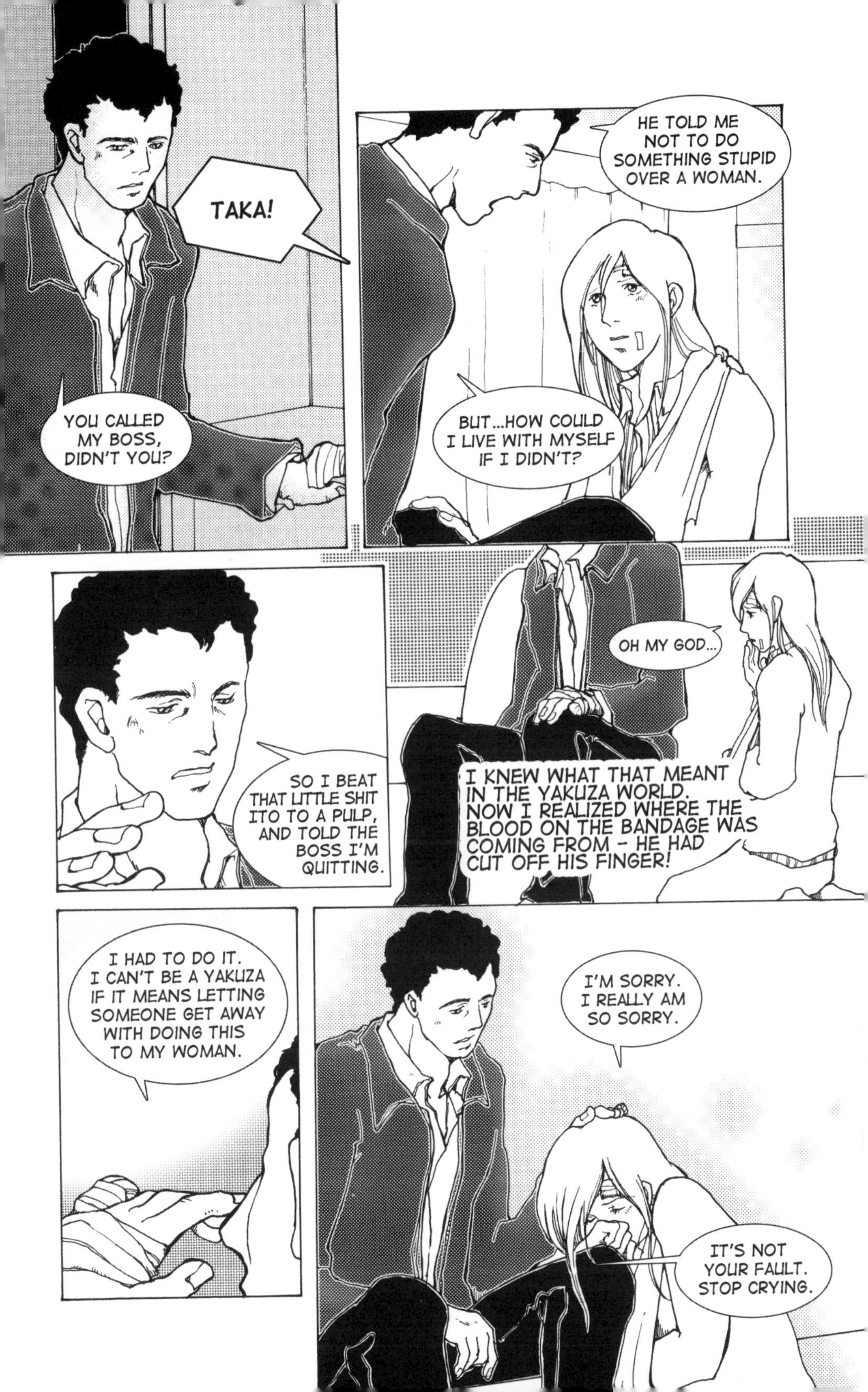
TAKA!
YOU CALLED MY BOSS, DIDN'T YOU?
HE TOLD ME NOT TO DO SOMETHING STUPID OVER A WOMAN.
BUT...HOW COULD I LIVE WITH MYSELF IF I DIDN'T?
SO I BEAT THAT LITTLE SHIT ITO TO A PULP, AND TOLD THE BOSS I'M QUITTING.
OH MY GOD...
I KNEW WHAT THAT MEANT IN THE YAKUZA WORLD. NOW I REALIZED WHERE THE BLOOD ON THE BANDAGE WAS COMING FROM - HE HAD CUT OFF HIS FINGER!
I HAD TO DO IT. I CAN'T BE A YAKUZA IF IT MEANS LETTING SOMEONE GET AWAY WITH DOING THIS TO MY WOMAN.
I'M SORRY. I REALLY AM SO SORRY.
IT'S NOT YOUR FAULT. STOP CRYING.

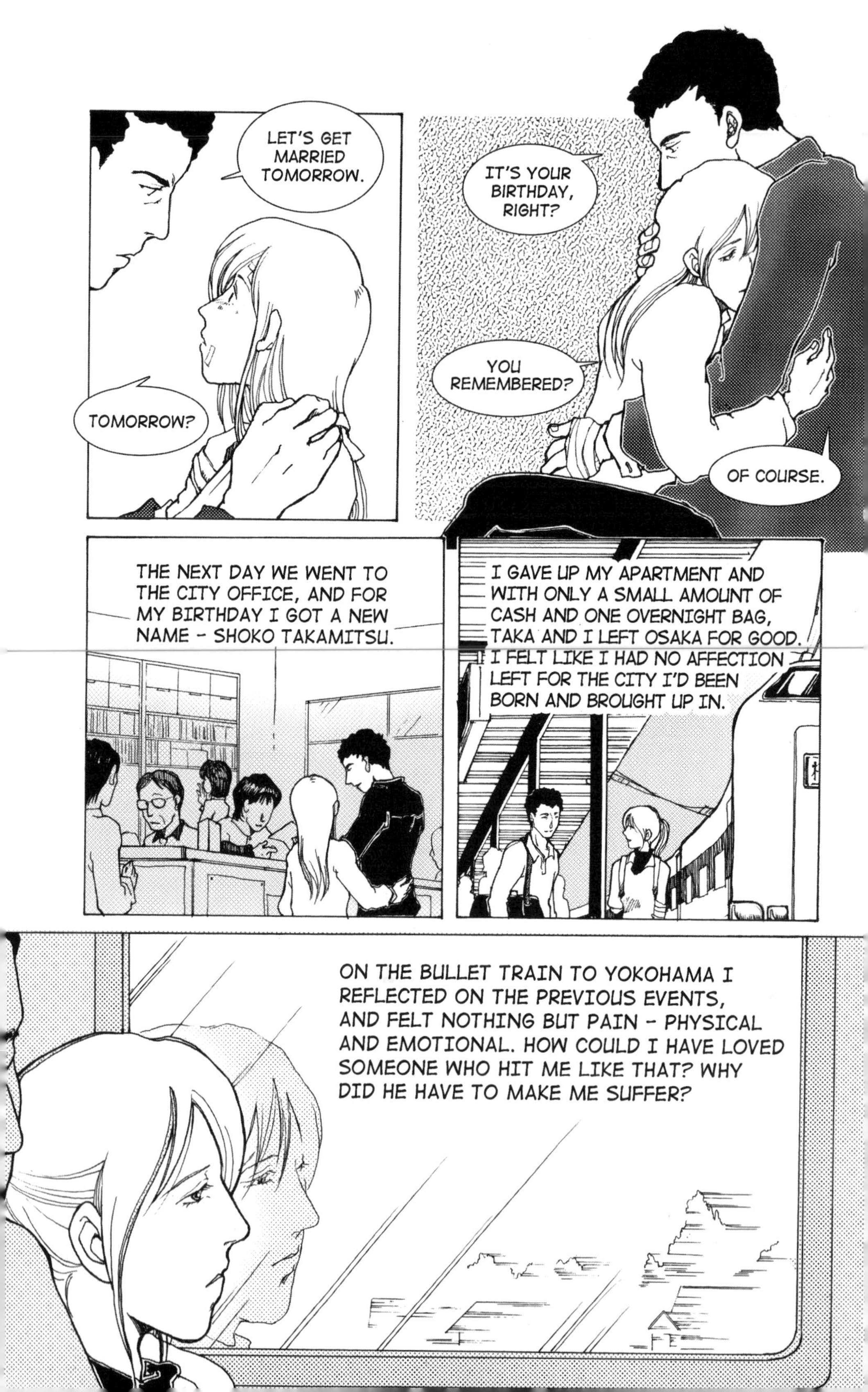
LET'S GET MARRIED TOMORROW.
TOMORROW?
IT'S YOUR BIRTHDAY, RIGHT?
YOU REMEMBERED?
OF COURSE.
THE NEXT DAY WE WENT TO THE CITY OFFICE, AND FOR MY BIRTHDAY I GOT A NEW NAME - SHOKO TAKAMITSU.
I GAVE UP MY APARTMENT AND WITH ONLY A SMALL AMOUNT OF CASH AND ONE OVERNIGHT BAG, TAKA AND I LEFT OSAKA FOR GOOD. I FELT LIKE I HAD NO AFFECTION LEFT FOR THE CITY I'D BEEN BORN AND BROUGHT UP IN.
ON THE BULLET TRAIN TO YOKOHAMA I REFLECTED ON THE PREVIOUS EVENTS, AND FELT NOTHING BUT PAIN - PHYSICAL AND EMOTIONAL. HOW COULD I HAVE LOVED SOMEONE WHO HIT ME LIKE THAT? WHY DID HE HAVE TO MAKE ME SUFFER?

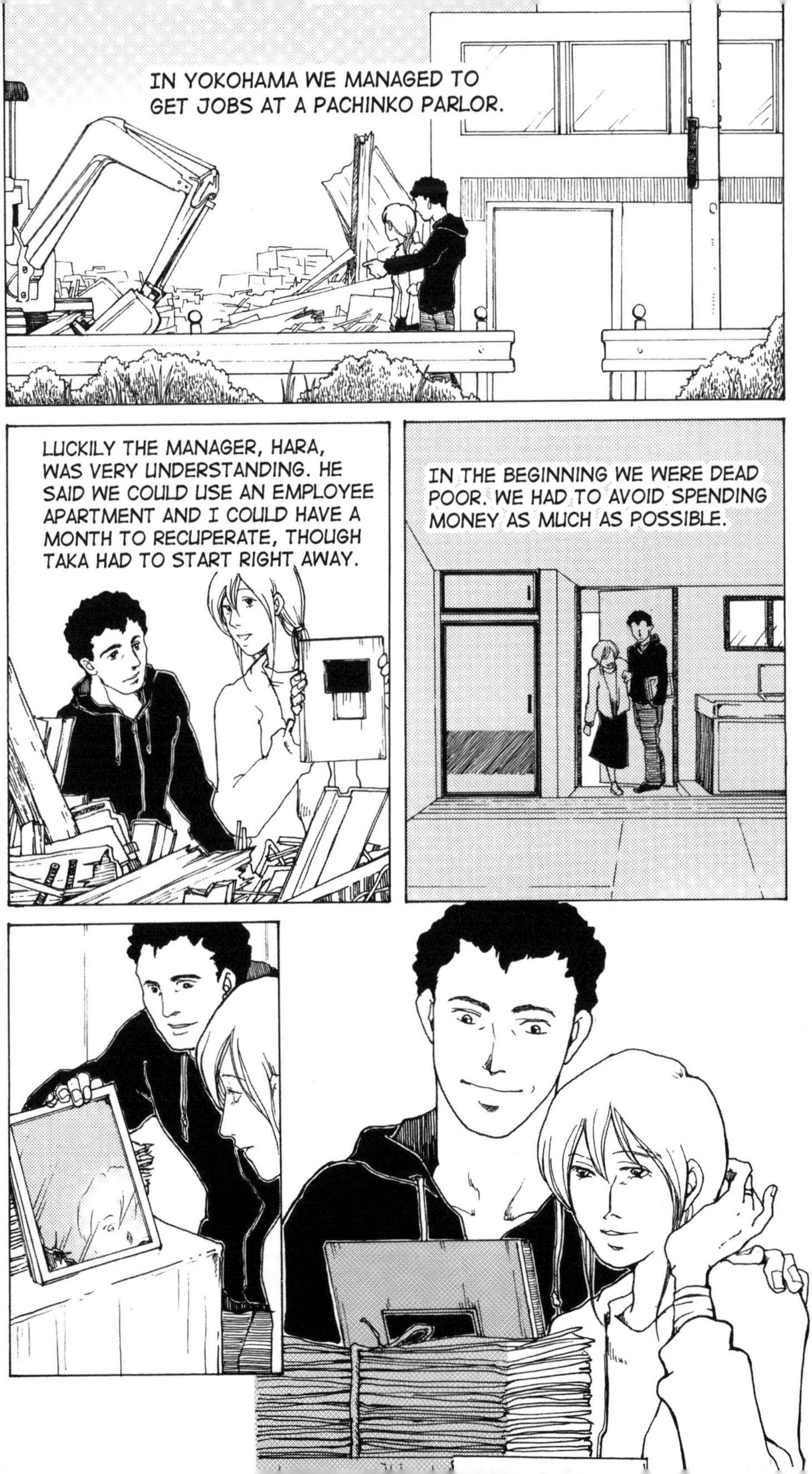
IN YOKOHAMA WE MANAGED TO GET JOBS AT A PACHINKO PARLOR.
LUCKILY THE MANAGER, HARA, WAS VERY UNDERSTANDING. HE SAID WE COULD USE AN EMPLOYEE APARTMENT AND I COULD HAVE A MONTH TO RECUPERATE, THOUGH TAKA HAD TO START RIGHT AWAY.
IN THE BEGINNING WE WERE DEAD POOR. WE HAD TO AVOID SPENDING MONEY AS MUCH AS POSSIBLE.

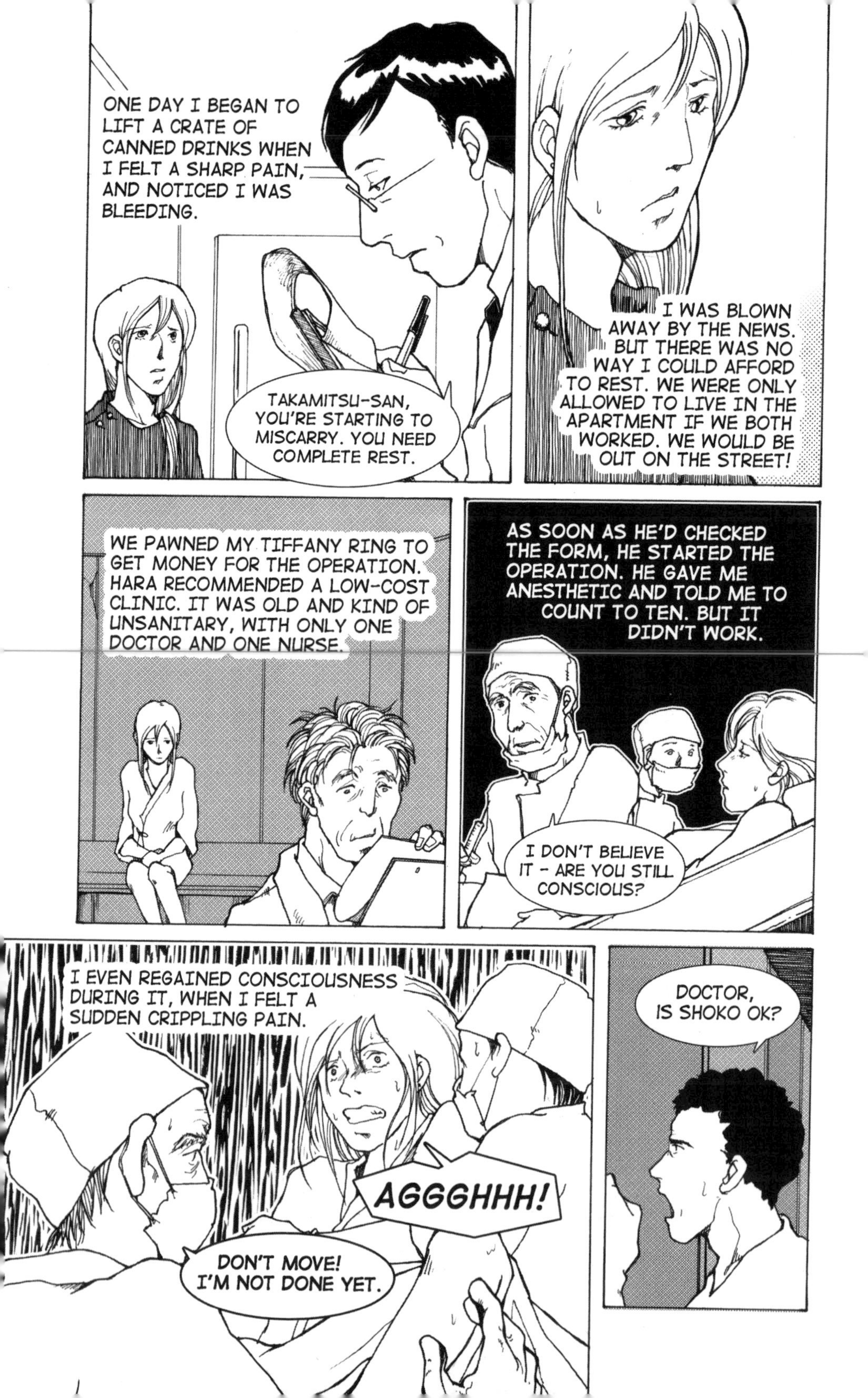
ONE DAY I BEGAN TO LIFT A CRATE OF CANNED DRINKS WHEN I FELT A SHARP PAIN, AND NOTICED I WAS BLEEDING.
TAKAMITSU-SAN, YOU'RE STARTING TO MISCARRY. YOU NEED COMPLETE REST.
I WAS BLOWN AWAY BY THE NEWS. BUT THERE WAS NO WAY I COULD AFFORD TO REST. WE WERE ONLY ALLOWED TO LIVE IN THE APARTMENT IF WE BOTH WORKED. WE WOULD BE OUT ON THE STREET!
WE PAWNED MY TIFFANY RING TO GET MONEY FOR THE OPERATION. HARA RECOMMENDED A LOW-COST CLINIC. IT WAS OLD AND KIND OF UNSANITARY, WITH ONLY ONE DOCTOR AND ONE NURSE.
AS SOON AS HE'D CHECKED THE FORM, HE STARTED THE OPERATION. HE GAVE ME ANESTHETIC AND TOLD ME TO COUNT TO TEN. BUT IT DIDN'T WORK.
I DON'T BELIEVE IT - ARE YOU STILL CONSCIOUS?
I EVEN REGAINED CONSCIOUSNESS DURING IT, WHEN I FELT A SUDDEN CRIPPLING PAIN.
AGGGHHH!
DON'T MOVE! I'M NOT DONE YET.
DOCTOR, IS SHOKO OK?

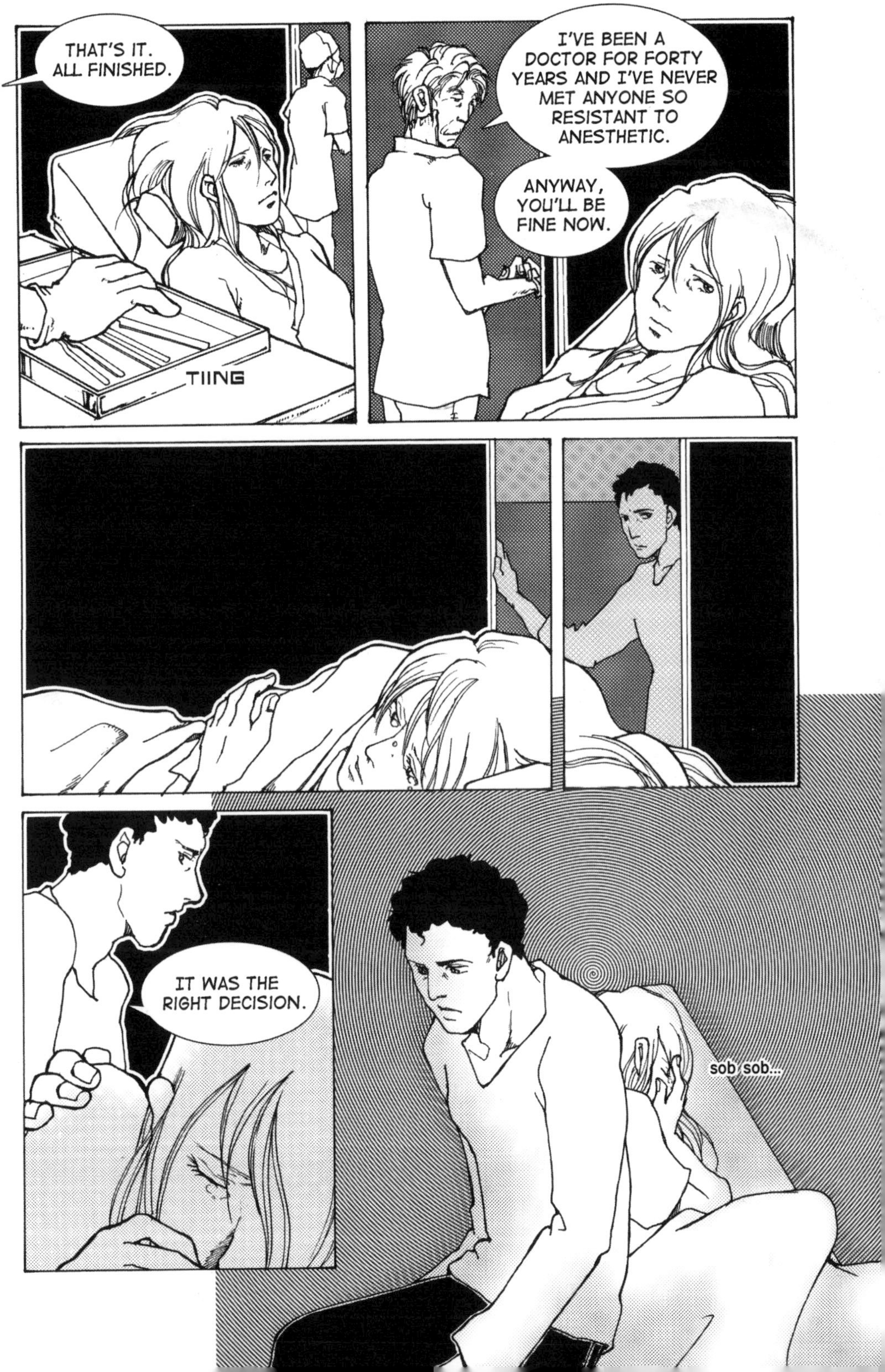
THAT'S IT. ALL FINISHED.
TIING
I'VE BEEN A DOCTOR FOR FORTY YEARS AND I'VE NEVER MET ANYONE SO RESISTANT TO ANESTHETIC.
ANYWAY, YOU'LL BE FINE NOW.
IT WAS THE RIGHT DECISION.
sob sob...

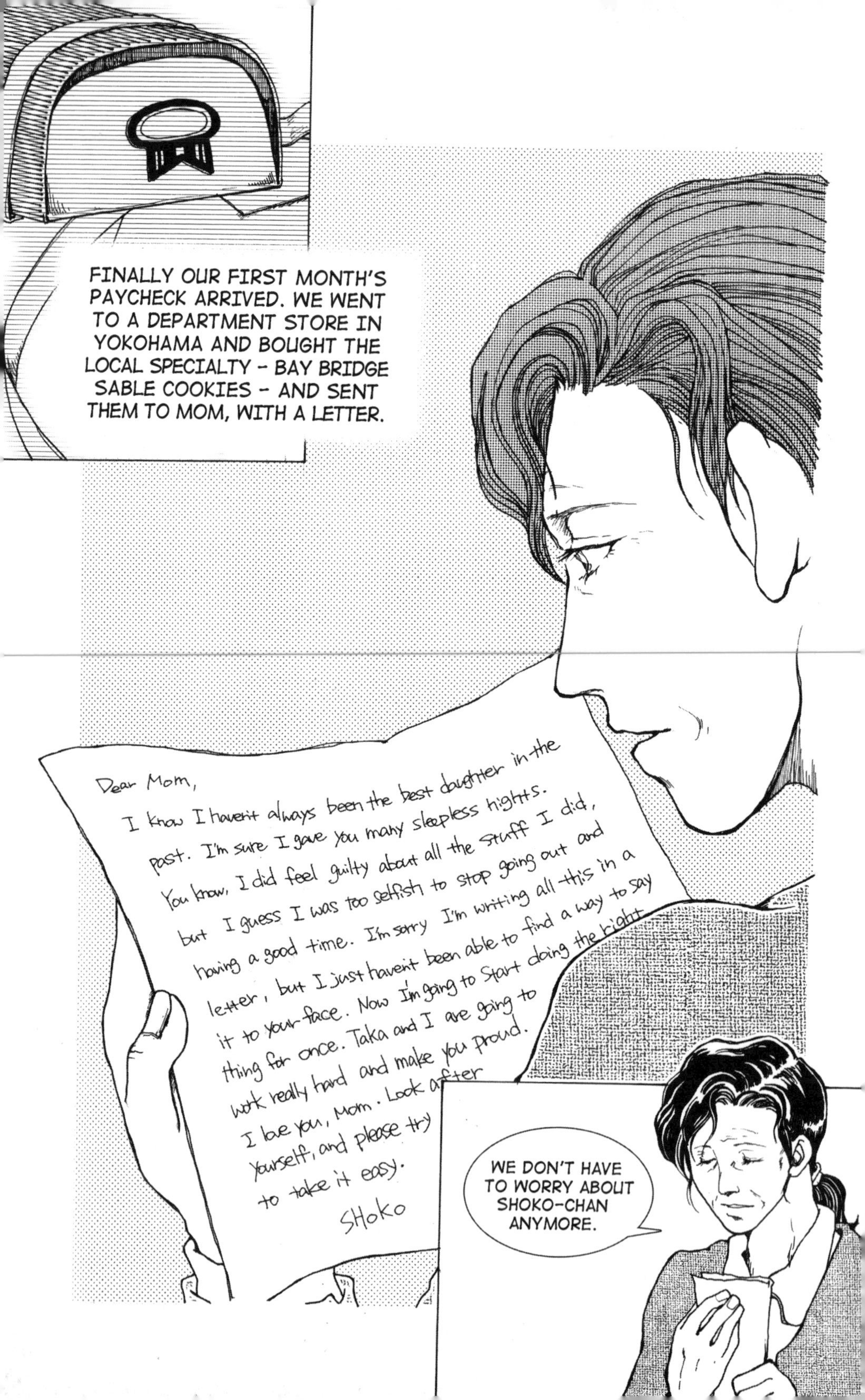
FINALLY OUR FIRST MONTH'S PAYCHECK ARRIVED. WE WENT TO A DEPARTMENT STORE IN YOKOHAMA AND BOUGHT THE LOCAL SPECIALTY - BAY BRIDGE SABLE COOKIES - AND SENT THEM TO MOM, WITH A LETTER.
Dear Mom,
I know I haven't always been the best daughter in the past. I'm sure I gave you many sleepless nights. You know, I did feel guilty about all the stuff I did, but I guess I was too selfish to stop going out and having a good time. I'm sorry I'm writing all this in a letter, but I just haven't been able to find a way to say it to your face. Now I'm going to start doing the right thing for once. Taka and I are going to work really hard and make you proud. I love you, Mom. Look after yourself, and please try to take it easy.
SHoko
WE DON'T HAVE TO WORRY ABOUT SHOKO-CHAN ANYMORE.

SHE SUFFERED A STROKE TWO DAYS LATER.

ONCE AGAIN, HARA WAS INCREDIBLY GENEROUS. HE LENT US 100,000 YEN OF HIS OWN MONEY, AND GAVE ME AS LONG AS I NEEDED TO BE WITH MY MOTHER.

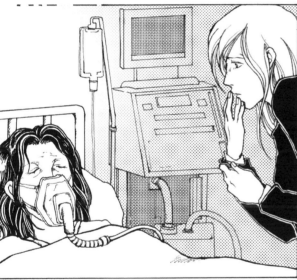

IS THERE ANYTHING WE CAN DO? WE'LL PAY ANYTHING IT TAKES, BUT HELP MY MOTHER!

A VEIN HAS RUPTURED IN THE REAR PART OF HER BRAIN THAT CAN'T BE OPERATED ON.

I'M AFRAID THERE IS NOTHING WE CAN DO.

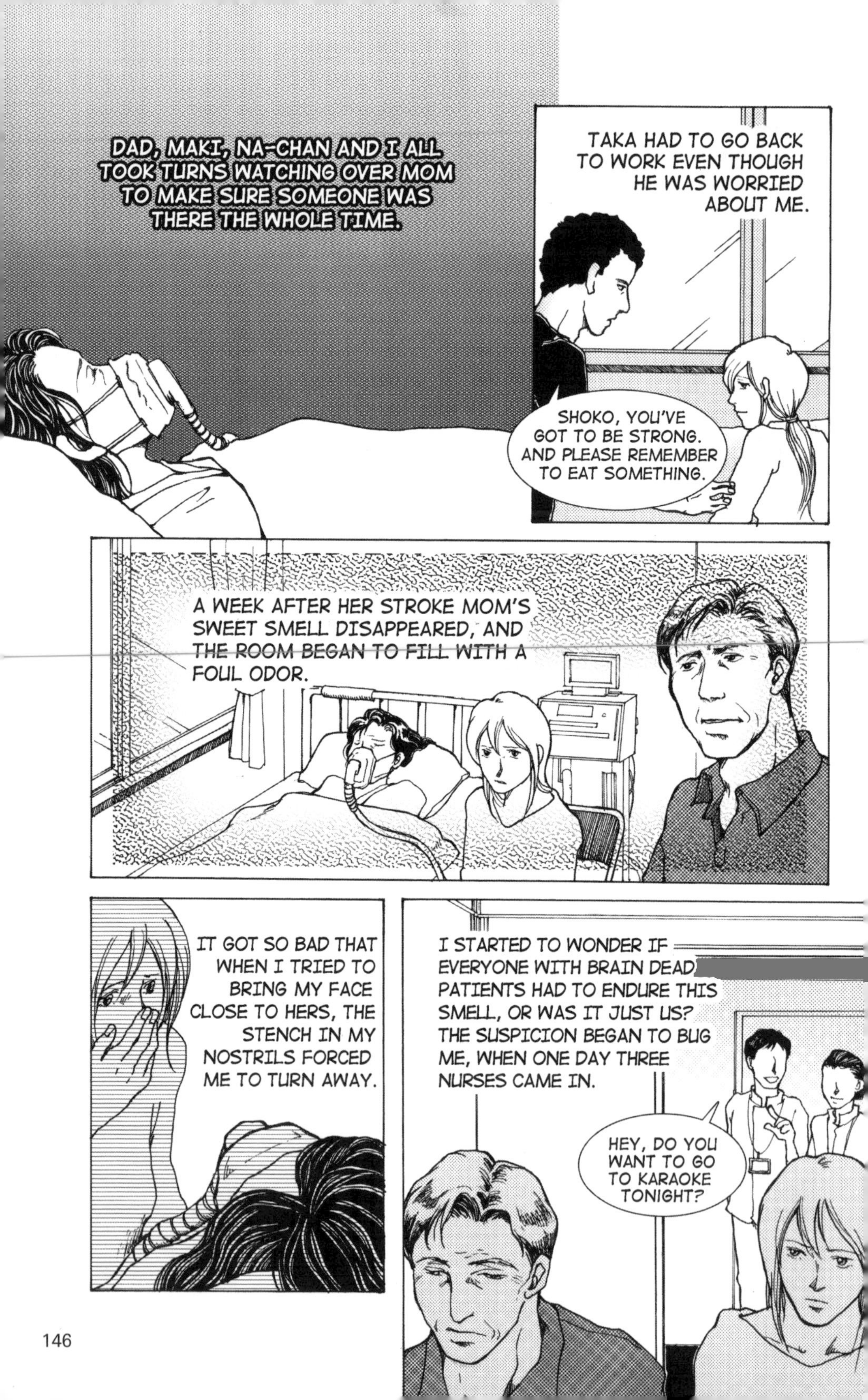
DAD, MAKI, NA-CHAN AND I ALL TOOK TURNS WATCHING OVER MOM TO MAKE SURE SOMEONE WAS THERE THE WHOLE TIME.
TAKA HAD TO GO BACK TO WORK EVEN THOUGH HE WAS WORRIED ABOUT ME.
SHOKO, YOU'VE GOT TO BE STRONG. AND PLEASE REMEMBER TO EAT SOMETHING.
A WEEK AFTER HER STROKE MOM'S SWEET SMELL DISAPPEARED, AND THE ROOM BEGAN TO FILL WITH A FOUL ODOR.
IT GOT SO BAD THAT WHEN I TRIED TO BRING MY FACE CLOSE TO HERS, THE STENCH IN MY NOSTRILS FORCED ME TO TURN AWAY.
I STARTED TO WONDER IF EVERYONE WITH BRAIN DEAD PATIENTS HAD TO ENDURE THIS SMELL, OR WAS IT JUST US? THE SUSPICION BEGAN TO BUG ME, WHEN ONE DAY THREE NURSES CAME IN.
HEY, DO YOU WANT TO GO TO KARAOKE TONIGHT?

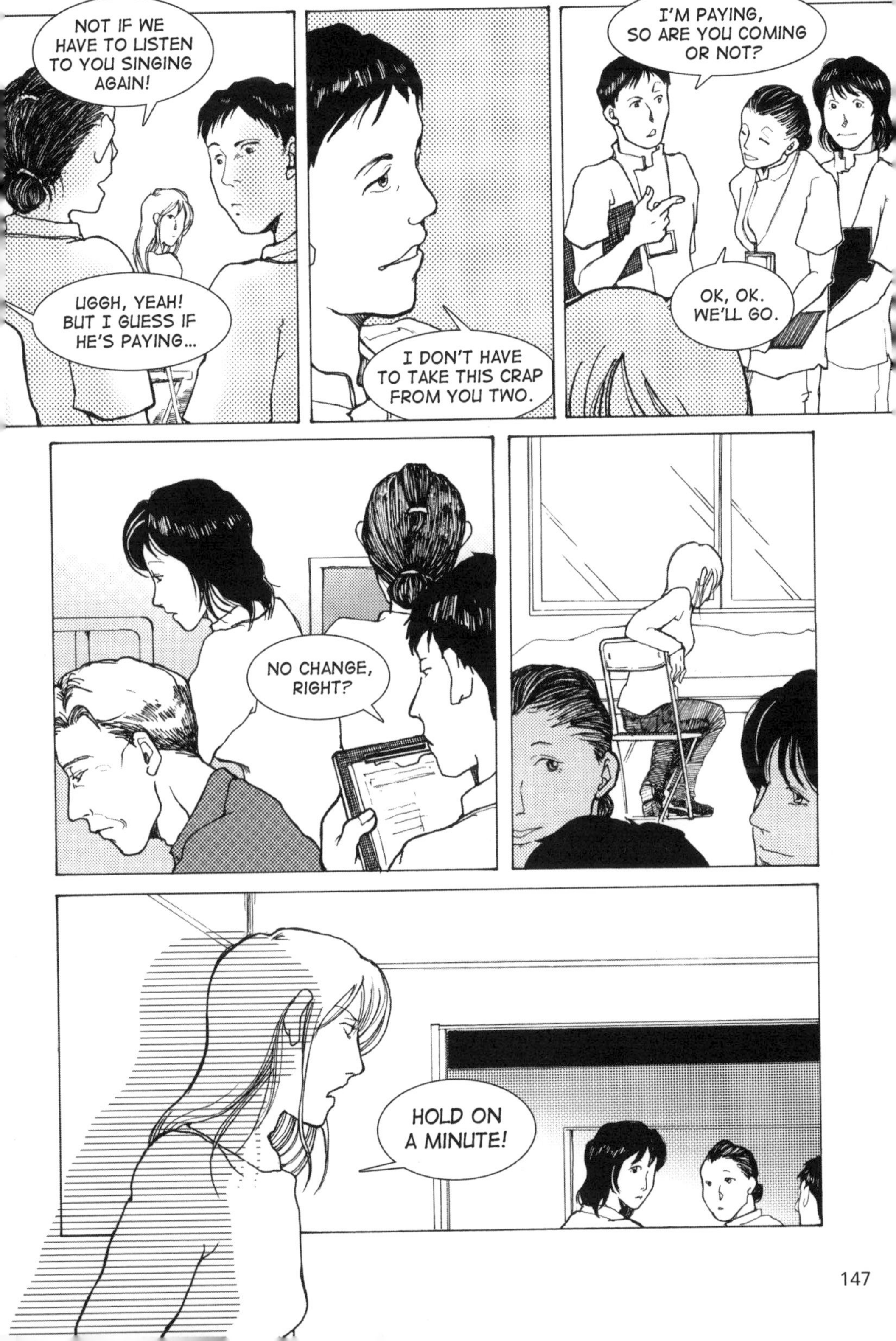
NOT IF WE HAVE TO LISTEN TO YOU SINGING AGAIN!
UGGH, YEAH! BUT I GUESS IF HE'S PAYING...
I DON'T HAVE TO TAKE THIS CRAP FROM YOU TWO.
I'M PAYING, SO ARE YOU COMING OR NOT?
OK, OK. WE'LL GO.
NO CHANGE, RIGHT?
HOLD ON A MINUTE!

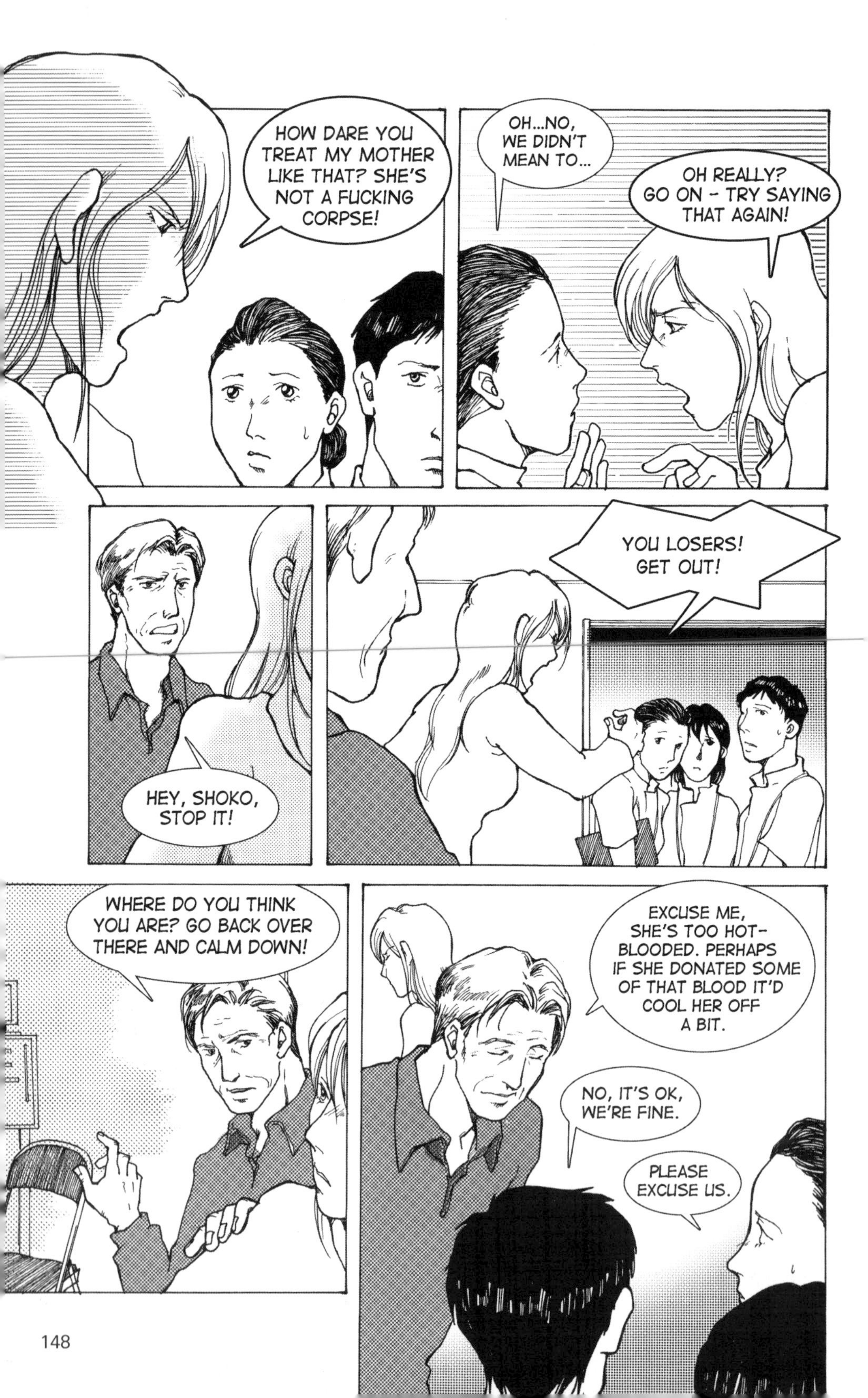
HOW DARE YOU TREAT MY MOTHER LIKE THAT? SHE'S NOT A FUCKING CORPSE!
OH...NO, WE DIDN'T MEAN TO...
OH REALLY? GO ON - TRY SAYING THAT AGAIN!
HEY, SHOKO, STOP IT!
YOU LOSERS! GET OUT!
WHERE DO YOU THINK YOU ARE? GO BACK OVER THERE AND CALM DOWN!
EXCUSE ME, SHE'S TOO HOT-BLOODED. PERHAPS IF SHE DONATED SOME OF THAT BLOOD IT'D COOL HER OFF A BIT.
NO, IT'S OK, WE'RE FINE.
PLEASE EXCUSE US.

I UNDERSTAND HOW YOU FEEL, BUT REMEMBER WHERE YOU ARE! WHY DO YOU LET PEOPLE LIKE THAT GET TO YOU?

YOU'RE RIGHT...

BUT A FEW DAYS LATER I NOTICED THAT MOM'S GROIN AREA WAS BRIGHT RED FROM BEDSORES.

EXCUSE ME, DO YOU HAVE ANY OINTMENT YOU COULD PUT ON THAT?

OINTMENT? SHE DOESN'T NEED IT. TENDO-SAN IS BRAIN DEAD, SO SHE CAN'T FEEL ANY PAIN.

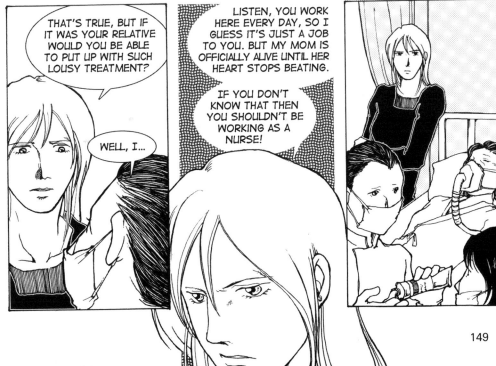

THAT'S TRUE, BUT IF IT WAS YOUR RELATIVE WOULD YOU BE ABLE TO PUT UP WITH SUCH LOUSY TREATMENT?

WELL, I...

LISTEN, YOU WORK HERE EVERY DAY, SO I GUESS IT'S JUST A JOB TO YOU. BUT MY MOM IS OFFICIALLY ALIVE UNTIL HER HEART STOPS BEATING.

IF YOU DON'T KNOW THAT THEN YOU SHOULDN'T BE WORKING AS A NURSE!

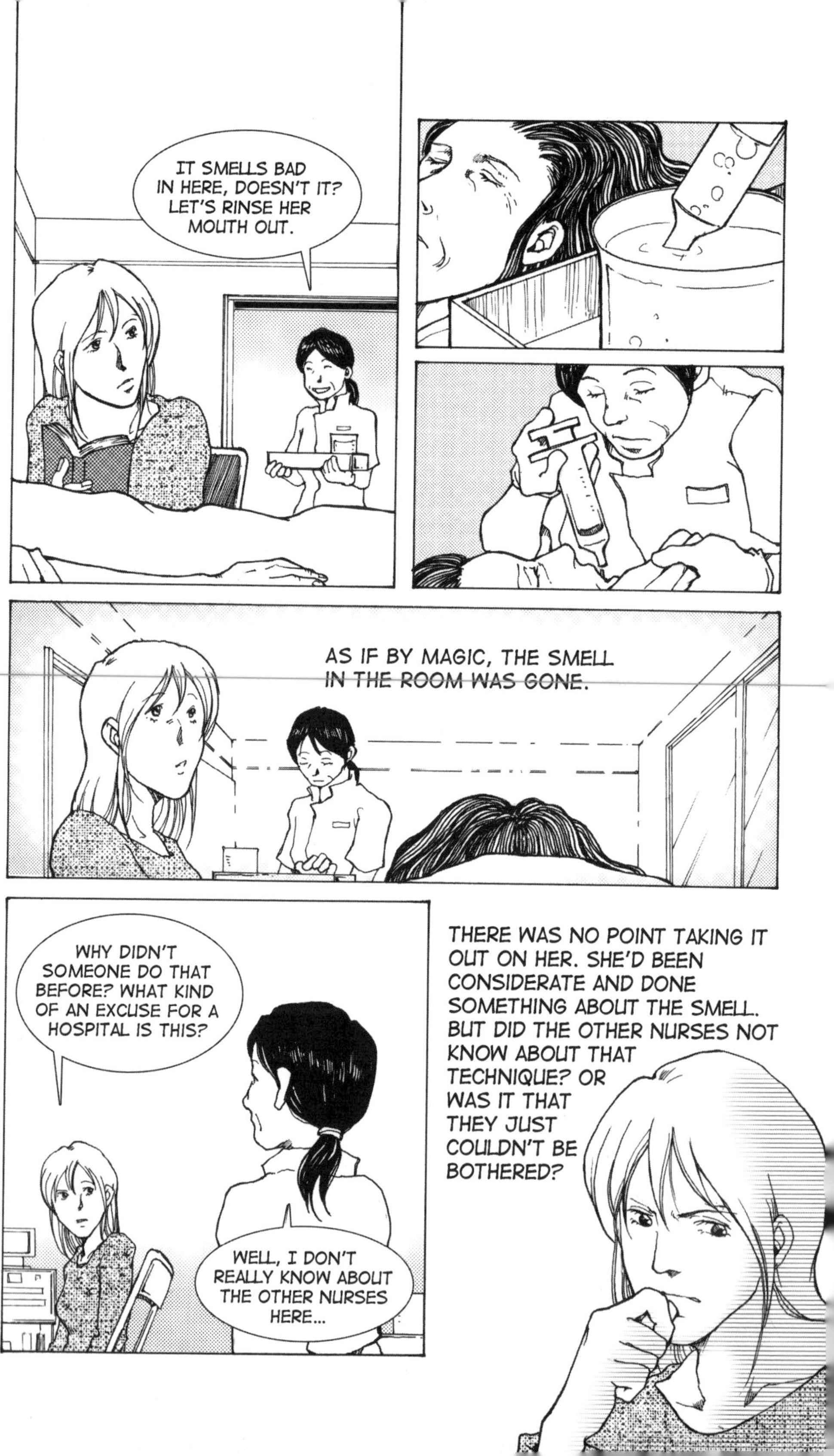
IT SMELLS BAD IN HERE, DOESN'T IT? LET'S RINSE HER MOUTH OUT.
AS IF BY MAGIC, THE SMELL IN THE ROOM WAS GONE.
WHY DIDN'T SOMEONE DO THAT BEFORE? WHAT KIND OF AN EXCUSE FOR A HOSPITAL IS THIS?
WELL, I DON'T REALLY KNOW ABOUT THE OTHER NURSES HERE...
THERE WAS NO POINT TAKING IT OUT ON HER. SHE'D BEEN CONSIDERATE AND DONE SOMETHING ABOUT THE SMELL. BUT DID THE OTHER NURSES NOT KNOW ABOUT THAT TECHNIQUE? OR WAS IT THAT THEY JUST COULDN'T BE BOTHERED?

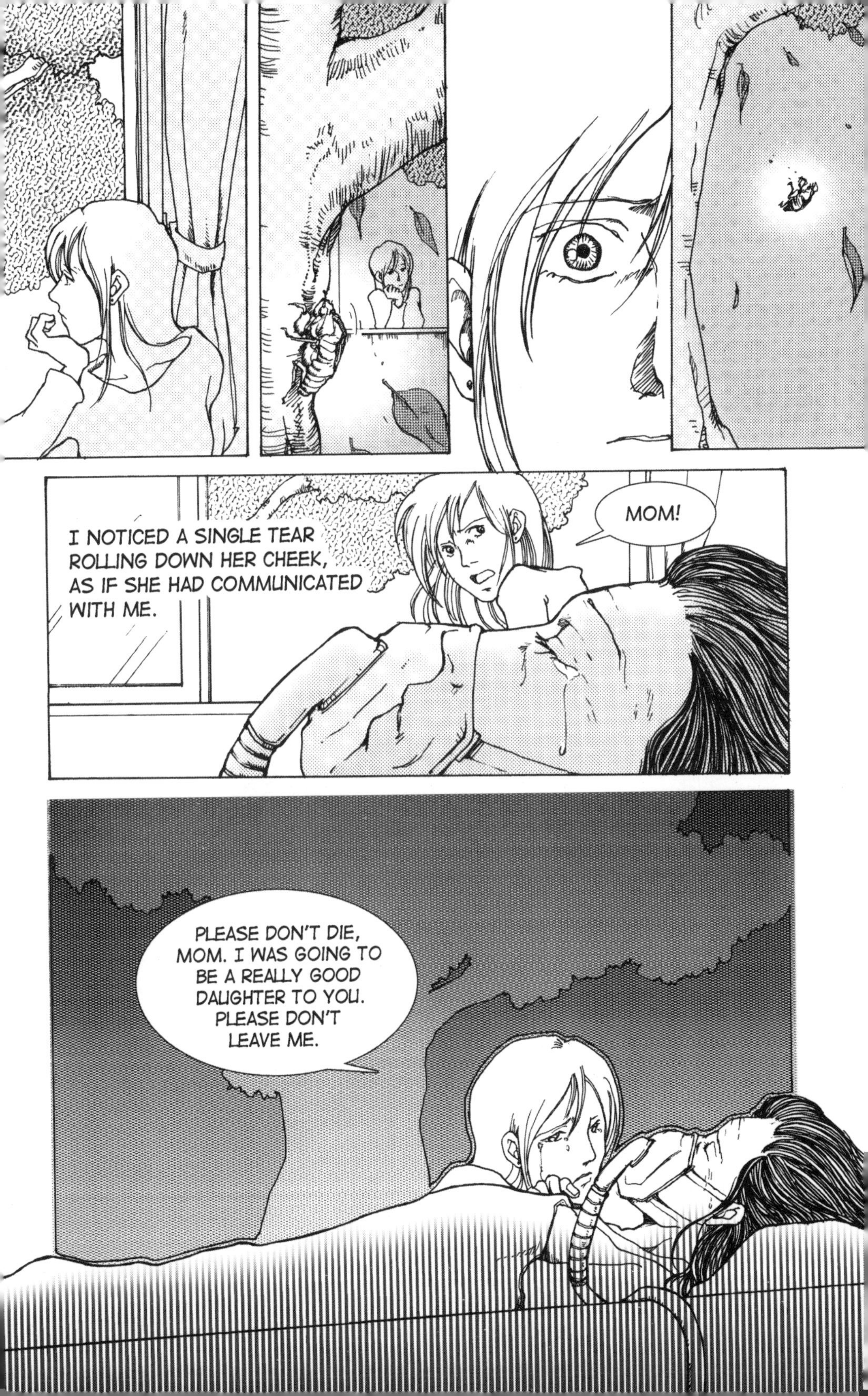
I NOTICED A SINGLE TEAR ROLLING DOWN HER CHEEK, AS IF SHE HAD COMMUNICATED WITH ME.
MOM!
PLEASE DON'T DIE, MOM. I WAS GOING TO BE A REALLY GOOD DAUGHTER TO YOU. PLEASE DON'T LEAVE ME.

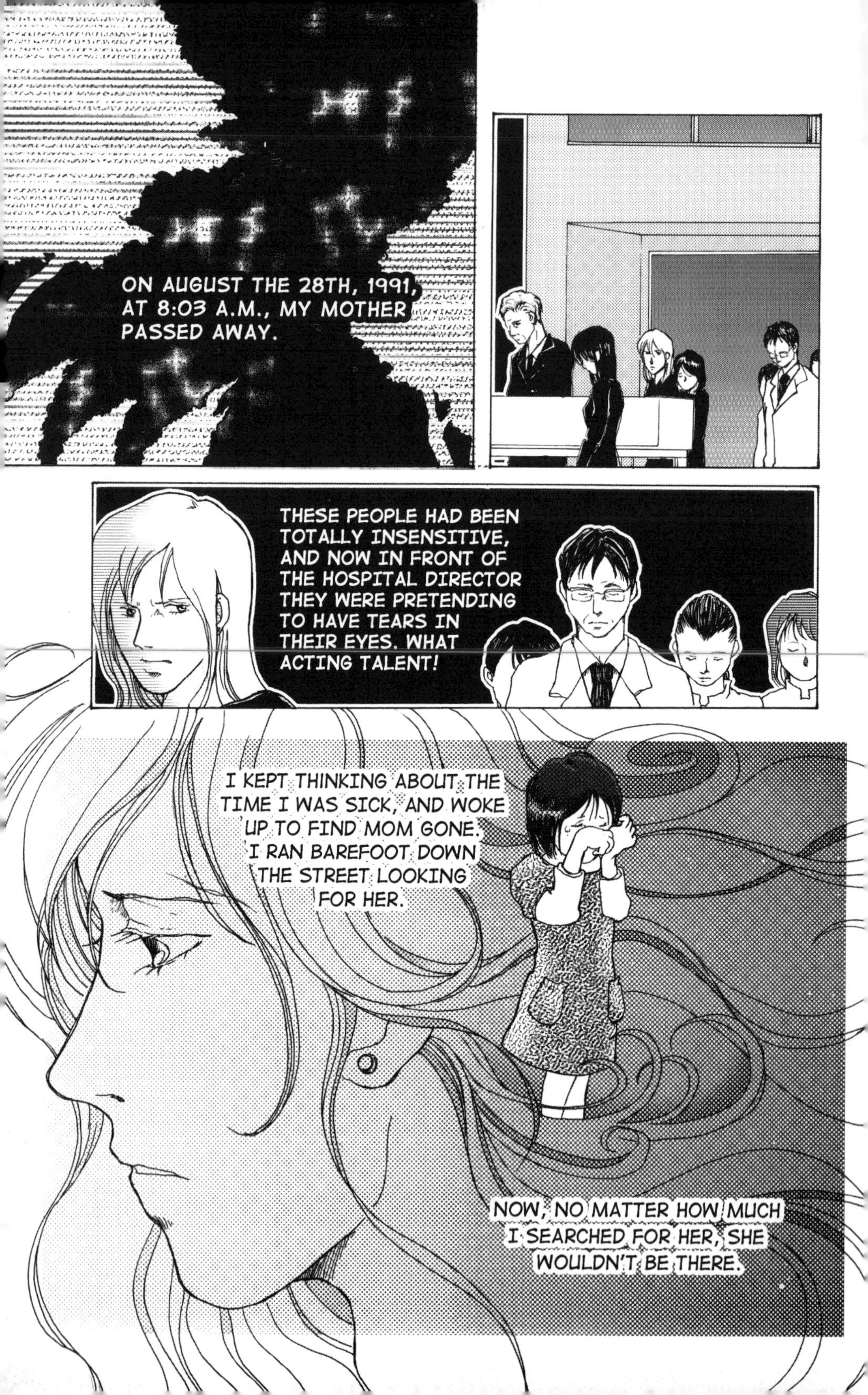
ON AUGUST THE 28TH, 1991, AT 8:03 A.M., MY MOTHER PASSED AWAY.
THESE PEOPLE HAD BEEN TOTALLY INSENSITIVE, AND NOW IN FRONT OF THE HOSPITAL DIRECTOR THEY WERE PRETENDING TO HAVE TEARS IN THEIR EYES. WHAT ACTING TALENT!
I KEPT THINKING ABOUT THE TIME I WAS SICK, AND WOKE UP TO FIND MOM GONE. I RAN BAREFOOT DOWN THE STREET LOOKING FOR HER.
NOW, NO MATTER HOW MUCH I SEARCHED FOR HER, SHE WOULDN'T BE THERE.

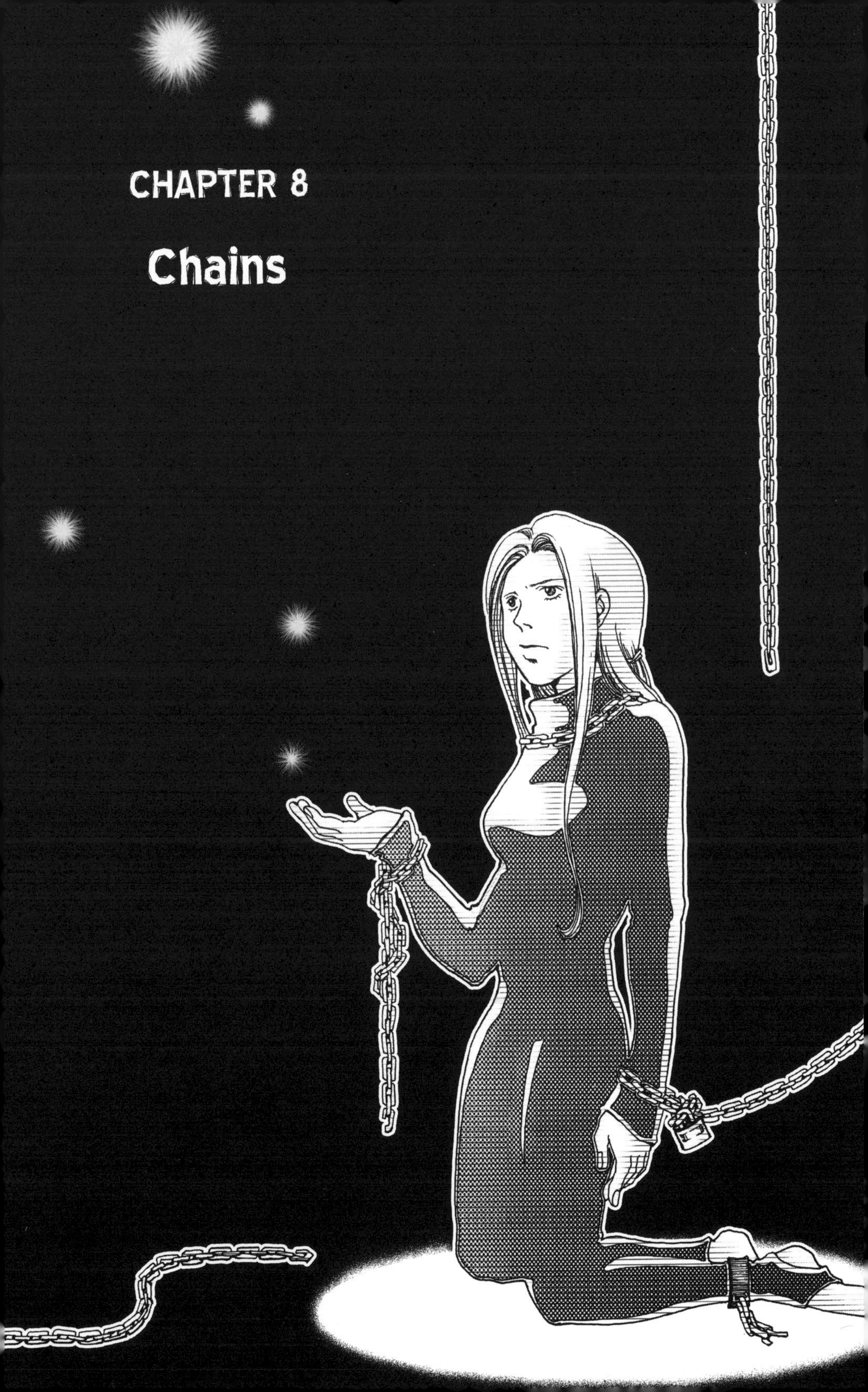
CHAPTER 8
Chains

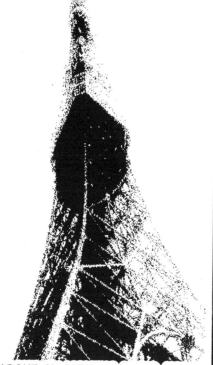

BUT AFTER A SHORT TIME HE HAD TO RETURN TO HIS HOMETOWN OF KUMAMOTO, IN SOUTHERN JAPAN. OUR CLOSE FRIEND WAS GONE.

ABOUT SIX MONTHS AFTER, HARA HAD SOME DISAGREEMENT WITH THE PACHINKO PARLOR OWNER, AND DECIDED TO GO TO TOKYO INSTEAD. BY NOW, WE LOVED HIM LIKE A BROTHER, SO WE WENT WITH HIM.

WE REALIZED WE HAD NO ONE IN TOKYO TO DEPEND ON, AND NOWHERE ELSE TO GO.

I THREW MYSELF INTO MY WORK AT A BAR IN SHINJUKU. BUT I WAS OFTEN SHORT OF MONEY BECAUSE MAKI AND ITCHAN BORROWED FROM ME EVERY MONTH.

CLOSED FOR BUSINESS

I WAS TWENTY-FOUR THEN. IT WAS THE BEGINNING OF THE 1990'S AND SOON THE ECONOMIC BUBBLE OF THE 80'S BURST. BUSINESS AT THE BAR SLOWED DOWN A LOT - CUSTOMERS JUST WEREN'T SPENDING LIKE THEY USED TO.

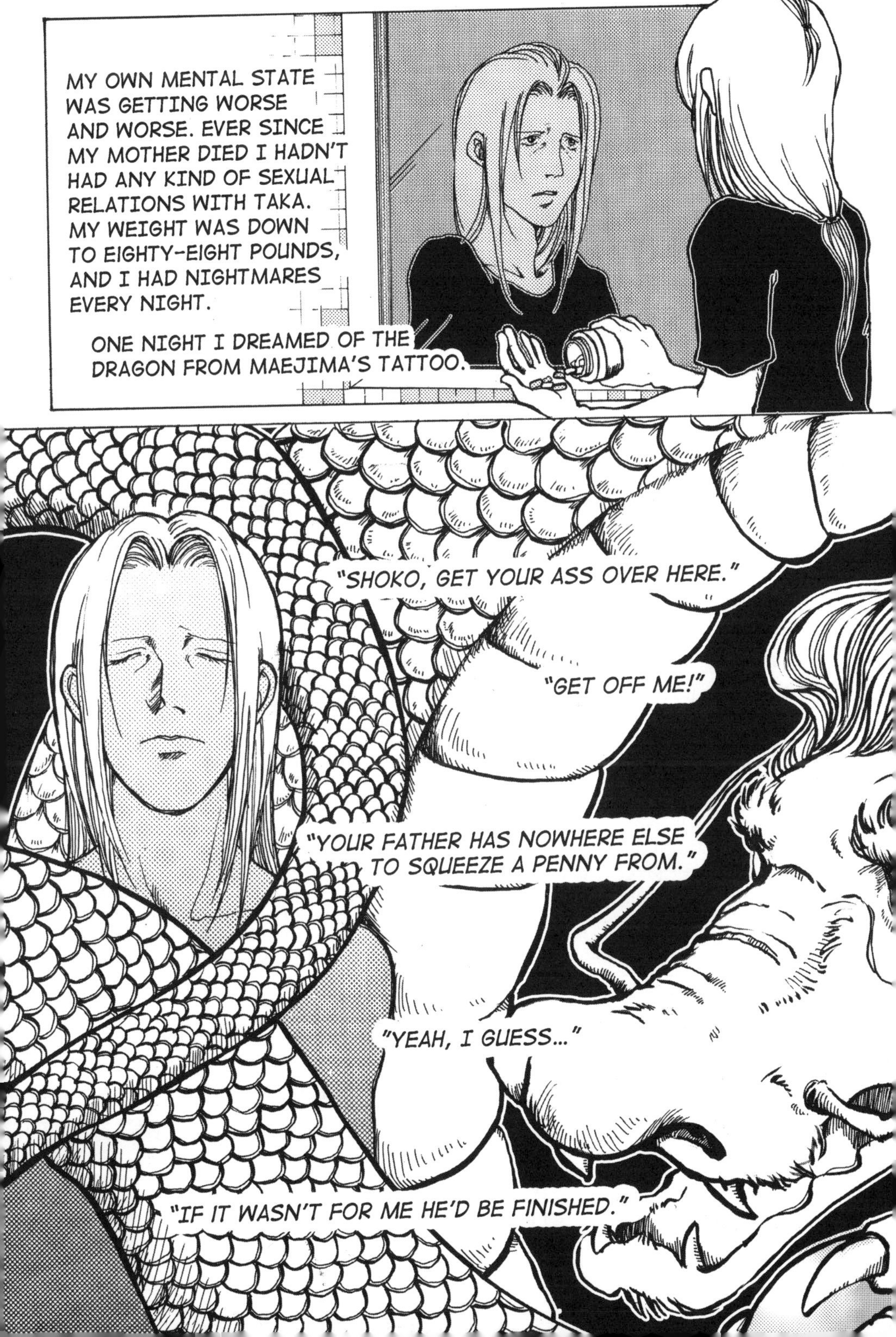
MY OWN MENTAL STATE WAS GETTING WORSE AND WORSE. EVER SINCE MY MOTHER DIED I HADN'T HAD ANY KIND OF SEXUAL RELATIONS WITH TAKA. MY WEIGHT WAS DOWN TO EIGHTY-EIGHT POUNDS, AND I HAD NIGHTMARES EVERY NIGHT.
ONE NIGHT I DREAMED OF THE DRAGON FROM MAEJIMA'S TATTOO.
"SHOKO, GET YOUR ASS OVER HERE."
"GET OFF ME!"
"YOUR FATHER HAS NOWHERE ELSE TO SQUEEZE A PENNY FROM."
"YEAH, I GUESS..."
"IF IT WASN'T FOR ME HE'D BE FINISHED."

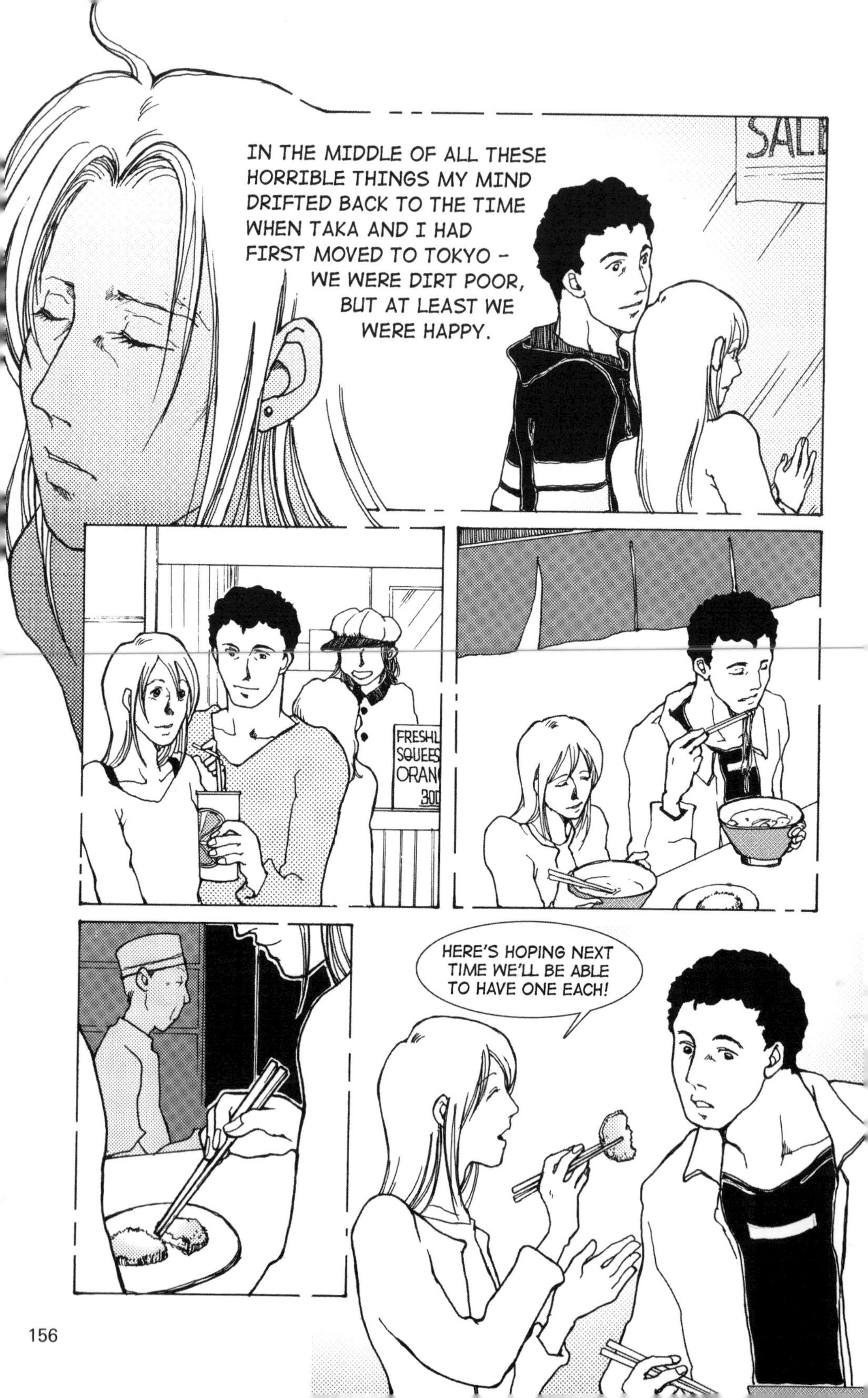
IN THE MIDDLE OF ALL THESE HORRIBLE THINGS MY MIND DRIFTED BACK TO THE TIME WHEN TAKA AND I HAD FIRST MOVED TO TOKYO - WE WERE DIRT POOR, BUT AT LEAST WE WERE HAPPY.
SALE
FRESHL SQUEES ORAN 300
HERE'S HOPING NEXT TIME WE'LL BE ABLE TO HAVE ONE EACH!

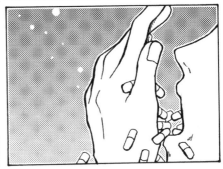

I'D HAD A FEVER FOR A WEEK AND WAS DIAGNOSED WITH A KIDNEY PROBLEM. BUT WE COULDN'T AFFORD THE COST OF DIALYSIS. TAKA WAS VERY KIND TO ME, BUT AFTER I SAW HIM OFF TO WORK ALL I WANTED TO DO WAS SLEEP, TO SEE NOTHING, TO HEAR NOTHING.

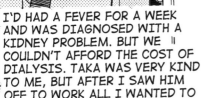

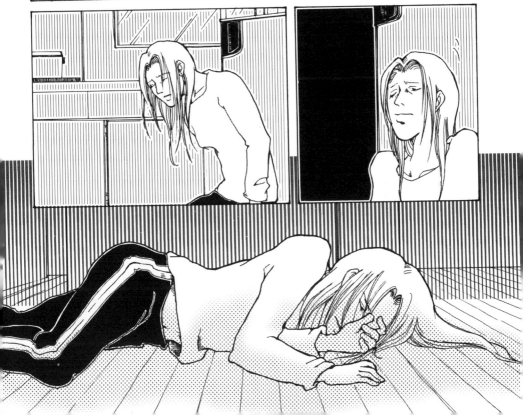

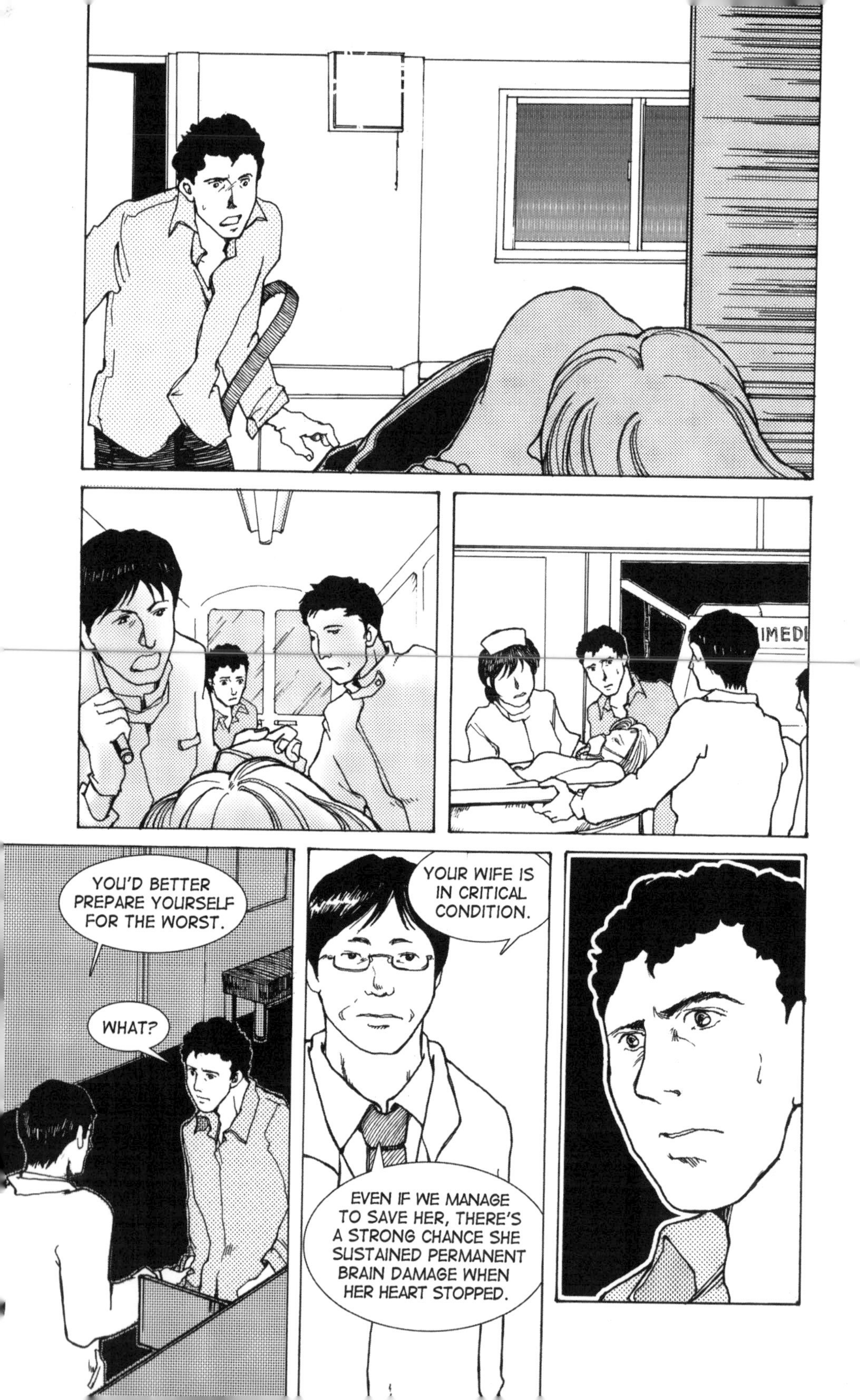
IMEDI
YOU'D BETTER PREPARE YOURSELF FOR THE WORST.
WHAT?
YOUR WIFE IS IN CRITICAL CONDITION.
EVEN IF WE MANAGE TO SAVE HER, THERE'S A STRONG CHANCE SHE SUSTAINED PERMANENT BRAIN DAMAGE WHEN HER HEART STOPPED.

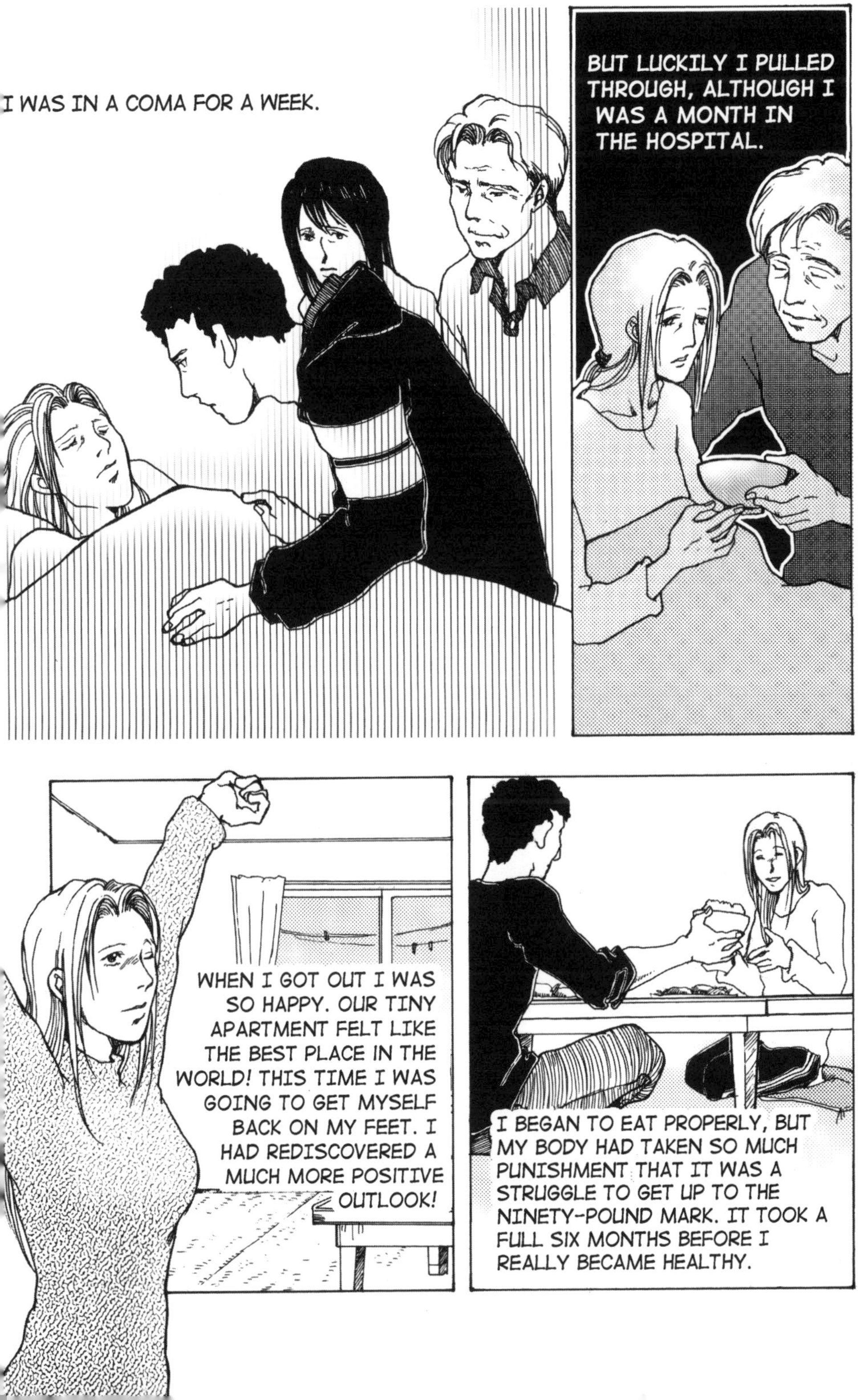
I WAS IN A COMA FOR A WEEK.
BUT LUCKILY I PULLED THROUGH, ALTHOUGH I WAS A MONTH IN THE HOSPITAL.
WHEN I GOT OUT I WAS SO HAPPY. OUR TINY APARTMENT FELT LIKE THE BEST PLACE IN THE WORLD! THIS TIME I WAS GOING TO GET MYSELF BACK ON MY FEET. I HAD REDISCOVERED A MUCH MORE POSITIVE OUTLOOK!
I BEGAN TO EAT PROPERLY, BUT MY BODY HAD TAKEN SO MUCH PUNISHMENT THAT IT WAS A STRUGGLE TO GET UP TO THE NINETY-POUND MARK. IT TOOK A FULL SIX MONTHS BEFORE I REALLY BECAME HEALTHY.

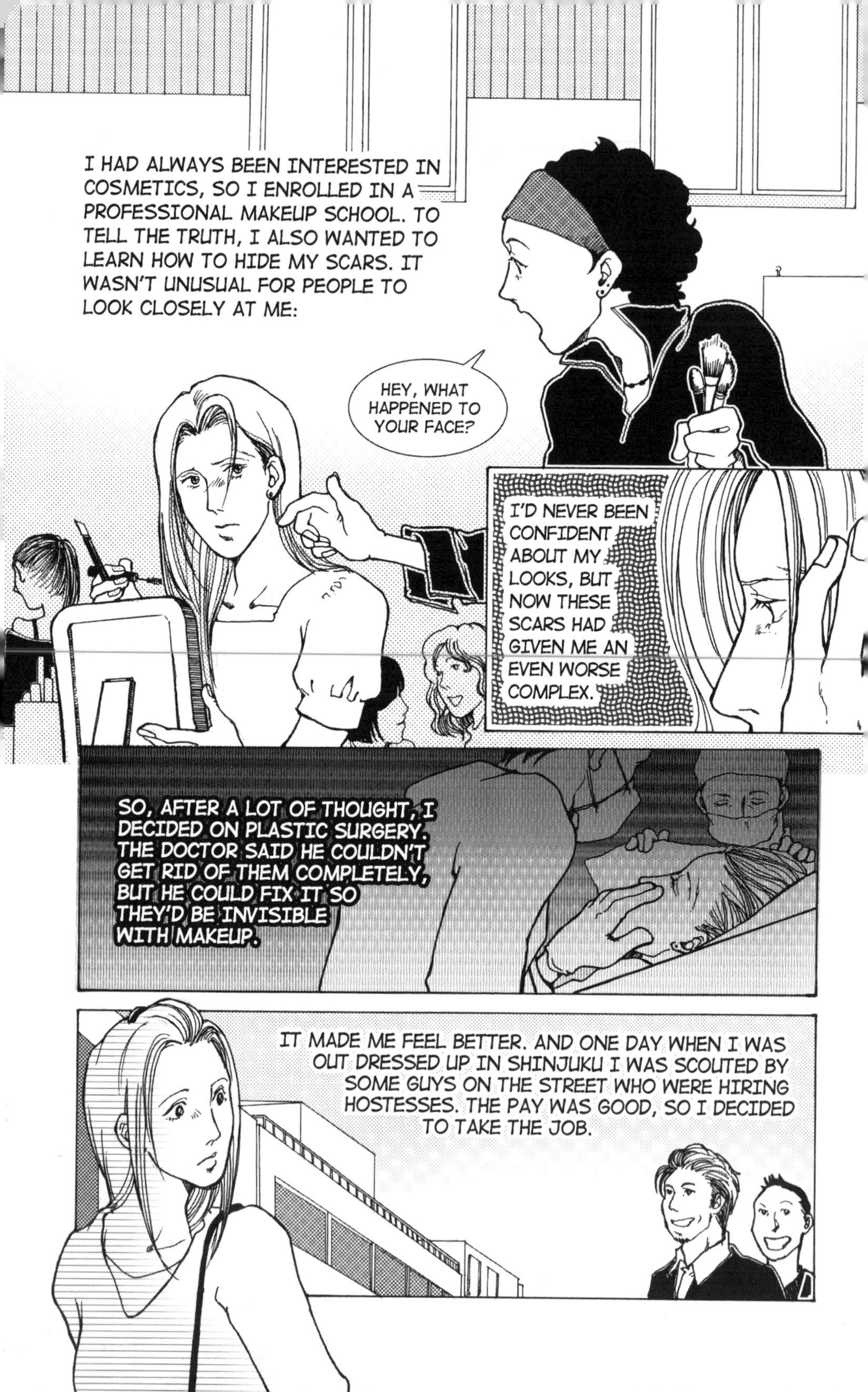
I HAD ALWAYS BEEN INTERESTED IN COSMETICS, SO I ENROLLED IN A PROFESSIONAL MAKEUP SCHOOL. TO TELL THE TRUTH, I ALSO WANTED TO LEARN HOW TO HIDE MY SCARS. IT WASN'T UNUSUAL FOR PEOPLE TO LOOK CLOSELY AT ME:
HEY, WHAT HAPPENED TO YOUR FACE?
I'D NEVER BEEN CONFIDENT ABOUT MY LOOKS, BUT NOW THESE SCARS HAD GIVEN ME AN EVEN WORSE COMPLEX.
SO, AFTER A LOT OF THOUGHT, I DECIDED ON PLASTIC SURGERY. THE DOCTOR SAID HE COULDN'T GET RID OF THEM COMPLETELY, BUT HE COULD FIX IT SO THEY'D BE INVISIBLE WITH MAKEUP.
IT MADE ME FEEL BETTER. AND ONE DAY WHEN I WAS OUT DRESSED UP IN SHINJUKU I WAS SCOUTED BY SOME GUYS ON THE STREET WHO WERE HIRING HOSTESSES. THE PAY WAS GOOD, SO I DECIDED TO TAKE THE JOB.

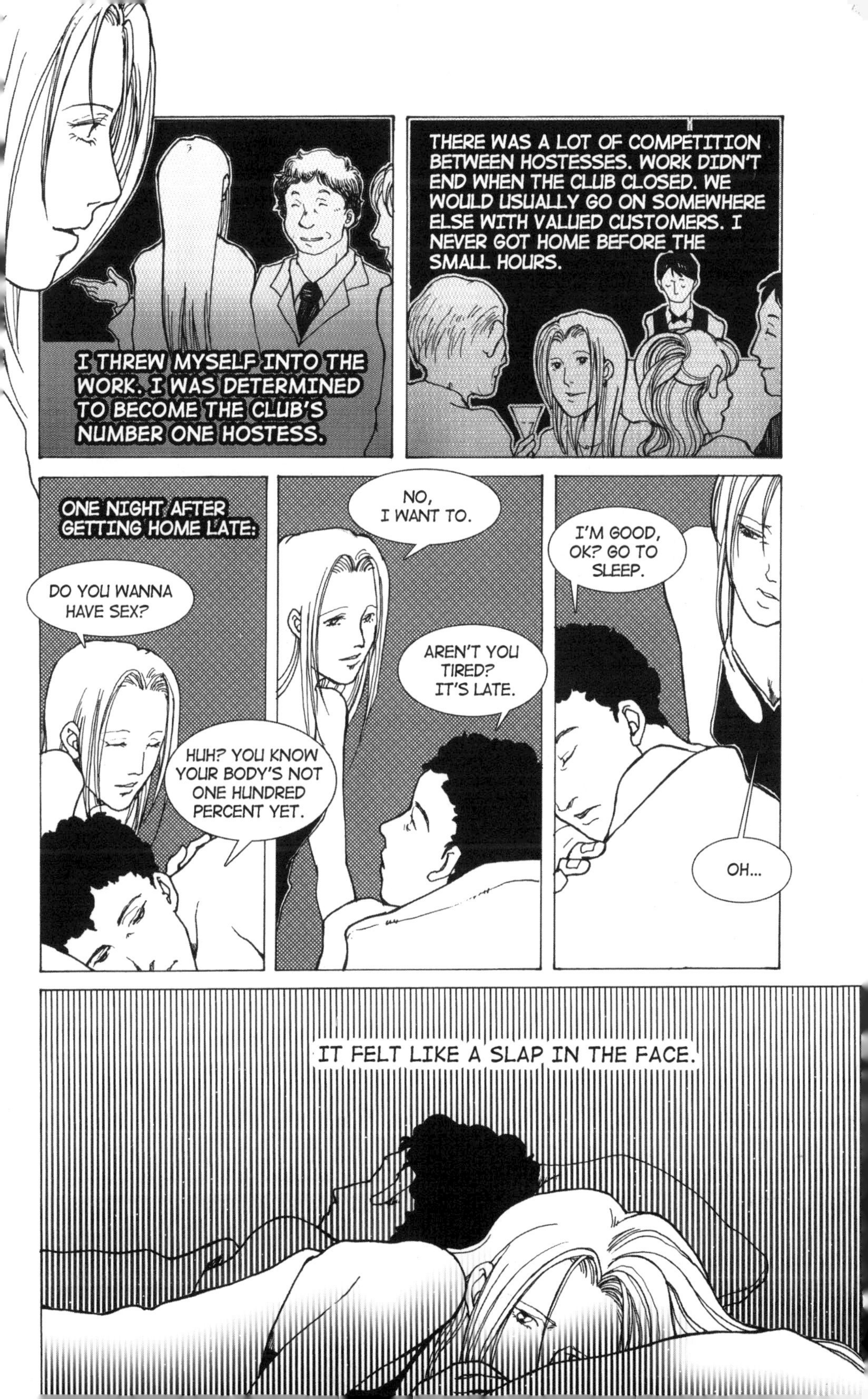
I THREW MYSELF INTO THE WORK. I WAS DETERMINED TO BECOME THE CLUB'S NUMBER ONE HOSTESS.
THERE WAS A LOT OF COMPETITION BETWEEN HOSTESSES. WORK DIDN'T END WHEN THE CLUB CLOSED. WE WOULD USUALLY GO ON SOMEWHERE ELSE WITH VALUED CUSTOMERS. I NEVER GOT HOME BEFORE THE SMALL HOURS.
ONE NIGHT AFTER GETTING HOME LATE:
DO YOU WANNA HAVE SEX?
HUH? YOU KNOW YOUR BODY'S NOT ONE HUNDRED PERCENT YET.
NO, I WANT TO.
AREN'T YOU TIRED? IT'S LATE.
I'M GOOD, OK? GO TO SLEEP.
OH...
IT FELT LIKE A SLAP IN THE FACE.

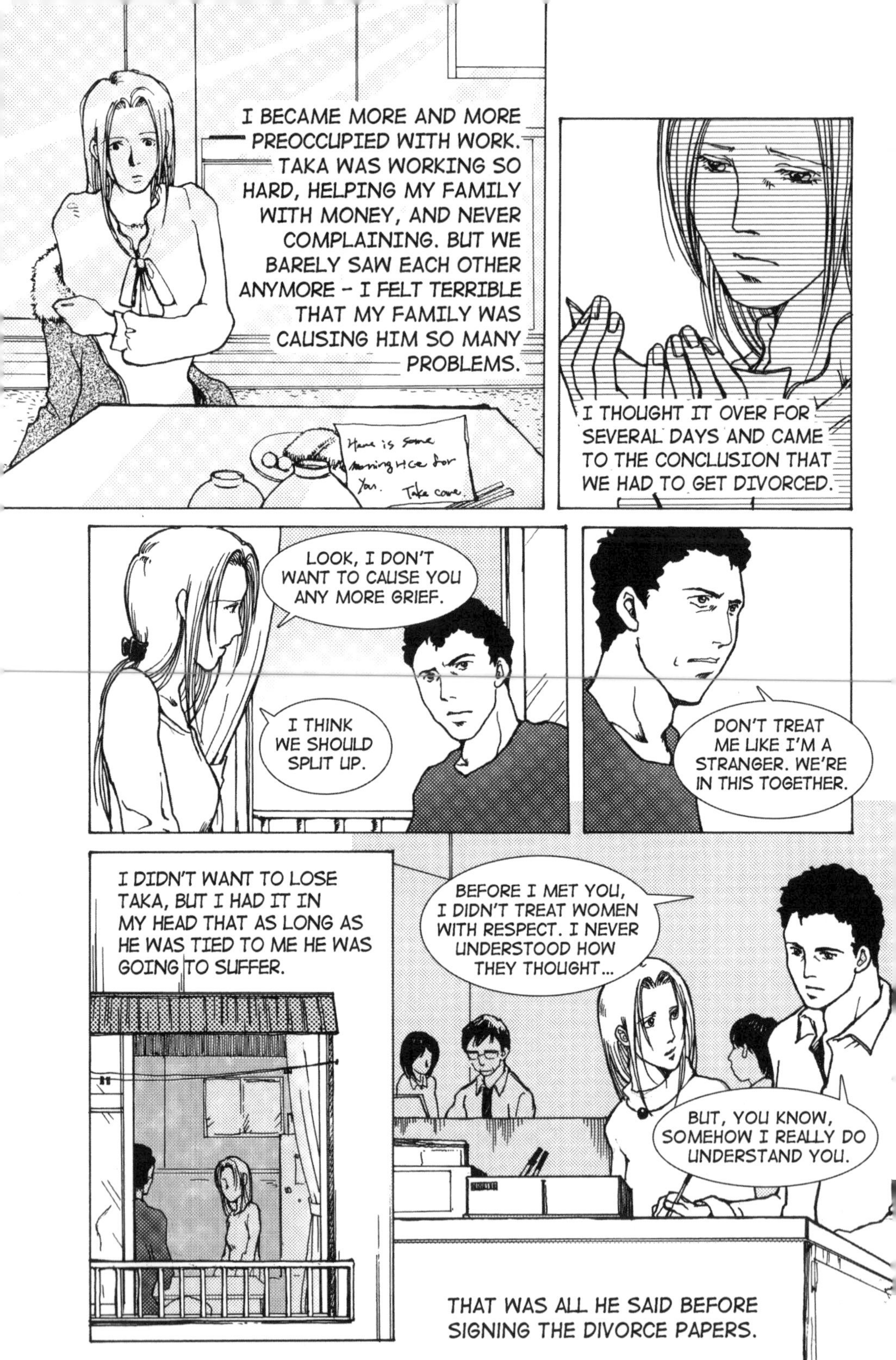
I BECAME MORE AND MORE PREOCCUPIED WITH WORK. TAKA WAS WORKING SO HARD, HELPING MY FAMILY WITH MONEY, AND NEVER COMPLAINING. BUT WE BARELY SAW EACH OTHER ANYMORE – I FELT TERRIBLE THAT MY FAMILY WAS CAUSING HIM SO MANY PROBLEMS.
Here is some morning rice for You. Take care
I THOUGHT IT OVER FOR SEVERAL DAYS AND CAME TO THE CONCLUSION THAT WE HAD TO GET DIVORCED.
LOOK, I DON'T WANT TO CAUSE YOU ANY MORE GRIEF.
I THINK WE SHOULD SPLIT UP.
DON'T TREAT ME LIKE I'M A STRANGER. WE'RE IN THIS TOGETHER.
I DIDN'T WANT TO LOSE TAKA, BUT I HAD IT IN MY HEAD THAT AS LONG AS HE WAS TIED TO ME HE WAS GOING TO SUFFER.
BEFORE I MET YOU, I DIDN'T TREAT WOMEN WITH RESPECT. I NEVER UNDERSTOOD HOW THEY THOUGHT...
BUT, YOU KNOW, SOMEHOW I REALLY DO UNDERSTAND YOU.
THAT WAS ALL HE SAID BEFORE SIGNING THE DIVORCE PAPERS.

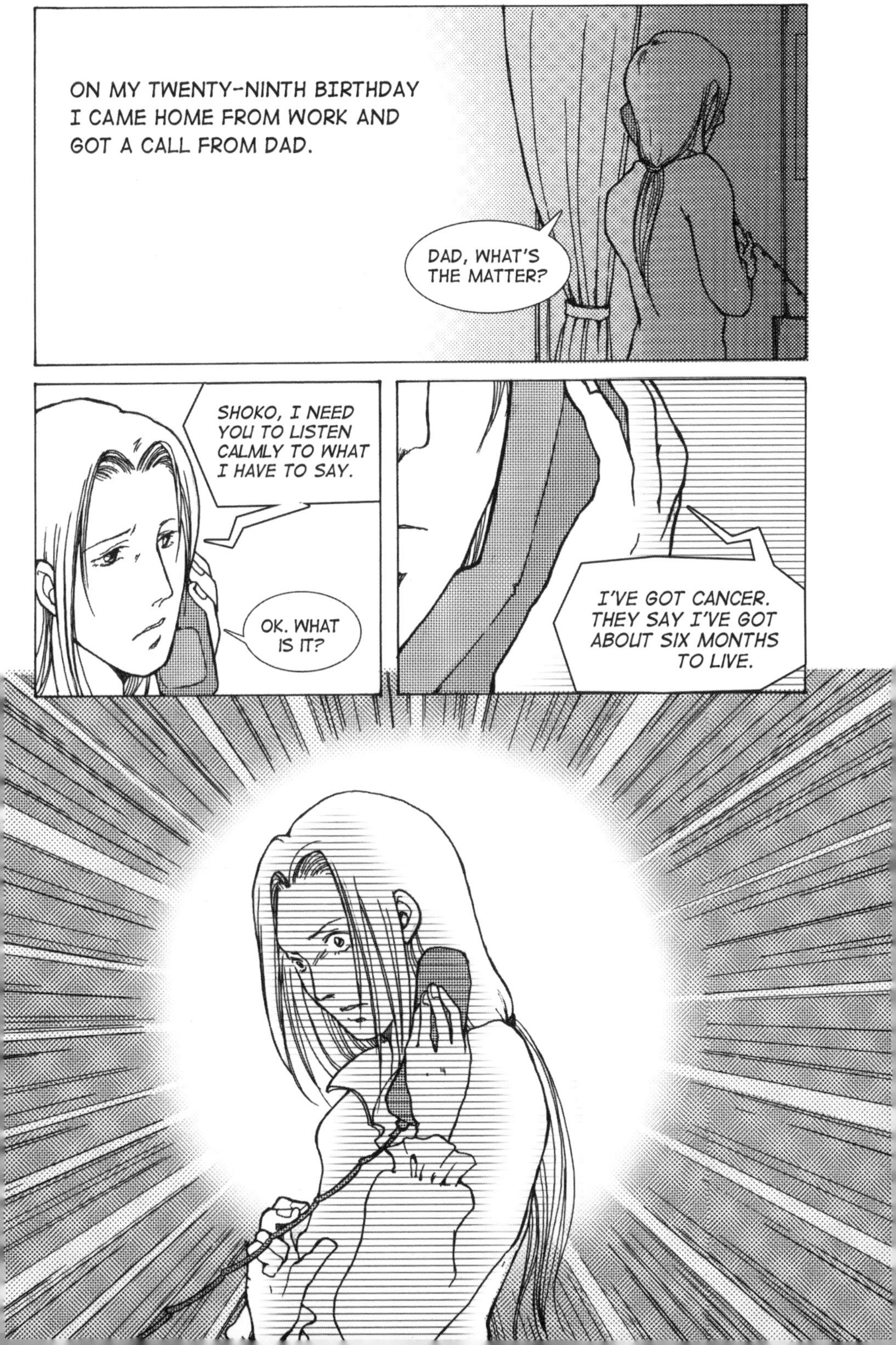
ON MY TWENTY-NINTH BIRTHDAY I CAME HOME FROM WORK AND GOT A CALL FROM DAD.
DAD, WHAT'S THE MATTER?
SHOKO, I NEED YOU TO LISTEN CALMLY TO WHAT I HAVE TO SAY.
OK. WHAT IS IT?
I'VE GOT CANCER. THEY SAY I'VE GOT ABOUT SIX MONTHS TO LIVE.

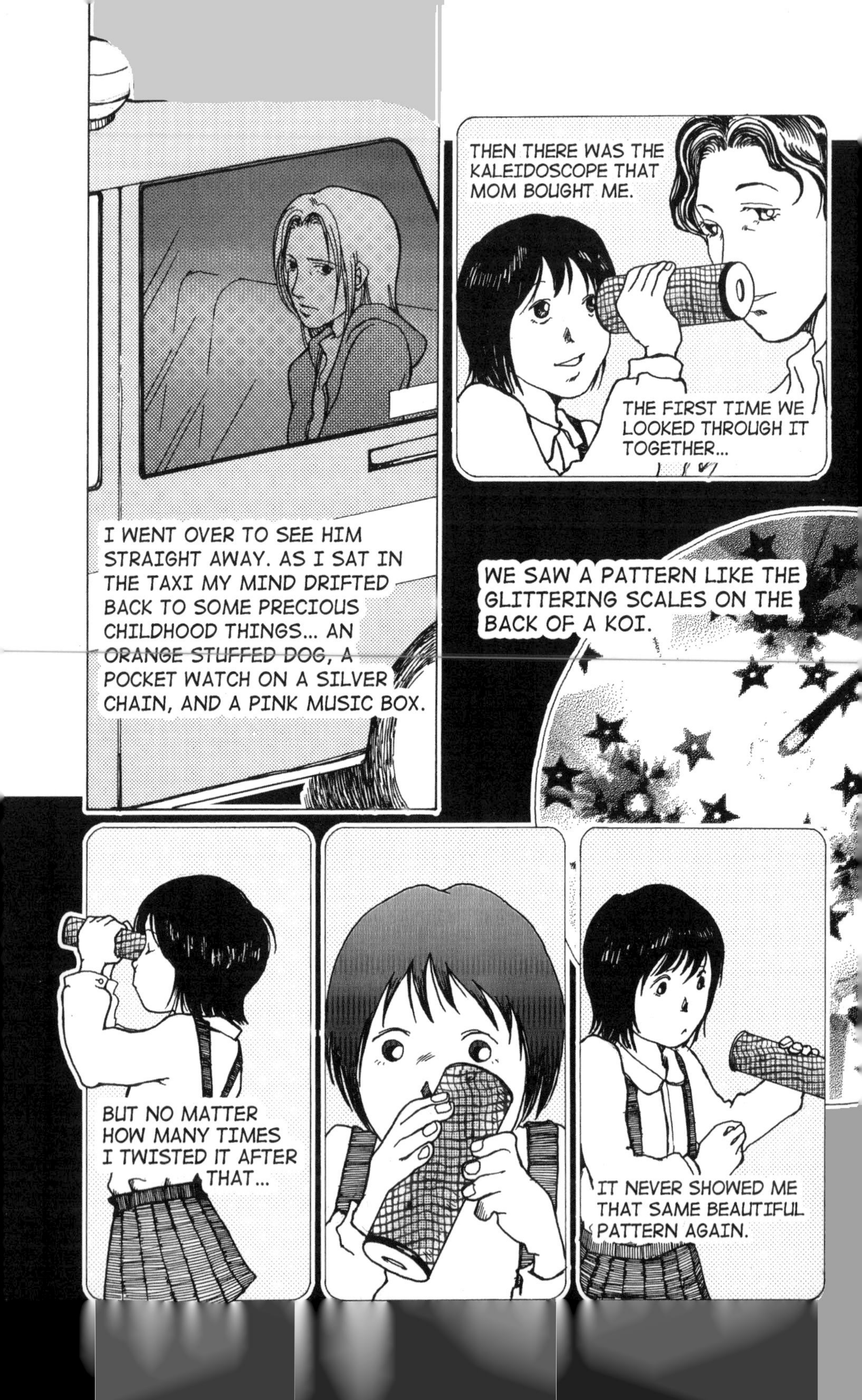
I WENT OVER TO SEE HIM STRAIGHT AWAY. AS I SAT IN THE TAXI MY MIND DRIFTED BACK TO SOME PRECIOUS CHILDHOOD THINGS... AN ORANGE STUFFED DOG, A POCKET WATCH ON A SILVER CHAIN, AND A PINK MUSIC BOX.
THEN THERE WAS THE KALEIDOSCOPE THAT MOM BOUGHT ME.
THE FIRST TIME WE LOOKED THROUGH IT TOGETHER...
WE SAW A PATTERN LIKE THE GLITTERING SCALES ON THE BACK OF A KOI.
BUT NO MATTER HOW MANY TIMES I TWISTED IT AFTER THAT...
IT NEVER SHOWED ME THAT SAME BEAUTIFUL PATTERN AGAIN.

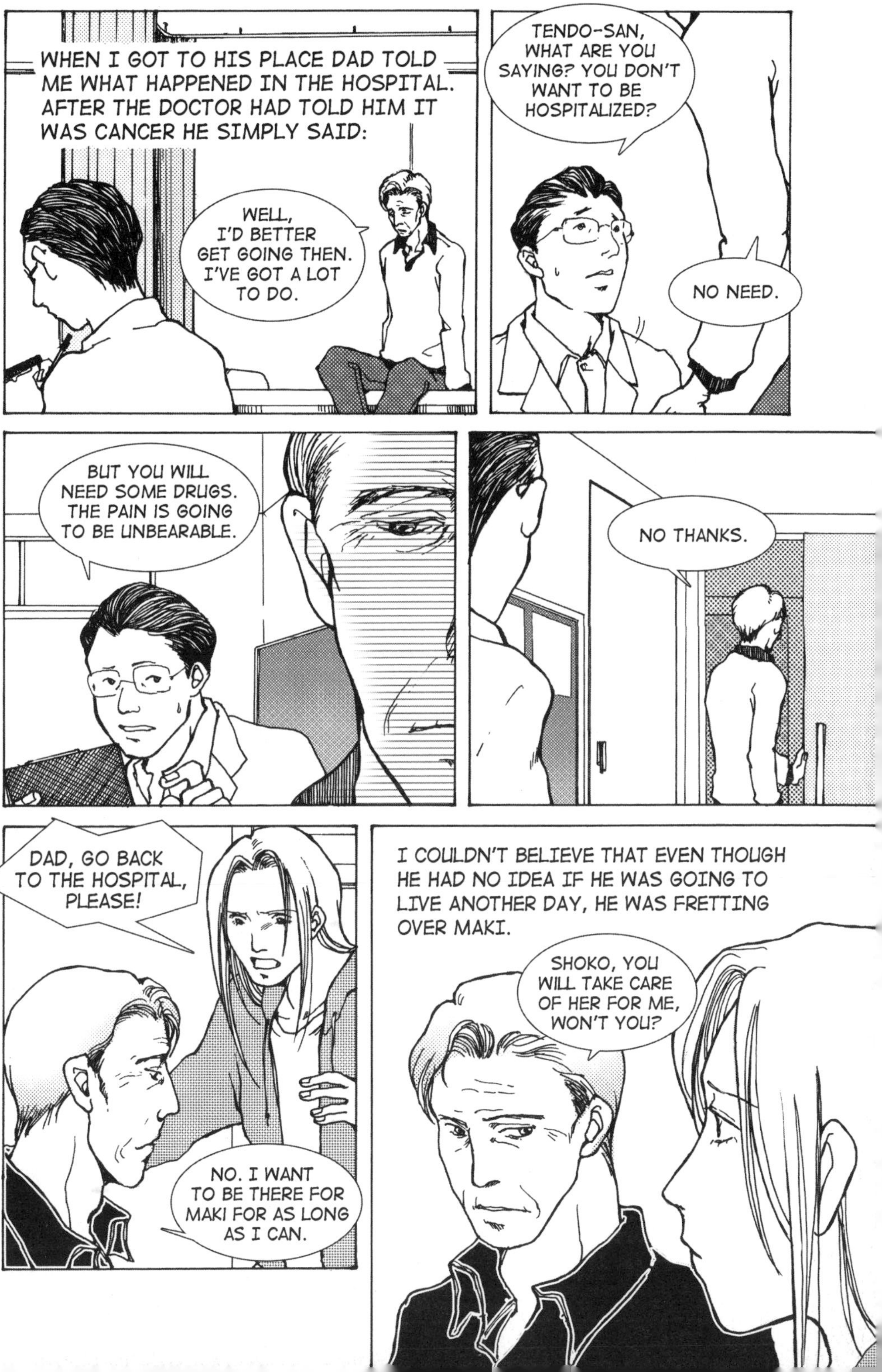
WHEN I GOT TO HIS PLACE DAD TOLD ME WHAT HAPPENED IN THE HOSPITAL. AFTER THE DOCTOR HAD TOLD HIM IT WAS CANCER HE SIMPLY SAID:
WELL, I'D BETTER GET GOING THEN. I'VE GOT A LOT TO DO.
TENDO-SAN, WHAT ARE YOU SAYING? YOU DON'T WANT TO BE HOSPITALIZED?
NO NEED.
BUT YOU WILL NEED SOME DRUGS. THE PAIN IS GOING TO BE UNBEARABLE.
NO THANKS.
DAD, GO BACK TO THE HOSPITAL, PLEASE!
NO. I WANT TO BE THERE FOR MAKI FOR AS LONG AS I CAN.
I COULDN'T BELIEVE THAT EVEN THOUGH HE HAD NO IDEA IF HE WAS GOING TO LIVE ANOTHER DAY, HE WAS FRETTING OVER MAKI.
SHOKO, YOU WILL TAKE CARE OF HER FOR ME, WON'T YOU?

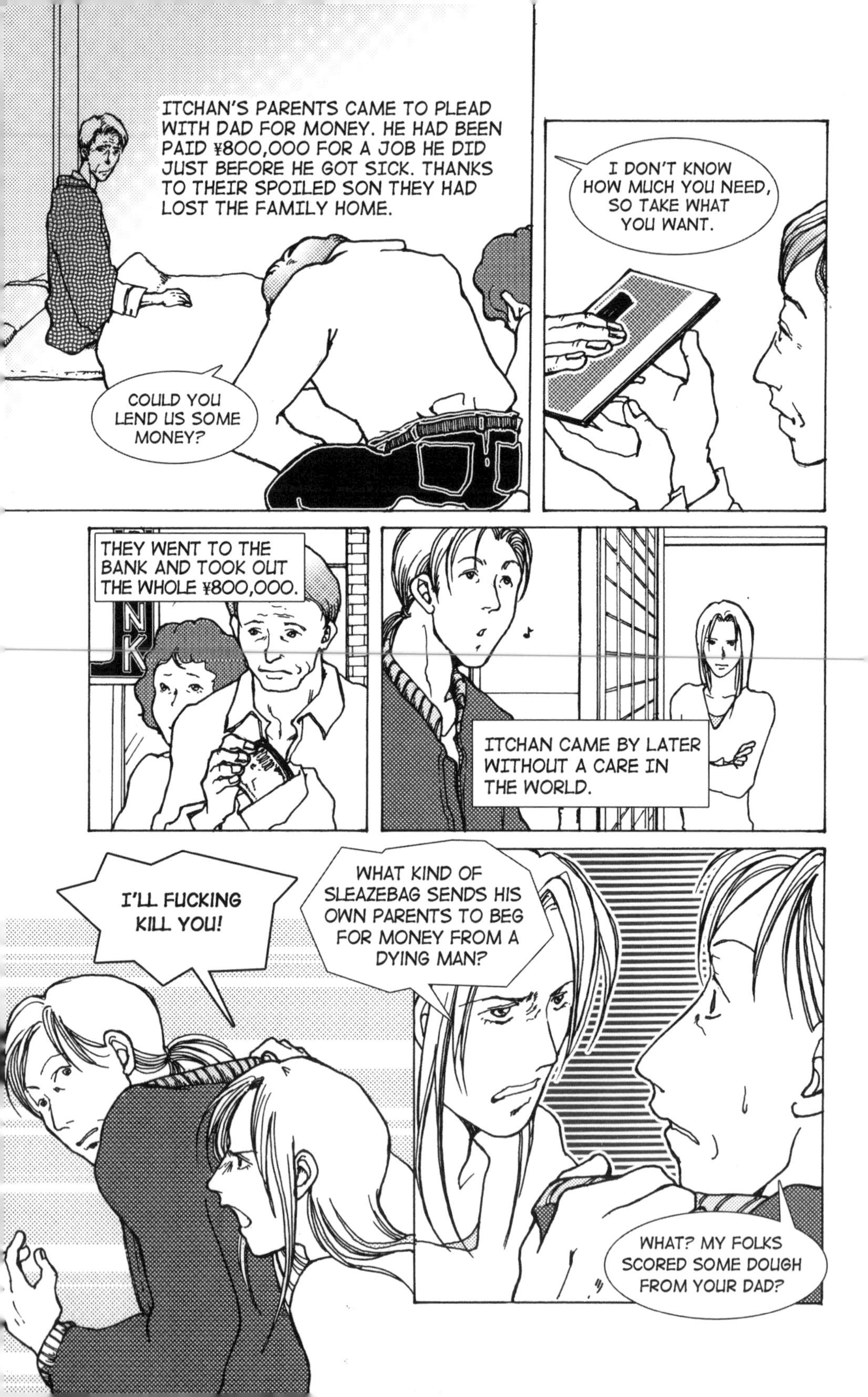

ITCHAN'S PARENTS CAME TO PLEAD WITH DAD FOR MONEY. HE HAD BEEN PAID ¥800,000 FOR A JOB HE DID JUST BEFORE HE GOT SICK. THANKS TO THEIR SPOILED SON THEY HAD LOST THE FAMILY HOME.
COULD YOU LEND US SOME MONEY?
I DON'T KNOW HOW MUCH YOU NEED, SO TAKE WHAT YOU WANT.
THEY WENT TO THE BANK AND TOOK OUT THE WHOLE ¥800,000.
NK
ITCHAN CAME BY LATER WITHOUT A CARE IN THE WORLD.
I'LL FUCKING KILL YOU!
WHAT KIND OF SLEAZEBAG SENDS HIS OWN PARENTS TO BEG FOR MONEY FROM A DYING MAN?
WHAT? MY FOLKS SCORED SOME DOUGH FROM YOUR DAD?

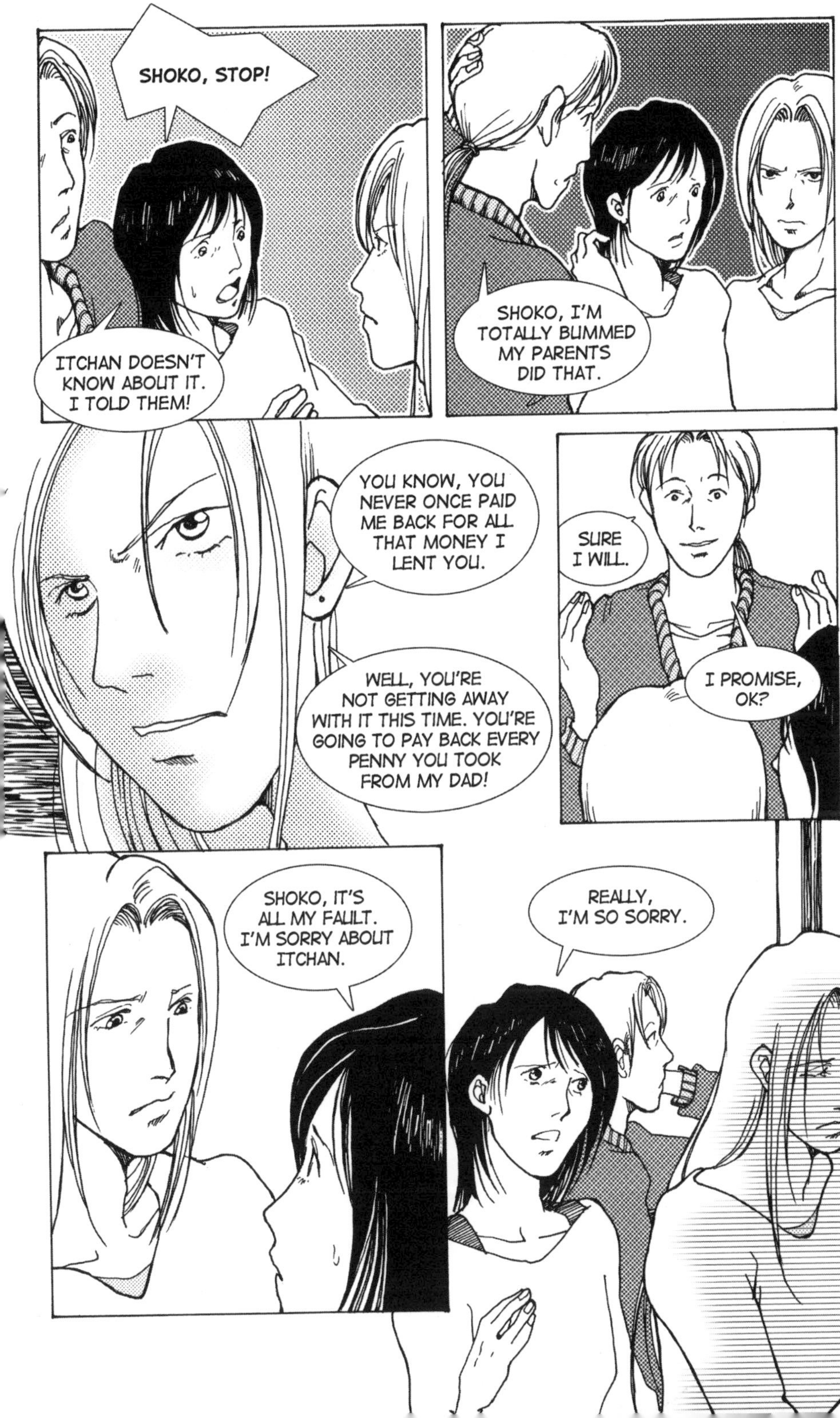
SHOKO, STOP!
ITCHAN DOESN'T KNOW ABOUT IT. I TOLD THEM!
SHOKO, I'M TOTALLY BUMMED MY PARENTS DID THAT.
YOU KNOW, YOU NEVER ONCE PAID ME BACK FOR ALL THAT MONEY I LENT YOU.
WELL, YOU'RE NOT GETTING AWAY WITH IT THIS TIME. YOU'RE GOING TO PAY BACK EVERY PENNY YOU TOOK FROM MY DAD!
SURE I WILL.
I PROMISE, OK?
SHOKO, IT'S ALL MY FAULT. I'M SORRY ABOUT ITCHAN.
REALLY, I'M SO SORRY.

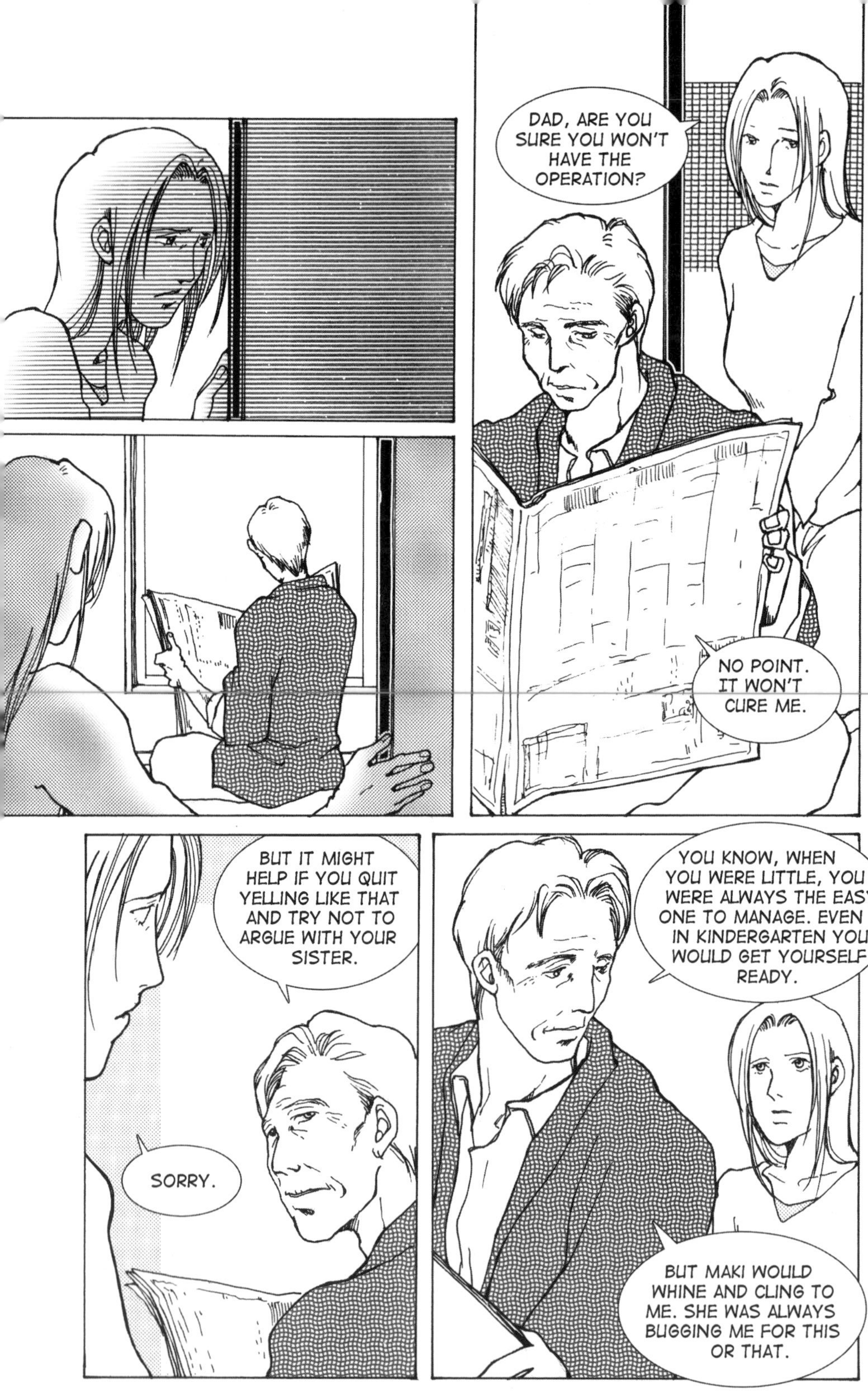
DAD, ARE YOU SURE YOU WON'T HAVE THE OPERATION?
NO POINT. IT WON'T CURE ME.
BUT IT MIGHT HELP IF YOU QUIT YELLING LIKE THAT AND TRY NOT TO ARGUE WITH YOUR SISTER.
SORRY.
YOU KNOW, WHEN YOU WERE LITTLE, YOU WERE ALWAYS THE EASY ONE TO MANAGE. EVEN IN KINDERGARTEN YOU WOULD GET YOURSELF READY.
BUT MAKI WOULD WHINE AND CLING TO ME. SHE WAS ALWAYS BUGGING ME FOR THIS OR THAT.

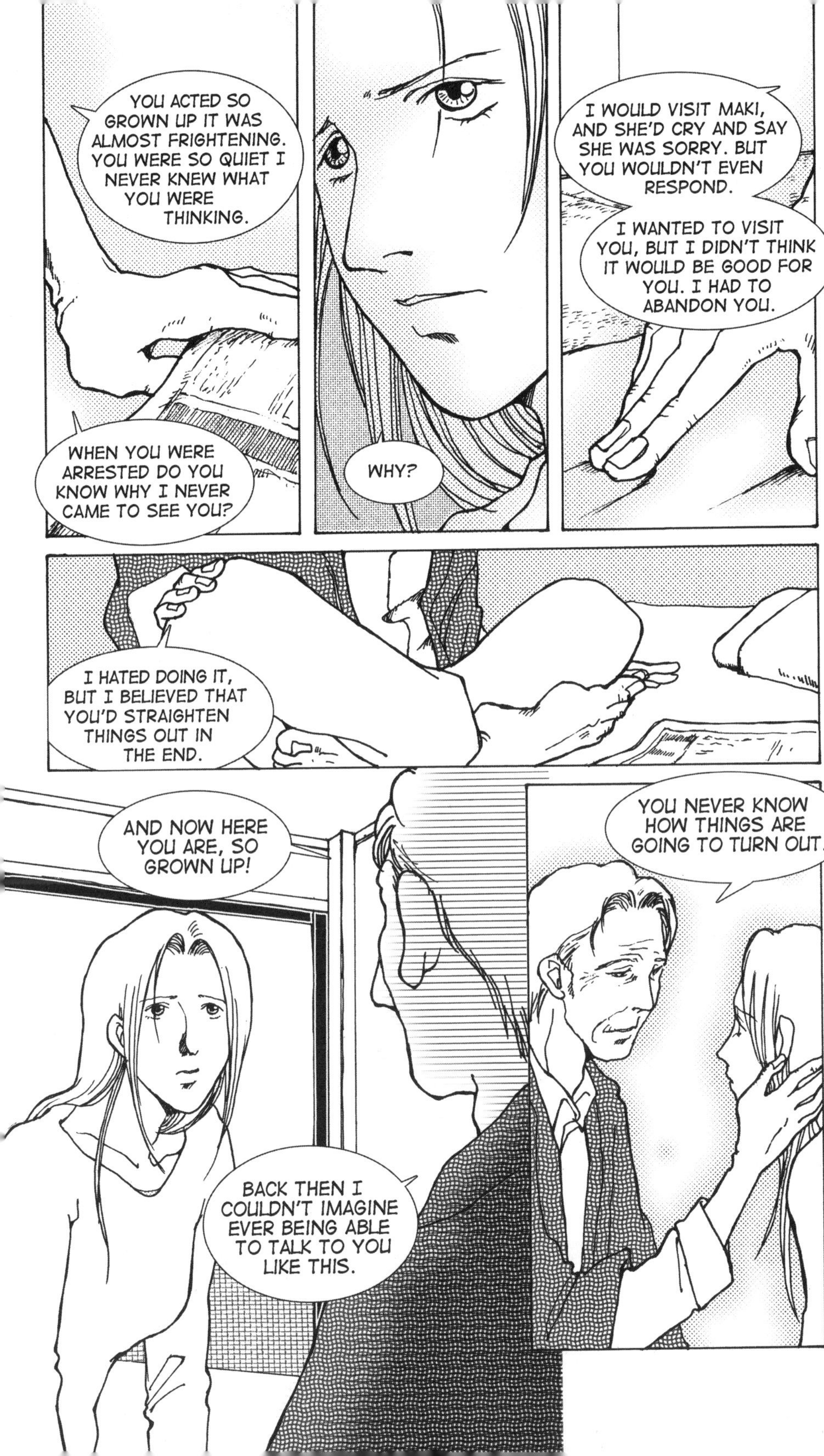
YOU ACTED SO GROWN UP IT WAS ALMOST FRIGHTENING. YOU WERE SO QUIET I NEVER KNEW WHAT YOU WERE THINKING.
WHEN YOU WERE ARRESTED DO YOU KNOW WHY I NEVER CAME TO SEE YOU?
WHY?
I WOULD VISIT MAKI, AND SHE'D CRY AND SAY SHE WAS SORRY. BUT YOU WOULDN'T EVEN RESPOND.
I WANTED TO VISIT YOU, BUT I DIDN'T THINK IT WOULD BE GOOD FOR YOU. I HAD TO ABANDON YOU.
I HATED DOING IT, BUT I BELIEVED THAT YOU'D STRAIGHTEN THINGS OUT IN THE END.
AND NOW HERE YOU ARE, SO GROWN UP!
YOU NEVER KNOW HOW THINGS ARE GOING TO TURN OUT.
BACK THEN I COULDN'T IMAGINE EVER BEING ABLE TO TALK TO YOU LIKE THIS.

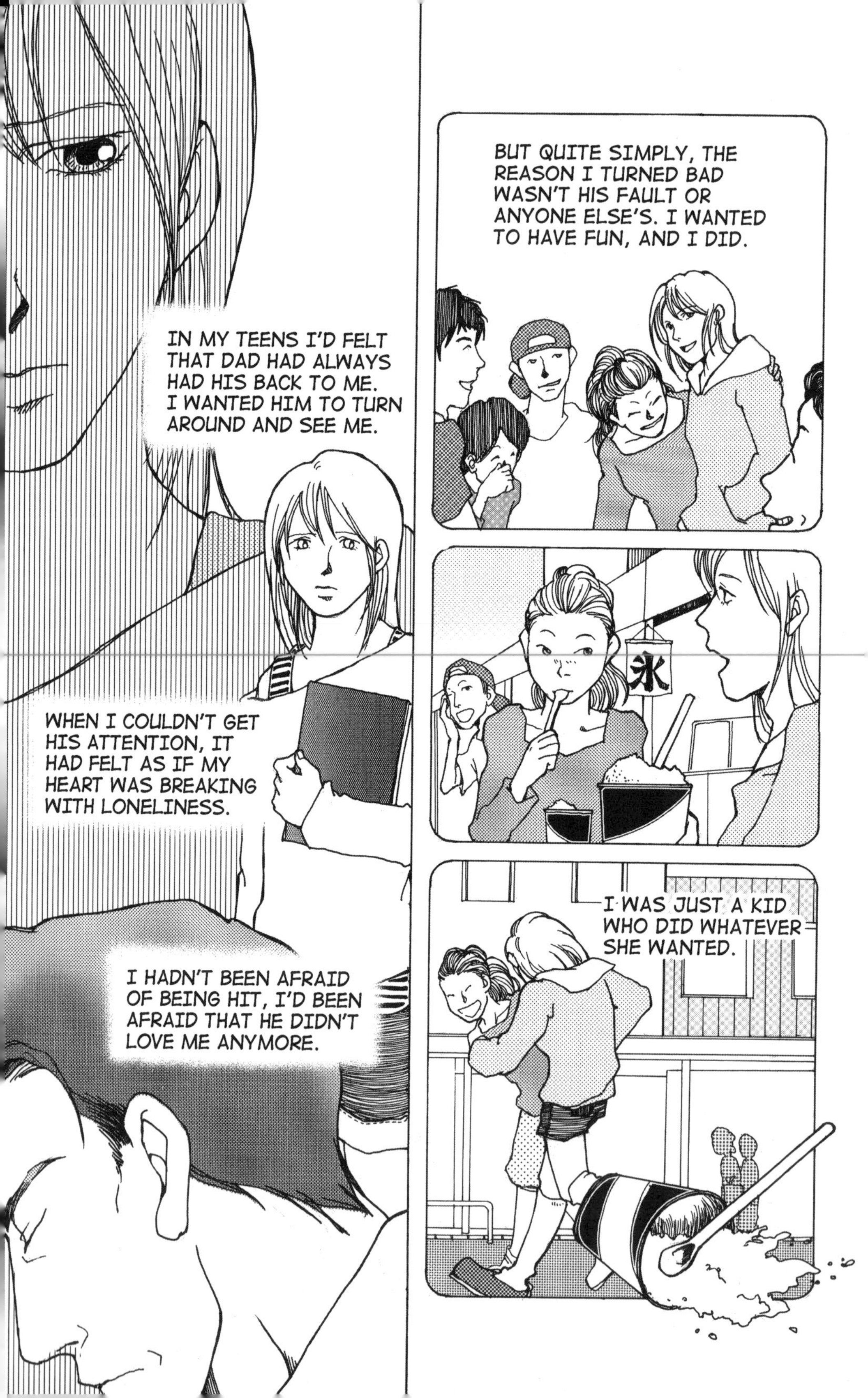
IN MY TEENS I'D FELT THAT DAD HAD ALWAYS HAD HIS BACK TO ME. I WANTED HIM TO TURN AROUND AND SEE ME.
WHEN I COULDN'T GET HIS ATTENTION, IT HAD FELT AS IF MY HEART WAS BREAKING WITH LONELINESS.
I HADN'T BEEN AFRAID OF BEING HIT, I'D BEEN AFRAID THAT HE DIDN'T LOVE ME ANYMORE.
BUT QUITE SIMPLY, THE REASON I TURNED BAD WASN'T HIS FAULT OR ANYONE ELSE'S. I WANTED TO HAVE FUN, AND I DID.
氷
I WAS JUST A KID WHO DID WHATEVER SHE WANTED.

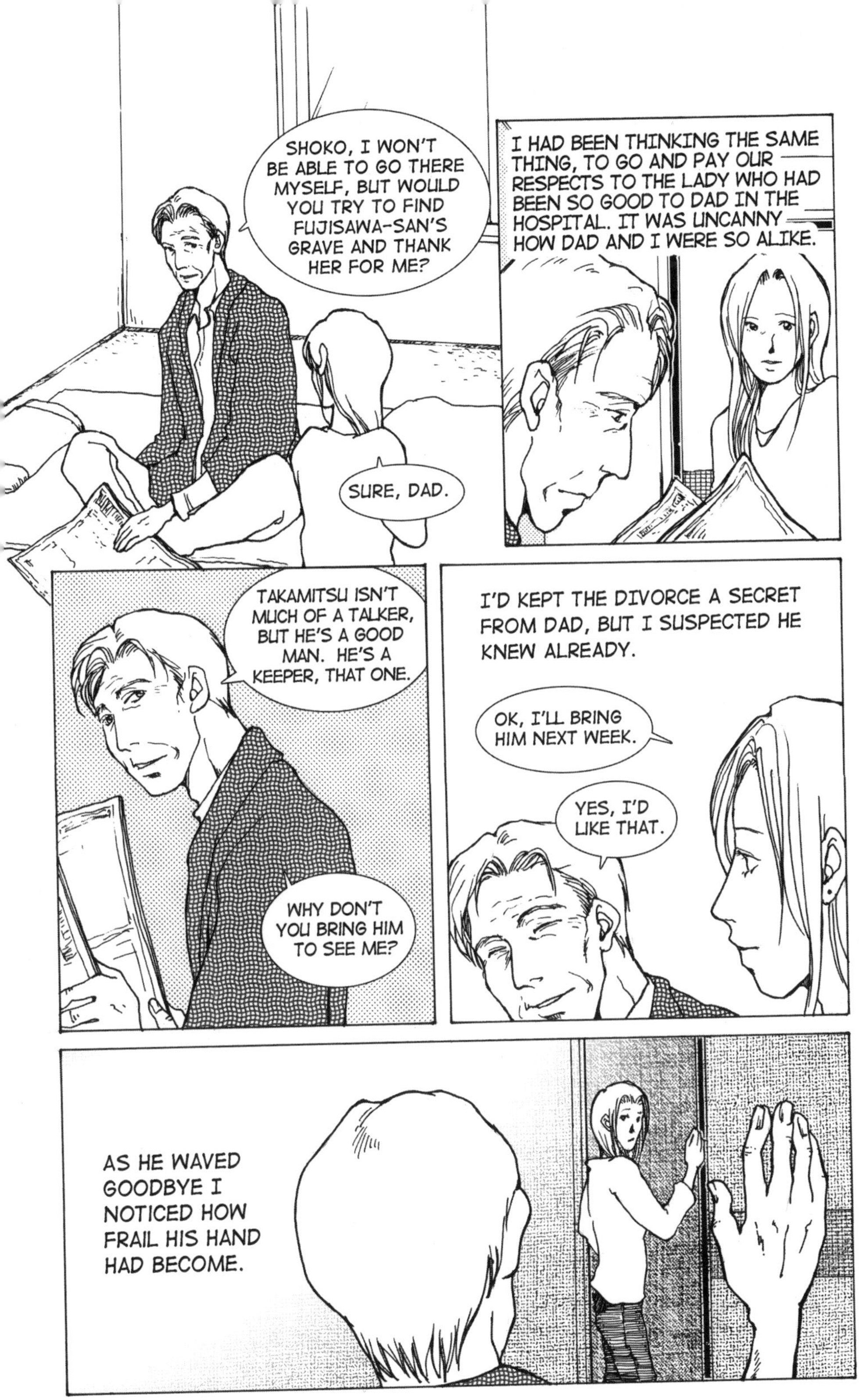
SHOKO, I WON'T BE ABLE TO GO THERE MYSELF, BUT WOULD YOU TRY TO FIND FUJISAWA-SAN'S GRAVE AND THANK HER FOR ME?
SURE, DAD.
I HAD BEEN THINKING THE SAME THING, TO GO AND PAY OUR RESPECTS TO THE LADY WHO HAD BEEN SO GOOD TO DAD IN THE HOSPITAL. IT WAS UNCANNY HOW DAD AND I WERE SO ALIKE.
TAKAMITSU ISN'T MUCH OF A TALKER, BUT HE'S A GOOD MAN. HE'S A KEEPER, THAT ONE.
WHY DON'T YOU BRING HIM TO SEE ME?
I'D KEPT THE DIVORCE A SECRET FROM DAD, BUT I SUSPECTED HE KNEW ALREADY.
OK, I'LL BRING HIM NEXT WEEK.
YES, I'D LIKE THAT.
AS HE WAVED GOODBYE I NOTICED HOW FRAIL HIS HAND HAD BECOME.

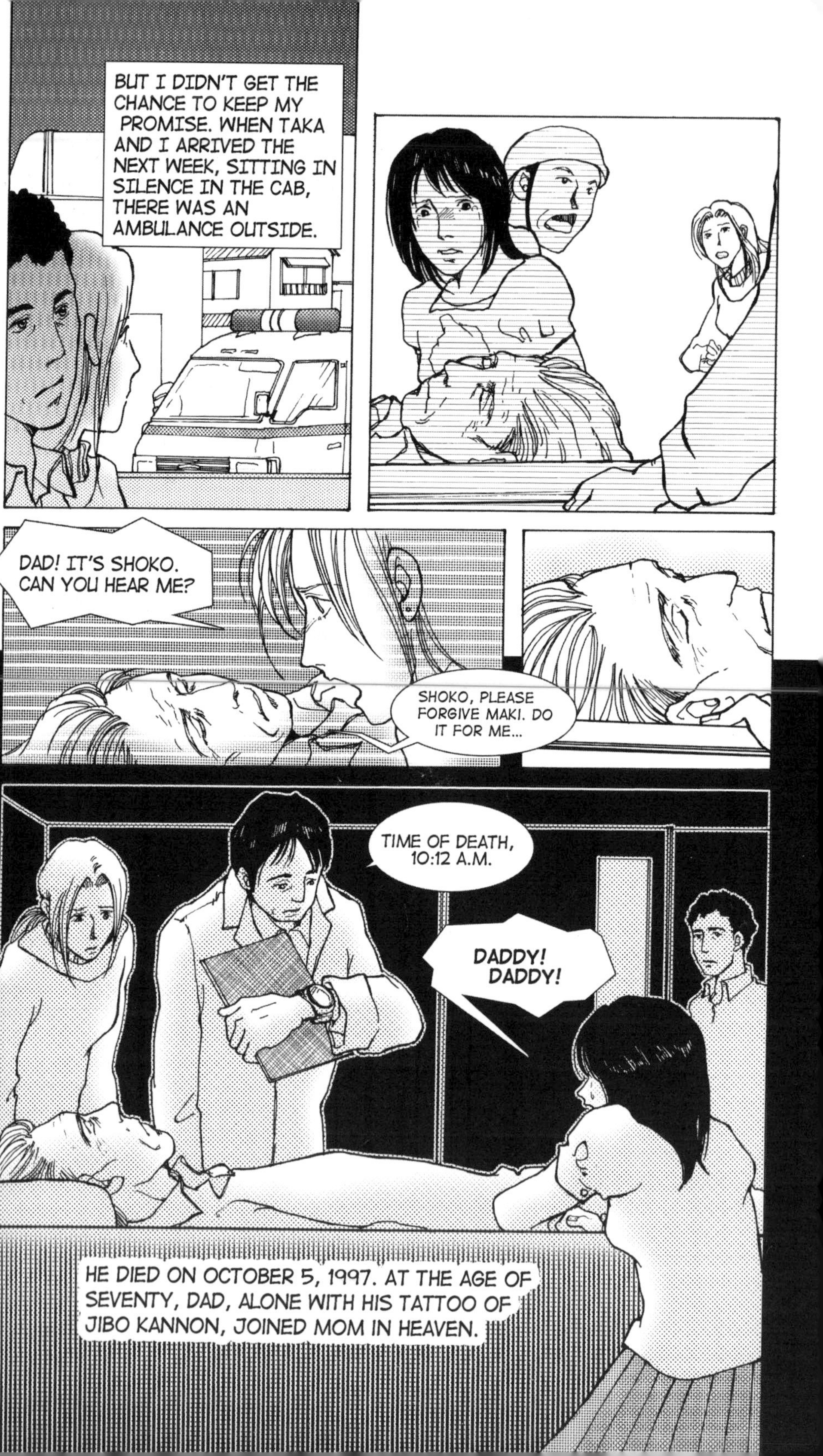
BUT I DIDN'T GET THE CHANCE TO KEEP MY PROMISE. WHEN TAKA AND I ARRIVED THE NEXT WEEK, SITTING IN SILENCE IN THE CAB, THERE WAS AN AMBULANCE OUTSIDE.
DAD! IT'S SHOKO. CAN YOU HEAR ME?
SHOKO, PLEASE FORGIVE MAKI. DO IT FOR ME...
TIME OF DEATH, 10:12 A.M.
DADDY! DADDY!
HE DIED ON OCTOBER 5, 1997. AT THE AGE OF SEVENTY, DAD, ALONE WITH HIS TATTOO OF JIBO KANNON, JOINED MOM IN HEAVEN.

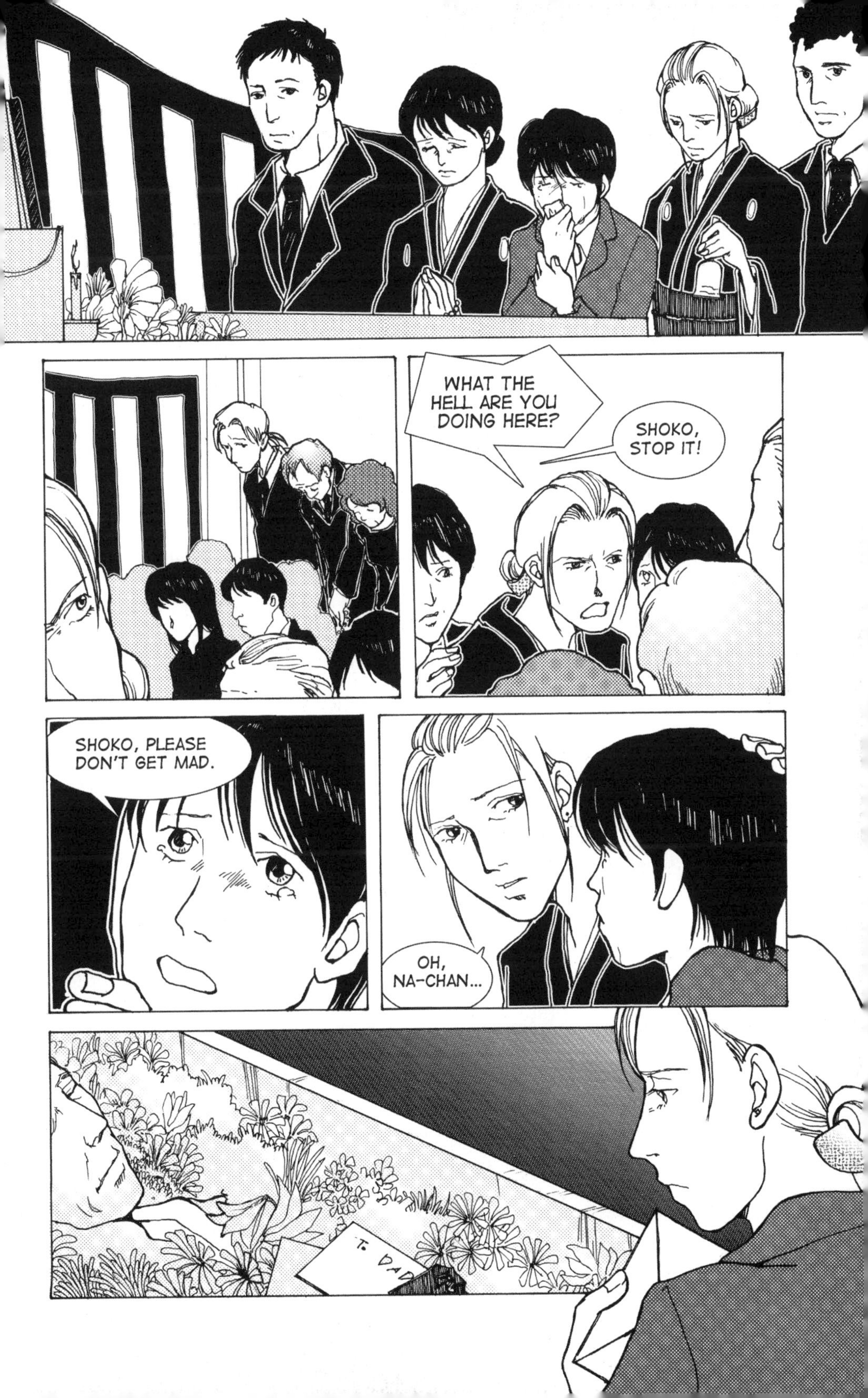
WHAT THE HELL ARE YOU DOING HERE?
SHOKO, STOP IT!
SHOKO, PLEASE DON'T GET MAD.
OH, NA-CHAN...
TO DAD

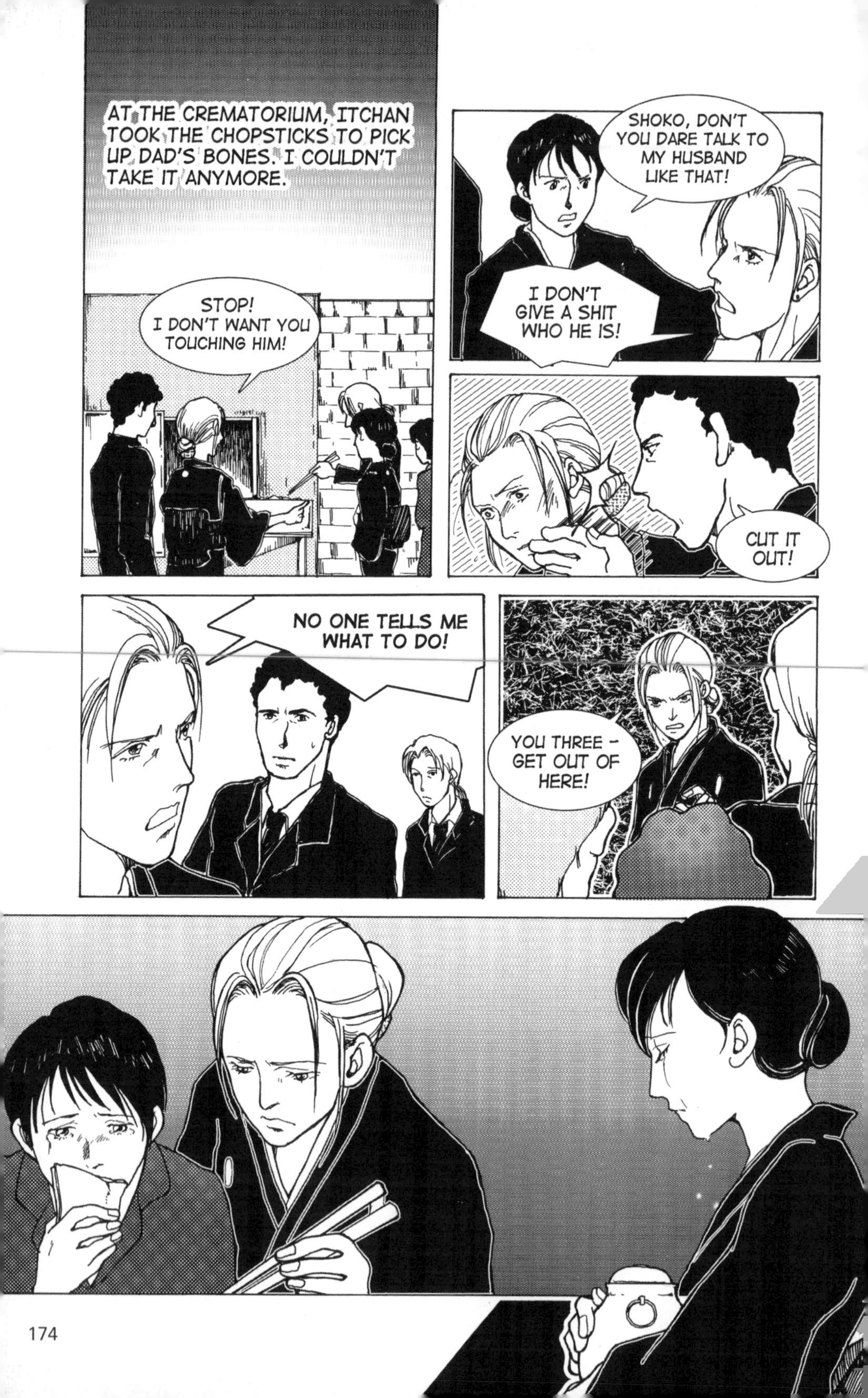
AT THE CREMATORIUM, ITCHAN TOOK THE CHOPSTICKS TO PICK UP DAD'S BONES. I COULDN'T TAKE IT ANYMORE.
STOP! I DON'T WANT YOU TOUCHING HIM!
SHOKO, DON'T YOU DARE TALK TO MY HUSBAND LIKE THAT!
I DON'T GIVE A SHIT WHO HE IS!
CUT IT OUT!
NO ONE TELLS ME WHAT TO DO!
YOU THREE - GET OUT OF HERE!

CHAPTER 9

Separate Ways

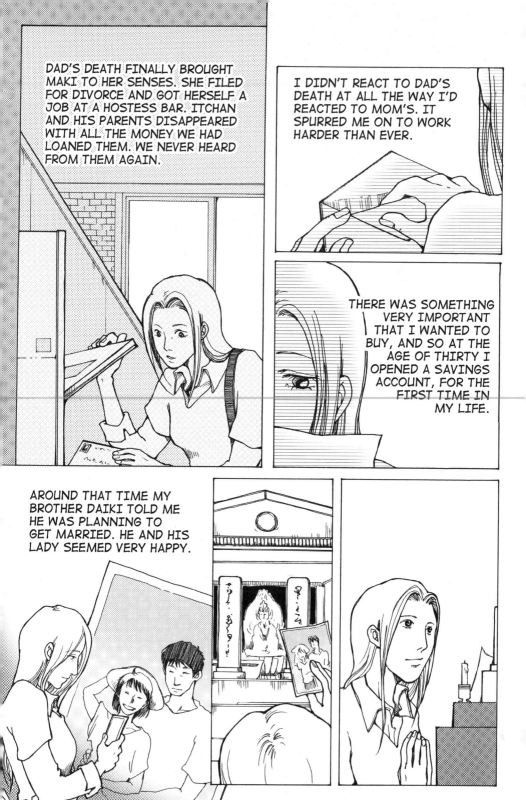

DAD'S DEATH FINALLY BROUGHT MAKI TO HER SENSES. SHE FILED FOR DIVORCE AND GOT HERSELF A JOB AT A HOSTESS BAR. ITCHAN AND HIS PARENTS DISAPPEARED WITH ALL THE MONEY WE HAD LOANED THEM. WE NEVER HEARD FROM THEM AGAIN.

I DIDN'T REACT TO DAD'S DEATH AT ALL THE WAY I'D REACTED TO MOM'S. IT SPURRED ME ON TO WORK HARDER THAN EVER.

THERE WAS SOMETHING VERY IMPORTANT THAT I WANTED TO BUY, AND SO AT THE AGE OF THIRTY I OPENED A SAVINGS ACCOUNT, FOR THE FIRST TIME IN MY LIFE.

AROUND THAT TIME MY BROTHER DAIKI TOLD ME HE WAS PLANNING TO GET MARRIED. HE AND HIS LADY SEEMED VERY HAPPY.

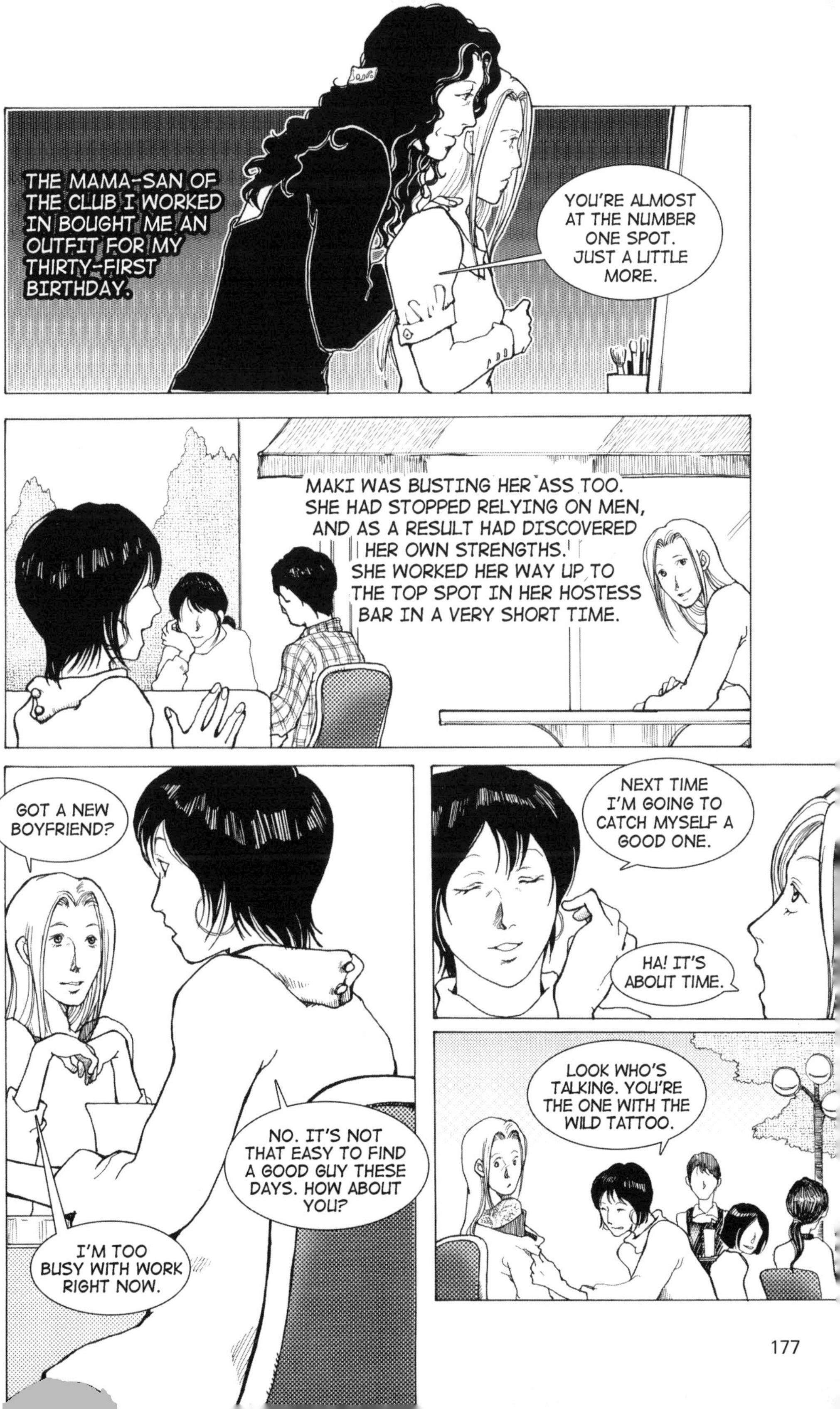
THE MAMA-SAN OF THE CLUB I WORKED IN BOUGHT ME AN OUTFIT FOR MY THIRTY-FIRST BIRTHDAY.
YOU'RE ALMOST AT THE NUMBER ONE SPOT. JUST A LITTLE MORE.
MAKI WAS BUSTING HER ASS TOO. SHE HAD STOPPED RELYING ON MEN, AND AS A RESULT HAD DISCOVERED HER OWN STRENGTHS. SHE WORKED HER WAY UP TO THE TOP SPOT IN HER HOSTESS BAR IN A VERY SHORT TIME.
GOT A NEW BOYFRIEND?
NO. IT'S NOT THAT EASY TO FIND A GOOD GUY THESE DAYS. HOW ABOUT YOU?
I'M TOO BUSY WITH WORK RIGHT NOW.
NEXT TIME I'M GOING TO CATCH MYSELF A GOOD ONE.
HA! IT'S ABOUT TIME.
LOOK WHO'S TALKING. YOU'RE THE ONE WITH THE WILD TATTOO.

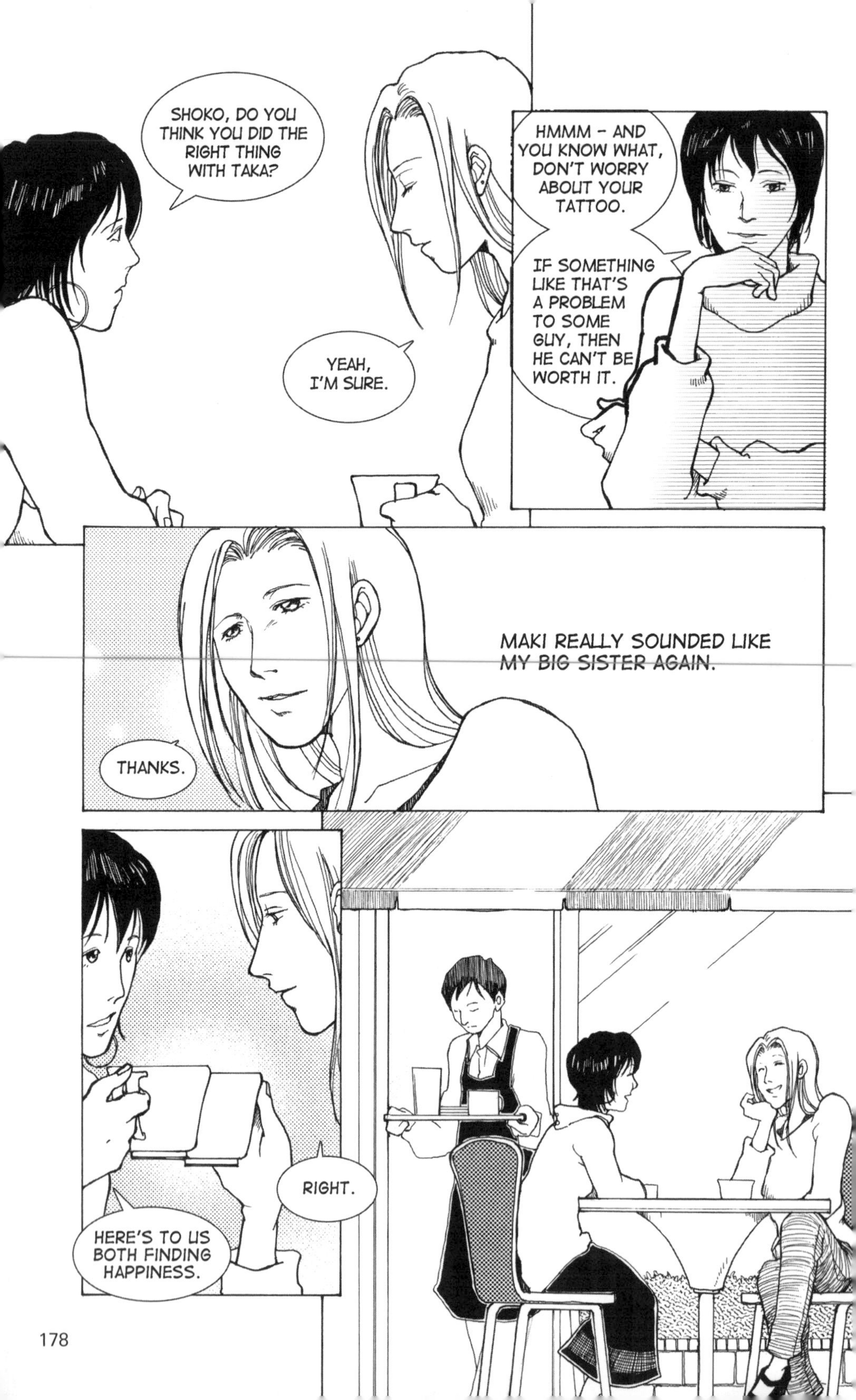
SHOKO, DO YOU THINK YOU DID THE RIGHT THING WITH TAKA?
YEAH, I'M SURE.
HMMM - AND YOU KNOW WHAT, DON'T WORRY ABOUT YOUR TATTOO.
IF SOMETHING LIKE THAT'S A PROBLEM TO SOME GUY, THEN HE CAN'T BE WORTH IT.
MAKI REALLY SOUNDED LIKE MY BIG SISTER AGAIN.
THANKS.
HERE'S TO US BOTH FINDING HAPPINESS.
RIGHT.

BY THE TIME I WAS THIRTY-TWO I HAD QUITE A LOT OF MONEY SAVED UP IN THE BANK. I BEGAN TO SEARCH FOR A GRAVE PLOT WHERE MOM AND DAD'S ASHES COULD BE LAID TO REST. I COULDN'T BELIEVE HOW EXPENSIVE THEY WERE!

STILL, I WASN'T GOING TO BE PUT OFF. SOMEHOW OR OTHER I WAS GOING TO GET A PLOT FOR THEM.

NA-CHAN HAD FOUND A NICE GUY, YAMAMOTO, A GRAPHIC DESIGNER, WHO SEEMED DECENT AND POLITE. HE EVEN INSISTED ON COMING TO FORMALLY ASK FOR HER HAND.

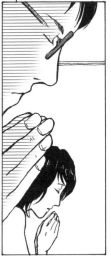

I KNEW THERE WOULD BE NO NEED TO WORRY ABOUT NA-CHAN.

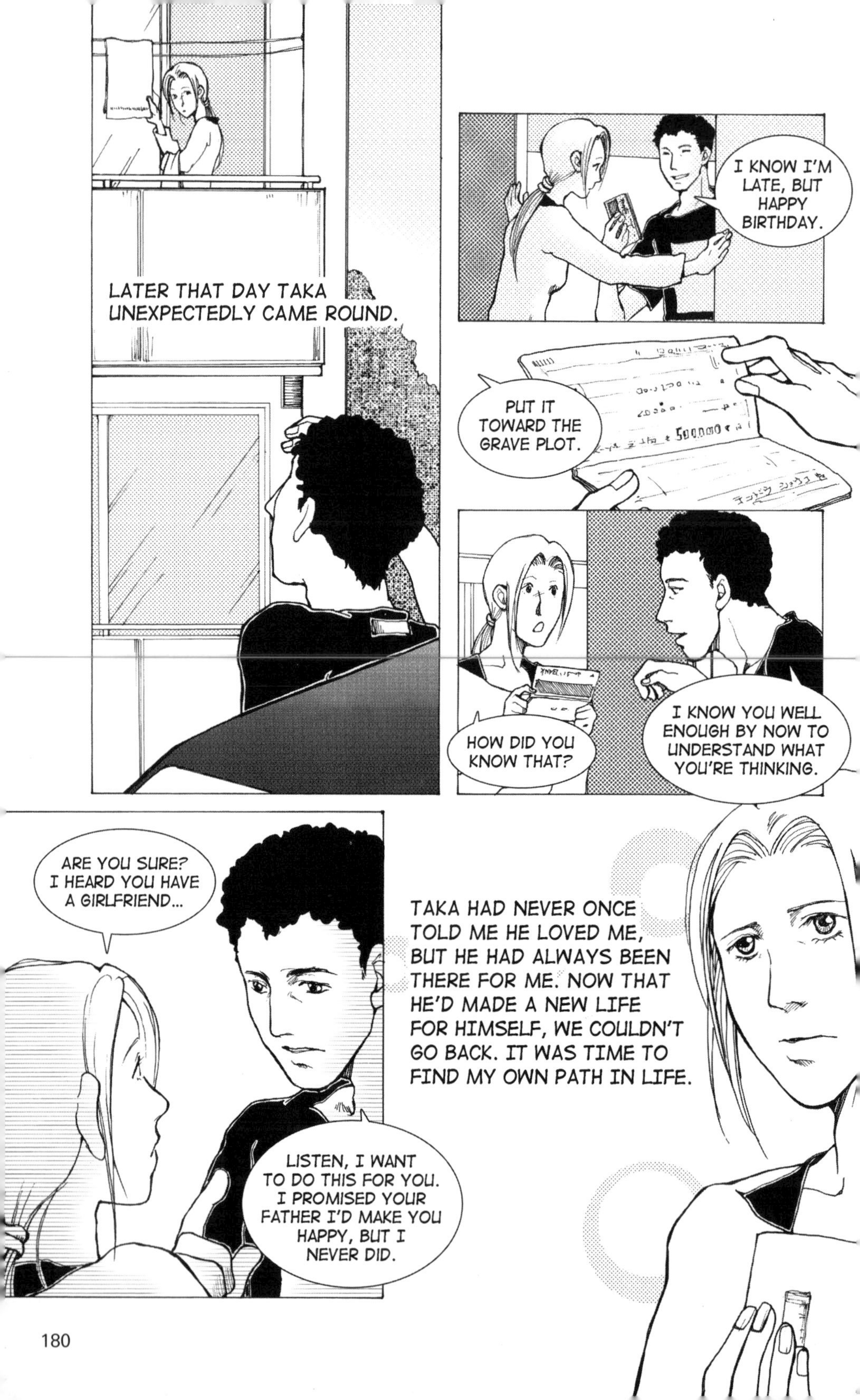
LATER THAT DAY TAKA UNEXPECTEDLY CAME ROUND.
I KNOW I'M LATE, BUT HAPPY BIRTHDAY.
PUT IT TOWARD THE GRAVE PLOT.
HOW DID YOU KNOW THAT?
I KNOW YOU WELL ENOUGH BY NOW TO UNDERSTAND WHAT YOU'RE THINKING.
ARE YOU SURE? I HEARD YOU HAVE A GIRLFRIEND...
LISTEN, I WANT TO DO THIS FOR YOU. I PROMISED YOUR FATHER I'D MAKE YOU HAPPY, BUT I NEVER DID.
TAKA HAD NEVER ONCE TOLD ME HE LOVED ME, BUT HE HAD ALWAYS BEEN THERE FOR ME. NOW THAT HE'D MADE A NEW LIFE FOR HIMSELF, WE COULDN'T GO BACK. IT WAS TIME TO FIND MY OWN PATH IN LIFE.

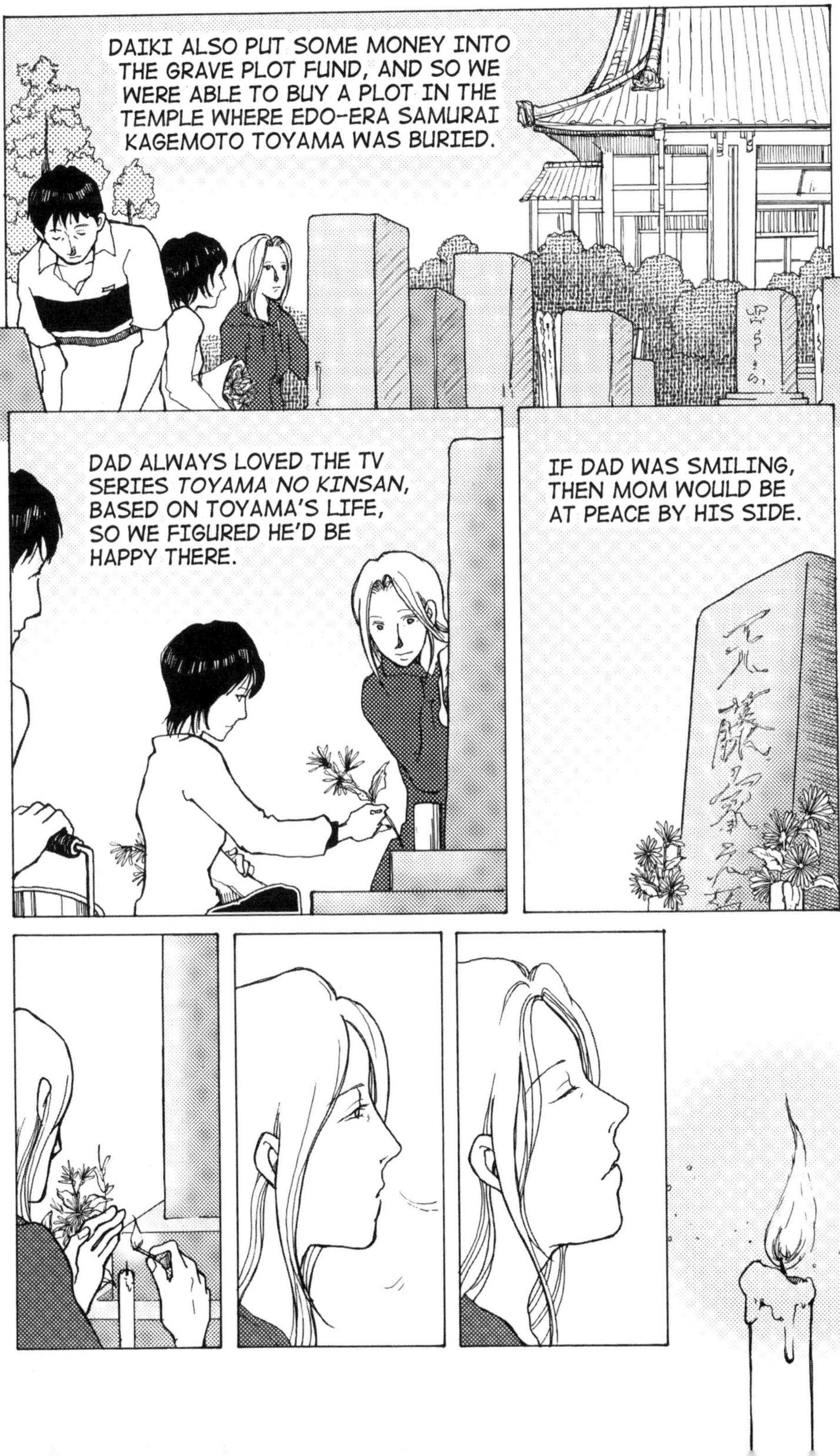
DAIKI ALSO PUT SOME MONEY INTO THE GRAVE PLOT FUND, AND SO WE WERE ABLE TO BUY A PLOT IN THE TEMPLE WHERE EDO-ERA SAMURAI KAGEMOTO TOYAMA WAS BURIED.
DAD ALWAYS LOVED THE TV SERIES *TOYAMA NO KINSAN*, BASED ON TOYAMA'S LIFE, SO WE FIGURED HE'D BE HAPPY THERE.
IF DAD WAS SMILING, THEN MOM WOULD BE AT PEACE BY HIS SIDE.

IT WAS TOO LATE TO BE A GOOD DAUGHTER TO THEM, BUT IN GIVING THEM THIS GRAVE, I'D BE ABLE TO STAY CLOSE TO THEM, AND THEY IN TURN COULD ALWAYS BE TOGETHER. I HOPED DAD WOULD FINALLY HAVE PEACE AND QUIET TO READ MY LAST LETTER TO HIM.

Dear Dad,

I always loved you so much. But when I saw you come home drunk with those hostesses on your arm, I couldn't stand it. I was terrified that you would abandon us and run away with one of those women. And I believed that if you went away, then Mom might have to leave us too. Because I was so afraid that would happen, and because I didn't want to make you mad, I did everything to try to stay on your good side when I was little. I didn't want to lose you.

In the end, we lost our house and everything in it, and Mom's dream of buying a new house for us all to live in together never came true. I really wanted to help you out with that, but I couldn't. I couldn't even keep my promise to you not to split up with Taka. I'm sorry for being such an ungrateful daughter. Please forgive me, Dad, for everything. I'm leaving you the talisman you bought me all those years ago. It's the only thing I have left now from when I was little, and it's my most precious possession. I want you to take it to remember me by. I know you'll be watching over us all from heaven. Tell Mom I love her too, okay?

Shoko

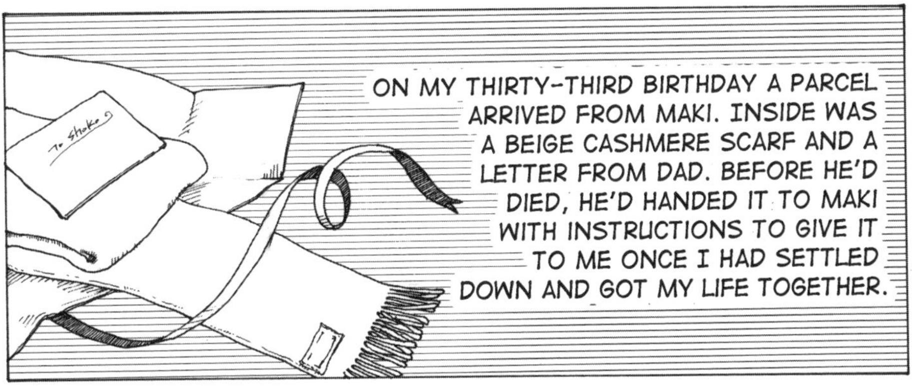
To Shoko
ON MY THIRTY-THIRD BIRTHDAY A PARCEL ARRIVED FROM MAKI. INSIDE WAS A BEIGE CASHMERE SCARF AND A LETTER FROM DAD. BEFORE HE'D DIED, HE'D HANDED IT TO MAKI WITH INSTRUCTIONS TO GIVE IT TO ME ONCE I HAD SETTLED DOWN AND GOT MY LIFE TOGETHER.

Dear Shoko,

Ever since you were little, you were such a kind and gentle child. You were the one who always looked after our pets. It brings tears to my eyes to think what a good heart you have. I wanted to meet Taka one more time and ask him to be sure to take good care of you, but it looks like I won't have the chance now. In my eyes, you're still as good hearted as you were as a kid. It's just your health that worries me. Please take extra care of yourself and make sure you don't work too hard. These are probably my last words to you, so Shoko, please continue to believe in yourself.

Dad

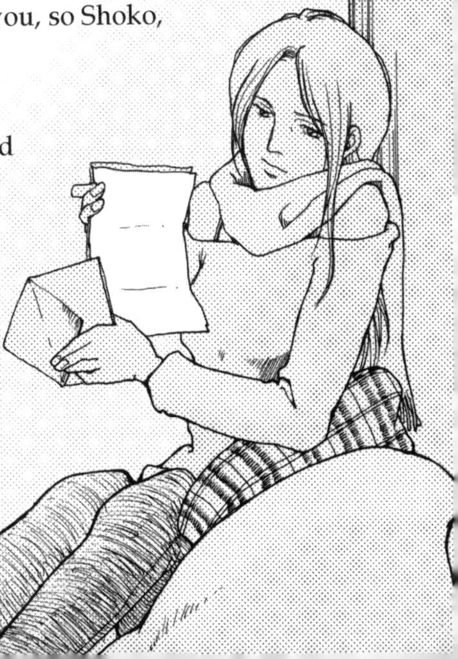

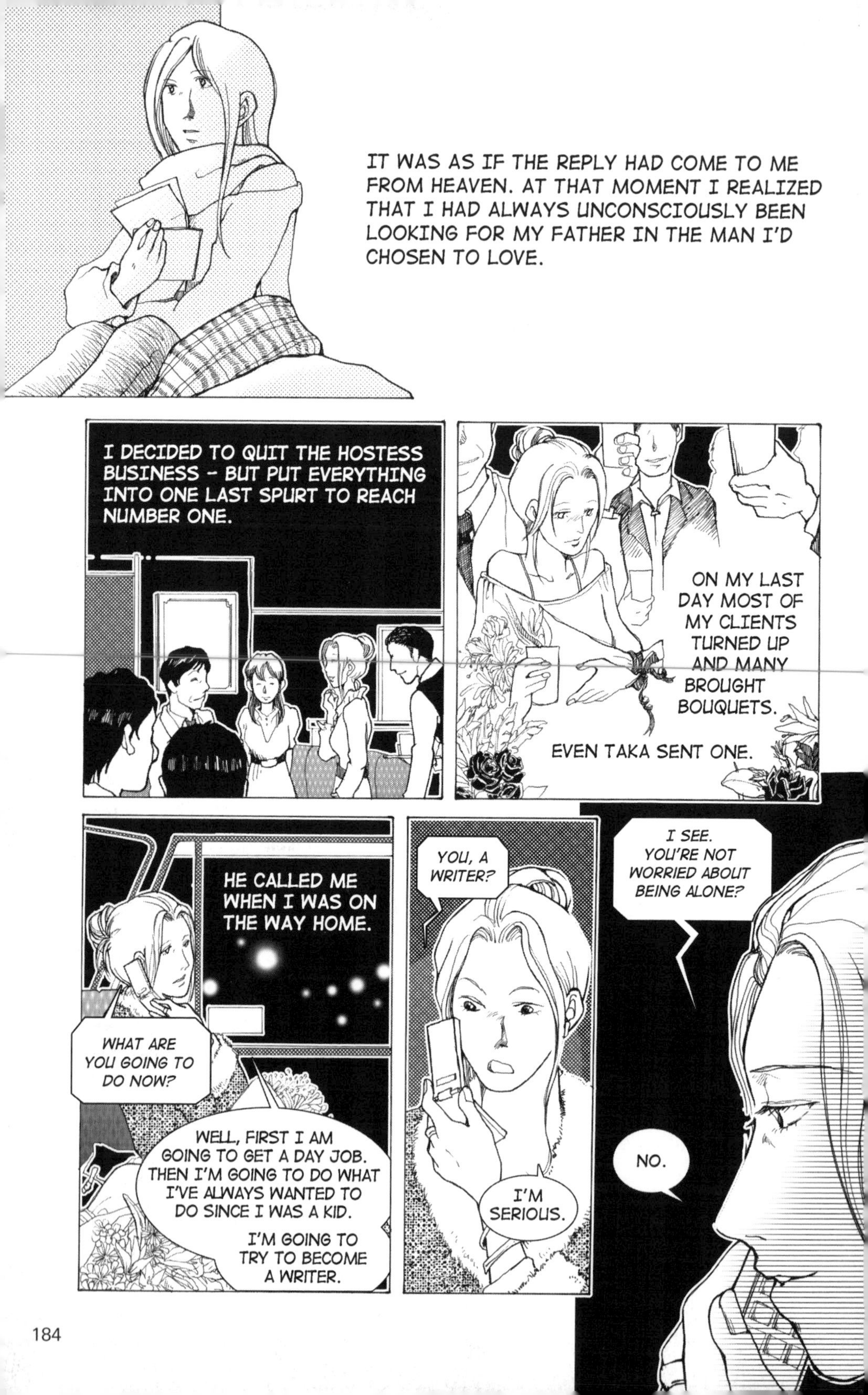
IT WAS AS IF THE REPLY HAD COME TO ME FROM HEAVEN. AT THAT MOMENT I REALIZED THAT I HAD ALWAYS UNCONSCIOUSLY BEEN LOOKING FOR MY FATHER IN THE MAN I'D CHOSEN TO LOVE.
I DECIDED TO QUIT THE HOSTESS BUSINESS - BUT PUT EVERYTHING INTO ONE LAST SPURT TO REACH NUMBER ONE.
ON MY LAST DAY MOST OF MY CLIENTS TURNED UP AND MANY BROUGHT BOUQUETS.
EVEN TAKA SENT ONE.
HE CALLED ME WHEN I WAS ON THE WAY HOME.
WHAT ARE YOU GOING TO DO NOW?
WELL, FIRST I AM GOING TO GET A DAY JOB. THEN I'M GOING TO DO WHAT I'VE ALWAYS WANTED TO DO SINCE I WAS A KID.
I'M GOING TO TRY TO BECOME A WRITER.
YOU, A WRITER?
I'M SERIOUS.
I SEE. YOU'RE NOT WORRIED ABOUT BEING ALONE?
NO.

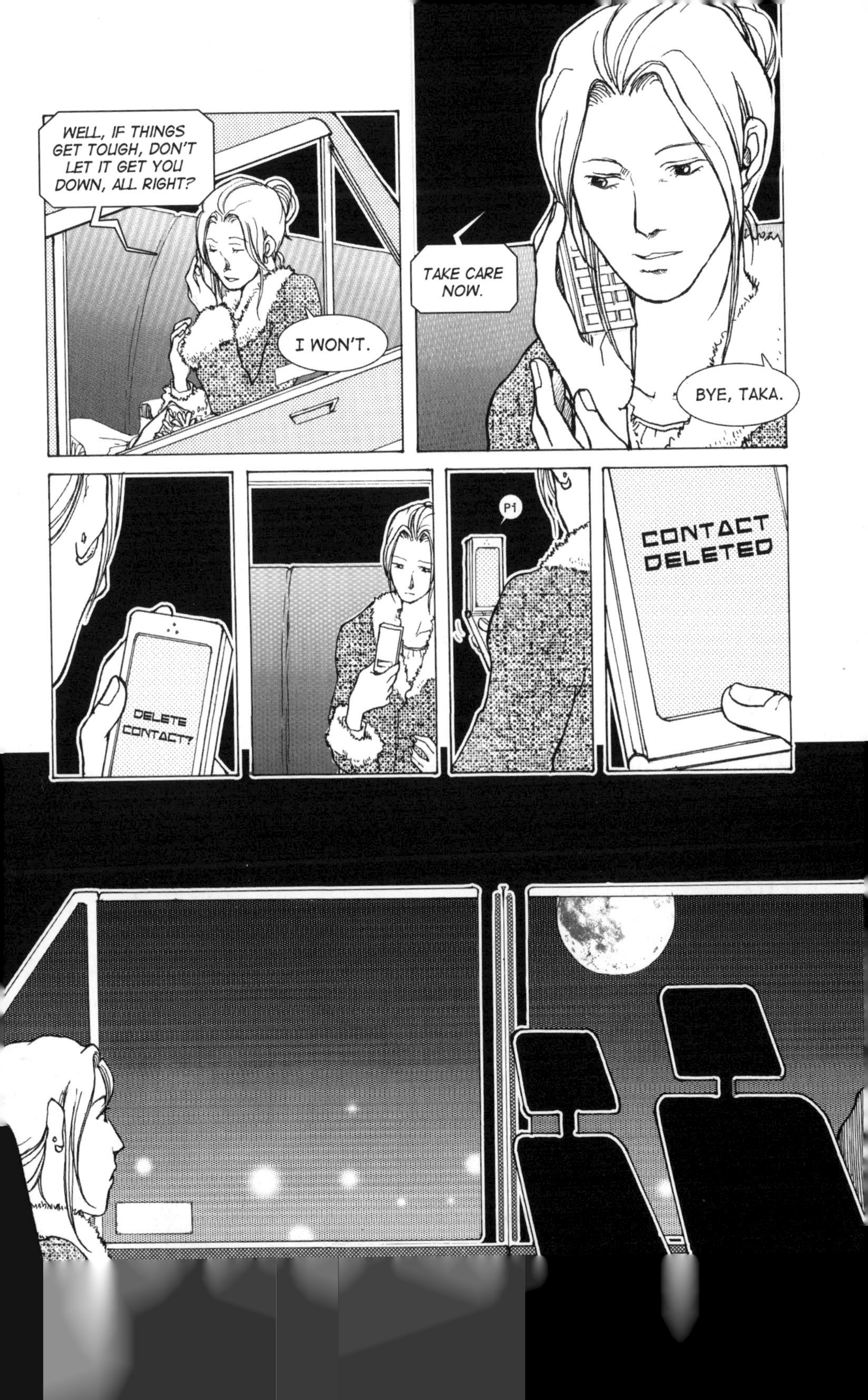
WELL, IF THINGS GET TOUGH, DON'T LET IT GET YOU DOWN, ALL RIGHT?
I WON'T.
TAKE CARE NOW.
BYE, TAKA.
DELETE CONTACT?
Pi
CONTACT DELETED

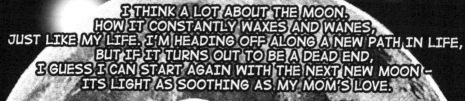

I THINK A LOT ABOUT THE MOON.
HOW IT CONSTANTLY WAXES AND WANES,
JUST LIKE MY LIFE. I'M HEADING OFF ALONG A NEW PATH IN LIFE,
BUT IF IT TURNS OUT TO BE A DEAD END,
I GUESS I CAN START AGAIN WITH THE NEXT NEW MOON –
ITS LIGHT AS SOOTHING AS MY MOM'S LOVE.

IT WON'T DO TO LIE OR CHEAT OR FAKE IT THIS TIME.
AND SOME DAY I'M SURE I'M GOING TO MEET "THE ONE,"
THE PERSON WHO WILL CARE ENOUGH ABOUT ME TO MAKE
ME THEIR NUMBER ONE. I KNOW THE MOON WILL SHINE
EXTRA-BRIGHTLY THAT NIGHT...

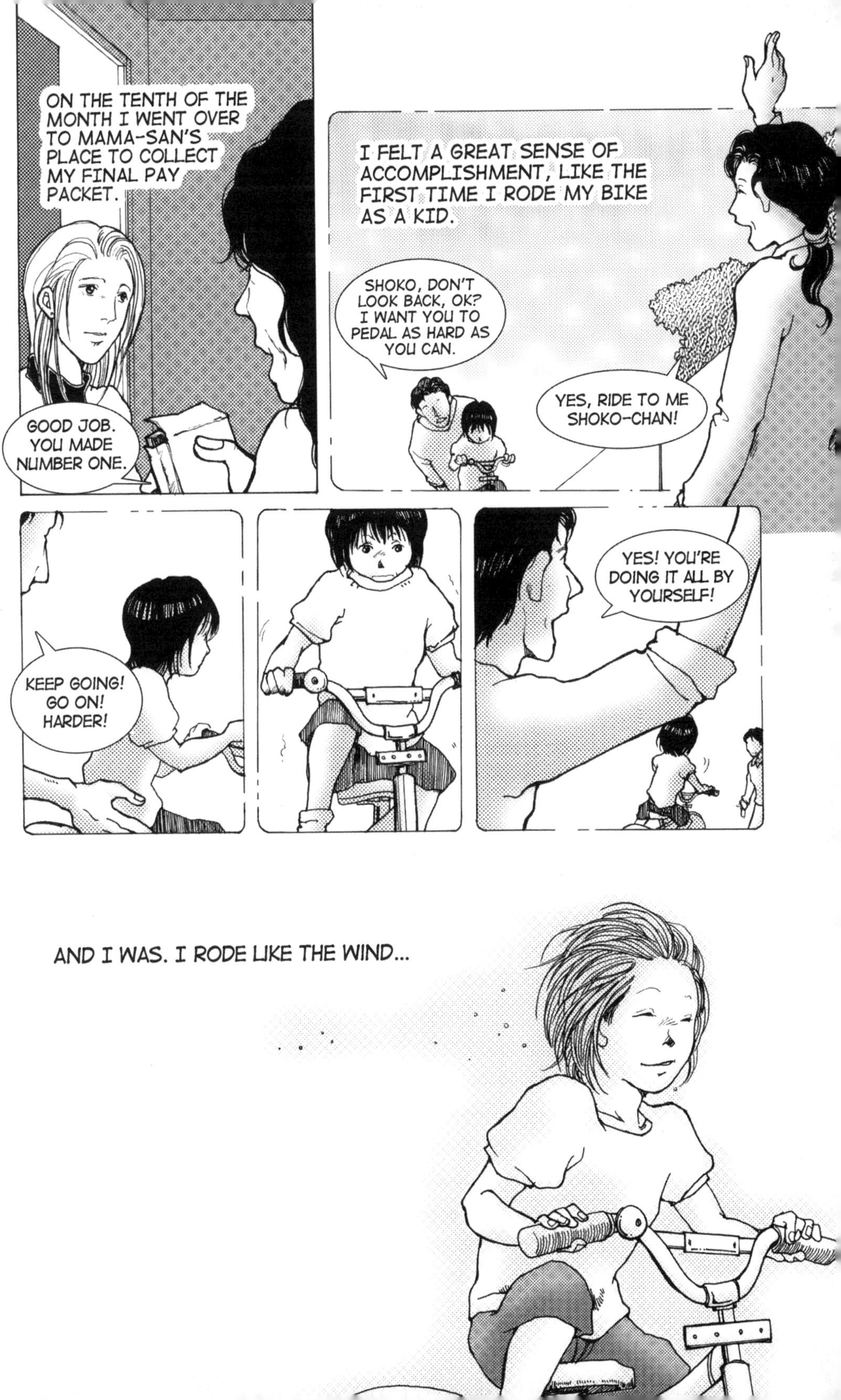
ON THE TENTH OF THE MONTH I WENT OVER TO MAMA-SAN'S PLACE TO COLLECT MY FINAL PAY PACKET.
GOOD JOB. YOU MADE NUMBER ONE.
I FELT A GREAT SENSE OF ACCOMPLISHMENT, LIKE THE FIRST TIME I RODE MY BIKE AS A KID.
SHOKO, DON'T LOOK BACK, OK? I WANT YOU TO PEDAL AS HARD AS YOU CAN.
YES, RIDE TO ME SHOKO-CHAN!
KEEP GOING! GO ON! HARDER!
YES! YOU'RE DOING IT ALL BY YOURSELF!
AND I WAS. I RODE LIKE THE WIND...

WRITING A MANGA OR COMIC SCRIPT

Even though manga and comic books are very popular art forms, the understanding of how they are made lags behind. I am often asked about the process, even in Japan. So here are some of the basics of how I work.

The first step is, of course, to have an idea for a story, scene or character. In my case, these tend to pop into my head anytime, anywhere—and I find the more I work, the more new ideas come to me. Working on a project and creating new ones go hand in hand. One feeds the other, and generating new ideas becomes a habit.

The next stage might be to write out a plot or synopsis of what happens, where, and to whom. My initial plot summaries tend be a bit "dry," just descriptions of A to B to C. It's in the script itself that I make things come alive. But jotting down the plotline helps me map out the story ahead of time. Some people work out the page breakdown at the same time they outline the story—figuring out how many pages the story might require and listing a basic description of what happens on each page.

PAGE BREAKDOWN

Page 8 [1st manga page]: Young Shoko with her mother, ring on her finger.

Page 9: Splash page [big opening page], her family getting into a car.

Page 10: Funeral, confrontation with an uncle.

In my case, I move on to the script immediately after my skeletal outline. At this stage, some writers prefer to do a "rough thumbnail sketch" of actual drawings on paper that they either send to the artist or use to help them visualize the script. I bypass this part and get right to the script. This has a few basic aspects, depending on the writer's style and his or her relationship with the artist.

Regardless of the course a writer takes, there are three essential parts to the script: the dialogue, the captions (or narrative), and the descriptions for the artist (this last does not surface in the finished work). The words that do appear on the page—the dialogue in the speech balloons and the narration in the rectangular caption boxes—are mostly the domain of the writer. Artists rarely change these, though they can if, for example, they feel there are too many words in a panel.

> DIALOGUE EXAMPLE
>
> SHOKO
>
> Who the hell do you think you're threatening?
>
> NARRATION EXAMPLE
>
> CAPTION: Shortly before I turned seventeen a bunch of us went to the office of a guy who had just become a yakuza himself.

The artist's role increases when it comes to the description. The descriptions are essentially guidelines for the artist. Some writers use a "page description"–type script, in which they outline what happens on one or more pages of a particular scene. They include the place, people, feeling, action, and other relevant information. The artist then blocks out the specific panels (or frames) of the actual art of the scene. In this instance, the artist is chiefly responsible for the panel-level visualization, with the writer having some say on it at this early stage. The other way—and this is what I normally do—is for the writer to describe things right down to the level of specific panels. He or she sets the scene, action, characters, and emotion, indicating what will happen in each panel, who or what the focus should be, and maybe even describing the framing (that is, directionals, often using terminology borrowed from film-making such as "zoom in close up to the character's face" or "pull back for a wide shot").

> SCRIPT: DESCRIPTION, PANELS
>
> PANEL 4: Big panel. Shoko from the front, playing the game, looking into the screen, but looking to the side, as she can feel Nakauchi looking at her about 10 feet behind. She feels uneasy. Perhaps we see the computer game she is playing a little bit, as if we are looking through the back of the computer screen at her. Also perhaps her sideways look could be in a small round insert panel inside this large one?

The transition between panels is also important. Panels should flow together smoothly as the readers read at whatever pace is set, whether fast or slow. Again, either the writer or the artist can do that. I usually have such panel-pacing issues in mind as I write. I've been told that it's one of my strengths (which is just as well, as I have plenty of weaknesses!).

The last aspect where writing plays a crucial role is in the overall arrangement of the panels on each page. I think most of this is the artist's domain, and I only comment on that part about a quarter of the time—when I have, for example, a clear idea of where I think a full-page spread might look good, or where the last panel should bleed off the page.

SCRIPT: DESCRIPTION, PAGE STRUCTURE

Page 186: This is an unusual, artistic-style page—please make this a page with many small boxes or circle-shaped panels, from different parts of her life. The background is the moon in the night sky, taking up the whole page, beneath the various small panels. Please put the captions at the top and the bottom, and—if possible—make the words curve around the edges of the moon at the top and the bottom.

NOTE: That was my original idea. Michiru adapted it eagerly, but added her touches, changing the visual rhythm to one she thought would work better.

So, all in all, the process of writing involves several stages, and can be approached in a few different ways. It's a rather subtle and complicated process, and quite under-appreciated as a form of writing. But I, for one, love it!

On to the Art

Once the script is passed to the artist (this is presuming there is a writer-artist team to start with), then the first step is often to sketch a page-by-page layout of the panels. As with the writing stage, the process is flexible, and different artists sometimes take different approaches. With that in mind, why don't I let Michiru step forward and explain how she works...

Sean Michael Wilson
Kumamoto, Japan

MICHIKO MORIKAWA

STEP 1

PLANNING THE PANEL LAYOUT

WHEN I CREATE MY OWN STORY, I USUALLY START FROM THIS STEP. I DON'T WRITE THE SCRIPT FIRST, BUT USE PANELS AND BALLOONS TO VISUALLY "WRITE" MY STORY. FOR *YAKUZA MOON*, I READ SEAN'S SCRIPT FIRST, THEN DOVE INTO VISUALIZING THE ACTION.

STEP 2

SKETCHING

I DON'T LIKE THIS STAGE SO MUCH! AFTER I FINISH STEP 1, THE IMAGE OF THE ART IS IN MY HEAD SO CLEARLY THAT I JUST FEEL LIKE STARTING THE INKING WITHOUT MAKING ROUGH PENCIL SKETCHES.

STEP 3

INKING

FOR INKING, I MAINLY USE BALLPOINT PENS (GEL INK TYPE), WORKING WITH MANY DIFFERENT SIZES OF PENS.

STEP 4

TONE

ADDING THE VARIOUS TONES BRINGS OUT THE DEPTH OF THE ART. I DO THIS STAGE ON MY COMPUTER.

STEP 5

LETTERING

THIS IS DIFFICULT! I OFTEN SET THE TYPE IN SEVERAL DIFFERENT POSITIONS BEFORE I FIND AN ARRANGEMENT I LIKE, AND THAT IS *AFTER* CHOOSING THE TYPEFACE!

I HAVE A GREAT RESPECT FOR ALL TYPOGRAPHERS!

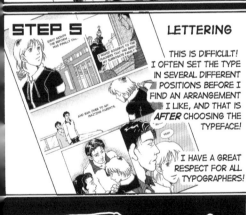

*THIS IS HOW MY DRAWING DESK LOOKS (A BIT MESSIER THOUGH!)

（英文版）漫画『極道な月』
Yakuza Moon

2011年3月29日　第1刷発行

著　者　天藤 湘子
作　　　ショーン・マイケル・ウィルソン
画　　　森川未知留

発行者　廣田浩二

発行所　講談社インターナショナル株式会社
　　　　〒112-8652　東京都文京区音羽 1-17-14
　　　　電話　03-3944-6493（編集部）
　　　　　　　03-3944-6492（マーケティング部・業務部）
　　　　ホームページ　www.kodansha-intl.com

印刷・製本所　大日本印刷株式会社

落丁本、乱丁本は購入書店名を明記のうえ、講談社インターナショナル業務部宛にお送り
ください。送料小社負担にてお取替えいたします。なお、この本についてのお問い合わせは、
編集部宛にお願いいたします。定価はカバーに表示してあります。

Printed in Japan
ISBN 978-4-7700-3146-4